D1124740

Grace Notes
for a Year

Grace Notes for a Year

Stories of Hope, Humor
& Hubris
from the World
of Classical Music

Norman Gilliland
NEMO Productions — Madison, Wisconsin

NEMO Productions
P.O. Box 260079
Madison, Wisconsin 53726-0079
First Edition.

Copyright (c) 2002 Norman Gilliland.
All rights reserved.
For permission to reprint from the following works, grateful acknowledgment is
hereby made to the following:

Excerpts from *Letters To His Family: An Autobiography*, translated by Galena
von Meck. First Cooper Square Press edition 2000. This Cooper Square Press
paperback edition of *Letters to His Family* is an unabridged republication of the
edition first published in Briarcliff Manor, New York in 1981. English language
translation copyright 1973 by Galena von Meck. Additional material copyright 1981
by Percy M. Young. Published by Cooper Square Press, an imprint of Rowman &
Littlefield Publishing Group, 150 Fifth Avenue, Suite 911, New York 10011.

Excerpt from *Selected Letters* by Ferruccio Busoni, edited by Antony Beaumont,
Copyright 1987 by Columbia University Press. Used by permission of
Columbia University Press.

Excerpts from *Selected Letters of Berlioz*, edited by Hugh Macdonald, translated
by Roger Nichols. Copyright (c) 1995 by Hugh Macdonald. Translation copyright
(c) 1995 by Roger Nichols. Used by permission of W.W. Norton & Company, Inc..

Excerpt from *The Bach Reader,* Revised Edition by Hans T. David and Arthur
Mandel. Copyright (c) 1966, 1945 by W.W. Norton & Company, Inc. Used by
permission of W.W. Norton & Company, Inc.

Excerpt from *Memoirs* by Mikhail Glinka, translated by Richard Mudge,
published by the University of Oklahoma Press, 1963. Used by permission of the
University of Oklahoma Press.

ISBN 0-9715093-0-1
LCCN 2001119571
Printed in the United States of America
Cover Design: Sarah Wolstenholme
ATTENTION: ORGANIZATIONS AND EDUCATIONAL INSTITUTIONS:
Quantity discounts are available on bulk purchases of this book for educational
purposes or fund raising.
For information, please call NEMO Productions at (608) 833-0988.

To Karl Schmidt,

Who breathes life into words.

Acknowledgments

It was fun to produce *Grace Notes* for broadcast. We recorded at the home studio of Don Sieb, high in the green hills of south central Wisconsin. When I looked out from the recording booth and saw his big shoulders shaking with mirth, I knew that I had just delivered an entertaining story-or else had blown a word in some spectacular way. Don's efficiency and outrageous sense of humor got us through many a session. I have no doubt that, had he lived to see this book come out, he would have been quick to put it in its place.

Most of the voices of *Grace Notes* belonged to veterans of Wisconsin Public Radio's *Chapter A Day*–Carol Cowan, Jim Fleming, and Karl Schmidt–each of whom brought a personal magic to the stories. Many thanks for those congenial evenings at the microphone.

My gratitude also to the apparently indefatigable Larry Knapp, distributor of the radio version of *Grace Notes*.

Many thanks to keyboard conversationalist Jeffrey Siegel for his kind words about this book, to composer and P.D.Q. Bach mastermind Peter Schickele for taking precious time to evaluate these stories, and to the delightful Studs Terkel for being such an inspiration.

As for the production of this book I'd like to thank Sarah Wolstenholme, Wendy Wink, and Dennis Ryan for valuable preparation, proofing, and advice. Thanks to my long-time bride, Amanda, for applying her auditor's meticulousness to yet another manuscript, to son Jordan for virtuosic computer assistance, and to son Ross for being so enthusiastic about the *Grace Notes* stories from the beginning. And finally, thanks to you for picking up this book and reading it.

Foreword

The purpose of *Grace Notes for a Year* is to shed light on the fragile and perilous process of inspiration, composition, and performance required to create classical music, whether the final product is a masterpiece or a mess.

The more one delves into the stories behind classical music, the more the personalities emerge—the rumbling Beethoven crossing words with his publishers, the headlong lovelorn Berlioz, the free spirited Mozart and his stern father—whom we follow through their quarrelsome letters of 1778—the urbane New Orleans-born virtuoso Louis Moreau Gottschalk, whose journal entries evoke vividly the cultural maelstrom of Civil War America.

In a way, of course, their stories of trial, triumph, and failure are similar to our own.

For the sake of clarity I've condensed some of the letters and have favored a contemporary American English. I hope that the errors are few and minor in these evocations of fascinating subjects. A contemporary of Beethoven's recalled that the composer could forgive the occasional wrong note in a performance of his music as long as the spirit was right. In that spirit I hope you'll enjoy these little stories and find that they enhance your appreciation of classical music.

Because *Grace Notes for a Year* began as a series of daily radio stories, this collection takes the form of a calendar, but it's not a musical almanac emphasizing composers' birthdays or the anniversaries of major musical events. On the other hand, the sequence of the stories does follow the changing seasons and their sometimes aggravating or amusing effect on music-making.

Along the way you will find, as promised, stories of hope, humor, and hubris from the world of classical music and the lively voices of the men, women, and children who dwell in it.

Norman Gilliland
Madison, Wisconsin
February 12, 2002

January 1st
Haydn's New Year

It was the beginning of a New Year and a grand adventure for Franz Joseph Haydn. On January 1, 1791, he left Calais for London, where he was to conduct his latest symphonies for English audiences. He wrote to a friend in Vienna:

My arrival set off a big commotion throughout the city, and I made the rounds of all the newspapers for three days in a row. Everybody wants to know me. I've already had to dine out six times, and if I wanted, I could dine out every day, but first I have to think of my health and my work. Except for the nobility, I receive no callers before two o'clock in the afternoon, and at four I dine at home with my host, Mr. Salomon. I have pleasant and comfortable, but pricey lodgings. My landlord is Italian—and a cook to boot—and serves me four very decent meals, but everything is awfully expensive here.

I was invited to a splendid amateur concert, but I got there a bit late, and when I showed my ticket they wouldn't let me in but led me to an antechamber where I had to wait until the piece being played was over. Then they opened the door of the concert hall and I was escorted on the arm of the entrepreneur up the center of the hall to the front of the orchestra to unanimous applause, and there I was stared at and hailed with many English compliments. I was assured that such honors had not been conferred upon anyone for fifty years.

After the concert, I was led to a handsome room, where I was supposed to be seated at the head of a table for 200 amateurs. But since I had dined out that day and had eaten more than I was used to, I turned down the honor with the excuse that I was feeling a bit under the weather. All the same, I had to drink the harmonious health—in Burgundy—of all the gentlemen there. They all returned the toast, and then I was permitted to be taken home.

January 2nd
A New Year's Letter from Tchaikovsky

On January 2, 1877, Peter Tchaikovsky chided his brother Modest for not being a better correspondent.

I don't know if you still remember my existence. I happen to be your own brother. I hold the position of professor at the Moscow Conservatoire and have written several compositions: operas, symphonies, overtures and so on. There was a time when you condescended to take an interest in me. We even took a trip abroad together last year, which has left an unforgettable memory in my heart. You often used to write frequent charming and interesting letters to me. But now it all seems to me nothing but a sweet dream. Oh, yes—you have forgotten me and don't want to know me any more!! But I am not like you. In spite of my antipathy toward keeping up correspondence, in spite of being very tired (it is midnight now), here I am sitting writing to you to remind you of my feelings of great love for you. And so, dear brother, I wish you a Happy New Year, health, happiness, and success very soon in all your new ventures....

As for me, dear brother, the holidays passed idly and not very happily. I wanted to work but was disturbed by friends. And now my relative Misha Assiere is on leave and staying with me. I must say, he is a very nice and sweet boy and I, dear brother, stay home with him every evening....

Before the holidays I became friendly, dear brother, with the writer Count Leo Tolstoy and have a very nice letter from him . And he listened, dear brother, to my first string quartet and during the Andante he shed real tears which, dear brother, makes me very proud. And you, my dear brother, do not be so presumptuous to forget that I, dear brother, am a "bird" of certain importance. And now, good-bye my dear brother.

Your furious brother,
Peter Tchaikovsky.

January 3rd
The Showman

When musicianship falters, an otherwise disastrous performance can be salvaged by showmanship. The Danish pianist Borge Rosenbaum was a fine musician and a natural showman.

He was born January 3, 1909, and began his professional career at thirteen. For twelve years he performed with most of the major orchestras in Europe. He had a delicate touch, but the poised young pianist also had a quick wit that was not to be suppressed.

One night Rosenbaum was performing with the Copenhagen Philharmonic. The piece was the big, romantic Second Piano Concerto of Sergei Rachmaninoff and Rosenbaum was playing with his usual sensitivity, but something was making the audience laugh. Confused and nervous, the conductor stepped up the tempo. The orchestra played faster and faster until they had left Rosenbaum a full three pages behind.

Rosenbaum had been responsible for the problem in the first place. The audience had been reacting to his expressive eyebrows as he played Rachmaninoff's soaring melodies. The pianist launched into a cadenza, a virtuoso cascade of notes that signaled the end of the movement. But suddenly, to everyone's astonishment, Rosenbaum broke off in the middle of the cadenza, left the piano, walked to the conductor's podium, and turned the score back three pages. Then he bowed to the orchestra, winked at the audience, and somberly finished the concerto.

He had already made a reputation for himself as one of Denmark's finest pianists. Now he became known as one of Europe's great comedians. But in 1940 when the German occupation of Denmark forced him to immigrate to the United States, he had to make a name for himself all over again. And the name Borge Rosenbaum picked was Victor Borge. For nearly sixty years Borge—and his eyebrows— toured the world, entertaining people with classical music.

January 4th
The Frozen Train

In January 1864 New Orleans-born pianist Louis Moreau Gottschalk was on a train, making a concert tour of the northern states. Stalled near Harvard, Illinois, and worn by war and weather, he found comfort where he could, as he relates in his diary:

Even though I had spent the night with my clothes on, with a woolen comforter around my neck and a fur cap on my head, lying all the while under a mountain of covers, when I woke up, my mustache was covered with frost. The thermometer sat at 32 degrees below zero! Our shoes are frozen. Our hats, too, and we have to put them under the stove to thaw them out. An old trapper guarantees a very rough winter to come. The muskrats on the Indian frontier have built their cabins two stories high, he tells us, and all the trout have abandoned the rivers to get to the deep water of the lakes.

We had a sick young soldier in the car with us. I'm eager to find out how he did during the night. Methodically I wrap myself in furs to go find out if I can do anything to comfort the poor young man. He is very weak. He's going back to his family.

By God's mercy there are noble hearts in this world of dollars and cents. I have found a young farmer who agrees to take care of him without payment.

The engineers and firemen have suffered more than anyone else. They had to stay on the engine all night to keep the fire going or the water in the boilers would surely have frozen. No chance of moving out today. Milwaukee is impossible. I can't even go back to Chicago.

I'm told that the ladies passed the night dancing. Somebody found a fiddler in the village. Luckily there's no piano, so I didn't have to perform.

January 5th
A Dangerous Reward

In 1853 the famed contralto Marietta Alboni was about to give a farewell concert, and the manager of New York's Broadway Theater was desperate to have her perform on his stage. He asked conductor Luigi Arditi to convince the star to sing the part of Norma at his theater. As a reward, the manager promised to buy Arditi the most handsome baton in New York.

Arditi wanted the handsome baton, but even more he wanted to hear Alboni sing Norma–a performance that would be an artistic triumph. As Arditi said later, "I knew the extraordinary extent of her command over her vocal powers. Her figure was not nearly so unwieldy as it afterwards became and, well, to make a long story short, I went to see her and pointed out the success she would no doubt obtain."

They tried the music together and Alboni allowed herself to be persuaded to perform the part of Norma at the Broadway Theater. The theater manager kept his word and presented Arditi with a baton that was a work of art in its own right. It had a topaz set at the bottom of it, and at the other end it sported a little golden Apollo playing on a harp.

Unfortunately the baton and the music collided. "I was very proud of the baton," Arditi recalled. "And must have struck up the opening bars of the overture with unusual energy because Apollo shook loose, flew off, and smacked a flute-player on his bald head."

The orchestra member kept on playing, but all during the first act of the opera Arditi's attention was divided between the score and the growing lump on the flutist's head. The next night, when Arditi took his place before the orchestra, the musicians were relieved to see him take out a perfectly simple, unornamented baton. Luigi Arditi had been right all along–the real reward for his efforts was the music.

January 6th
Varèse & the Apache

Edgar Varèse dared to challenge traditional notions of harmony. His early years in Paris also required considerable daring and were less than harmonious.

At the turn of the 20th century, Varèse's colleagues in Paris acted as his bodyguards as he walked home from rehearsals in a rough part of the city. They wanted to protect him from young toughs known as *Apaches* who frequented the streets. But Varèse was confident that he would have nothing to fear from the Apaches once they got to know him. He felt that he could get along with almost anyone, from aristocrats to working people—to gang members.

Varèse had a friend who was an intern in one of the Paris hospitals. Occasionally the composer would visit the young doctor on night duty. One night an Apache who had been knifed was brought in, bent almost double and holding his hat over his belly just to keep his guts from falling out. He was in great pain. Varèse lit a cigarette and put it in the young Apache's mouth. The young man was sullen and suspicious, not believing that the hospital staff cared whether his kind lived or died. "You'll see," Varèse assured him. "My friend is good and he's going to operate on you. Don't worry. You're in good hands."

Months later a stranger came to Varèse's door. "You don't know who I am," he told the composer, "but I know you. You saved my life." It was the wounded Apache. "Didn't I tell you my friend would pull you through?" Varèse asked. "It wasn't your friend," the man replied. "It was you and the cigarette you gave me and the way you talked. I just came to say that if you ever need a job done, if anyone ever messes with you, I'm your man."

Whether in the concert hall or the streets of Paris, Edgar Varèse was not one to shy away from confrontations.

January 7th
The Beethoven Conspiracies

Ludwig van Beethoven is said to have described composing as ten percent talent and ninety percent work. On January 7, 1809, he wrote from Vienna to his publisher in Leipzig suggesting that the hardest work comes *after* composing.

I am forced through intrigues and conspiracies and dirty tricks of all kinds to leave the Only German Fatherland. I'm going at the invitation of his majesty the King of Westphalia as the Kappellmeister with an annual salary of 800 ducats in gold.

There will probably be some abusive articles in the newspapers about my last concert. By no means do I wish everything said against me to be suppressed, but people should know that no one has more personal enemies here than I do. And that's all the easier to understand since the state of music here is becoming worse and worse.

We have conductors who understand as little about conducting as they do about conducting themselves. At the Wieden it's the worst. I had to give my concert there, and on all sides stumbling blocks were put in my way. There was a terrible trick played out of hatred for me, for Herr Salieri threatened to expel any musician belonging to their company who played for me, but despite several flaws that I couldn't prevent, the public received everything most enthusiastically. Nevertheless, scribblers will not fail to write wretched stuff against me in the newspapers.

The musicians were particularly enraged that careless mistakes cropped up in the simplest, plainest piece. I abruptly called out to them in a loud voice to stop and begin again. Nothing like that had ever happened before. The public made its delight known.

January 8th
The Cure

One night in 1994, 72-year-old pianist Abbey Simon and his wife were in The Hague, crossing a street in a rainstorm when an inattentive driver smashed into them. Simon's wife was badly injured. His own injuries were not life-threatening, but he had four broken fingers. The pianist's doctor was blunt. "The bad news," he said, "is that you'll never play the piano again. The good news is that we can experiment because we have nothing to lose."

The "good news" gave Simon little comfort. "I was in hysterics," he recalled a few years later. "I used to come home from the hospital after a day spent caring for my wife and doing my physical therapy and just sit around and cry. I couldn't figure out what to do with the rest of my life."

The doctor's experimental therapy included micro casts for each finger and playing chess with pieces attached to the board by Velcro. Simon began by teaching himself to play five notes in a row without pressure. Some of the damage proved permanent. The second finger of his right hand remained very crooked, requiring him to re-finger everything he played, and his hand span had shortened, making some kinds of chords particularly hard to play. If a chord was otherwise impossible, he allowed himself to roll it, and in extreme cases, settled for omitting a note.

Simon made a remarkable comeback. Just three months after the accident, he was in Carnegie Hall performing Liszt's virtuoso Transcendental Etudes. By the turn of the 21st century he was giving fifty concerts a year.

The cure had required determination, hard work, and a few compromises. It also required Abbey Simon to trust the doctor and his experimental treatment. So it was all for the best that, only after his recovery, a friend told Simon that she blamed that same doctor for ruining her daughter's hand.

January 9th
The Adventuresome Soprano

Anna Rivière was one of the most admired of 19th century English sopranos. She was also one of the most adventuresome.

She was born in London on January 9, 1810. She entered the Royal Academy of Music at the age of 14. Seven years later, just after her professional debut, Anna married Sir Henry Bishop, who was 24 years her senior. Her reputation as a singer grew rapidly, based largely on her tours with Sir Henry and harpist Nicholas Bochsa. After a tour of Dublin, Edinburgh, and London, Anna Bishop deserted her husband and three children and eloped with Bochsa—who was reputed to be a forger and bigamist.

From then on, Madame Bishop—as she continued to be known—traveled and sang as if her life depended on it. Between 1839 and 1843 she traveled to every major town in Europe, where she sang in 260 concerts. In the course of two years in Naples, she performed in 20 operas. In 1855 she and Bochsa sailed for Sydney, Australia. He died there the following year, and Anna went on to tour South America before returning to New York, where she married a diamond merchant.

Then she began what proved her most dangerous adventure. After another American tour in 1866, she and her husband set sail across the Pacific. They were shipwrecked on a small coral reef, and for more than a month they drifted in a small boat before finally reaching Guam. She had lost her music, her wardrobe, and her jewelry, but Madame Bishop was not to be stopped. She went on to Manila and began a concert tour that led to Hong Kong, Singapore, and India before she went back to England. After another two-year world tour she returned, eventually, to New York, where she gave her last public performance in 1883—at age 73.

Meanwhile the husband she left behind, Sir Henry, had become famous for writing the music to lyrics that might eventually have been meaningful to Anna Bishop—"Home, Sweet Home."

January 10th
Weber's Conducting Ordeal

In 1804, Carl Maria von Weber was not yet 18 years old. But he already had some distinguished compositions to his credit, and though he had little conducting experience, he was invited to lead the theater orchestra in Breslau. The salary was small and the position modest, but it would help Weber to support his unproductive father. He accepted the invitation. Within two years that decision would cost him dearly.

Weber started off badly in Breslau, although he didn't know it. An influential violinist had wanted Weber's conducting job, and before Weber even arrived in town, the violinist did his best to blackball Weber from important musical opportunities. Weber demanded many more rehearsals than the orchestra members were used to, and, coming from a teenager, the demand was particularly galling.

His most unpopular move was to change the seating of the orchestra. Traditionally the winds had been in the front with the strings behind them. Weber put the first violins, oboes, horns, one cello and one double bass at the right, the second violins, clarinets, bassoons, and violas to the left, and, in the back, the trumpets and kettledrums. Breslau audiences were partial to brass, and they complained that they couldn't hear the music.

Weber also was faulted for his insensitivity when it came to replacing old incompetent musicians with fresh talent. Many of the longtime musicians, the "dead wood," were popular with the townspeople. And there was no good way to finance the incoming musicians that Weber wanted. Weber insisted that the improved orchestra and a more exciting repertory would pay for themselves, and he pressed on with great enthusiasm. The orchestra directors responded by vetoing every suggestion that required extra spending.

And Weber's ordeal in Breslau was by no means over. His worst experience there was yet to come, and it would have little to do with music. To be continued....

January 11th
Weber & the Wrong Bottle

In the midst of this series of temporary professional setbacks, Weber suffered a personal calamity that would last a lifetime.

One evening early in 1806, Weber asked a friend, Friedrich Wilhelm Berner, to come to his lodgings to go over the score of an opera Weber was writing. Berner agreed, but was delayed until long after Weber had gotten home.

Arriving home, Weber was thirsty, and, seeing a wine flask, he picked it up and took a long drink. But the fluid in the flask was not wine. It was acid—an etching solution Weber's father had carelessly poured into a wine bottle.

It was late by the time Berner arrived but, seeing a light in the window, he knocked on the door. When there was no reply, Berner tried the door and found it unlocked. Entering the dark room, he smelled a sharp odor. Then he tripped over a body. It was Weber. Berner cried out and Weber's father, clad in a night-shirt, came running from the next room. They called doctors but Weber's mouth and throat were badly burned, and it was a long time before he could even explain what had happened. He was sick for two months, and, when he recovered, his beautiful singing voice had been forever burned away.

When he finally returned to the theater, Weber found that all of his reforms had been reversed and, fearing that he would be blamed for the worsening performances to follow, he resigned and retreated from Breslau. But years later he would take some comfort from words that he had written before accepting the post: "Nothing harms me which affords me experience."

January 12th
Handel's Fighting Prima Donnas

The evening of January 12, 1723, was one of the most remarkable in London theatrical history. On that night Handel's opera *Ottone* premiered, and the star was soprano Francesca Cuzzoni–a force to be reckoned with.

She had arrived from Italy the previous December, already a celebrated singer–and a temperamental one. During rehearsals for *Ottone* she decided that one of Handel's arias didn't suit her and she refused to sing it. No shrinking violet himself, Handel seized Cuzzoni by the waist and told her that if she didn't sing the aria he would throw her out the window. She sang it and *Ottone* was a sensation. During the next three seasons, Cuzzoni became quite wealthy singing in other Handel operas in London. Her undivided acclaim was not to last though. In 1726 soprano Faustina Bordoni joined Handel's opera company, and she and Cuzzoni became intense rivals. One bone of contention–Bordoni was beautiful while Cuzzoni was anything but. According to parliamentarian Robert Walpole, Cuzzoni was short and squat with a doughy, cross face but fine expression." He added that she was not a good actress, dressed ill, and was "silly and fantastical."

One night in 1727, the rivalry between the two came to a head. At a performance of the opera *Astianatte,* ovations from the Bordoni faction of the audience were answered with catcalls and whistles from the Cuzzoni partisans. Before long the sopranos themselves got into a fistfight on stage, in full view of the audience, which included the Prince of Wales. Wits and wags had a field day with the fracas. Ambrose Philips–better known as Namby-Pamby–wrote satirical verses about Cuzzoni before her angry departure for the Continent. But the most fitting lampoon came from John Gay, who satirized both singers as Polly and Lucy in his runaway success of 1728, *The Beggar's Opera.*

January 13th
War and Peace at the Opera

Leo Tolstoy enjoyed opera, but he also enjoyed making fun of it. In his novel *War and Peace,* in a scene set in 1811, we see the opera through the eyes of 19-year-old Natasha Rostova, and it becomes a strange and amusing spectacle:

In the center of the stage sat some girls in red bodices and white shirts. One very fat girl in a white silk dress sat apart on a bench with a piece of green cardboard glued to it. They all sang something. When they had finished their song, the girl in white went up to the prompter's box and a man wearing tight silk trousers and holding a plume and dagger went up to her and began singing and waving his arms.

For a while he sang alone, then they both paused while the orchestra played and the man fingered the girl's hand, apparently awaiting the downbeat as a cue to start singing with her. They sang together and everyone in the theater began clapping and shouting while the man and woman on the stage—lovers apparently—began smiling, spreading their arms and bowing.

After her life in the country and in her present serious mood, all of this seemed grotesque and funny to Natasha. She couldn't follow the plot or listen to the music. She only saw the painted cardboard and the queerly dressed men and women who moved, talked, and sang so strangely in that brilliant light. At first she felt embarrassed for the actors and then they amused her. She studied the faces in the audience, looking for the same reaction, but they all seemed intent on the stage and expressed delight that, to Natasha, seemed contrived.

Feeling the bright light and the air warmed by the crowd, Natasha gradually passed into a state of giddiness, and she was seized by strange impulses. She wanted to jump onto the stage and sing with the actress, to reach out with her fan and touch an old gentleman sitting nearby, and then to lean over and tickle the beautiful Hélène.

January 14th
The Dangerous Host

Music-making can be hard enough for those whose instruments are mainstays of the orchestra. For harmonica-player Larry Adler the early years were tough–and a little scary.

In 1928 or so, at age 14, Adler left his home in Baltimore to audition in a New York harmonica band. He played the *Poet and Peasant Overture*. The bandleader's evaluation–"Kid, you stink." Finally Adler landed a job with a road show. After playing at the Oriental Theater in Chicago the performers were invited to a party. The host, a stranger to Adler, asked him, "You're Jewish, aren't you?"

"Yes," Adler said.

His host said, "I'm Catholic."

"That's nice," Adler replied.

"You go to shul–to temple?"

"I do five, six or seven shows a day," Adler told the man. "I can't go to shul."

The host was outraged. He made Adler promise to get up early and go to shul the next Saturday, no matter how many shows he had. He asked if Adler's parents were living and, told that they were, asked, "You write to them every day, huh?" Adler said no, he wrote once every two weeks or so.

"I don't like that," the man said. "Look, get your coat and go on home. I'd rather not see a kid like you here. At home you're going to sit down and write your parents a nice letter. You promise?"

Adler promised. Then he went over to comedian Harry Ross and asked," Who is that busybody?"

"Come on, Larry," Ross said. "You've got to be kidding."

"No, no–what's his name?"

His host's name was Al Capone. Larry Adler quickly went home, went to shul, and wrote his parents a long letter.

January 15th
Indoor and Outdoor Culture at the White House

Although the President was a noted outdoorsman, he also enjoyed the subtleties of chamber music. And sometimes the wild and the refined met cheek to jowl in the White House of Theodore Roosevelt.

When he came into office in 1901, Roosevelt brought a new sophistication to music-making in the executive mansion. Roosevelt enjoyed the Marine Band Symphony Orchestra, the Washington Symphony, the Philadelphia Symphony, and the renowned Kneisel Quartet.

But the best-remembered performance in the White House of Theodore Roosevelt took place on the evening of January 15, 1904, when the 27-year-old cellist Pablo Casals played a Boccherini sonata, "The Swan" from *Carnival of the Animals* by Saint-Saëns, and "Spanish Dance" by Czech composer David Popper. After the concert, the President put his arm around Casals' shoulder and led him among the guests, introducing him to everybody and talking all the while. "I felt that in a sense he personified the American nation," Casals said later, "with all his energy, strength, and confidence." Even so, it was hard for Casals to picture the President galloping on a horse or hunting big game–widely reported activities of Theodore Roosevelt.

But the President's cultivated tastes in music didn't set so well with some of his rough and ready cohorts. One of them, Captain Seth Bullock of Deadwood, South Dakota, when asked what he thought of the music after one concert, replied, "It's most too far up the gulch for me." To which Theodore Roosevelt replied, "All I've been afraid of was that Bullock might draw his gun and begin shooting the fiddlers."

As for Pablo Casals, he survived many an American engagement and gave his last White House recital for President John F. Kennedy.

January 16th
Breaking In

In his native land, Fernando Sor learned how to make music and developed a career as a performer and composer. He was a gifted guitarist and also wrote an opera, a motet, and songs. But Spain wasn't in the mainstream of music-making, and so in 1813, at the age of 35, Sor went to Paris to become an opera composer.

Despite his versatility, Sor was still known as a composer of guitar music, and the guitar was thought of as a purely Spanish instrument. There was no telling how well guitar music would go over in Europe beyond Spain. Sor listened carefully to the operas being performed in Paris and felt that he could do justice to the genre, and in fact, thought that he could help to turn grand opera away from some trends that he didn't care for. He started looking for a libretto and discovered that the best librettists, prizing their reputations as great poets, were not easy for a composer to approach unless he had already done well with an opera in Paris.

Sor went to visit one of them, the poet Marollier, who opened Sor's portfolio and listened to some portions of an opera by the aspiring composer. He said that the music was thoroughly Italian and not at all suitable for the French theater. He suggested that Sor take some time to study with an expert so that he might become more capable of writing for the theater.

The young Spaniard blew his top. He counted off everything that he thought was wrong with works that were being praised to the sky in Paris, and he launched into an attack on dilettantes who could listen to truly beautiful music without recognizing its value.

The poet closed the composer's music portfolio, and, to this day, Fernando Sor, composer of operas, is best known as the writer of outstanding works for the guitar.

January 17th
Mendelssohn in Rome

In the 19th century, many a composer made a pilgrimage to Rome and was awestruck by the greatness of its ruins. When 22-year-old Felix Mendelssohn made the trip, he saw ruins, but little greatness. To his family in Berlin he reported on January 17, 1831:

The night before last a theater opened with a new opera by Pacini. There was a tremendous crush. The boxes were full of the most elegant people. Pacini took his seat at the piano and received an ovation. He had not written an overture. The opera began with a chorus during which a tuned anvil was beaten in time to the music. The Corsair appeared, sang his aria, and was applauded.

The Corsair up on stage and the maestro down in the pit both bowed. Many other pieces followed and the thing became tedious. The audience agreed, and when Pacini's grand finale rang out, the musicians in the pit rose to their feet and started talking in loud voices and laughing and turned their backs to the stage. The Countess in the box next to mine fainted and had to be carried out. Pacini vanished from the piano, and amid a good deal of chaos the curtain came down.

Next came the great Bluebeard Ballet and then the last act of the opera. Once it began, the audience hissed the entire ballet from start to finish and accompanied the second act of the opera, likewise, with hisses and laughter. At the end they called for the manager, but he didn't show.

That is a sober account of a first night and theater opening in Rome. If the music had caused a sensation, I would've been perplexed because it is sad stuff, beneath criticism. But it also perplexes me that they should suddenly turn their backs on Pacini, their big favorite, whom they wanted to crown in the Capitol, and instead make fun of his tunes and sing parodies of them. On another occasion they had carried him home on their shoulders.

January 18th
The Faust Stratagem

For one reason or another some operas fail to draw crowds. When it happened to Charles Gounod's opera, *Faust* in London in 1863, the composer was lucky enough to have the services of a clever and daring impresario.

With the opera's London debut just a few days away, only a handful of tickets had been sold. Impresario James Henry Mapleson was faced with the prospect of a complete failure. He took a bold step and told the box-office manager that *Faust* would be performed four nights in a row. The box-office manager assured him that he was mad, that one performance of *Faust* would be more than enough.

Mapleson went even further. He told the manager that for the first three performances of the opera not one ticket would be made available other than those already sold. Then he collected all of the unsold tickets in several carpetbags and mailed them to selected people throughout the city and suburbs of London.

Next Mapleson took out an ad in the London *Times*, saying that a death in the family had made available at a bargain price some hard-to-get opening night box seats, adding that all other box seats had been sold. He saw to it that the opening night box seats were sold.

In the meantime, people who were turned away at the box office started spreading the word that a *Faust* ticket was a valuable commodity. As the day of the debut approached, more and more people wanted tickets.

The first performance—well attended by the people to whom Mapleson had mailed tickets—received polite applause. The impresario arranged for Gounod to take several bows on stage just to build up the excitement.

The second performance stirred a little more enthusiasm, and by the time the paying public got to see *Faust,* demand had swollen to the point that the theater was filled night after night—all because of the stratagem of an imaginative and daring impresario.

January 19th

Why Bother to Get Up?

Gioacchino Rossini was one of the most active opera composers of all time, but, according to a story from one of his contemporaries, he could be spectacularly lazy. In 1824 the celebrated author Stendahl wrote a biography of Rossini in which he suggested that it was easier for Rossini to compose than to get out of bed on a cold day.

During the winter of 1813, Rossini was lodging at a cheap inn in Venice. He was composing in bed to avoid paying for a fire. He was just finishing a duet when the sheet of paper slipped through his fingers and fluttered to the floor. Rossini leaned over and tried to find it, but in vain. It had slipped beneath the bed.

Suddenly chilled, Rossini pulled back under the blankets muttering, "I'd rather write the whole thing over again. I can do it in no time. All I have to do is remember it." Unfortunately his mind went completely blank. He sat there for a good quarter of an hour, getting more and more annoyed as he failed to recall a single note of the duet.

Finally he burst out laughing. "I'm a fool," he declared. "I'd do better just to write another duet. Rich composers can afford to have fires in their rooms, but I have my own form of self-indulgence. I absolutely refuse to get out of this bed to go crawling around for a runaway duet. And even if I did, it would probably bring me bad luck."

Just as he was finishing up the second duet, a visitor stopped by and Rossini asked him to retrieve the duet under the bed. "Now listen," said Rossini. "I'm going to sing you both duets and you tell me which one you like better." The visitor preferred the first, thinking the second duet too fast. Rossini nodded, and right on the spot wrote a trio for the same opera, wrestled into his clothes, swearing all the while about the cold, and went downstairs for a cup of coffee.

January 20th
The Runaway Horn Player

For two centuries it was fashionable for composers to have Italian names. But fashion wasn't the first thing on the mind of composer Jan Vaclav Stich when he changed his name. He wanted to avoid having his front teeth knocked out.

Stich was born in 1740 into a family of Czech peasants who lived on the estate of Count Joseph Johann von Thun. The boy was a talented violinist. But when it came to playing the horn, he was a standout. In fact, he was so good that Count von Thun sent him to Prague to study with the very best horn players available.

But the gifted young musician wasn't entirely grateful. He was headstrong and independent. Soon after he returned to the service of the Count, he and four other musicians ran away. The Count flew into a rage, and sent his soldiers after the runaways with orders to knock out the horn player's front teeth so that he'd never be able to play again. Jan Vaclav Stich kept one jump ahead of them, though, and escaped across the border into the Holy Roman Empire. There, at the age of 20, Jan Vaclav Stich became Giovanni Punto.

Within ten years Punto was famous as one of the best horn players in Europe. He played in the private orchestra of England's King George III and in various court orchestras. He became so successful that in 1788 he made a concert tour of Germany in his own coach. In Paris, Punto met Mozart, who was so taken with his playing that he wrote a sinfonia concertante for him. In Vienna, he met a young German composer who wrote a sonata that the two performed in Vienna and Budapest. After the Budapest performance, a music critic wrote of the pianist-composer, "His name is not well-known in music circles," then he added, "Of course, Punto is very well-known."

But soon the young pianist-composer would become a good deal better known than the horn player who had changed his name to save his teeth. *His* name was Ludwig van Beethoven.

January 21st
The Devil's Trill

For centuries the violin has been thought of as an instrument of the devil. In 1770 the English music historian Charles Burney came across the remarkable story of "The Devil's Trill."

Burney's primary interest was contemporary music, and he was disappointed to arrive in Padua a few months after the death of the city's famed composer, Giuseppe Tartini. But from Tartini's friends Burney pieced together a profile of the composer. The recollections included the strange story of how Tartini had come to write his celebrated violin sonata known as "The Devil's Trill."

According to Tartini, he dreamed one night in 1713 that he had made a compact with the Devil, who promised to be at his service on all occasions. And during this dream his wishes were anticipated and surpassed with the assistance of his new servant. Finally, he imagined that he presented the Devil his violin in order to discover what kind of musician he was. To his astonishment, he heard the Devil play a solo so singularly beautiful, with such superior taste and precision, that it surpassed all the music that he had ever heard or conceived in his life. Tartini was breathless with admiration.

Awakening, Tartini seized his violin and tried desperately to recreate what he had just heard, but in vain. Then he composed a piece that may be his very best work. He called it the "Devil's Sonata," but it was so inferior to what his sleep had produced that he declared he would have broken his instrument and abandoned music forever if he could have made a living by any other means.

Apparently Tartini did get over his brush with the devil because he went on to perform and compose violin music for another 57 years. Charles Burney, the possessor of a keen, analytical mind, dismissed the devil story. He said that it showed how much Tartini's imagination was influenced by his powers of composition.

January 22nd
In the Presence of Greatness

On the night of January 22, 1937, the Greek conductor Dimitri Mitropoulos gave the fourth of five dazzling concerts in Boston. Particularly impressed was a young Harvard student whose life was about to be changed by the performances.

During three previous concerts, Mitropoulos had impressed everyone with his triple talent. In one concert he conducted his own arrangements of music by Purcell and Beethoven, conducted–and soloed in–Ottorino Respighi's *Toccata for Piano and Orchestra*, and ended with a suite from Alfredo Casella's opera *La Donna Serpente*. Mitropoulos had conducted the entire program from memory.

The young Harvard pianist had met his musical idol a few days earlier, while playing background music at a reception in his honor. Shortly afterward, Mitropoulos had spoken of the greatness and genius that he saw in the 18-year-old. After the final concert in Boston's Symphony Hall, the overflow audience and orchestra members alike poured out their admiration for the conductor. Ladies unpinned their corsages and threw them toward the podium. Mitropoulos took 13 bows. He picked up each bouquet and kissed it. The young pianist joined the crush in the conductor's dressing room. Mitropoulos made his way to him and steered him into the one place where the two could talk in private–the bathroom.

Mitropoulos put his hands on the shoulders of the breathless young man and said, "you must make me proud one day." He spoke of the young man's gift for composing. He spoke of the hard work ahead and the need not to be swayed by the flattery of friends. "You have everything to make you great," he said. "It is up to you only to fulfill your mission."

Before long, the young man would begin doing just that, and soon audiences around the world would know the name of another conductor, composer, and pianist–Leonard Bernstein.

January 23rd
The Scandalous Salome

Richard Strauss' opera *Salome* tells the lurid story of King Herod's stepdaughter and her lust for John the Baptist. Early performances of the opera were almost as sensational.

On January 23, 1907, the day after *Salome* was introduced at New York's Metropolitan Opera House, the press attacked it as "diseased in mind and morals." But before the curtains had parted, Strauss' opera was already linked to a scandal because Oscar Wilde, the author of the play on which it was based, had spent two years in prison for homosexual practices. The opera left little to the imagination. Piling scandal on top of scandal, it exposed its Victorian audiences to Salome's sensuous "Dance of the Seven Veils" and featured the brandished head of John the Baptist.

Four days after the New York premiere, the directors of the Metropolitan Opera denounced the opera and barred a repeat performance. Two days later, the New England Watch and Ward Society took steps to prevent its being staged in Boston. In March, the Congregational ministers of Boston labeled the opera "debauching and brutalizing." Somehow a Boston performance was scheduled anyway until the Governor and Bishop Lawrence issued a protest, leading the mayor of Boston to ban it entirely.

The Baptists and Methodists of Philadelphia chimed in with their own prohibitions. And on it went for several years in several countries. The censors canceled the Vienna premiere. In Berlin the Kaiser tried to prevent its performance, and in London, in 1910, the Lord Chamberlain asked that certain lines be deleted. But it may have been the opera's success that caused Richard Strauss his greatest discomfort. When *Salome* was presented in Dresden, in 1905, a ballerina performed the "Dance of the Seven Veils." Much to Strauss' dismay, once the opera caught on, the hefty soprano who sang Salome's part insisted on doing the dance herself.

January 24th
Liszt's Wild Party

Eighteen forty-eight. Piano virtuoso Franz Liszt was dazzling Europe in one concert after another. The slender, dark-haired virtuoso was the heartthrob of many a lady. But one day the arch romantic became a little too flamboyant.

The occasion was a farewell party for a friend leaving Weimar. The partygoers toasted the guest of honor by passing around a boot of champagne, and, before long, the gathering became very merry. As the proceedings progressed, Liszt took off his jacket and tie. It occurred to him that the doctor sitting next to him had promised to sound his chest when the opportunity arose. Liszt tore open his shirt and invited the doctor to do the procedure right then and there.

The doctor had been enjoying the champagne too. Laughing, he took a piece of paper from his coat pocket, formed it into a stethoscope, and placed it uncertainly on Liszt's bared chest.

At this point a Professor Wolff, realizing that he was supposed to be giving an English lesson to Princess Wittgenstein's daughter, decided to slip away from the party. He was most of the way down the stairs when Liszt noticed his absence. Still half-dressed, Liszt leaped from his chair and chased after the professor in an effort to bring him back to the party. Not finding him, Liszt ran all the way to the corner of the next street. Now bare-chested, with his hair flying about his face, Liszt caught sight of a pretty girl standing in a doorway, knitting. He stopped and spoke to her passionately, trying to embrace and kiss her.

The frightened girl fled across the courtyard, through the cellar door, and down the steps with Liszt in pursuit. Just then, a servant drawing water from a well came to the girl's defense by emptying the bucket on Liszt's head.

His friends quickly marched the doused pianist back to the party. But the incident caused a scandal. Only the intervention of the Grand Duchess–and the girl's assurance that she had been unharmed by the presumed madman–prevented damage to the dashing virtuoso's career.

January 25th
The Wedding March

One 19th century musical masterpiece brilliantly evokes the English character even though it was written by a 17-year-old who had not yet been to England.

As a boy, Felix Mendelssohn experienced English sensibilities through the plays of Shakespeare. Using the latest German translations, his family often acted them out for their own entertainment. So it was natural for Mendelssohn, at 17, to write his overture *A Midsummer Night's Dream*. Sixteen years later–in 1842–after he had traveled in England–Mendelssohn encountered another fervent admirer of Shakespeare–the King of Prussia. With an enthusiasm not to be denied, the king demanded that Mendelssohn write incidental music to four plays, including Shakespeare's *The Tempest* and *A Midsummer Night's Dream*. With unwavering style, Mendelssohn returned to Shakespeare's play of magic and star-crossed lovers and wrote complete incidental music for an 1843 performance in Potsdam.

Most popular of all his incidental music was the wedding march that sets the scene for the beginning of Act five. When that final Act opens, the Duke of Athens and the Queen of the Amazon have married and everyone assembles for the festivities.

Mendelssohn's wedding march turned out to be more effective than anyone could have imagined, largely because of a single event: On January 25, 1858, in London, the march was perfect for an event that was both English and German–the marriage of Queen Victoria's eldest child to the Crown Prince of Prussia. Victoria, Princess Royal and the prince–who would later become Frederick III–were the first to have an organist perform the march at their wedding. To this day the wedding march from *A Midsummer Night's Dream* is the music most often heard at weddings.

January 26th

Chopin in High Society

At age 21, Polish composer Frédéric Chopin left his native country, little knowing that the departure would be permanent. Within a year, he was a great success in Paris as a pianist and teacher. But he retained his modesty and good humor in a letter to a friend back home:

I have gotten into the highest society. I sit with ambassadors, princes, ministers, and don't even know how it has happened because it didn't result from any effort of mine. It is necessary for me because good taste is supposed to depend on it. Right away you supposedly have a bigger talent if you've been heard at the English or Austrian embassy. You play better if princess so-and-so was your protector.

Although this is only my first year among the artists here, I have their friendship and respect. People with huge reputations dedicate their compositions to me before I do so to them. People compose variations on my themes. Finished artists take lessons from me and compare me with John Field.

If I were even more stupid than I am, I would consider myself at the pinnacle of my career, but I know how much I still lack to attain perfection. I see it all the more clearly now that I live only among first-rate artists and know what each one of them lacks.

Anyway, maybe you haven't forgotten what my personality is like. I am today what I was yesterday, with just this one difference: I now have one whisker. The other still refuses to grow.

I have five lessons to give today. You think I'm making a fortune? Carriages and white gloves cost more, and without them I wouldn't be in good taste. Otherwise I care nothing for money, only for friendship, and I pray that I still have yours.

January 27th

The Young Critic

The brilliant but playful young composer had traveled with his father to Milan hoping to lay the foundation for a European reputation. On the eve of his fourteenth birthday, January 27, 1770, Wolfgang Amadeus Mozart wrote to his 18-year-old sister Nannerl in Salzburg:

I rejoice that you had such a good time at the sleigh ride, and I wish you a thousand opportunities for pleasure so that you can spend your life merrily. But one thing bothers me, namely that you allowed your admirer, Herr von Molk, to sigh and sentimentalize, and that you didn't go with him in his sleigh, thinking that he might pester you. What a lot of handkerchiefs he must have used that day to dry the tears he shed for you! No doubt he also swallowed at least three ounces of cream of tartar to drive away the awful evil humors in his body.

The opera at Mantua was very good. The prima donna sings well, but she's inanimate, and if you didn't see her acting, but only singing, you might imagine she wasn't singing at all because she can't open her mouth so she whines everything. The seconda donna may look like a grenadier, but she has a very powerful voice and really doesn't sing badly considering that this is her first appearance.

In Cremona the orchestra is good. The prima donna is very passable, but rather ancient and as ugly as sin. She doesn't sing as well as she acts. The seconda donna is not ugly on the stage. She's young but nothing wonderful. The male lead has a fine voice and a beautiful cantabile. The tenor has a pleasing exterior and looks like the king at Vienna. The lead ballerina is good, but an ugly dog. There was a ballerina who danced far from badly, and what's more, is far from plain, either on or offstage. The rest are the usual so-so.

The 14-year-old composer signed his letter "Wolfgang de Mozart—Noble of Hohenthal and attached to the Exchequer."

January 28th

Orange Plantation Composer

"That man has music in his mind, but when he sets it down it's almost impossible to play it." So said an American friend of a young English composer named Frederick Delius. It's not surprising that Delius' music was unusual. He had found his calling in a very unusual way: managing an orange plantation in Florida.

At 22, Delius longed to be a musician but he was stuck with a desk job that he found increasingly boring—a job in his father's wool business. When he came across an article about Florida, he pleaded with his father to let him go there. The elder Delius did better than that. He bought an orange plantation to give his son some means of support during his retreat.

Delius loved the wilderness on the banks of the St. Johns River, and he quickly took to the exotic life of canoeing and alligator hunts and listening to the songs of former slaves. He enjoyed those diversions so much that he let the oranges rot on the trees.

One day in 1886, Delius made the three-day trip to Jacksonville to buy a piano. While he was trying out various instruments in a store, a stranger approached him and introduced himself. He was a music teacher, a former New Yorker named Thomas F. Ward, and he had been intrigued by the strange and wonderful harmonies Delius was playing. Delius persuaded him to come to the plantation. Ward stayed six months, teaching Delius harmony and counterpoint. Delius later recalled that those were the best lessons of his life.

In 1886, Delius went back to Europe to take up more formal studies at prestigious institutions. But as a composer he had already been formed in a far less likely way. A teacher discovered in a Jacksonville piano store had sowed the seeds of Frederick Delius' career on a remote plantation in Florida.

January 29th

Compromises

For a long time the Spanish composer Manuel de Falla had wanted to compose a work based on the novel *The Three-Cornered Hat*. His original idea was to make an opera of it, but the author's will did not permit it, so Falla opted to write it as a ballet. Early on he learned important lessons about the compromises that come with performance.

Choreographer Serge Diaghilev had suggested Falla's *Nights in the Gardens of Spain* for the ballet, but Falla doubted that the music—with its intricate orchestral detail and abstract feeling—could be applied to ballet, so he suggested *The Three-Cornered Hat* and went to work on it. But World War I prevented Diaghilev from presenting the first performance. He authorized it to be performed as a mime, and it premiered that way in Madrid in 1917, conducted by Joaquín Turina. Despite the scaling-down of the production, Falla was quite taken with the performance.

By the time Diaghilev was able to choreograph the work, he decided that Falla would have to make cuts and additions to speed the whole thing up. Falla obliged. One of the highlights of the ballet is the final song and dance, a jota inspired by the dances of Aragon. And in order to get into the spirit of writing the piece, Falla accepted an invitation to a school dedication in an Aragonaise village. After the ceremony, a prominent Polish soprano sang one of Falla's jotas from a balcony overlooking the town plaza. The finer points of the jota were lost on the crowd and the people in the plaza reacted to it with silence, apparently unable to recognize it as something Aragonaise. Falla felt as if he were suffering a long slow death until at last the singer finished.

Later that night, though, in the village streets, Falla heard young men singing his jota with a rough native gusto, and the experience prompted him to compose the lively and authentic jota that closes *The Three-Cornered Hat*.

January 30th

The Feast

The winter of 1937 was a tough one for the Spanish composer Joaquín Rodrigo and his wife Victoria. Having grown up blind, Rodrigo was accustomed to difficulties, but as an exile in France during the Spanish Civil War, he was struggling just to get enough to eat. The couple was staying in an inexpensive hotel in Paris. A friend referred them to a woman who might be interested in buying some of their antiques. Weak with cold and hunger Rodrigo and Victoria went to see the prospective buyer. She apologized for having a dinner guest. "You'll have to wait a little while," she said. "I assume you've already eaten?"

Rodrigo assured her that they had, being too polite to mention the meager plate of rice and half a banana that was their usual supper. The composer and his wife sat down in the corner and waited. The dinner seemed to go on and on. "Try some of these wonderful slices of ham," the hostess said to her guest. "How do you like them?"

"Absolutely delicious," was the guest's reply.

The hostess offered Burgundy and duck with orange sauce. "It's too bad that the dessert is only an apple tart," she said, "and fruit and coffee." When the feast finally came to an end, the hostess said to Rodrigo and his wife, "I'm sorry that you couldn't join us. But don't you think it's a little late now to talk business?" She referred them to an antique dealer, adding, "he doesn't pay much because right now there is such a huge supply. We have so many refugees in France who need assistance."

A few years later, after World War II, Rodrigo and his wife encountered the woman again. Rodrigo was successful and famous for his *Concierto de Aranjuez*. Their former hostess had been blacklisted as a collaborator and was destitute. Rodrigo and his wife shared with her their relatively sumptuous dinner of potatoes and cabbage.

January 31st

Busoni Arrives in New York

On January 31, 1915, one of Italy's great composers, a homesick Ferruccio Busoni had just arrived in New York, and in a letter to pianist Egon Petri he turned his thoughts to the latest musical events.

I sent you two long letters from on board ship and the same vessel took them back to Europe. I posted the letters in full view of the giant buildings of the N.Y. waterfront. The morning was made magical by a light fog and that haze which I have described as sun-particles...

For each of us this arrival is in its way confusing yet stimulating. I too was moved by the spectacle and the ideas which one associates with it-but by the time we had gotten to the center of town, my heart had sunk as far below zero as it had been above it. And so it has remained until the twelfth day...

My friend Walter Rothwell has been relieved of his post as conductor in St. Paul, Minnesota. The orchestra was financed by a railway company that used it to inform cities on its line that St. Paul was a cultural center worth visiting. But evidently St. Francis found a more willing audience amongst the birds than did St. Paul among the cities of Minnesota, for the orchestra, being deemed unprofitable, has been disbanded. To the great joy of the neighboring city of Minneapolis, which is now proclaiming its orchestra as the cultural figurehead of the entire state and sending it about...

Yesterday I heard Fidelio *and was moved by the music. What a pity that the singers are such a distraction in opera performances. And one has to listen to them! The public goes to the opera because of the singers, not the music...*

February 1st

The Stingy Virtuoso

The two had been an inseparable duo. Their music had taken the concert halls of Europe by storm. Now one of them was about to go under the knife and the other insisted on being present during the entire operation. It would be enough to rattle the nerves of any surgeon—being asked to save the violin of the great virtuoso, Niccoló Paganini.

The "surgeon," the restorer of fine violins, was the Parisian J.B. Vuillaume. As his chisel began opening the instrument, there was a slight cracking noise and, in a heartbeat, Paganini was out of his chair, bending nervously over the workman. Each new movement of the tool made the violinist more and more nervous. He said it was if the chisel were entering his own flesh.

Both violin and violinist survived, but it's unlikely that the restoration brought Vuillaume any musical reward because Paganini was not free with his playing. The conductor, Sir Charles Hallé, could testify to that. He recalled seeing Paganini often in a Paris shop. In the 1830's, Hallé was a young pianist and Paganini often got him to play simply by pointing a bony finger at the piano.

From his earliest childhood, Hallé had heard about the playing of Paganini, had heard it described in supernatural terms, and longed to hear it for himself. On one memorable occasion, after Hallé had played for Paganini, a long silence ensued. Finally, Paganini rose and approached his violin case. Hallé felt he was on the threshold of the experience of a lifetime—a personal performance from the great Paganini.

Paganini opened the case. He took out the violin and carefully began to tune it. Hallé waited for him to pick up the bow and play, waited until the suspense was almost unbearable. Apparently satisfied, Paganini stopped tuning. Hallé held his breath for the first note. Carefully, the virtuoso put the violin back and shut the case, ending the only Paganini "performance" Hallé would ever get to hear.

February 2nd
The Philosopher Fraud

Jean-Jacques Rousseau was one of the most celebrated men in 18th century Europe. As far as many musicians were concerned, he was also one of the most hated.

The great Swiss philosopher began his professional life as a musician. In 1732 the 20-year-old Rousseau was long on boasting and short on ability. Though he was unable to write down the simplest drinking song, he claimed to be a composer. Meeting an influential law professor who held concerts at his house, Rousseau set about composing something for him. After two weeks of work, Rousseau considered the piece done and confidently distributed copies to the musicians who were to play it.

On the night of the concert, young Rousseau gave the musicians careful instructions regarding timing, interpretation, and cues for repeats. They tuned for five or six minutes. Finally all was ready and Rousseau gave several raps on the conductor's desk with a costly roll of paper. The room grew quiet. Gravely, Rousseau began to beat the time.

Years later, Rousseau recalled that in all the history of French opera there was never such a discordant racket. The musicians choked with laughter. The audience sat bug-eyed. The orchestra, out to make the most of the composer's embarrassment, saw to it that their scraping was loud enough and shrill enough to pierce the eardrums of the deaf. Rousseau pressed on bravely, sweating visibly, lacking the nerve to break and run. He heard the audience whispering, "It's absolutely unbearable. What mad music! What a hell of a racket!"

Rousseau did go on to compose a widely successful opera, *The Village Sage*. But, even then, he had his awkward moments. While he was supervising rehearsals of the opera, he got along so badly with the musicians that they hanged him in effigy. To which indignity Rousseau replied, "I don't wonder they should hang me now, after having tortured me so much."

February 3rd
The Confederate Composer

Among those who survived—but never recovered from—the Civil War was a promising young composer and flutist named Sidney Lanier.

Lanier was born in Macon, Georgia, on February 3, 1842. As a young man, he was a talented musician and poet, but when the Civil War broke out he set aside his flute and enlisted as a private in the Confederate army. For nearly four years he endured the hardships of war, but his harshest experiences began just before the conflict ended, in the autumn of 1864, after he was captured. During his four months as a prisoner-of-war in the Federal prison at Point Lookout, Maryland, Lanier contracted tuberculosis—consumption as it was then known. He later recalled that in the years to follow, "pretty much the whole of life had been merely not dying."

He became fascinated by the relationship between poetry and music, and, in 1876, he wrote innovative words for composer Dudley Buck's cantata—*The Centennial Meditation of Columbia*, which was performed at the opening of the Centennial Exhibition in Philadelphia.

Beset by ill health, Lanier spent the winter of 1872 in San Antonio, Texas, where he enjoyed the local German choral societies. But his financial worries became more pressing than ever, and the next year he moved north again. He joined the Peabody Orchestra in Baltimore as a flutist, a position he held off and on for the next five years. To make ends meet, Lanier wrote and lectured on poetry at the Johns Hopkins University. Along the way, he also composed several slender works for flute and small ensemble. In 1875 he wrote a large poem, "The Symphony," which later—much later—was recognized as a remarkable demonstration of his theory of the resemblance between poetry and music.

Sidney Lanier lived to be only 39, having shown much more talent than he could deliver. His promise had been cut short 16 years earlier, not on the battlefield, but by a four-month stay in a Federal prison.

February 4th

Kreisler's Other Hoax

Fritz Kreisler is known for perpetrating one of the great hoaxes in music history—passing off his own compositions as the works of early masters. But long before that scandal broke in 1935, Kreisler involved two major composers in a clever hoax.

Born on February 4, 1875, Kreisler was only seven when he entered the Vienna Academy in 1882. His teacher for harmony and music theory was the great Anton Bruckner, a strong supporter of the music of Wagner. Kreisler and some other boys decided to make a case against Wagner.

Bruckner had a chubby dog named Mops who stayed with the boys during the lunch hour while Bruckner took off for more serene surroundings. The boys put Mops to work. They made a habit of slapping and chasing the dog as they played music by Wagner. Then they would play a theme from Bruckner's *Te Deum*, during which they'd feed the dog. After a while they had Mops conditioned so that the mere sound of the Wagner would make him run from the room, while the Bruckner brought him trotting back joyfully.

One day when Bruckner returned from lunch, the boys put their joke to the test. "Master Bruckner," they said, "we know that you're devoted to Wagner, but we don't think he can even compare to you. Why, even a dog would know that you're a greater composer than Wagner." Bruckner blushed at the praise and asked what they meant.

Out came Mops. The boys played their Wagner. Howling, the dog ran from the room. Then they played their theme from Bruckner's *Te Deum*. Back came Mops, wagging his tail and pawing expectantly at their sleeves. Bruckner was convinced and visibly moved.

A young Fritz Kreisler and his friends had decided one of the great musical controversies of the 1880's—with the help of a dog named Mops.

February 5th

Victor Herbert's Revenge

Victor Herbert was America's foremost composer of operettas. He was also involved in one of the most notorious lawsuits in the history of music.

Herbert was born in Dublin in 1859. He came to New York as a cellist in 1886 and soon began a career as a conductor and composer. In 1898, he became conductor of the Pittsburgh Symphony. He had long since learned to take good reviews and bad in stride. But nothing prepared him for what he read in *the New York Musical Courier* one day in 1901. It was a review, not of an individual work of Herbert's, but of his entire career:

"All of Victor Herbert's made-to-order comic operas are pure and simple plagiarism," the review said. "There is not one single aria, waltz movement, polka, galop or march in those operas that has touched the public ear, and the street pianos and organs have ignored them–the best evidence that the people do not find them palatable. He became popular suddenly by attaining command of a brass band and joining a rollicking club of actors and Bohemians known as the Lambs, who–removed entirely from any musical comprehension–accepted the good-natured band leader as their musical dictator, and American fashion immediately paralleled him with serious-minded composers. How Pittsburgh intelligence could ever select this clever bandmaster as its symphony director passes comprehension."

Herbert hit the ceiling. He sued the *Musical Courier* for libel, asking the court for $50,000 in damages. For the next 15 months the lawsuit was headline news, largely because of the absurdity of statements made by defense witnesses, particularly one claiming that part of Herbert's operetta *The Wizard of the Nile* was note for note taken from Beethoven's Ninth Symphony–a claim easily refuted by the eminent conductor Walter Damrosch.

Herbert ultimately received just over $5,000 as a result of that successful libel suit against the *Musical Courier*. But, above all, he was vindicated as a respected –and popular–composer.

February 6th

Berlioz' Headlong Love

Hector Berlioz expressed himself in a grand way, both musically and romantically. In 1828 he was smitten with Harriet Smithson, an Irish actress who was playing Juliet and Ophelia with an English theater company in Paris. Full of unrequited love, Berlioz wrote to his friend Humbert Ferrand on February 6, 1830:

Again, without warning and without reason, my ill-fated passion awakens. She is still in London, yet I feel her presence all around me. I listen to my heartbeat. It's like a sledgehammer. If only she could dream of the poetry, the infinite extent of a love like mine, she would fly into my arms, even though she would die in my embrace. I was just going to begin my symphony Episode in the Life of an Artist *to portray the course of this misbegotten love of mine. I have it all in my head but I can't write down a thing.*

Can you tell me what it is—this overwhelming emotion, this flair for suffering which is killing me? Wait a minute—my fire is going out.

Oh, my friend, to re-light it I have burned the manuscript of my elegy! Always tears, sympathetic tears. I see Ophelia shedding them. I hear her tragic voice. The rays from her sublime eyes consume me.

I have spent quite a while drying the floods that have fallen from my eyes, while I saw Beethoven looking at me severely....All of this is crazy—completely crazy, from the viewpoint of a domino player in the Café de la Regence or a member of the Institute.

No, I still intend to live. Music is a heavenly art, nothing surpasses it but true love. The one will always make me as unhappy as the other, but at least I shall have lived.

Berlioz did live long enough to marry—and separate from—Harriet Smithson.

February 7th
A Virtuoso Visitor

Wherever he performed, Franz Liszt caused a stir. We get a vivid close-up of the dazzling pianist from the celebrated Russian composer Mikhail Glinka, who describes a visit by the 30-year-old Liszt to St. Petersburg in February 1842:

He played Chopin's mazurkas, nocturnes, and etudes and, in a word, all brilliant and fashionable music very nicely but with terribly affected "elegant" touches.... Less satisfactory, though (in my opinion) was his playing of Bach (whose Well-Tempered Clavier *I knew almost by heart) and a Beethoven symphony which he himself had transcribed for piano. In Beethoven's sonatas and in classical music as a whole his execution was not of the requisite quality, and his way of striking the keys was jerky, as if he were chopping cutlets. His playing of Hummel's Septet suggested something close to contempt, and I thought that Hummel had played it incomparably better and more simply. Liszt played Beethoven's E Flat Major Concerto much better. In the last analysis, I cannot compare his manner of playing with that of Field, Charles Mayer, or even Thalberg, especially in the scales....*

Liszt sight read several numbers from Ruslan *from an autographed score of mine, not known to anyone before, and to the general astonishment he didn't miss a note....*

Aside from his very long hair, in society he sometimes resorted to a sort of dainty affectation and at other times to an arrogant self-confidence. For the rest, despite a certain patronizing air, he was generally well liked, especially among artists and young people; he gladly and wholeheartedly took part in the general merriment and was not at all loath to carouse with us.

*From *Memoirs* by Michail Ivanovich Glinka. Translated by Richard B. Mudge. Copyright 1963 by the University of Oklahoma Press. Reprinted by permission.

February 8th
Verdi Doesn't Exist

Giuseppe Verdi was a composer who fought for political causes. But his official role in politics came against his will. On February 8, 1865, he wrote to librettist Francesco Maria Piave:

I received a letter from Count Cavour urging me to accept the nomination to parliament that several citizens were offering me. I went to see him in Turin and he laughed at my speech about how unsuited I was for Parliament. Then he proposed some convincing arguments of his own.

"All right," I said at last. "I accept on the condition that I may resign after a few months."

"Very well," he said. "Just inform me beforehand."

I became a Deputy and at first I went often to the Chamber. Then came the ceremonial session when Rome was proclaimed the capital of Italy. After casting my vote I went up to the Count and said, "I think the time has come for me to bid farewell to the assembly."

"Wait till we go to Rome," he said. "Meanwhile I'm off to the country."

Those were the last words I heard him utter. A few weeks later he died! After several months I left Rome, traveled around, and finally settled in Paris for professional reasons. So I was away from parliament for over two years and I've hardly ever set foot there since. Several times I've tried to hand in my resignation, but for some reason or another I am still a Deputy against all my wishes and tastes, without any political position, any gift for the work, and completely lacking in the necessary patience.

So there you are. If you ever need to write my biography as a Member of Parliament all you have to do is print in the middle of a blank page: "The 450 are really only 449 because Verdi as a Deputy doesn't exist."

February 9th
The Chow Hound

On February 9, 1790, Joseph Haydn had just returned to the Hungarian country estate of his long-time employers, the Esterházy family, and to his friend Frau von Genzinger he wrote longingly of the comforts and congeniality of Vienna.

Now–here I sit in my wilderness–deserted–like a poor orphan, almost without human companionship. Sad. Full of the memory of precious days gone by. And who knows when those pleasant days will return? That charming company in which a whole circle shares one heart, one soul, and all of those fine musical evenings that can only be remembered, not described in writing.

Where is all the enthusiasm? Gone. And gone for a long time. At home I found everything in confusion. My whole apartment was in disarray. My forte-piano, which I used to love, was out of order, disobedient–and perturbed rather than soothed me. I got little sleep. Even my dreams were a persecution, for when I dreamed I was hearing an excellent performance of The Marriage of Figaro, *that wretched North wind woke me up and almost blew my nightcap off my head....*

Here at Esterház nobody asks me, "Do you take chocolate with milk or without? Would you like coffee, black or with cream? What can I get you, my dear Haydn? Would you like vanilla ice or a pineapple one?" If only I had here a piece of good Parmesan cheese, especially on fast days to help the black dumpling and noodles down more easily. This very day I ordered our porter to send me down a few pounds of it.

Forgive me, dearest lady, if on this occasion I waste your time with such outrageous stuff in my wretched scribbling. Forgive me as a man to whom the Viennese were too kind. But I am already gradually beginning to get used to country ways. Yesterday I did some studying for the first time, and it was quite in the Haydn manner.

February 10th
The Poet Prophet

One of the most memorable scenes in Russian opera is in Tchaikovsky's *Eugene Onegin*—the scene in which two friends engage in a fatal duel. The opera was based on a narrative poem written in 1831 by Alexander Pushkin, who in many ways was predicting his own death.

Pushkin was a celebrated poet, and his wife Nathalie one of the most beautiful women in Russian society. In the fall of 1836, a young Frenchman, Baron George d'Anthes, began a flirtation with Nathalie. Being a foreigner, he had no particular reverence for Russia's great national poet. Nathalie by no means discouraged his attentions, and their relationship soon became common knowledge. The situation grew dangerous when a practical joker sent Pushkin a letter in French informing him of his unanimous election as Grand Master of the Most Serene Order of Cuckolds.

Wild with jealousy, Pushkin jumped to the conclusion that the Baron was behind the insult and sent him a note challenging him to a duel. Then events took a strange twist. The Baron wrote to Pushkin, declaring that his affections were not for Nathalie but for her sister Catherine. The duel was averted and the Baron married Catherine, becoming Pushkin's brother-in-law. But it was not to be a happy family. Soon the Baron and Nathalie resumed their relationship. Furious, Pushkin dashed off an accusing and insulting letter to the Baron's father, and this time the Baron challenged Pushkin to a duel.

The encounter was set for 4 p.m. on February 10, 1837. Pushkin and his second, a friend from school days, drove through St. Petersburg, greeting many unsuspecting friends on their way to the appointed place, the Black Brook. Pushkin and the Baron arrived at the same time. The poet grew impatient with the preliminaries, and finally the two walked through the snow, turned, and aimed their pistols. The Baron fired first and Pushkin fell, wounded in the abdomen.

Two days later, Alexander Pushkin passed into history, best remembered for his poem *Eugene Onegin*, in which he had foreshadowed his own death in a duel.

February 11th
The Child Adventurer

He was playing the piano at age one. At four, he improvised at public concerts. At six, he auditioned for admission to the Paris Conservatory and would have been admitted if it hadn't been for one impulsive mistake.

Young Isaac Albéniz was a parent's dream and a nightmare rolled into one. He was born in Comprodón, Spain, in 1860. His father was an administrator in Gerona. After the failure at the Conservatory, the elder Albeniz launched his six-year-old son on a three-year tour of intensive concertizing–with a heavy emphasis on showmanship. The boy made a specialty of playing with the keyboard covered, with his back to the piano. And, to attract even more attention, young Albeniz performed dressed as a musketeer, with a sword at his side.

When he was eight, his father's strictness and Jules Verne's adventure novels prompted Albéniz to run away from home–still dressed as a musketeer. He sneaked aboard a train, where he chanced to meet the mayor of Escorial, a kindly man who arranged for him to perform at the local casino, then put him and his earnings on the return train to Madrid. But Albéniz sneaked onto a train going in the opposite direction. Bandits attacked that train. Albéniz didn't want to go home penniless, so he performed throughout Spain and Portugal. He was 12 when the mayor of Cádiz had him arrested in order to return him to his parents at last. But Albéniz stowed away on a ship bound for Buenos Aires. A year later, when he was playing a concert in Santiago, Cuba, he was arrested again and taken to Havana. Small world–his father had just become the comptroller of taxes there.

The elder Albéniz allowed the boy to continue his world travels. Eventually returning to Paris, Albéniz applied again to the Conservatory and this time was accepted, in part because he avoided his previous mistake of pitching a ball through a window pane.

February 12th
Tchaikovsky on the Road

On February 12, 1888, Peter Tchaikovsky was traveling from Leipzig to Prague and coping with fame. He wrote to his brother Modest.

On Sunday the 12th, we left for Prague. At the frontier, I already felt the coming celebrations. The chief of guards asked if I was Tchaikovsky, and when I said that I was he became most deferential. In the last station before Prague, a delegation and an entire crowd were waiting for us and accompanied us to Prague. At the station in Prague—another delegation, children with flowers, two speeches—one in Russian, another long one in Czech. I replied and walked to a carriage through a thick wall of people all shouting 'Slava!' (Hail.) At the hotel I was given a splendid suite. In the evening Verdi's opera Otello *at the Opera House; a crowd of new acquaintances and more welcomes. After the opera, supper at my hotel.*

Yesterday morning a visit from Dvořák who stayed for more than two hours. A tour around the town and a look at some of the important sights, accompanied by the director of the museum and a Russian priest. Supper at the home of a prominent bookseller. A ball in the best hall in town, where I sat in a box and everybody looked at me.

Today a service in our Russian church at 10:30, a visit to the Students' Club, dinner at Dvořák's, another drive through the town with the museum director—he speaks very good Russian—and a big evening reception in my honor, all of which is very nice, very flattering, but you can imagine how tired I get and how I suffer. I'm in a fog.

It seems that my stay here makes sense, not so much because I am a good composer but because I am a Russian composer. I'm sending clippings from the paper. Good-bye, Modinka. Be pleased for my sake but also feel sorry for me.

February 13th

Carnaval!

In February 1917, composer Darius Milhaud left war-torn France for Rio de Janeiro as the secretary to the newly appointed French Minister to Brazil. His experiences there would not affect French politics, but they would influence French music.

Milhaud arrived in Rio in the middle of Carnaval, and the holiday was his introduction to Brazilian folklore. In his autobiography *My Happy Life*, Milhaud described the excitement in the streets as the time for Carnaval approached:

One of the dancers' favorite amusements is to improvise words to a melody that's repeated over and over. The singer is supposed to keep coming up with new words, and as soon as he starts to run out of ideas, somebody new takes over. The monotony of this unending chorus and its persistent rhythm end up creating a hypnotic effect and the dancers fall under the spell of it.

He recalled ladies going to the ball in their formal attire, leaning on their husbands' arms. Since most of the dancers were servants, they borrowed their masters' clothes, and sometimes even their names and titles. One night, he heard "The President of the Senate" and "The British Ambassador" announced and saw two servant couples, dressed to beat the band, come forward proudly. Milhaud summed up the musical impact of the event:

For six weeks the entire population throws itself into singing and dancing. One song that becomes the most popular is designated the Carnaval song. We heard the one for 1917 wherever we went, cranked out by little orchestras in front of movie theaters, played by military bands and town orchestras, whistled and sung in every house—and it followed us around all winter long.

The rhythms and melodies of Rio stuck with Milhaud longer than that. Some of his best music was inspired by the sounds he heard in Brazil during Carnaval.

February 14th

Nothing But You

Robert Schumann on his way to Zwickau, wrote to Clara Wieck on the eve of Valentine's Day, 1836:

It's all I can do to keep my eyes open. For the last two hours I've been waiting for the express mail coach. The roads are so bad that it may be two in the morning before we get underway. How clearly I can see you, my own beloved Clara. You seem so near that I can almost touch you. Once upon a time I could express my feelings in pretty phrases, but no more....

I may as well tell you that my future is now much more secure. Of course, I can't just sit on my hands and I still have plenty to do if I'm going to earn the image you see in your mirror. You'll want to continue with your art, to share my work and my burdens, my happiness and my sorrow.

My priority in Leipzig will be to put my material affairs in order. I am at peace with myself. Who knows? Maybe your father won't refuse his blessing when I ask for it. There is still plenty to think about, but for now I trust in our good angel. Fate created us for each other. I've known that for a long time, even though I didn't have the nerve to speak to you sooner or to come to an understanding with you.

Later on I'll give you a fuller explanation of today's jottings, and if you can't make them out, then be assured that I love you more than I can say. It's getting very dark in this room, and my fellow passengers are sleeping. Outside there's a snowstorm. As for me, I'll take refuge in a corner, bury my head in a cushion, and think of nothing but you.

February 15th

Bach Draws His Sword

In the summer of 1703, an 18-year-old organist began his duties at the New Church at Arnstadt. His contract included an excellent salary, and things might have gone very well if church officials had stuck to the contract. But they added one more duty, and the result was a confrontation that could have been fatal.

The organist was a temperamental genius named Johann Sebastian Bach. In addition to all of his other responsibilities, he was expected to train a small group of pupils from the Latin school. The pupils were such hard cases that the City Council called their behavior "scandalous." Because he was younger than most of them, Bach had a hard time maintaining discipline. For two years, the short-tempered teacher and the unruly class clashed.

One of the more unruly musicians was a bassoonist named Geyersbach. He was three years older than Bach and made a point of being offensive. One dark night he confronted Bach on the street and began hitting him with a stick and calling him a "dirty dog." Bach was not altogether blameless. He had poked fun of Geyersbach and called him a "nanny goat bassoonist." Not one to take a beating lightly, Bach drew his sword and the fight was on. Dodging the stick, Bach made several thrusts that pierced Geyersbach's jacket before passers-by rushed in to prevent bloodshed.

Church officials urged Bach to work with the choir despite the "imperfect conditions." But after the street fight, Bach became so disgusted with the offending group of students that he eventually managed to get out of teaching them.

Bach's conflicts weren't over though. Soon he would be at odds with the congregation, and the conflict would bring two great changes in his life. To be continued...

February 16th

Bach Takes His Leave

Eager to forget the embarrassments at Arnstadt, Bach asked the church officials for a four-week leave of absence so that he could travel to Lübeck to visit the famous organist Dietrich Buxtehude. With permission granted, Bach set out for Lübeck, 230 miles away, probably traveling mostly by coach.

He was most interested in a set of evening concerts Buxtehude conducted. He arrived just in time for them and found that they surpassed his highest expectations.

The high level of musicianship in Lübeck held Bach in awe. The four weeks turned into four months. At one point it was even suggested to him that he might become Buxtehude's successor, if only he would marry Buxtehude's 30-year-old daughter Anna Morgana, but Bach politely declined. Back in Arnstadt he had fallen in love with Maria Barbara Bach, a distant cousin.

When he finally returned to Arnstadt, Bach was a new musician. Encouraged by all the new ideas he had heard in Lübeck, he became inventive as he accompanied hymns, inserting long improvisations between verses—much to the confusion and dismay of the congregation. The church officials, still aggravated by his long absence, ordered him to stop embellishing the music, and Bach overcompensated by making the preludes too short. Then church officials complained about rumors that Bach had been using the church in off-hours to accompany the singing of "an unknown maiden"—namely Maria Barbara.

So by June 1707, Bach had had enough. He took a job as organist in Mühlhausen, and, in October, he settled into married life with his bride, Maria Barbara.

February 17th
Grieg Plays for Liszt

Edvard Grieg, writing from Rome, February 17, 1870.

Dear Parents! Yesterday as I was sitting in the Scandinavian Club playing whist I received a message that Liszt would like to see me at his house.

This wasn't my first meeting with him. Recently he was in town and expecting me, so I rushed out to see him. He lives close to the Titus Triumphal Arch and the old Roman Forum, in a monastery. I was told that he likes for people to bring something with them so I took my last violin sonata, wrote on the outside "To Dr. F. Liszt with admiration," also took my funeral march for Nordraak and a booklet of songs and hurried down the street with butterflies in my stomach. But I could have spared myself the anxiety because it would be hard to find a more lovable man than Liszt.

Grieg recalled that Liszt's eyes looked hungrily at the sonata tucked under his arm and his long spidery fingers drew so close that Grieg thought it best to open the packet at once. Liszt began to turn the pages, gave the first part of the sonata a cursory reading, nodding occasionally with a "Bravo!" or "very lovely." Then, Grieg confessed, Liszt put him on the spot:

My spirits began to soar, but when he asked me to play the sonata my courage failed me completely. Never had I tried to put the whole thing together for the piano, and I would gladly have avoided making a mess of it in front of him, but I was stuck. So I began on his beautiful Chickering grand piano. Right at the beginning, where the violin breaks in with a little baroque but national passage, he exclaimed, "How bold! I like it. Let's hear it again."

And when the violin the second time slips into the adagio, he played the violin part higher up on the piano in octaves with such beautiful expression, so remarkably true and singing, that I smiled inwardly. Those were the first notes I heard from Liszt.

February 18th

Father Mozart's Command

In February 1778, Mozart was long past his days as a child prodigy and trying to make a name for himself as a mature composer and performer. His long-suffering manager was his father Leopold, and letters between the two show that they often failed to see eye-to-eye.

Leopold was eager for his son to build his reputation by going to Paris but, after a few letters crossed in the mail, the elder Mozart was dismayed to discover that Wolfgang was not in Paris but in Mannheim, where he was keeping company with his attractive young cousin, Aloysia Weber. When Wolfgang wrote from Mannheim of his desire to go to Italy, the agitated Leopold was tested to the breaking point. He wrote a stern letter trying to get his son back on track:

The object of your journey was to help your parents and to contribute to your dear sister's welfare, but above all, to acquire honor and fame in the world, which to some extent you did in your boyhood.

Now it falls entirely on you to raise yourself by degrees to one of the highest positions ever achieved by any musician. It's a duty you owe to a kind Providence for the extraordinary talents He has given you, and it depends entirely on your own good sense and good conduct whether you become a commonplace artist the world will forget or a celebrated master which future generations will read about in books.

On the one hand, infatuated with some pretty face, you may one day breathe your last on a straw sack with your wife and children starving. On the other hand, after a well-spent Christian life, you may die peacefully in honor and independence with your family well provided for. Go off to Paris without delay! Nothing ventured, nothing gained. The very idea of Paris should have guarded you from all distractions.

February 19th

Amadeus Fires Back

Having been taken to task by his father, Mozart fired off a defensive letter:

I always thought that you would disapprove of my trip with the Webers, but I never had any such intention. When people lose confidence in me I'm likely to lose confidence in myself. The days when I stood on a stool and sang some nonsense Italian and kissed the tip of your nose are long gone. But have you ever lost my reverence, love, and obedience?

The bitter way you write about my innocent relationship with your brother's daughter makes me justifiably indignant. But since it's not what you think I see no need to respond to you on the subject.

But never mind. You wrote in a moment of irritation. Everything you write about Mademoiselle Weber is true, but her singing goes to the heart. But when I wrote you I knew as well as you do that she is still too young and first must be taught to act and has to rehearse often on stage. Lately I have made her practice the passages in the Grand Aria because if she goes to Italy she'll have to sing bravuras. The cantabile she'll certainly never forget because that's her natural inclination.

So now you know everything. I still recommend her to you with all my heart and I beg you not to forget about sending the arias, cadenzas and other things I asked for. I embrace my sister lovingly. She's not supposed to worry about every little trifle or I won't come back to her.

Aloysia soon spurned Mozart, and four years later he married her younger sister Constanze.

February 20th
Weber Pans Der Freischutz

Reviewers have long been vilified for being rough on performers. But this letter from Carl Maria von Weber shows that sometimes the harshest critics are composers. Weber wrote to his wife from Vienna on February 20, 1822:

Finally, in the evening, was the performance of my Freischütz. *What can I say about it? Where can I begin? No two passages in the opera were played at the correct tempo. Everything was either hurried or dragged out. The conductor had rehearsed it without the least artistic insight or expression. I sat there in a fever. The house was quite full. Otherwise everything went well. The choruses were outstanding, the scenery very pretty although most of it was irrelevant. The most basic elements of stagecraft were ignored. The stage wasn't even darkened at the end of Act I. And so on. The Overture—taken too fast. The Introduction was good! The ensemble number went excellently and was rousingly sung by the chorus.*

Forti did well. He has a different approach to the character but it's consistent, and his singing is excellent. Schröder was charming. She has a lovely voice and acts in character. Her intonation is clean but she is by no means a completely developed singer yet. As for Mademoiselle Vio, she is completely lackluster and the duet dragged dreadfully.

The great aria, the prayer—rushed but not without expression. The trio went head-over-heels. The Wolves' Glen scene was just sort of glued together, but with a lot of attractive touches. Agatha's cavatina was the only thing that was quite good. The finale was all helter-skelter.

On top of all that, for the sake of policy, I had to put the best face on things and pretend to find it all just gorgeous. I can't understand how people could have liked that opera. At the same time, though, I have to give everyone credit for doing their best, and their enthusiasm is unbounded.

February 21st

Second Thoughts

Even the best composers can stumble on the first step to writing an opera–coming up with a subject! Giacomo Puccini wrote from New York to his publisher in February 1907:

Regarding Conchita, *I still have major doubts about the subject. When I think of the novel I have no doubts, but when I think of the libretto, I have plenty. The structure and the murky psychology scare me.*

The development is drab and treacherous to put into music. The first and second scenes are all right, but the scene at the window in the dance café and the last scene both seem to me unsatisfactory.

Give this boat a good going-over and see if you can find any leaks. I can see them. But what can I do? The world is expecting an opera from me and it's past time to have one ready. We've had enough of Boheme, Butterfly, *and* company. *Even I am sick of them!*

I'm writing all of this to prepare you for my doubts about Conchita. *You'll ask, "Why did you pick up the subject in the first place?" My dear boy, I've been wracking my brain and my soul for three years to find a place to lay my four notes and I have latched onto the most impressive one like a hungry cat.*

The scene with the naked dance has to be disguised. The virginity question, which is the focus of the book, cannot be made clear in a spoken version of the story. I'm afraid of the last scene, which–unless it's unusually realistic–will be just an ordinary duet. And the scene the way I've imagined it won't be accepted by the public. So I assure you that my life is not a bed of roses.

Puccini never wrote the planned opera.

February 22nd

Music-Making at Mount Vernon

During the quiet years between his wartime experiences, George Washington enjoyed relaxing at home with music.

When he married widow Martha Custis in 1759, Washington encouraged her to take keyboard lessons, though she seems not to have pursued them for long. In 1761 Washington bought a London-made harpsichord for his stepdaughter, Patcy, who was four years old at the time. For her less inspired older brother Jack, Washington bought a violin and a boxwood flute trimmed with silver. During the 1760's, Mount Vernon was usually full of guests and Washington liked to coax young Patcy into giving recitals. In 1766, when music teacher John Stadler came to Mount Vernon, Martha took keyboard lessons with her children.

Washington liked the music of Joseph Haydn and Johann Christian Bach, and that of Ignaz Joseph Pleyel and Johann Baptist Vanhall, as well as country fiddle tunes and the otherworldly sounds of the glass harmonica, an instrument perfected by Benjamin Franklin. He tried to persuade any musically inclined guest to play.

Washington was well known as an accomplished dancer, and once a month he sponsored dancing lessons in the big drawing room at Mount Vernon. It wasn't all fun and games though. Dancing master John Christian took the lessons so seriously that, in the presence of their mother, he struck two young ladies when they made mistakes in their dancing. And when he thought that one of the young men was acting "insolent and wanton," he told him to straighten up or leave the classes. The uncooperative young man was almost certainly Jack Custis, the stepson of the accomplished dancer and music-lover, George Washington.

As for Washington's own musical abilities, he confided to Philadelphia composer Francis Hopkinson, "I can neither sing one of the songs nor raise a single note on any instrument."

February 23rd

Augusta

"What's that music you're playing? I emphatically dislike it." So said César Franck's wife when he played a piano version of his Quintet. She may have been reacting to the unusual passion in the piece–passion aroused by an extraordinary student of Franck's.

The student was Augusta Holmes, the daughter of an Irish army officer. At 22, she was eager to break away from her family, so Augusta set out for Bayreuth to satisfy her craving for the music of Wagner. Among her companions was Catulle Mendès, whose bride had taken a fancy to Wagner. Mendès wasted little time in becoming Augusta's lover.

Returning to Paris, Augusta established a salon where she entertained an entourage of admiring writers, painters, and musicians with her remarkable singing. Among them was one of France's most distinguished composers, Camille Saint-Saëns. "We were all in love with her," he recalled many years later. "Any one of us would have been proud to have made her his wife." Saint-Saëns wrote two sonnets in praise of her beauty. Saint-Saens' disdain for Franck's Quintet may well have came from the jealousy he felt when she began taking lessons from Franck.

It was a perfectly respectable relationship, but the attention Franck lavished on his new student made Franck's marriage less than comfortable. Vincent d'Indy admitted to falling under her spell after she sang her version of the *Danse Macabre*. Nikolai Rimsky-Korsakov was struck by her appearance, which he described as "very décolleté."

Before long, Augusta's musical ambitions drew her on to bigger things, including composing operas, without much success. By the turn of the century, she was a shadow of her former self, keeping a small apartment near the Paris Opera where she maintained a roomful of souvenirs to remind her of her years among the brightest artists France had to offer.

February 24th
Handel's Blunder, Part 1

When George Frederick Handel's oratorio *Deborah* premiered in London in 1733, it could have made the composer a lot of money if he hadn't made several blunders having little to do with music.

King George II and the Royal Family were present, and all of them liked the oratotio except for Frederick, Prince of Wales, who had taken to condemning anything his father praised. Diarists of the day wrote that the oratorio was charming and magnificent. But the blessing of the king was a curse for *Deborah,* because the king was not a popular man in 1733. King George had just spent a long sojourn in Hanover, confirming suspicions that he had no great love for England.

Prime Minister Robert Walpole had just reinstated a salt tax, was about to impose a tax on tobacco, and planned to raise the taxes on spirits and wine. At the same time, Walpole had reduced the land tax, playing into the hands of the well-to-do at the expense of the masses.

Without any apparent sensitivity, Handel chose to raise admission prices to his oratorios. The people could not do without salt, tobacco, or wine. They *could* do without Handel. And at the opening night of *Deborah*, only 120 of them showed up. Most patrons had resolved to boycott his theater. Handel tried to make excuses: the cost of new lights for the theater. People laughed and stayed away.

His temper became so violent that most of the singers kept their distance from him. One of Handel's librettists published a letter which spoke of Handel having been thrown into a fit of deep melancholy, "interrupted sometimes by raving fits, in which he sees ten thousand opera devils coming to tear him to pieces, then he breaks out into frantic incoherent speeches, muttering 'sturdy beggars, assassinations, etc.'"

And the situation would get worse before it got better.

February 25th
Handel's Blunder, Part 2

Handel had never written more brilliantly, but when his oratorio *Deborah* opened in London in 1733, once-loyal audiences boycotted it, in part because of exorbitant ticket prices and, in part, because of a notorious misadventure with a case of Burgundy.

Handel had invited a scene-painter named Goupy to dinner at his house on Brook Street. The artist had created the scenery for several of Handel's latest operas and was the drawing-master to the Prince of Wales. He was also a cartoonist with a bent for withering satire.

During the walk to dinner, Handel carefully explained that he was losing most of his money because of reversals at the theater, was practically in the poorhouse, and so dinner would be slim, indeed. Handel was true to his word. The supper was minimal. Afterward, Handel excused himself, saying that he had some writing to do. He said that he had received an inspiration that he was eager to put down on paper. Goupy sat at the table and waited. And waited, but still Handel didn't return.

Then, chancing to look out the window, the artist caught sight of Handel in an adjoining room. He was enjoying a glass of Burgundy, having just been given a case of it by a highly-connected friend. Being a wine-lover himself, the artist was offended, and he left the house resolving to take revenge the best way he knew how.

Soon afterward, two notorious cartoons were circulating around London. One of them was called "The Charming Brute," and it showed a hog seated at the organ surrounded by fine foods and wine. The hog's face was that of George Frederick Handel. Before long, the cartoons had been published throughout England. Shopkeepers offered copies for sale. Handel had become the joke of the year, and Goupy was celebrated as a David who had slain a musical Goliath–a giant who had dared to raise ticket prices above the reach of the common man.

February 26th
Sir Thomas Quells a Neighbor

Music-making is a congenial form of art, but Sir Thomas Beecham discovered that sometimes the congeniality needs a little lubrication. During a tour of Australia, the English conductor was relaxing in his hotel room, playing the piano and applying his less-than-sonorous voice to some of Wagner's forging songs. At about midnight there was a rapping on the wall. Sir Thomas went to the room next door and knocked. "Shut that bloody row at this time of night," his Australian neighbor said. "How do you expect anybody to go to sleep?"

Sir Thomas replied, "I don't expect it. This is not the time for sleep." He went on to inform the Australian that to go to bed after midnight was to go to bed at a reasonable hour.

The Australian was not convinced. "How do you expect a fellow to get any sleep in all that hell row? I've got to get up early and do a day's work."

Sir Thomas remained cheerful. "My dear fellow, I have to get up early and conduct the Brisbane Orchestra at a rehearsal, which is worse. Come, come, and rouse ye. Thou art a scholar; let us therefore eat and drink."

Perhaps he was too incredible to be resisted, the urbane and persistent Englishman lingering at the businessman's hotel door at midnight. The groggy Australian came into Beecham's suite and sat there in his pajamas, taking in whatever entertainment Sir Thomas dished up, drinking champagne until, dead to the world, he was carried back to his room by Sir Thomas.

The next day, the Australian checked out of the hotel. But not before leaving Sir Thomas a note declaring that he had never enjoyed himself so much in his life and lamenting that he had passed out so quickly. Showing the note to a friend, Sir Thomas remarked, "The Australian is a heavy, but not a strong drinker."

February 27th

Paderewski's Revenge

The great Polish pianist, Ignacy Jan Paderweski, took the opportunity to get even with an agent named Wolff who mistreated him on his way to the top. And he wondered ever after what it had cost him to even the score.

In Berlin, in 1890, Paderweski was an international sensation, and he was to perform his piano concerto with the eminent conductor, Hans von Bülow. Wolff's agency was the most powerful in Europe. In 1889 Paderewski had asked Wolff to manage his German concert tour and Wolff had flatly refused. Some years before, when Wolff had been manager for Anton Rubinstein, he had forbidden Paderewski even to stand in the hall during Rubinstein's Paris concert.

Now, on the eve of Paderewski's Berlin debut, Wolff invited Paderewski to come under his management. He made no mention of the previous encounters. Paderewski reminded him of them point by unpleasant point and steadfastly refused. "Oh, well," Wolff laughed, "that is business my dear sir—business! Don't regard it so seriously. Join me now and you'll be very glad you have.

You'll never regret it, never if you come to me." Wolff added solemnly, "If no is your answer, I must tell you very frankly that you will regret it."

The next day, during the performance of Paderewski's concerto, the orchestra played abominably. Once they had gotten through the concerto, which Paderewski later described as a massacre, a further indignity was waiting. Paderweski was playing a series of solos. Von Bülow had been sitting by the piano. During a funeral march by Schubert, he suddenly jumped up, pushed his chair back, and ran from the stage. It was impossible for Paderewski to continue. The program ended in a complete fiasco.

Was von Bülow conspiring with Wolff to ruin the concert? Paderewski never found out, but he came to consider Schubert's funeral march a funeral march for his debut in Berlin.

February 28th

Like Son, Like Father

Johann Strauss the Younger is known as the waltz-king, but his father was worthy of the title before him, according to an eyewitness account from Vienna in 1833:

Under illuminated trees and in open arcades people sit at countless tables eating and drinking, chatting, laughing and listening. In their midst the orchestra plays new waltzes that stir the blood like the bite of a tarantula. In the middle of the garden, on the orchestra platform, stands the modern hero of Austria, the Austrian Napoleon, the conductor Johann Strauss.

The power wielded by the black-haired musician may be very dangerous. He's particularly lucky that there's no censorship for waltz music and the thoughts and emotions it stirs up.

The motley crowds bump each other. The girls, warm and laughing, push their way through groups of lively youths, their hot breath like the perfume of tropical flowers.

A long rope is put up to separate those in the center of the hall from the dancers. It's an unsteady barrier though, and the only way to distinguish the dancers is to watch the girls' heads going round and round. The couples waltz right through anything that gets in the way of their joyous enthusiasm. Nothing holds them back, not even the intense heat, which pours forth in waves as if driven by African winds.

These orgies go on till early morning, then Austria's musical hero, Johann Strauss, packs up his violin and goes home to sleep for a few hours and to dream of new battle plans and waltz themes for the next afternoon. The steamy couples stream out in the warm night airs of Vienna and disappear with happy giggles in all directions.

February 29th
He Wasn't That Precocious

One of the most successful opera composers of all time retired from writing operas at the age of 37. By then he already had a long career behind him. In fact, Gioacchino Rossini began composing enduring works just after his second birthday.

In the summer of 1804, Rossini and two cousins named Morini were staying at a country house near Ravenna. Their host was the 23-year-old Agostino Trossi, member of a well-to-do family of grain merchants. Trossi was an amateur bass player, and the group thought it would be fun to make music together. Rossini rose to the occasion and in three days dashed off a series of six sonatas for two violins, cello, and double bass.

Years later, Rossini described the performances, saying that the others "played like dogs" and that he was "not the least doggish, by God." In the only surviving manuscript he referred to the works as "six dreadful sonatas."

The musical establishment knew about the existence of the sonatas almost from the beginning, but the whereabouts of the pieces was a mystery for years. Most experts assumed that they had long since been destroyed when, in 1954, Rossini's original manuscript turned up in the Library of Congress in Washington.

Although Rossini was the first to disparage the sonatas and may well have touched them up in later years, they show how precocious the young composer was. In fact, technically, he wrote them just after his second birthday. Rossini was born on February 29, 1792. His first birthday wouldn't come until February 29, 1796. Because 1800 was a century year not divisible by 400 it was not a leap year. And so the composer's second birthday didn't occur until 1804, just a few months before the 12-year-old Rossini wrote his charming and enduring sonatas for strings.

March 1st

Gluck Takes It from the Top

Christoph Willibald von Gluck was so intent on the music that he was unaware of anything else. His friend, painter Johann Christian Mannlich, described a rehearsal in Paris in the 1770's.

Every day from nine until noon Gluck attended the rehearsals of his opera. When he returned from them, always in the company of Madame Gluck, he was awash in sweat from his exertions. Without saying a word to him Madame Gluck would take off his wig, rub his head with a towel, and change his clothes. He was flat on his back and didn't say a word again until mealtime.

At one rehearsal the overture and two thirds of the opera had gone passably well although the composer did find about a thousand things to repeat twenty times "from the top." But when the time came to work on the third part, Gluck ran around like a man possessed, from one end of the orchestra to the other. Sometimes the violins were the culprits, sometimes it was the basses or the horns or the violas and so on.

He cut them off, sang the passage with the expression he wanted.

During one of these incidents Gluck was downstage in the vortex of it all, listening to each instrument, when the basses made a mistake. He turned his head so fast that his old round wig couldn't keep up and fell to the floor. In his enthusiasm for the music he wasn't even aware of the loss and noticed only that the lead soprano, with exaggerated gravity, picked up the wig from the floor with two fingers, the other fingers extended, and put the wig back on his head.

In his excitement Gluck had once again "taken it from the top."

March 2nd
Truth or Legend?

Truth or legend? Either way, one story about Archangelo Corelli has come down from generation to generation, from Corelli's time to our own. The story takes place about 1709, when Corelli was at the height of his reputation as a composer and a violinist. It goes like this:

The King of Naples invited Corelli to come and perform for him. Supposedly Corelli was fearful and reluctant, but finally was convinced to come from Rome to Naples to perform for the king. Although he was nervous because there wasn't time to rehearse the members of the king's orchestra, Corelli agreed to perform one of his concertos with them. He was stunned when the king's players read his concerto at sight almost as well as his own ensemble did after many rehearsals.

Next he was cajoled into playing one of his violin sonatas for the king, who found the slow movement too long and drab and left before it was over. Then Corelli was asked to lead in the king's presence a performance of a masque by Alessandro Scarlatti. Corelli found Scarlatti's violin part awkward and difficult. He stumbled on a high F and was shaken to hear the king's violinists carry the note gracefully. After that they were to perform a song in C Minor. Corelli began in C Major. "Start over," Scarlatti said cheerfully, but Corelli went on in C Major until Scarlatti raised his voice and got him to play in the right key.

The 18th century English music historian Charles Burney tells the end of the story: "So mortified was poor Corelli with this disgrace and the general bad figure he imagined he had made at Naples, that he stole back to Rome in silence."

True or false, the story implies that in a time of cutthroat competition among musicians, someone played a trick on one of the greatest—Archangelo Corelli.

March 3rd
The Violinist Revolutionary

He was a composer and one of the finest violinists of the 18th century, but the times he lived in forced Joseph Boulogne to set aside music and embrace revolution.

He was the son of a French government official and an African woman from the Caribbean island of Guadeloupe. For a time, the family lived in Haiti. Then, when Joseph was about 10, his life took a sudden turn when they moved to Paris. Young Joseph became skilled in all the pursuits of a gentleman—riding, dancing, swimming, and skating. He developed into one of the most adroit swordsmen in Europe.

Although he may have begun studying the violin with his father's plantation manager, Joseph now moved in high musical circles, may have studied with the distinguished composer Jean-Mairie Leclair, and, by 1769, was performing as an orchestral violinist under the direction of the famous François-Joseph Gossec. In 1772, he made his debut as a soloist performing his own violin concertos. The violin parts required spectacular virtuosity, but Joseph Boulogne impressed his audiences most with the sensitivity and expressiveness of his playing. Within a year, he was director of one of the finest orchestras in France. In the 1770's, he continued to compose. His string quartets were among the first written in France.

The 1780's were not to be so auspicious for music-making. When the French Revolution broke out in 1789, Joseph Boulogne—now known as the Chevalier de Saint-Georges—sided with the young Republic and assembled a military force in northern France. In those unsettled times he was wrongly accused of misspending money supplied to his troops, was relieved of his command and imprisoned. As soon as he was released, he set out for his old home, Haiti, where a slave rebellion had erupted. By the time Saint-Georges returned to Paris in 1797, he was ready to resume music-making, but two years later he would die almost penniless, having given most of his resources to the cause of revolution.

March 4th

The Joke That Became Famous

Some musical works are written from inspiration, some for money. Ignzey Jan Paderweski wrote his famous Minuet in G as a practical joke.

An elderly doctor named Chalubinski had befriended the 26-year-old Paderewski, and often invited the young pianist to his house in Warsaw. The doctor and a writer friend invariably asked Paderewski to play something by Mozart. Paderewski got tired of playing nothing but Mozart and decided to put a stop to it. He went home and improvised a minuet in a vaguely Mozartean style. The next night, he showed up at the doctor's house, eagerly awaiting the customary invitation to play Mozart. Sure enough, the golden moment soon came.

"Won't you play a little Mozart?" the doctor asked.

Paderewski cheerfully agreed, sat down and played his minuet. "Oh, Mozart!" the doctor cried. "What a wonderful piece! Tell me, Paderewski, is there any one now alive who could write such beautiful music?"

Paderewski laughed at this unexpected bonus. "Yes, there is such a person," he said. "I have written it."

At first the doctor and his friend were very annoyed at being tricked, and suddenly the Mozart concert was over for that night. But, a few nights later, they asked to hear genuine Mozart and then asked to hear the minuet again, and soon it became a regular part of the Mozart evenings. Before long, Paderewski realized that the minuet could make him a popular composer, and very soon it did just that.

March 5th

The Irresistible Bandleader

An enduring story, probably part fiction:

At the sight of the grim-looking procession peasants ran for their lives. In that part of Romania and Hungary, robbers were everywhere and these appeared to be some of the worst.

They were actually a band of 34 young musicians who had fallen on hard times. Authorities had come close to confiscating their instruments in the middle of a performance because of unpaid debts, and they had sold a couple of violins to buy a few rusty pistols, though ammunition had been beyond their means. They had come east from Vienna full of high hopes that fell quickly in empty concert halls that led to empty pockets and empty stomachs. Now they were broke and so ratty-looking that no innkeeper would give them a place to perform.

Winter had set in, and the band's instruments rode in an open hay wagon across the Carpathian Mountains as a troop of soldiers escorted the group to the Wallachian frontier. The musicians mutinied against their 19-year-old leader and vowed not to take another step. "We must see this thing through together," he declared. "One for all and all for one! We'll give a farewell concert at the nearest town, divide the profits and get back to Vienna however we can."

Eventually they straggled into Bucharest, where they managed to make good money in a series of performances. Success was cut short, though, when the young bandleader proved irresistible to a local lady of distinction. She had a rendezvous with him at the house of her washerwoman. Unfortunately, her husband also showed up with six of his servants, who beat up the charming bandleader.

Did the hotheaded husband know the name of the young man he had run out of town? Perhaps not, but he later heard it many times because within a few years much of Europe had fallen under the bandleader's charm, while dancing to his waltzes—the waltzes of Johann Strauss.

March 6th

A Dubious Honor

Jean Sibelius must have had mixed feelings. He had been commissioned to compose a cantata for a solemn state occasion—the Finnish celebration of the coronation of Czar Nicholas II. It was a major opportunity for the young composer, but, as a Finnish nationalist, he had no desire to glorify the ruler of an empire that had long controlled Finland.

The Finnish observance of the event took place in a courtyard at the University of Helsinki. The students assembled and removed their hats. Like Sibelius, the students were no friends of Czar Nicholas. But, by tradition, the Czar was chancellor of the university. Their only consolation during the ceremony would be new music from the man earning a reputation as Finland's finest composer.

The rousing, sonorous music of Sibelius began—but not as Sibelius intended it. The trumpet player was making a hash of his part. Then he began to play notes that had nothing to do with what Sibelius had written. Then he began to improvise. The trumpet player was drunk.

The supposedly solemn ceremony degenerated into a farce. Although Sibelius must have been horrified at what happened to his cantata, he must have shared in the secret pleasure the students felt at throwing a sour note into the coronation of the detested Czar.

That was in 1894. Five years later Sibelius would again run afoul of the Russians when he wrote a series of pieces to accompany re-enactments of patriotic scenes. The last of the pieces became a rallying cry for Finnish freedom, and the Russian authorities outlawed any further performances of it. But the piece made its way to Germany, where it was known as "Fatherland", and to France under the title "Patrie." When Sibelius managed to have the piece performed in Russian-controlled Latvia, the authorities insisted on giving it the bland title "Impromptu." But soon enough all the world would know it as *Finlandia.*

March 7th

The Case of the Disappearing Operas

Writing an opera requires a great deal of time and energy for the composer and the librettist. The payoff, of course, comes when the opera proves a success or at least gets performed. But in the case of some operas planned by Giacomo Puccini, the work of composer and librettist simply evaporated.

Just after the success of his opera *Manon,* Puccini was working with a librettist named Giovanni Verga on an opera called *Lupu.* It was a Sicilian story, and both the publisher and the young Puccini thought it would make a wonderful opera. Puccini sailed to Sicily and met the author. The two of them agreed on everything, right on down to the details of the libretto. Full of enthusiasm, Puccini sailed for home.

On the voyage home Puccini met the stepdaughter of Richard Wagner. He told her of his plans for a new opera and described some of it. She advised him to come up with some other idea and by the end of the voyage his plan for the opera had crumbled away.

With the promising subject of Marie Antoinette, Puccini fared far worse. The librettist, Luigi Illica, began with an epic scenario spanning fourteen episodes. When he and Puccini began working on it, Puccini cut and condensed, and within a month it was down to eight scenes.

On they went, with Puccini trimming and condensing until they had just three acts, an acceptable number for an opera, with the climactic prison scene at the end. The librettist no doubt thought that they had stopped chopping at last.

But then Puccini cut the other two acts, eliminating months of the librettist's research and writing. The librettist was known for his temper and he vented it against Puccini's publisher, against Puccini, against Marie Antoinette and art in general, because by then it had become apparent that the opera *Marie Antoinette* had evaporated entirely.

March 8th

The Color Bar

Samuel Coleridge-Taylor, the son of a West African and an Englishwoman, became a world-famous composer and conductor by the age of 30. In the fall of 1904, he was touring the United States by train, conducting performances that drew thousands. But one thing about America troubled him. When he returned to London he spoke to an interviewer about it.

As soon as people found out I was English, they were quite different. Of course, at first they could not reconcile the absence of the Yankee twang in a man of color like myself. At the same time, I was sorry for colored people generally. I heard some pitiful stories about their treatment. I met a young colored lady of great educational attainments and of refined tastes. She was traveling south of Washington, and was turned out of the car. Colored people and white are separated when traveling on the other side of a line drawn south of Washington.

Other indignities, too, were perpetrated, for which there was absolutely no redress. Think of it if the aggrieved parties were whites! When I go to Tuskegee, it will be in Mr. Booker Washington's own private car, and consequently I shall avoid being insulted. What is so deplorable to me is that there is as yet very little discrimination between the educated and decent-minded black and the idle and semi-civilized man of color. This, understand me, is from an English point of view. And the fact is, no Englishman can get quite inside the question, it is really so subtle.

In traveling from Washington to Chicago, Coleridge-Taylor found that there was one kind of equality on American trains. "Human life," he remarked, "seems very cheap when in transit. I happened to pass the scenes of three recent smashes. Naturally I did not trust myself with blithesome confidence to the tender mercies of the railway staff and the rolling-stock."

March 9th

An American Escape

In 1906, European immigrants flocked to America looking for new opportunities. The Russian pianist and composer Alexander Scriabin came to find new possibilities and to escape old problems.

His most recent difficulties included a desperate need for money and a break with fellow composer Anatol Liadov, who suggested appallingly low prices for Scriabin's smaller piano pieces.

A conservatory friend convinced Scriabin to make the American tour. Scriabin played his piano concerto in Carnegie Hall and performed with modest success in Cincinnati, Chicago, and Detroit.

The money was a little disappointing, but even more disappointing was Scriabin's effort to get away, at least temporarily, from his mistress, Tatyana Schloezer, who had become increasingly domineering.

Scriabin did everything he could to convince Tatyana not to come to America with him. He warned her that if she came to America, their newborn second child would starve. He told her how terrible the ocean voyage would be. He scared her with stories about writer Maxim Gorky, who was deported from America on morals charges because he had arrived with his mistress. Tatyana came anyway, and the couple somehow avoided deportation.

Although Scriabin didn't speak English, his manager arranged an interview with the press and answered all the questions himself. When Scriabin read the newspaper accounts of his tour he found them quoting things he had never said. "I don't know if anyone wanted me because of my music," Scriabin remarked, "but wherever I went I met with triumph. America loves noise and publicity...after great success."

In a more formal pronouncement Scriabin offered faint praise, declaring, "I was very favorably impressed by America, and I think that Europeans judge America most immaturely and one-sidedly. Americans are far from insensitive and untalented in art, as is generally thought."

Alexander Scriabin left America with a few dollars and a lot of unpaid bills, but for a few months, at least, he had put some of his problems behind him.

March 10th
Weber's Hopes & Fears

Carl Maria von Weber was 30 years old and beginning to settle down professionally and socially. On March 10, 1817, he wrote from Dresden to a friend:

I should have written to you long ago to tell you about my appointment as Kappellmeister to the King of Saxony and Director of the German Opera here, but I have really been too busy. Anyway, I am at last settled here, and my wonderful travel plans have all evaporated. Sure, I have an annual vacation, but if I get married in the autumn–God willing–it will be harder for me to leave the nest.

I had many frustrations and intrigues to overcome when I got here and several times was on the brink of leaving again, but in the long run it showed them they were dealing with a man who was too independent to allow his rights to be trampled. Now everything's going along smoothly. Those who don't love me at least fear me.

Soon I'll be trying my hand at a new opera, written for me by the well-known poet Friedich Kind. It's The Hunter's Bride, *a very romantic, captivating and beautiful work. For the most part I lead a solitary, maybe even melancholy life because even though I have plenty of acquaintances and am generally respected, I lack a real friend, have no one to talk with about music, and that's really sad.*

My appointment here is only for a year. That's customary. And though it's never been known not to lead to a lifetime engagement, I know my own star so well that I'm still nervous but I trust in God and do not tremble, although in the future I'll have more than just myself to take care of. The arrangement with my fiancée's mother is also settled now. She's going to her son at Mainz and I'm to give her 100 thalers a year. It's worth the sacrifice to have peace and quiet at home.

Within four years he would be famous throughout Germany for his opera *Der Freischütz.*

March 11th

Concert at Gunpoint

Pianist George Antheil got used to his concerts turning into riots. After all, he made a habit of ending each evening with a set of ultra-modern pieces. But he wanted his music to be heard, and he started taking dangerous measures to see that it was.

Like many young American artists in the 1920's, Antheil went to Europe to further his career. His tour included cities in the former Austro-Hungarian Empire, and Antheil carefully deleted from his publicity any reference to his World War I status as an aviator. But between the controversy of his music and the instability of post-war politics, Antheil took no chances. In a silk holster under his left arm he carried a .32 caliber automatic pistol.

His first concert in Budapest had deteriorated into violence. At the second, Antheil walked on stage, bowed, and said, "Attendants, will you please close and lock the doors?" Once they had complied, he pulled out his pistol, laid it on the Steinway, and began his concert. Every note was heard.

It was not so easy in Munich. It was March 1922, and the concert agency received a note saying: "If the American pianist attempts to play French works in the Munich concert hall, the place will be bombed." Antheil asked who might be responsible for the threats. The agency had no doubt. "A bunch of local hoodlums known as the National Socialist Party led by an Austrian maniac, Adolf Hitler." Antheil got so mad that he insisted on doing the concert. Knowing that his .32 wouldn't be much help, he fortified himself with something else—half a bottle of red wine. The next thing he knew, he was playing the opening piece, Bach's Fugue in E Minor.

The next day, the Munich critics observed that Antheil had played the Bach with uncommon coldness and lack of feeling. The rest of the performance, they noted, had been merely acceptable. It was the last time Antheil drank anything before a concert.

March 12th

An Honest Opinion

Johannes Brahms disliked insincere flattery. But he sometimes went to great lengths to get an honest opinion of his composing and his playing.

In his autobiography, composer Karl Goldmark mentions receiving an invitation to a house where two new Brahms compositions were to be performed for the first time–a piano trio and a string quintet. After the performances, just about everyone came forward to compliment Brahms. Knowing that Brahms tended to brush aside polite flattery, Goldmark held back. The next morning, Brahms invited him to walk with him to visit some friends. As they walked along a mountain ridge at the edge of the woods, Goldmark realized that Brahms had invited him on the walk in hopes of getting a sincere evaluation of the pieces.

They came to a friend's house and found all the doors open in the morning sunshine. No one was in sight. Goldmark and Brahms walked into the music room. On the piano they found volume one of Carl Czerny's technical studies–*The School of Velocity*–the bane of many a struggling student. Brahms sat down and played the first etude in scales. He made a hash of it–striking some notes three times while he tried to figure out where to go next.

A woman's voice called out from the next room, "Why, Franzi, what are you doing? Play more slowly." Brahms played faster, stumbling even worse. "Franzi, you are slurring terribly!" came the voice, "Why are you playing F Sharp? It's F. F! Play more slowly." Brahms persisted, playing worse than ever. "This is too much," the woman said. "You played so well before. You're just being spiteful." She came rushing into the room, expecting to find a child pianist and was greeted instead with a chorus of laughter from two great composers.

On the way home, Brahms was in a particularly good mood, and Goldmark took the opportunity to offer him his second sincere critique of the day, telling him how much he admired the newly written trio and quintet.

March 13th

From the Earth to the Moon

It was an extremely popular subject–science fiction. The music was by France's leading operetta composer, Jacques Offenbach, and the story by the father of science fiction, Jules Verne. The French stage had never seen anything like *From the Earth to the Moon.*

The Franco-Prussian War of the 1870's had demoralized France, and the country was looking for new hope. The leading thinkers looked to science. One writer remarked that bright, gas-lit streets and wide traffic arteries had done more to cut crime than any moralizing could. Technology had become the fascination of France.

The extravagant pantomime *Le Voyage dans la lune* delivered it in spades. The producer had a large, state-of-the-art relief model of the moon erected in floodlights on the theater facade. The first act of the pantomime featured the enormous gun that shot the lunar travelers skyward. The gun was so huge that it rested on mountains and stretched across valleys, towns and rivers.

The scenery for the second act was just as fantastic. It was the lunar landscape, and it included a tobacco plant that burst into bloom in seconds.

In Act Four, just as the lunar travelers were sentenced to hard labor in the interior of the moon, there was a peal of thunder, the ground quaked, lava flowed and flames rose up all around. One of the travelers took refuge in a gigantic rock, which was then struck by a ball of fire and flung into space. Ashes came raining down and the burned-out crest of the volcano came into view, then the earth, growing larger and larger until it filled the entire sky.

As for Offenbach's music, it did its share to draw in the crowds and keep them happy, the most notable exception being Jules Verne, who was not amused, and considered suing Offenbach for stealing his idea.

March 14th
Haydn Takes London

Joseph Haydn had been in London for three months and was succeeding mightily with English audiences. On March 14, 1791, he wrote to a friend in Vienna:

I have plenty to do because of all the concerts and opera, and I am hounded all the time by the subscription concerts. Our opera hasn't opened yet, and since the king won't grant the license, the director of the opera plans to open it as if it were a subscription concert because if he doesn't he just may lose twenty thousand pounds sterling. I won't lose anything because my bankers in Vienna have already received my money.

My opera, which is called The Philosopher's Mind, *will be staged at the end of May. I've already finished the second act, but there are five acts, the last two of which are quite short. In order to show the public his theater, his opera and his ballet, the director of the opera came up with the shrewd idea of arranging a few days ago a dress rehearsal just as if it were opening night. He distributed four thousand tickets and more than five thousand people showed up.*

The opera Piero *by Paisiello was a great success. Only their prima donna is a salami and I'm not going to use her in my opera. The ballet was absolutely magnificent. Now we are waiting for a yes or no from the king. And if our theater is opened, the other theater–that of our competitors–will have to close its doors because the castrato and the prima donna are too old and their opera didn't appeal to anyone.*

At Mr. Salomon's first concert I created a furor with a new symphony and they had to repeat the Adagio–which had never before happened in London. Just imagine what it means to hear such praise from the mouths of Englishmen!

March 15th
The Ill-Fated Symphony

That first symphony can be intimidating for a composer. Sergei Rachmaninoff was a long time recovering from his.

He was pleased with his symphony, confident to the point of arrogance. He played a piano version for composer Sergei Taneyev, who expressed his displeasure with it. Undaunted, Rachmaninoff sold it to a publisher for 500 rubles. He was convinced that an entirely new path of music had opened up to him. He took the symphony to St. Petersburg to be performed. During rehearsals Rachmaninoff became painfully aware of two things. The symphony was being played very badly and was, in the first place, full of flaws. "Forgive me," said conductor Nikolai Rimsky-Korsakov, "but I do not find this music at all agreeable."

On March 15, 1897, as the time for the debut approached, Rachmaninoff grew increasingly uncomfortable. He left the artists' room and found his way to a fire escape where he huddled, trying not to hear his symphony in what he later called "the most agonizing hour of my life." Occasionally he stuck his fingers in his ears, tortured by the discords he was hearing. He kept asking himself, "How is it possible?"

As the last chords of the symphony died out, Rachmaninoff fled horrified into the street, and drove back and forth through wind and mist until he had calmed down enough to attend a dinner in his honor. But all evening long, he was aware above all of his shattered self-confidence.

The injury didn't end there. Composer and critic César Cui wrote in the *St. Petersburg News:* "If there were a conservatory in hell, Rachmaninoff would gain the first prize for his symphony, so devilish are the discords he has dished up for us." As a parting shot, he pointed out that the ill-fated symphony had been given the Opus number 13.

March 16th
Gershwin's Early Setbacks

Recognition came early to George Gershwin, but first came some humbling moments.

At 21, Gershwin wrote a piano piece called "Swanee." It debuted in a band arrangement at the Capitol Theater in New York where 60 chorus girls with electric lights on their slippers danced to it. Gershwin hung around outside the theater to see how sheet music sales of "Swanee" were going in the lobby. There were very few takers.

Gershwin set his sights on something loftier, a national anthem called "O Land of Mine," with lyrics by Michael E. Rourke. He submitted it anonymously in a major contest sponsored by the *New York American*. The contest judges were some of the top names in music–John Philip Sousa, John McCormack, and Irving Berlin. The first prize was a heady $5,000. The prize they awarded Gershwin was dead last–a paltry 50 bucks.

That same year, Gershwin wrote a lullaby for string quartet. The lullaby featured graceful part writing, sublime harmonies, and a lilting melody. In 1923 Gershwin spent several months chafing under the rules imposed by his harmony teacher, Rubin Goldmark. He dusted off his lullaby from four years earlier and showed it to Goldmark. The teacher, mistaking it for a new work, took credit for its creation. "Good," he told Gershwin, "very good. I can see that you are already beginning to profit from your harmony lessons here." The lullaby would remain unpublished and unperformed for half a century.

As for "Swanee," it caught on a good deal faster. Gershwin was playing some of his songs at the party of a singer friend in New York. When he came to "Swanee," the singer, Al Jolson, snapped up the song and turned it into a worldwide hit. Jolson might well have been introducing George Gershwin to the world with his famous words, "You ain't seen nothing yet."

March 17th

The Cold Irish Pianist

He was traveling with one of the most famous and successful composers of the day, but the young Irish pianist was not having a good time.

His name was John Field and he was touring Europe demonstrating Muzio Clementi's new pianos. Soon he would become known as one of the great teachers and performers of the day and a composer in his own right. But, in 1802, the 20-year-old was only the protégée of the stingy Clementi.

In Paris, Clementi rented two of the cheapest rooms available, quarters overlooking an inner courtyard, where they lodged for several dreary months. Then they took off for new territory–St. Petersburg, Russia. The colder the weather, the stingier Clementi became. Young John lost his hat and several months passed before Clementi saw fit to replace it. He also thought it would be uneconomical to buy heavy clothing that would be unnecessary once they left Russia. So John walked through the snowy streets without an overcoat.

When the German violinist and composer Louis Spohr came calling at their hotel room, he found both John and Clementi up to their elbows in soapsuds doing their weekly wash. Clementi maintained his dignity by advising Spohr that he should follow their example since the washerwomen of St. Petersburg charged far too much and ruined clothes in the bargain.

While Clementi spent more and more time with aristocratic students, John was left to fend for himself to stretch a small food allowance at the local market. One day he decided he had had enough. He invited twenty friends to his hotel and tricked Clementi into paying for it. The next day, when Clementi received the bill, teacher and student almost had a complete falling-out. Shortly afterward, Clementi left the city, leaving John to his own devices. But by then the young pianist had impressed many well-to-do patrons with his playing. He spent the rest of his life in St. Petersburg–in relative warmth and comfort.

March 18th
Brutally Frank Advice

How direct should an established composer be when appraising the work of an up-and-comer? Vincent d'Indy would have had two answers to the question—one before and one after getting advice from César Franck. D'Indy recalled:

Once I had played a movement of my string quartet for him—which I naively thought would win his approval—he was silent for a moment. Then, turning toward me with a mournful look, he said something that I've never been able to forget because it's had a decisive influence upon my life. He said, "there are some good things in it. It shows spirit and a kind of instinct for dialogue between the parts. The ideas wouldn't be bad—but that's not enough. The work isn't finished. Then Franck added, "in fact, you really know nothing whatsoever."

Seeing that I was shocked and horrified by his opinion, Franck went into some specifics and concluded, "Come and see me if you want to work together. I could teach you composition."

The visit had taken place very late in the evening. When I got home, I lay awake, balking at the severity of his opinions. I told myself that Franck was an old-fashioned musician who knew nothing of youthful and progressive art. And yet, in the morning, after I had calmed down, I picked up my poor quartet and went over the master's criticisms one by one as he had scrawled them on the manuscript. And I had to admit to myself that he was completely correct: I knew nothing.

I went to him, a bundle of nerves, and asked if he would be good enough to take me on as a student, and he let me into the organ class at the conservatory, of which he had just been appointed professor.

The humility helped. Vincent d'Indy soon became a major French composer in his own right.

March 19th
The Italian Marine Band

The group of 16 Italian musicians didn't know what to think. Their leader, Gaetano Carusi, had brought them to America, the land of promise. But when they arrived in Washington, their first thought must have been to go back home.

The year was 1805, and Carusi himself described the capital city of the new republic as "a desert, a place containing two or three taverns and a few scattered cottages and log cabins." The Italians were supposed to form a band to represent the United States Marines and President Thomas Jefferson. Apparently the band came with few perks. Upon their arrival, the Italians were trooped off to their residence—an area in the Marine barracks where the musicians and their families—30 in all—had to bundle together in a single room and sleep on a bare floor.

Somehow they mustered their dignity for their first American performance at a banquet celebrating the victory of the American Navy over the Tripoli pirates.

The members of the band were in for a three-year hitch, but after only 18 months all of them were dismissed from the corps. Carusi was outraged. He took legal action against the federal government, claiming to have been duped into his position through false and deceitful promises and complaining that the commandant had confiscated his music. At the age of 72 he was still at it. He petitioned Congress for $1,000 in compensation and was turned down.

But Gaetano Carusi prevailed in the long run. His three sons grew up in Washington and went on to become very successful concert promoters, and several of his musicians made their way back into the military where they left a lasting influence on the Marine Band.

March 20th
The Dazzling Liszt

At the age of 29, Robert Schumann was one of many pianist composers who were dazzled by the virtuosity and personality of the 28-year-old Franz Liszt. He reported to his fiancee Clara Wieck, from Leipzig on March 20, 1840:

I wish you could have been with me this morning to see Liszt. He is quite extraordinary. He played some of my Novelettes and passages from the Fantasy and the Sonata in a way that kept me completely enchanted. A lot of it wasn't what I had in mind, but his genius showed through in all of it, plus a tenderness and daring display of emotion that he probably doesn't reveal every day....

The second Novelette in D Major was particularly delightful. Believe me, it was very, very effective. He plans to play it at his third concert here.

If I tried to tell you about all the commotion that's going on here it would fill volumes. He hasn't given his second concert yet. He opted to go to bed, and two hours ahead of time announced that he was under the weather. I can readily believe he was, and so was not up to speed, but his illness was also a matter of procedure. I can't go into all of it for you here.

But for me it was all very pleasant since he is now in bed all day and aside from me will admit only Mendelssohn, Hiller and Reuss. If only you had been there this morning, my girl!

Would you believe that at his concert he played one of Härtel's pianofortes that he had never seen before? I find it charming that he has such confidence in those precious ten fingers of his. But don't follow his example, my dear Clara Wieck. You stay just as you are because you're unsurpassable.

March 21st
The Hardest Thing in the World

On March 21, 1864–in the thick of the Civil War–New Orleans-born composer Louis Moreau Gottschalk was in the middle of a concert tour of the northern and western states. Although he was a southerner, he was loyal to the Union cause. But he wasn't impressed with many of the men who fought for it. In his journal he wrote:

En route to Baltimore. Our car is filled with very noisy soldiers who sing songs and smell of the eternal whiskey. At first we ignore them but they become increasingly disagreeable. One starts smoking, then a second, and a third imitates him. We ask them please to abstain from it for the sake of Madame Variani and a young lady accompanying her who find the smoke disagreeable. They waste no time informing me with a torrent of epithets taken from the rogue's dictionary that we are no gentlemen, that these are no ladies, that as soldiers they have the right to do as they please, and that they would prove it to us.

After this lecture–remarkable more for its vulgarity than its logic–all the soldiers in the car started whistling, screaming, and howling like Chinese or like savages when they wish to show their irrepressible courage. An officer there wisely declined to interfere–the whiskey bottle that had been going around the awful circle of our "heroes" had made many stops at his lips–and it was clear that an officer would be unwelcome to reclaim an authority which had drowned in a flood of spirits.

"We will do whatever we please." The words ring in my ears. I admit that I was choked with anger–a disagreeable anger because it had to be silent, like right before brute force. To have to sit by quietly when you know you are right is the hardest thing in the world; and I experienced it at that moment.

March 22nd

Lully's Last Maneuver

Jean-Baptiste Lully was extremely devoted to his music. In fact, he died for it.

Lully was hands down the staunchest promoter of his own music. He was so taken with his compositions that he declared he would kill anyone who said they were bad. When his opera *Armide* failed to get the enthusiastic reception he thought it deserved, Lully had it presented for an audience of one–himself. In a scene worthy of an Alexandre Dumas novel, King Louis XIV decided that the opera must be all right if Lully would go to such lengths to have it performed. So he, too, arranged for a private showing. He decided that it wasn't half bad–and turned the tide of public opinion.

Later, when the king was gravely ill, Lully was obliged to write a Te Deum. Into this hymn of praise Lully poured all his skill and effort. He lavished great care on the preparations for the performance, and as a special show of devotion, he beat the time himself, using the customary long heavy staff. In the heat of excitement, Lully accidentally pounded his foot with the staff. The result was a blister. Lully's physician advised him to have his little toe cut off. Lully resisted, and after a few days the physician recommended amputating Lully's entire leg. Soon the time for decision-making had passed. Lully's days were numbered.

But he still faced one more fight for his music. His confessor refused to absolve him of his sins unless he would burn his opera *Achilles et Polixeme*. Lully gave in and allowed the opera to be burned. A few days later, Lully was feeling a little better, and a visitor asked him why he had been so foolish as to burn a perfectly good opera to humor a grim priest.

"Shhhh!" whispered Lully. "I have another copy of it." It was Lully's last blow on behalf of his craft. He died soon afterward, on March 22, 1687.

March 23rd
Good and Bad Advice

John Ireland became one of England's great 20th century composers. As a young man he received advice from another major composer—Edward Elgar. Fortunately for English music, Ireland ignored some of it.

In 1900, Ireland attended a party at the house of one of Elgar's friends, the subject of one of Elgar's *Enigma Variations*. Elgar asked Ireland, "Young man, do you intend to become a composer?"

Rather timidly, Ireland said that he did.

Elgar had been "discovered" by Richard Strauss. His advice: "For God's sake, let it alone. I have been composing for years, yet no one in England took any notice of me till a German said my music was good."

Ireland later received more advice from Elgar. One of his orchestral works was being performed at a Queen's Hall concert where Elgar was conducting his Second Symphony. Elgar listened to Ireland's piece and said some kind things about it. Ireland asked if he could show Elgar the score and Elgar arranged to have him bring it over the next morning to his chambers at St. James Street. They spent a couple of hours looking at Ireland's composition and Elgar gave Ireland many helpful pointers on orchestration, ideas that Ireland had never seen in text books. Ireland came to think of that get-together as the most important lesson he'd ever had.

John Ireland ignored Elgar's first advice and kept right on composing, but for the rest of his 60-year career, he remembered the rest, both the explicit and the implied.

March 24th

Waldstein

Waldstein. The name is best remembered because Beethoven wrote one of his greatest piano sonatas for his friend and patron. The sonata remains a monument to Waldstein. The friendship and patronage were a good deal less enduring.

Count Ferdinand Ernst Gabriel Waldstein und Wartemberg von Dux, Knight of the Teutonic Order, was born eight years before Beethoven, on March 24, 1762. He met the 20-year-old Beethoven in Bonn at the home of mutual friends. Waldstein was handsome, erudite, poised, charming and witty. He was a pianist and fancied himself a composer.

In 1791 Waldstein commissioned young Beethoven to write an evening's musical entertainment, a Knight's Ballet. Waldstein had the ballet performed at his Bonn palace during Mardi Gras, attributing the music to himself. At the same time, Waldstein was one of the first to recognize Beethoven's genius, and he took steps to secure Beethoven employment as a court musician and saw to it that he received some discreet financial aid.

But the darker side of Waldstein's personality—his impetuousness, his susceptibility to get-rich-quick schemes, and his recklessness—put him on a collision course with disaster. And when years of war undermined the financial stability of Europe, the finances of the aristocracy shook with it. By 1818 Waldstein had sunk deeply into debt. He was entitled to substantial benefits, but by the time he died in 1823, he was so poor that his estate couldn't pay his doctors' bills, and a friend had to pay for his funeral.

By then Beethoven and Waldstein had long since gone their separate ways. But Beethoven wasn't the only artist Waldstein had taken under his wing. Back in 1785 he had hired an aging Italian adventurer as his librarian. The librarian had used his years of tranquility to write torrid memoirs that had turned a librarian's name into a household word—Casanova.

March 25th

A Royal Pain

An invitation to perform for a king. Most musicians would see it as a grand opportunity. Louis Spohr found it a royal pain.

In 1807 Spohr and his bride Dorette were touring Germany. Spohr was one of the best-known violinists in Europe and his wife a splendid harpist. In Stuttgart, a representative of the king invited the young couple to give a concert. But Spohr had heard that the king and court liked to play cards during concerts and so he agreed to play only if the king agreed *not* to.

"You presume to give orders to my most serene master?" the king's representative asked. "I would never dare to give him a message like that."

"Then I must forego the honor of being heard in court," Spohr replied.

Yet the representative did bring himself to convey the message. The king agreed,. but only on condition that the pieces be performed in one series so that his card playing would be interrupted only once. So the concert was on. The members of the court seated themselves at their card tables. The concert began with performances by local musicians—an overture, followed by an aria. During these "preliminaries" the servants clattered around and the card-players called out "I bid" and "I pass" so loudly that nobody could hear much of the music. Then the king's representative came over and told Spohr to get ready to play. King and court listened attentively but the only acknowledgment of the music was the king's gracious nod at the end of each piece. No one else in the audience dared to applaud.

Then the card-playing continued with the music of the locals in the background, but when the king finished his game and pushed his chair back, the concert was over—in the middle of an aria. The musicians, accustomed to the king's abruptness, obediently put away their instruments, while Louis Spohr quietly held his temper, none the happier for having the honor of playing for royalty.

March 26th

The Presidential Performer

It was a time when a president of the United States was in sore need of soothing music, and Woodrow Wilson brought some of the best performers into the White House. He had the added advantage of being a pretty fair musician himself.

As a young man, Wilson had played the violin. He sang tenor in the Princeton University Glee Club and later at the Johns Hopkins University Glee Club. He seems to have set the violin aside, but even as president, Wilson had a reputation as a fine tenor. While singing "The Star-Spangled Banner," he liked to hold the high note at the end of the phrase "the land of the free," which thrilled many a visitor to the home of the brave.

Wilson's singing particularly impressed a harpist named Melville Clark who recalled a "velvety soft moonlit night" in 1914 when he was performing at a White House reception for European diplomats. After the guests took their leave, Wilson asked the harpist to take his harp and follow him to the rear portico. The audience for this impromptu concert consisted almost entirely of secret service agents–about 35 of them–hiding in the bushes.

The president was clearly concerned about the prospect of a war between the United States and the countries whose diplomats had just left the reception. He wanted to unwind a little and he asked the harpist if he could play "Drink to Me Only with Thine Eyes." When the harpist obliged, the president began singing in "a clear, lyric tenor voice." Wilson asked for more songs, Scottish and Irish melodies and tunes by Stephen Foster, all of which he sang with perfect diction. They went on until nearly midnight, when the president stood up looking relaxed and renewed.

Wilson found music so satisfying that, seeing a minstrel dancer named Primrose, he expressed a wish to swap jobs with him.

March 27th

The Modest Virtuoso

On March 27, 1830, a 20-year-old Polish pianist, Frédéric Chopin, was concertizing in Warsaw, and he wrote to a friend in a nearby town:

About the first concert: The hall was full, and all the boxes and stage seats were sold out three days in advance, but most of the audience didn't get the impression I expected. Only a few of them appreciated the first Allegro from my concerto. There were some bravos but I think only because they were puzzled and had to pose as connoisseurs. The Adagio and Rondo had some effect, elicited some spontaneous shouts. But the Potpourri on Polish themes, as far as I could tell, didn't fly. They applauded in the spirit of "let him go away knowing that we aren't bored."

That evening the critics–the "gods"–and the people in the orchestra seats were quite content, but the people in the pit complained that I played too softly. They would have preferred to be in the café hearing the discussions about me. The Polish Courier, *while praising me to the skies for the Adagio, advised more energy. Guessing where that energy lies, in the next concert I played a Viennese piano instead of my own, so the audience–even larger than before–was happy.*

Clapping, exclamations that I had played better the second time than the first, that every note was like a pearl, and so on. Calling me back, yelling for a third concert. The Krakowiak Rondo had a tremendous effect. Applause broke out four times.

Finally I improvised, but not the way I wanted to–that wouldn't have been for the public. You'll notice that all the major newspapers were pleased. I was sent a laurel wreath and some verses. Mazurkas and waltzes have been written on themes from my concerto. An accompanist asked me for my portrait, but I couldn't allow that–it would've been too much at once, and anyway I don't want anyone to wrap butter in me.

March 28th

What Went Wrong?

In 1601, at the age of 25, Thomas Weelkes was one of England's most promising musicians. He joined the choir of Chichester Cathedral as an organist and church official. The position came with prestige and money and for several years Weelkes prospered. He married the daughter of a wealthy merchant and settled into a life of performing and composing. Then his life took a turn for the worse.

The first indication of trouble came in 1609 when Weelkes was censured for being absent from the cathedral during a visit from the bishop, but there is no indication of what the punishment was. The arrival of a new bishop brought tighter discipline at the cathedral and absences on Sundays and holy days brought the forfeiture of wages for offenders. The crackdown included a warning to Weelkes that he had to spend at least three hours a day teaching the choristers—or lose his position.

The charges against Weelkes continued, citing instances of inefficiency, neglect of duty, and drunkenness. Weelkes denied the charge of drunkenness and nothing much happened as a result of it. But in 1615, he was in trouble again when the church's highest-ranking bishop arrived and singled out Weelkes and ten other choir members as being chronically absent. Later he was accused of being "a common drunkard and a notorious swearer and blasphemer."

In 1617 Weelkes was dismissed from his position but, perhaps because he was hard to replace, he seems to have continued with an unofficial standing in the church. By 1623, church officials were again calling his conduct into question, but Weelkes slipped beyond their jurisdiction once and for all by dying at the age of 49.

Because Thomas Weelkes' first three books of madrigals had promised such a brilliant career, it has been said that the decline of his later years appears all the more tragic.

March 29th

Eccentric to the End

He was a strange man, a macabre man, the composer of the "Funeral March for a Papagallo." Everything about Charles-Valentin Alkan seemed eccentric—even his death on March 29, 1888.

After more than 100 years, the circumstances of Alkan's death are still controversial. The most common story has it that he was found "crushed beneath his upturned bookcase from which he had been extracting a Hebrew religious book."

In 1909 Alexandre de Bertha published an article describing a more mundane death for Alkan. According to Bertha, Alkan was found stretched out on his kitchen floor, in front of the stove, which he had probably been about to light in preparation for his evening meal. But this account tells neither how Alkan died nor who discovered the body. All it gives us is a curious allusion to a fatal situation in Alkan's apartment "brought on by his unusual habits."

All references to an accident have been traced to a single source—one Isidore Phillipp who was 23 years old at the time of Alkan's death, and who claimed to have been one of the group that pulled Alkan's body from beneath the bookcase. Phillipp was known to be essentially a truthful person who liked to emphasize the grotesque.

Yet the police archives from the time mention no accident in Alkan's apartment. The primary reaction to his death seems to have been surprise that the aged composer hadn't already been dead for years. Aside from his immediate family, only four mourners attended his funeral at Paris' Montmartre Cemetery on a damp, dreary Easter Sunday. The four were a business associate, a violinist, Bertha and Phillipp—the authors of the two contradictory accounts of Alkan's death. It was a case worthy of an investigator who made his debut in that year of 1888—Sherlock Holmes.

March 30th

Cherubini Takes on Napoleon

He conquered most of Europe but, for a time, Napoleon met his match when he entered the realm of music and took on composer Luigi Cherubini.

Napoleon was as opinionated about music as he was about politics. One evening in the 1790's, when an opera of Cherubini's was being performed, Napoleon and Cherubini were sitting together. Napoleon turned to the composer and said, "My dear Cherubini, you are certainly an excellent musician, but usually your music is so noisy and so complicated that I can make nothing of it."

Cherubini replied, "My dear general, you are certainly an excellent soldier, but when it comes to music I hope you'll excuse me if I don't think it necessary to adapt my compositions to your comprehension."

In 1797, Napoleon returned from Italy full of praise for Italian composers, and he brought with him a drab little march by Giovanni Paisiello as an example. After a performance, Napoleon made a point of going up to Cherubini and praising the mediocre little march without mentioning a more ambitious effort by Cherubini. The next year, on the eve of Napoleon's departure for Egypt, he again praised Italian composers in general but managed to say only unflattering things about Cherubini's music, to which Cherubini replied, "Citizen-general, occupy yourself with battles and victories and permit me to apply my talent to an art of which you know nothing."

Napoleon walked away. But a few years later, Cherubini's candor would cost him dearly. After signing the Treaty of Pressburg in 1805, Napoleon—now Emperor—invited Cherubini to accompany him to Paris, but Cherubini had committed himself to write a work for the Viennese and declined to go. When he arrived in Paris, Napoleon conferred upon Ferdinando Paër an honor he had apparently intended for Cherubini—the lucrative post of court musician.

March 31st

Schubert Down on His Luck

Franz Schubert writing from Vienna to a friend in Rome, March 31, 1824:

I feel like the most miserable, most unhappy being in the world. Imagine a man whose health will never entirely recover and whose despair about it only makes matters worse. Imagine a man whose brightest hopes have amounted to nothing, to whom the joys of love and friendship can offer only the greatest pain, whose enthusiasm for beauty is dying away. Then ask yourself if that man isn't the most wretched of beings.

"My peace has gone, my heart is heavy." I could sing those words every day because every night I go to bed hoping that I won't ever wake up again, and each morning only brings back the grief of the day before. So I spend my days joyless and friendless, except that Schwind sometimes drops by and brings a ray of sunshine from happy days gone by.

As you probably already know, our literary society committed suicide by drinking too much beer and eating too much sausage. But I have hardly been to a meeting since you left. Leidesdorf, whom I have come to know very well, is a good man indeed but so melancholy that I think I've been unduly affected by him. Anyway, his business and mine are going so badly that neither of us has any money. Your brother's libretto was declared to be useless, the result being that my music wasn't wanted either.

Cantelli's libretto to The Conspirator *had been set to music in Berlin by a local composer and received with applause, so I seem to have written two more operas for no reason. The latest news in Vienna is that Beethoven will be giving a concert at which his new symphony, three pieces from a Mass, and a new overture are to be performed. God willing, I've a notion to give a similar concert in the year to come.*

April 1st

The Tricksters

Niccoló Paganini was the most famous violinist in Europe. He was also more versatile than anyone would have guessed–at work and at play.

Gioacchino Rossini was at his wits' end. The conductor of his new opera *Mametto the Second* had died suddenly, and in the entire city of Rome there was no suitable substitute to be found. Paganini offered his services and conducted the rehearsal and the first two performances with such panache that the performers were dazzled. And that wasn't all. A horn player with a particularly difficult solo had taken ill at the last minute. Paganini played his part on the viola while continuing to lead the orchestra.

Shortly afterward, toward the end of carnival season, Paganini postponed one of his own concerts for one day. The only explanation–"extraordinary circumstances." The circumstances being that Paganini wanted to take the night off to have a little fun. He and Rossini and two singer friends dressed up in the costumes of blind street musicians. The rotund Rossini wrapped himself in such thick folds of material that he looked like an elephant. The thin and ghostlike Paganini squeezed into clinging feminine clothing that made him appear downright supernatural.

Clowning and singing and probably armed with a fiddle and a guitar, the duo made their way along palace-lined thoroughfares bedecked in flowers and brocade. Several times they were invited to sing in upper crust homes, and apparently none of their highborn hosts knew that their entertainment was coming from the greatest violinist and the greatest opera composer in Europe.

April 2nd

Fed Up in Rome

Love, politics, and music. In April 1831, Hector Berlioz was in Florence, Italy, and he was disgusted with all three. He wrote to a friend:

You speak to me of music and of love! What do you have in mind? I don't get it. Is there something on earth called music and love? I thought I'd heard those doomed words in a dream. You're condemned to misery if you believe in them. As for me, I no longer believe in anything. I intended to travel to Calabria or Sicily and join some gang of bandits. That way at least I would have seen some magnificent crimes, thefts, assassinations, rapes, and burnings instead of all these miserable little crimes, these acts of feeble treachery, which are a disease of the soul. Outrageous rabble!

And they ramble about art, thought, and imagination, about fair-mindedness, about poetry–as if they had anything to do with that. What more can I tell you? About Rome? Well, nobody got killed. Only the bold locals who wanted to slit all our throats and set fire to the Academy because we were supposedly in league with the revolutionaries to banish the Pope. We had no such idea. The Pope was absolutely safe from us....Nonetheless we were all armed, and if the locals had come they'd have gotten a warm reception.

What else? Ah yes. Here in Florence during my first visit I saw an opera about Romeo and Juliet by a little no-good named Bellini. And Shakespeare's ghost didn't show up to eliminate the little upstart! The dead don't come back.

There was a wretched eunuch called Pacini who had written an opera called Vestal. *I had just enough strength left after Act One to escape. I pinched myself on the way out to see if it was really true–and it was!*

April 3rd

The Swedish Nightingale Meets Barnum

The famed soprano Jenny Lind had plenty of talent and determination. And when she came to America in 1850 she had more than enough publicity. Her promoter was the biggest showman of them all–P.T. Barnum.

Eager to rise above his reputation as a promoter of sideshows and freaks, Barnum had risked his entire fortune on the singer that he dubbed the Swedish Nightingale, a singer whom he had never heard or seen. He saw to it that the risk paid off. When she arrived in New York, her admirers mobbed Jenny Lind. By midnight, when she arrived at her hotel, a crowd of 30,000 had gathered just to get a look at her. At one o'clock, a fire brigade 700 strong ushered in a band of 130 musicians who came to serenade her.

Tickets for her first American concert were in such demand that they were auctioned off. The first ticket went to a hat maker named Genin who paid $225 for it and got several days' worth of fame in the bargain. At the concert 7,000 shouting people crammed into Castle Garden to hear Jenny Lind sing. She received 10,000–all of which she gave to New York charities. She repeated her success in Philadelphia, Washington, Richmond, Charleston, and Baltimore.

In Baltimore something happened that may have made Jenny Lind decide that things had gotten out of hand. She was on the balcony of her hotel, bowing to the masses below, when her shawl fell. Instead of returning it, the crowd fought over the shawl, tearing it to shreds and pocketing the pieces as souvenirs. Soon afterward she backed out of her contract with Barnum–at a cost of $30,000–and completed her American tour. Several years passed before she returned to the concert stage.

As for P.T. Barnum, he went into a profession for which he may have been supremely well qualified–politics.

April 4th

Nettles Instead of Roses

"This profession, my dear boy, is not what people imagine." So wrote violinist Eugène Ysaÿe to his son Gabriel about 1901. "Everybody thinks it's all honey and roses," Ysaÿe continued, "but the truth is that you get nettles instead of roses and vinegar instead of honey."

"I'll give you a couple of examples," Ysaÿe added. "I've just given four recitals in four days, each one in a different town, which meant traveling four or five hours a day. On the train a person has vague fears of an accident or that his traveling companions are assassins. And of course, for their part, they're thinking the same thing about you." As soon as Ysaÿe played the four recitals, he left for Nuremberg at 6:30 a.m. and didn't reach Hanover until 2:30 a.m. the next morning. He threw himself on the bed, but at 9:30 somebody came to get him for the rehearsal with the Grand Opera orchestra. " And I was expected to be in good form!" he remarked.

"There are good sides to it all," he told his son. "But something always seems to get in the way of complete satisfaction. A string breaks, the heat melts the resin or the cold freezes your fingers. Suddenly you're afraid you've forgotten everything. Or maybe when you're on stage you take out what you think is a handkerchief and mop your brow with it, only to find out that it's a sock you tucked into your pocket at the last minute when you packed. That actually happened to a conductor in Geneva. He realized it only when the audience began to laugh."

Ysaÿe had a bigger concern than embarrassment. During a Munich concert his hand began to freeze up. He was afraid that his days as a soloist were over. Although the Munich concert worked out, from then on, Eugene Ysaÿe was haunted by the fear that one day in the middle of a concert, his hand would fail him.

April 5th

Footloose in Paris

In April 1778, 22-year-old Wolfgang Amadeus Mozart was in Paris hoping to build an international reputation. His father had found it necessary to prod him a good deal to get Mozart to go to Paris, largely because Mozart had fallen in love with Aloysia Weber. But once he got to Paris, Mozart plunged into his work—teaching, visiting important people and composing for the well-to-do.

He had been in Paris for only a week or two when a man named Le Gros, the director of the Concert Spirituel, asked him to write some choruses to improve a Miserere for an upcoming concert. On April 5, Mozart wrote to his father in Salzburg:

I must say that I'm right glad to have that task behind me because it really is awful not to be able to write at home and to be rushed at that. But now—God be praised—it's finished. I hope it will prove effective. Monsieur Gossec, when he saw the first chorus, said to Le Gros—I wasn't present—that it was charming and could not fail to be successful, that the words were wonderfully arranged, and above all, admirably set to music. He's a kind friend of mine, but very reserved.

I am not merely to write an act for an opera, but an entire two-act opera. Noverre, the ballet master with whom I dine as often as I wish, made it happen, suggested the idea in fact. I think it's to be called Alexander and Roxana.

I'm about to compose a Sinfonie Concertante. The flutist will be Wendling, the oboist Ramm, the French hornist Punto, and the bassoonist Ritter. I must say, Punto plays splendidly. I have just this moment returned from the Concert Spirituel. Baron Grimm and I often pour out our wrath on the music here. You can be sure though that it's only between the two of us. In public we cry out, "Bravo! Bravissimo!" and clap our hands until our fingers tingle.

April 6th

Our Family Honor

On April 6, 1778, Leopold Mozart responded to a letter from his son Wolfgang Amadeus in Paris, hoping to prod the young genius into gainful employment:

If, like Honauer or the late Schobert, you could rely on a monthly salary from some prince in Paris and on top of that, work every now and then for the theater, the Concert Spirituel and the Concert des Amateurs, and occasionally have something engraved for subscription, and if your sister and I could give lessons and she could perform at concerts and musical entertainments, then we would surely have enough to live comfortably.

You would like for me to be completely chipper in my letters. My dear Wolfgang! You know that honor is more dear to me than life itself. Think about all that has happened. Recall that even though I hoped—with your help—to get out of debt, so far I have only sunk in deeper and deeper. As you know, my credit with everyone here is solid. But the moment I lose it, my honor will evaporate too. Furthermore, the kindness and sympathy of the trades people lasts only as long as you are paying them, and if payment is late, well then—you can kiss the friendship of the world good-bye.

And then there's the Archbishop. Is he going to get the satisfaction of hearing that things are going badly with us so that he can laugh at us and make fun of us? I would sooner drop dead on the spot than face that. When I received your letter and read it I was right away in the best mood, and to everyone who had been asking about you we passed on the good news that you had arrived safely in Paris. All of them send their greetings.

Can you blame me if such an urgent matter affecting all of my loved ones is on my mind, night and day?

April 7th

The Convert

One of the most influential musicians of the 1880's and '90's was the conductor and critic Hans von Bülow. He had made and broken more than one career. He was also big enough to admit being wrong—or changing his opinion. On April 7, 1892, von Bülow wrote to Giuseppe Verdi:

Illustrious Maestro, please condescend to hear the confession of a repentant sinner. Eighteen years have passed since the undersigned committed a sin of journalistic boorishness in regard to the last of the five great kings of modern Italian music. He has repented in grievous shame countless times!

When the sin at hand was committed—and in your kindness you may have forgotten it—he wasn't quite in his right mind. His mind was fogged by an extreme Wagnerian fanaticism. Seven years later the light slowly dawned on him. His fanaticism was distilled into enthusiasm. Fanaticism is an oil lamp. Enthusiasm is an electric light. In the intellectual and ethical world light means justice. Nothing is more injurious than injustice, nothing more intolerable than intolerance.

I've started to study your later works Aida, Otello, *and the* Requiem, *a rather lackluster performance of which not long ago brought me to tears. I've been studying them not only to the letter, which stifles everything, but also in the spirit, which brings life! Well, there you have it, illustrious Maestro. I admire you, love you!*

A week later Verdi wrote back to von Bülow, saying graciously, "There's no need to talk of repentance and absolution. If your earlier opinions were different from today's you had every right to express them and, who knows, maybe you were right then. If artists in the North and South have different inclinations, then let them be *different*. They should all further the characteristics reflecting their respective nations, as Wagner said."

April 8th
Pay Up!

Ludwig van Beethoven's music has many stormy moments, and it's likely that some of them were inspired by his dealings with his publishers. In the spring of 1805, he wrote to Breitkopf and Härtel in Leipzig a letter that shows his Olympian anger:

Only yesterday did I receive your letter dated January 30th. Although I can readily understand your long delay, the whole affair is too embarrassing for me to waste a single word on it. If there was a fault here, it was a mistake my brother made regarding the time allowed for the copying. The honorarium is far less than what I usually take. Beethoven makes no boast and despises everything that he has not expressly received through his art and merits. So send back all the manuscripts you have received from me, including the song. I cannot and will not accept a smaller fee.

There are no middlemen between us to prevent us from coming to an agreement. No, the impediments are in the issue itself–which I neither can nor care to alter.

The publisher hung on to the manuscripts, and Beethoven wrote again:

I must insist that you print at once the works you have already received, so that the symphony and sonatas appear within two months. The delay in publishing my works has often been very harmful to my business relations, so I am resolved to stick to such deadlines in the future. As to the payment, it would be fairest if you pay the 700 florins for the three works you already have and when you get the other two, pay the balance of 400 florins. If, for some unforeseen reason, you find that these terms aren't to your liking, my only recourse will be to break off negotiations and demand the immediate return of the works you've already received.

In this instance the publisher agreed. But the stormy Beethoven temper would come into play many more times in his turbulent business dealings.

April 9th
The Quarrelsome Handful

They were known as "The Mighty Handful"–five 19th century Russian composers who supposedly constituted a "school" of Russian nationalist writing. But sometimes the "handful" took the shape of a fist.

Two of them–César Cui and Modest Mussorgsky–became bitter adversaries. In 1874 Mussorgsky's opera *Boris Godunov* premiered in St. Petersburg. It was the product of six years' work and a good deal of discussion among the members of "The Handful." When it was performed, the opera was lavishly and tastefully staged. It was a great success with the public. The composer and the performers took many bows and curtain calls after each act.

It was widely known that Cui was the spokesman for the "Mighty Handful," and everyone waited eagerly to see what he would say about this major effort of one of its members. What they got was a big surprise. Whatever praise Cui had for the opera was so laced with acid criticism that the result was devastating. He referred to the opera's "slender musical interest" and "coarse splashes of color" and to the "musical portrayal of unimportant details."

Then there was the incident of the wreath. On opening night, three ladies had attempted to deliver a laurel wreath on stage to Mussorgsky. The management had thwarted them. They complained in a newspaper: "Is it necessary," they asked, " to send in a formal petition, stamped and sealed, before one can get a wreath handed up to the stage?" When Mussorgsky attempted to take blame for the incident, Cui said that the composer had been frightened at the very thought of the wreath–and of the ladies attempting to bestow it.

The opera itself was to be the object of a similar tug-of-war. After Mussorgsky's death, it was released in at least three editions–two by Rimsky-Korsakov and one by Shostakovich. Today, the greatest Russian opera is generally considered to be the original *Boris Godunov* upon which Mussorgsky had lavished so much care.

April 10th

The Singer Is Always Right

Performer and accompanist may practice hard to develop a common approach to a piece of music. But when the night of the performance arrives, the best intentions may go out the window if nervousness throws the performer into old habits. In his memoir *Am I Too Loud?* the great accompanist Gerald Moore says that when the performer goes astray, it's the accompanist's duty to play along.

Moore mentions a couple of instances in which he had to move quickly and with imagination to salvage a performance. In one case a popular tenor was singing "The Cloths of Heaven" by Thomas Dunhill. The song moves through a succession of keys, and during an unaccompanied passage the tenor sang a tone too low. Moore jumped in and transposed the rest of the song, so that what had begun in E flat ended in D flat.

On another occasion, Moore was hired by a Fine Arts Society to accompany a cellist in a program of contemporary music. The president of the society requested that they perform Frank Bridge's "Melodie," and they learned it just for the occasion. During the concert they were halfway down the first page when Moore realized that he and the cellist had parted ways. The cellist was playing a low C fortissimo, which comes on the last page of the work. Moore flipped through several pages and joined the cellist, who was still hanging onto the C for dear life. After the concert, audience members told Moore that "Melodie" was "the gem of the evening."

Moore's favorite "life-saving" story concerns a pianist and a singer who were performing Hugo Wolf's "Song of the Wind." The soprano forgot a huge part of the middle of the song, the pianist improvised, and the two performers managed to finish at the same time. The audience liked the piece so much that they demanded a repeat performance and seemed none the wiser when the second rendition turned out to be a good deal longer than the first.

April 11th
The Texan

April 11, 1958. A boyish-looking 23-year-old from Kilgore, Texas walks on stage to compete in the final round of the Tchaikovsky International Piano Competition. Fifteen hundred people are packed into the Great Hall of the Moscow Conservatory. Thousands more wait outside. Still more are watching via one of Russia's first live musical TV broadcasts.

The young Texan is Van Cliburn and he is poised to be the first American to win the first prize in this highly prestigious competition. He's the first American many of the Russians have seen, but he has already won over many in Moscow with his playing.

In this final round of the competition, he is to play Tchaikovsky's First Piano Concerto. No one seems to notice the bandage covering a cut on his right index finger. Kiril Kondrashin begins to conduct the orchestra. Van Cliburn's performance transcends everything he has done so far. Next he plays a new rondo by Dmitri Kabalevsky. After a timeout to replace a broken string, he takes on the fiercely difficult Rachmaninoff Third Piano Concerto.

The crowd in the Great Hall goes wild. The ovations continue even after Van Cliburn leaves the stage. Emil Gilels, president of the jury, brings him back for an unprecedented second appearance. The minister of culture takes his dilemma straight to Premier Nikita Khrushchev.

"Is he the best?" the formidable Khrushchev asks.

"Yes," he's the best," the minister of culture assures him.

"In that case," Khrushchev nods, "give him the prize."

Soon afterward, a symbolic photograph circulates worldwide showing a smiling Khrushchev embracing the young American whose artistry has helped bring a thaw in the Cold War.

April 12th
A Dangerous Detour

Charles Burney was 18th century England's foremost musicologist, and in 1770 he traveled through Italy, learning all he could about Italian music and manners. He couldn't resist a dangerous detour. He wrote:

Mr. Hamilton proposed a journey into the neighborhood of Mount Vesuvius–a journey on it was not advisable when red-hot stones and sulphurous smoke may come down in any direction depending on the way the wind shifts. We therefore set off only with the intention to visit the lava of former eruptions, and to coast round the foot of Vesuvius as far as we could with safety by keeping always to the windward. Captain Forbes and I set off in Mr. Hamilton's chaise while he preceded us on horseback. We had two servants behind.

It began to rain on us before we had gotten two miles. We stopped at a gentleman's house in a rich vineyard within a mile of the mountain, and leaving there our chaise and horse, we ventured towards it on foot. I was prepared for the worst by having on a flannel waistcoat, leather stockings, and old good-for-nothing shoes, with a greatcoat. Captain Forbes had on a silk suit.

I had before taken shelter under the leaves of a remaining bit of another vineyard and found it impossible to resist the tempting ripe clusters. We heard the mountain roar, felt its throes under our feet, and saw the huge red-hot stones thrown up within a mile of us.

After visiting the different kinds and streams of lava, and going to the foot of Vesuvius, we returned to the house where we had left the chaise and horses. Two gentlemen came out to greet Mr. Hamilton. They seemed under great apprehension of a new eruption by the symptoms of the previous night. They had heard the mountain roar and seen it throw out huge stones and cinders all night.

Despite the risks, Charles Burney would live until April 12, 1814–his 88th birthday.

April 13th
The Ill–Tempered Accompanist

Performing for the great Henri Vieuxtemps was bad enough, but violinist Leopold Auer also had to put up with one of the worst accompanists imaginable–the wife of Vieuxtemps.

It happened about 1859, when Auer was a student. Auer and his father went to visit Vieuxtemps and the violinist received them cordially, but his wife–who was also his accompanist–was icy. After some small talk about his studies, Auer was allowed to take out his violin–not a very good one–and play. Madame Vieuxtemps sat down at the piano, looking bored. Auer had a nervous disposition as it was and he was trembling as he began to play Vieuxtemps' "Fantasie Caprice."

Years later when he told the story, Auer couldn't remember whether he had played well or not so well, but he remembered pouring his whole soul into each note even though his technique wasn't the best. Vieuxtemps encouraged him with a friendly smile.

Suddenly, in the middle of the performance, Madame Vieuxtemps jumped up from the piano and began prowling around the room, bending to the floor, looking underneath the furniture, and under the piano as if she had lost something.

Auer was at a complete loss. He stood open-mouthed, feeling as if he had been knocked from a bright pinnacle by a fiery explosion from a pit. Even Vieuxtemps seemed amazed as he watched his wife scouring the room. Finally he asked her what she was doing.

"A cat or two must be hiding in the room," she said, "meowing in every key."

When Auer realized that she was referring to his playing, he fainted. His father caught him before he fell to the floor. Vieuxtemps turned the entire debacle into a joke, though, patted Auer on the cheek and told him everything would be all right. Leopold Auer went on to become one of the world's great violinists, but he would never forget the setback he suffered at the age of 14.

April 14th

Rescued By Robin Hood

At the beginning of 1938, the main concern of Erich Wolfgang Korngold was the upcoming production of his opera *Die Kathrin*. Within a few months the Austrian composer would find his world–and his priorities–turned upside down, and he would owe his life to an unlikely rescuer–Robin Hood.

Korngold was attending a performance of his third piano sonata by a gifted student named Robert Kohner when his wife broke the news that Korngold had been offered a contract to write the music for the Errol Flynn move, *The Adventures of Robin Hood*. The astounded composer looked at his wife and said, "This is an omen." But the offer from Warner Brothers required him to be in Hollywood within a few days, and Korngold was reluctant to leave with the debut of his opera hanging in the balance. He called the Director of the Vienna Staatsoper for advice, and was surprised to hear his own words coming back to him: "Take this as an omen and go!"

After a dangerous drive over icy roads, a stormy trans-Atlantic crossing, and a train accident, Korngold and his wife and son arrived in Hollywood just twelve days after leaving Vienna. The composer had been sketching out ideas for the movie during trip, but when he saw the fast-pasted adventure film, he balked, convinced that he would be unable to write music for it. Within days, his bridges were burned behind him, though, as Hitler's troops marched into Austria. As the work of a non-Aryan, Korngold's opera was no longer eligible for production, and his house in Vienna was occupied by German troops.

The young pianist who had played Korngold's sonata was one of the first to die in the concentration camps, and Erich Korngold had no doubt that were it not for Robin Hood, he and his family would have suffered the same fate. He returned the favor by writing music that won the film an Oscar.

April 15th

Steel Fingers

It had recently worked for Sergei Rachmaninoff. Sergei Prokofiev thought it might work for him too. So, in 1918, he arranged an American concert tour. He was overlooking some important differences between Rachmaninoff and himself and between Europe and America.

When Rachmaninoff came on stage he overwhelmed everyone with his six-foot-plus height, his disdainful face and aristocratic manner. He played piano pieces that were romantic and melodic, easily enjoyed and remembered. He was an artist of noble origins who was fleeing a revolution Americans had come to distrust.

Prokofiev, on the other hand, bore none of the stamp of the tragic exile. He was a citizen of the dangerous new Soviet State. When he walked before the audience in New York's Aeolian Hall he strode on stage smiling, low-key, businesslike. He sat down at the piano and proceeded to play without drama and without flourishes. He had the audacity to play a program that was practically all Prokofiev. Unlike Rachmaninoff, he included not one classical work. It was only at the manager's insistence that he slipped in a little Rachmaninoff and Scriabin.

"Too little," Prokofiev later lamented. "Rachmaninoff had more sense. He added only one or two of his preludes to a program that was otherwise all classical." The critics worked him over good. One said that his mechanical playing sounded as if he had "steel fingers, steel wrists, steel biceps, steel triceps—sounded in fact like a music machine."

At the cheap hotel where Prokofiev was staying, the elevator operator touched his sleeve and remarked with awe, "Steel muscles!" Prokofiev recalled, "Evidently he thought I was some kind of boxer."

First round results: American critics, one; Prokofiev, zero. But the contender would be back.

April 16th
The Orange Plan

Sergei Prokofiev's previous trip to America had not gone very well. The critics had panned his piano pieces and playing as "Bolshevism in art" and "the epitome of Godless Russia." Worse, he had become known as a performer with a mechanical style.

Now it was 1920 and Prokofiev came to America with a plan. He had two compositions in hand. His Third Piano Concerto and his comic opera *The Love for Three Oranges*. If the opera succeeded, he could use the concerto to show his versatility. If the opera failed, he could use to concerto to divert attention from the failure. But right away his plan ran into trouble. Preparations for the opera's Chicago debut ran behind schedule, and word got out that a small fortune was being spent on its production. On top of that, an orange-growing company offered to advertise the opera as the inspiration of someone who liked their oranges. Prokofiev turned down the offer, and the resulting publicity overshadowed both the Third Piano Concerto and the opera.

When the opera finally was performed, its humor found the mark. The Chicago audience not only laughed, they went away humming two hit tunes–the scherzo and the celebrated march from Act Two.

But not so in New York. The press tore into Prokofiev and his oranges. Prokofiev summed up his American experience by saying, "I was left with a thousand dollars in my pocket, a bad headache, and an overwhelming wish to get away to some quiet place where I could work in peace."

He had also made it easier for the next "modernists" to come to America. And for himself. The next time, both Prokofiev and America would be better prepared.

April 17th
The Blessing of a Broken Leg

Sometimes a musician has to make a tremendous effort just to go through with a performance. In the case of pianist Oscar Levant, a broken leg helped.

By 1955 Levant had a 30-year performing career to his credit, but in recent seasons he had become better known for his cancellations than for his playing. In June of 1955, Howard Mitchell did what few other conductors would do. He invited Levant to perform with Washington's National Symphony. A year earlier Mitchell had run afoul of Levant's nervousness when the pianist ran from the stage during a rehearsal. That concert had never taken place.

Touched by this new vote of confidence, Levant accepted the invitation and began an effort to regain the coordination in his fingers. He practiced a few basic yoga breathing exercises and freed himself from all but one of the tranquilizers that he had come to rely on.

The orchestra he faced for the rehearsal was the same one that had seen him run from the stage a year before. Much to his relief, Oscar Levant played beautifully, had never played better in his life. The orchestra stood up and cheered.

The next night, for the performance, the auditorium was filled. Levant waited nervously in the wings as the big concert Steinway was wheeled on stage. Then its back leg snapped and the instrument crashed to the floor. Would it become a symbol of Levant's career?

Stage hands returned and propped the Steinway up with a sawhorse. The sight of the glamorous piano leaning on its ungainly crutch made Levant laugh, and in that instant his tension broke. He walked on stage to thunderous applause, shrugged at the tilting Steinway, sat down and delivered a magnificent performance of Gershwin's piano concerto. It was a flash of the old brilliance for a man at the twilight of his career, thanks to the support of a friend, the performer's own determination, and a broken piano leg.

April 18th

The Conductor Who Invented Himself

It must have been the radio interviewer's nightmare. In 1955 the world-renowned conductor Leopold Stokowski arrived for a live interview before he was to conduct a concert with the Miami University Symphony Orchestra. The interviewer began by stating that Stokowski was born in 1882. Stokowski interrupted and said that he had been born in 1887. The interviewer began again, saying that Stokowski's father was Polish and his mother Irish. Stokowski cut him off again, insisting that he had no Irish ancestry and questioned the interviewer's source of information. Sixty seconds into a half hour interview Stokowski walked out.

There was a good reason for the confusion. Stokowski was constantly re-inventing his life story. At various times he maintained that he had been born in Poland. Actually he was born in a lower middle-class neighborhood of London on April 18, 1882. In 1968, at the age of 86, he spoke of having developed his interest in music at the age of seven when his grandfather bought him his first violin. Actually that grandfather had died three years before Stokowski was born. Stokowski stated variously that his grandfather was either a peasant or a prosperous landowner deprived of his property by the Czar. The truth was that his grandfather, also named Leopold, was neither. He was a cabinet-maker who had emigrated to London and married a British woman named Jessie Sarah Anderson

Their son, also a cabinet-maker, married an Anglo-Irish woman, and a year later, Leopold Stokowski was born into a household where Polish was never spoken.

Despite Stokowski's claim that he was of Polish birth, friends noticed that he had the odd habit of adjusting his speech pattern to match the place he was discussing. But they also observed that when he was excited or under stress, the cosmopolitan—and imaginative—Leopold Stokowski often lapsed into his original lower-middle class London accent.

April 19th

Trust Your Players

Every now and then, a conductor has to give his players the benefit of the doubt. In fact, André Previn once remarked, "The more you trust your players–whether you're doing a Haydn symphony or something with the ink still wet–the better off you'll be."

As a beginning conductor, Previn was inclined to stop a rehearsal to correct any wrong note, ill-timed entry or lapse of time or pitch. But he soon realized that about half the time, a really good player would recognize the mistake right away, and correct it the next time through without being told. That enabled him to concentrate on the more subtle mistakes during the next rehearsal, which was harder for the conductor, but saved wear and tear on the orchestra.

In return, he noted, good players–players to be trusted–could sometimes come to the rescue of a conductor, because sooner or later, most conductors lose their place during a performance.

In the 1960's, when Previn became conductor the London Symphony Orchestra, principal hornist Barry Tuckwell gave him some advice that stuck. He said, "When you get lost in a piece–and you will–make nice, vague motions for a while, and we'll sort it out for you." He added, "But if you start flogging away at us, we're screwed."

Eventually Previn got a chance to put Tuckwell's advice to the test. He was conducting–from memory, he thought–a complicated piece by Peter Maxwell Davies, and suddenly realized that he didn't know what was happening. "So I just kind of looked elegant for four bars" he recalled, "and the orchestra fixed it for me." He concluded, "If I'd gone on, wildly beating eleven-sixteenths, we would never have got out of the hole."

For André Previn, a performance is very much a team effort, one based on mutual trust between the conductor and the orchestra.

April 20th

A Manager's Legacy

David Blakely was John Philip Sousa's manager for only five years, but–in life and death–he had a major impact on the history of American band music.

Blakely ran the first tour of the Marine Band led by Sousa. The tour began in the spring of 1891 and lasted five weeks. Blakely had done his work well. The response was gratifying. But Sousa suffered a nervous breakdown and the Marine Corps Surgeon sent him to Europe to recuperate.

By the time he returned to the United States, though, Sousa was planning another tour in cooperation with Blakely. Toward the end of that tour, Blakely approached Sousa with the idea of resigning from the Marine Corps and organizing a civilian concert band. Sousa was reluctant to give up the security of the Marine Corps but he had always dreamed of having his own band. When Blakely offered him four times his Marine Corps salary plus a percentage of the profits, he was quick to agree.

The gamble paid off handsomely. During the next three years the new Sousa Band was in constant demand.

Again Sousa sailed to Europe for a vacation, but the retreat was short-lived. In Italy, Sousa received word that David Blakely had died.

Full of concern for the future of his band, Sousa rushed to England, where he departed for America. All during the crossing he walked the deck of the steamship, brooding on an uncertain future. As he paced, worried and homesick, he began to hear in his imagination a band playing a new march. As soon as he arrived in New York, Sousa wrote it down. It turned out that the death of David Blakely had inspired him to write one of the greatest marches of all time–"The Stars and Stripes Forever."

April 21st

The Composer Knight

On April 21, 1738, between four and five o'clock in the afternoon a man appeared before the high altar of a convent in Madrid to take his vows as a knight of Santiago. He was not an adventurer or a soldier. He was not even Spanish by birth. He was an Italian-born composer named Domenico Scarlatti.

The honor may well have come via the influence of Scarlatti's former pupil Maria Barbara, daughter of the King of Portugal. Scarlatti had lived and worked in Spain for nine years. Maria Barbara had been unable to obtain honors for him at the Spanish Court. But she may have convinced her father to declare Scarlatti eligible for knighthood in the Portuguese Order of Santiago and arranged for the ceremony to take place in Madrid.

A priest asked Scarlatti if he was willing to change his life, even to the point of eating, drinking, and sleeping as a different man. When Scarlatti agreed, the priest continued, "You know that the order promises you neither horse nor arms, nor food other than bread and water, and the mercy of the Order, which is great. Additionally, we ask you if you are prepared to defend the gates against the Moors, and to maintain such obedience and humility that even if we sent you to keep the pigs you would do it."

Scarlatti responded, "I so promise."

Further questioning determined that Scarlatti had obtained his wife's consent, was guilty of no form of sacrilege or crime, and that his ancestry was free of Moorish blood. After confession and communion, Scarlatti returned to take his vows of devotion, obedience, and conjugal fidelity. Then he put on the white cloak of a full-fledged knight.

Scarlatti's descendants later allowed all of his musical manuscripts to disappear, but from generation to generation, they jealously preserved the records of his knighthood. As for Maria Barbara, she later had great influence in the Court at Madrid—as the Queen of Spain.

April 22nd

Ravel's American Comforts

It was finally settled. The famous French composer Maurice Ravel was coming to the United States. He was shy and withdrawn, but he was about to be embraced by a nation.

His most immediate concern was cigarettes. Ravel smoked almost constantly and he was hooked on French Caporals. Bringing a three-month supply into the United States would cost a fortune in customs duties. An American cigarette-maker gallantly offered to manufacture his cigarettes from the same blend of tobacco used in the Caporals. The next need was easier to arrange—Ravel's favorite French wines would accompany him in his travels.

Ravel had wanted his arrival kept quiet, but when he stepped onto the pier in New York, in 1928, a crowd of newspaper reporters met him. From then on admirers surrounded him. He was besieged with telephone calls and telegrams, and invitations to lunch, dinner, and tea. He received flowers and letters. The reclusive Ravel was overwhelmed.

But at least he had come prepared to be seen. His wardrobe included dozens of bright shirts and vests and 20 pairs of pajamas. His ties had arrived at the last minute, and he was in for a shock when he unpacked them. They were all half an inch too long. One of his entourage who cheerfully volunteered to shorten the ties counted 57 of them.

Shortly after he arrived in New York, he was the guest of Mrs. Thomas Edison at a Carnegie Hall concert where the audience acknowledged him by rising to their feet, clapping, whistling, and throwing their programs into the air. When the retiring Maurice Ravel finally was persuaded to come on stage, he received a thunderous ovation that went on for a full ten minutes.

April 23rd
The Handshake

It was a brief and simple encounter, but it made a big impression. In his 1952 autobiography *My Life*, Alexander Gretchaninoff looked back more than 60 years to his first meeting with his musical idol.

In the 1880's, when Gretchaninoff was a student at the Moscow Conservatory, the celebrated composer of the day was Peter Tchaikovsky. Each new Tchaikovsky symphony was included in the concerts of the Russian Imperial Musical Society. As soon as his songs were published, music lovers snapped them up. As a boy, Gretchaninoff was lucky enough to attend the first performances of Tchaikovsky's operas *Eugene Onegin* and *The Queen of Spades*.

For the Moscow symphony concerts, the orchestra was usually beefed up with conservatory students. Theory students were sometimes drafted to play the percussion instruments if the parts weren't too prominent. Gretchaninoff was excited and nervous when he was assigned the glockenspiel part in a performance of Tchaikovsky's orchestral suite *Mozartiana*. The prospect was all the more thrilling because the conductor was to be none other than Tchaikovsky himself.

Despite Gretchaninoff's nervousness, the practices went well. During the intermission in the last rehearsal Gretchaninoff was talking to a friend when he saw Tchaikovsky coming toward him. The friend introduced them. Tchaikovsky shook hands with Gretchaninoff and commented, "These parts should always be given to young musicians. Professionals never play them as conscientiously as these young performers do."

Long after receiving the compliment from his idol, Gretchaninoff was walking on air. His friends made fun of him by saying that for an entire week Alexander Gretchaninoff had not washed the hand that had touched Tchaikovsky.

April 24th

The Composing Machine

Today he is best known for his technical studies such as *The School of Velocity*—methodical, mechanical approaches to piano mastery. Carl Czerny was actually an extraordinarily prolific composer whose curiously mechanical way of working made his vast output possible.

The English writer John Ella visited Czerny in Vienna in 1845 and asked the composer how he could possibly find the time to publish so much music.

Czerny replied, "I'll surprise you all the more when I tell you that I was 28 years old before I published my first work, but I have written more music in my lifetime than any living copyist. In fact, I have written more than 1,000 pieces that have never been printed, yet I've never employed a copyist to prepare any of my publications."

The Englishman had heard that Czerny was also in the habit of working on four different publications at once, and he couldn't help asking Czerny about that. Smiling, Czerny showed Ella around his study. Each corner of the room had a desk with an unfinished score on it. "You see, my dear Ella, that here I am working for the English," Czerny said. At the first desk was a long list of English national tunes to be arranged for the firm of D'Almaine and Company. At the second desk was a half-finished set of Beethoven's symphonies that Czerny was arranging for piano duet for another publisher. At a third desk, Czerny was working on a new edition of Bach's fugues, and at the fourth desk he was composing a Grand Symphony.

Czerny's method of operation? After finishing a page at the first desk, he would pass on to the second and so on, and when he had written a page at the fourth desk, he went back to the first desk and started all over again.

The industrial revolution was in full swing, and Carl Czerny had applied its principles to his art.

April 25th
Overwhelmed in London

Felix Mendelssohn's trip to England inspired some of his finest music. But sometimes the 20-year-old composer was so overwhelmed by his surroundings that Mendelssohn the musician took a backseat to Mendelssohn the tourist. He wrote to his family on April 25, 1829:

I have taken leave of my senses. London is the grandest and most complex monstrosity on earth. Picture this. You step out of my lodging and turn right, down Regent Street. Look at that magnificent wide street lined with porticos–unfortunately behind a thick fog again today. Look at the shops with their inscriptions in letters as tall as a man, and the coaches stacked high with passengers, and see how one line of vehicles is outpaced by pedestrians because it's been halted by some elegant carriages.

See over there a horse rearing up because its rider has acquaintances in a nearby house. See men carrying around posters promoting graceful and artistic performances by trained cats. See the beggars and the Negroes and the fat John Bulls with a slender, pretty daughter on each arm. Oh, those daughters! But have no fear. I'm not in any danger in that department, either in Hyde Park with its crowds of young ladies or at the concert or at the Opera.

The only danger is at street corners and crossings where I often murmur to myself, "Be careful not to fall under the wheels."

Here I am sitting near the divine grand piano that the Clementi firm has just sent over for the duration of my stay. Here I am beside a cheerful fire, within my own four walls. Under my window a beggar has just struck up a song and is almost drowned out by the cries of the hawkers. From here to London itself is a three-quarter hour drive and all along the way, down every street, you find a constant din. But that's only about a quarter of the city. Imagine all that and you can imagine why I'm half out of my senses.

April 26th

The Loner

Peter Tchaikovsky wrote some of his best music during long trips to Italy. But even there music and friends could put him out of sorts. To his brother Modest he wrote from Rome in April 1890.

For two days running I have been in a bad humor, even in despair, and have lost both appetite and any desire to work, etc. The Palens have announced all over Rome that I am here and the first to arrive was Alexei Golitzin. It cannot be helped, I like him very much and, even after the first moment of horror at seeing a new face, I was glad to see him. But immediately after him Sgambati appeared. I managed to give the instruction that I was receiving no one and he was not allowed in, but he left a note and a ticket for a quartet recital, for the next morning at which my first quartet was to be played. This has brought me to absolute despair, which proves how wild I have become.

I had to go to the quartet recital and listen to a mediocre–not to say a bad–performance, go to the artists' room with Sgambati in view of all the gaping audience and mutter polite trivialities, etc.

I must say, though, that Sgambati–knowing I am a solitary person and working hard–says he does not want to intrude and so will not invite me to his house. But he begged me to come next Friday to hear his quartet. (The same we heard when Liszt was present.) All the same, the pleasure of my stay in Rome is quite poisoned…

I do not know if I will be able to stand another week although I am terribly anxious to finish what I had planned.

The quartet was a big success and the papers were full of praise for it. Well, the papers here praise everything! Oh! The sooner home the better. Fancy! I have pains in my stomach at the mere thought of traveling home. Everybody is leaving and it will be difficult to get seats.

April 27th

Dangerous Peace

George Frederick Handel wrote some of his most successful music for a peace celebration that erupted into a battle.

In 1749, late in his long career, Handel wrote his *Royal Fireworks Music* to celebrate the Peace of Aix-la-Chapelle which ended the eight-year War of Austrian Succession. England had spent much on the war and won little. Hoping to bolster the government's image, King George II and his court embarked on a series of public relations events. The festivities were to be topped off by a spectacular pyrotechnical display in London's Green Park. Six months in advance work began on a colossal fireworks pavilion. When it was finally completed the day before the big ceremony, the pavilion stretched 410 feet long and 114 feet high. The central section held giant figures of Neptune and Mars and King George presenting peace to Britain. Above it all–200 feet above the ground–was a giant disc representing the sun.

Accompanying all the brouhaha would be the *Royal Fireworks Music* of Mr. Handel, completed just six days before the grand event. With a band of 100 musicians, he rehearsed the score at Spring Gardens, Vauxhall, before a crowd of 12,000. All around, traffic came to a standstill. Apparently the king's publicists had done their jobs well.

Then came the big night–April 27, 1749. King George and his court watched eagerly from The Queen's Library. At six o'clock Handel's overture began. As it came to a close, the Royal Salute erupted from 101 brass cannon, and the pavilion burst into fireworks. Unfortunately, it also burst into flames. The music may have gone on for a few more movements before the rest of the pavilion went up in smoke, but the masses who had come to celebrate the peace soon found themselves in a battle for their lives.

Handel, nonetheless, continued to enjoy a reputation as the composer whose music best represented English sensibilities, even though he always considered himself a German.

April 28th
The Power Struggle

They were some of the greatest composers France had ever heard—Camille Saint-Saëns, Vincent d'Indy, and César Franck—and they were locked in a power struggle over fame and love.

Needless to say, music also played a part in their conflict. The setting was the Societé Nationale that Saint-Saëns had founded 15 years earlier. The year was 1886 and Saint-Saëns, at 51, was considered an old reactionary by many of the newer composers at the society. Foremost among his musical offenses was Saint-Saëns' opposition to the music of Richard Wagner. He also disliked 64-year-old César Franck, who was the idol of d'Indy and his followers.

Saint-Saëns was undoubtedly jealous of César Franck the composer, but his jealously of Franck was not entirely musical. In fact, Saint-Saëns had taken part in the performances of many works by Franck. The falling-out had more to do with a young woman named Auguste Holmes to whom both Franck and Saint-Saëns were attracted. The affair of Mademoiselle Holmes had come to a boil during one such performance—the premiere of the great D Minor Piano Quintet by Franck. The quintet was dedicated to Saint-Saëns, but it expressed a good deal of Franck's passion for young Auguste, and Saint-Saëns, having heard rumors about a relationship between Franck and Auguste, may well have been performing the quintet while trying to cope with increasing jealousy. When the performance was finally over, Saint-Saëns hurried from the stage, leaving the manuscript on the piano.

That sort of thing had been going on for six years, and d'Indy decided it was time to oust Saint-Saëns from the Society. He hit on a plan to do just that. Knowing how adamant Saint-Saëns was about a Society devoted exclusively to French music, d'Indy led his young cohorts in passing a resolution to include foreign music at the Society's concerts. Pressed to the limit, Saint-Saëns promptly resigned his presidency, and a new president was chosen—his rival for the affections of Auguste—César Franck.

April 29th
The Dresden Gamble

The same piece of music can draw very different reactions from city to city, as Carl Maria von Weber reported from Dresden to a friend in Berlin in April 1824:

I've been going through a rough patch, and maybe it's just as well that my enormous workload didn't give me much time to think. But still I couldn't help feeling a sustained bitterness. At Prague Euranthe *was a flop. At Franfurt it caused an uproar. Everyone was dumfounded by the notorious scrawlings of the Viennese gossip columnists.*

So I was very curious to find out what kind of response it would get from our cool, subdued, and particular public here in Dresden. The attitude was unfriendly rather than accepting. So Euranthe *was performed last night–and the triumph was beyond imagining! Never had I seen a Dresden audience so roused, so enthusiastic. The excitement grew from one act to the next. When it ended they called for me and then they called for the entire cast.*

I have to admit that it was a top-flight performance. In particular, Devrient–who played Euranthe–and Mademoiselle Funk as Eglantine outdid themselves as actors and singers. Mayer as Lysiart and Bergman as Adolar both did quite nicely. The chorus was top notch. The orchestra played with a precision and subtlety to be found here only.

Now everybody is saying that the opera is even better than Der Freischütz. *Tieck, among others, was supposed to have attended a party after the opera but declared that his head was already filled by it. He said–to other people naturally–that there were things in the opera that Gluck and Mozart would be jealous of. I know that I can relate such things to you without being misconstrued. I wouldn't dare tell anyone else in the world.*

April 30th

Liszt Plays Grieg

Edvard Grieg was 25 years old when he wrote his masterpiece, the *Piano Concerto in A Minor*. One of the first to see it was Franz Liszt, who not only played it and critiqued it, but afterward offered Grieg advice to last a lifetime.

The occasion came one evening in 1865. Grieg had just received the manuscript from the printer and was hoping that Liszt would play it at a gathering of friends. "Will you play it?" Liszt asked, to which Grieg quickly replied, "No, I can't. I haven't practiced it."

Liszt took the manuscript, went to the piano, smiled and said to the guests, "All right then, I'll show you that I can't either." He took the first part of the concerto so quickly that it came out a jumble, but after a little tempo coaching from Grieg, he brought out the beauty of the work, playing the most difficult part—the cadenza—best of all. Liszt began to make comments to Grieg and the guests as he played, nodding to the right or left at the parts he particularly liked.

As Liszt approached the end of the finale, he suddenly stopped, stood up, left the piano with big theatrical strides, raised his arms, and walked across the large hall, roaring out the theme. When he got to the place where the first tone is changed in the orchestra from G-Sharp to G, he stretched his arms grandly and shouted, "G, G, not G-Sharp! Magnificent! That is the real Swedish Banko!"

He went back to the piano, repeated an entire section, and finished, whereupon he handed Grieg the manuscript and said warmly, "Keep boldly on. I tell you. You have the ability—and don't let them get you down!"

Edvard Grieg later recalled that Liszt's final advice about the critics proved very important to him and that it had the air of a sacred pronouncement.

May 1st
The Cold-Hearted Duchess

The 22-year-old Wolfgang Amadeus Mozart had arrived in Paris to build an international reputation. He wrote to his father Leopold in Salzburg on May 1, 1778:

Responding to an invitation of eight days prior, I drove to the house of the Duchesse de Chabot. I waited half an hour in a large room without any fire and as cold as ice. At last the Duchess came in. She was very polite, and implored me to excuse her piano since none of her instruments were in good order, but she asked me at least to give it a try. I said I'd be happy to play something but couldn't right then because my fingers were completely numb from the cold, so I asked her to take me to a room where there was a fire.

"Oh, yes, yes, you are right," she answered. She then seated herself and spent an entire hour drawing in the company of several gentlemen all sitting in a circle around a large table, while I had the honor of waiting.

The windows and doors were open so that not only my hands, but my body and feet were cold, and my head also began to ache. At last, to cut matters short, I played her miserable piano. What annoyed me most of all was that the Duchess and the gentlemen never stopped drawing for a moment, but coolly continued what they were doing, so that I had to play to an audience of chairs and tables and walls.

Finally I got up and said I'd be glad to come back when some better instrument could be found, but the Duchess persuaded me to wait until her husband came in. He sat down beside me and listened with great attention, and I forgot all about the cold and the headache, and in spite of the miserable piano, played as I can play when I'm in the right mood.

May 2nd
No Deal!

As World War II raged in Europe, English composer Arthur Bliss was director of music at the BBC. His family was in America and he was looking for a way to go over so that he could arrange to bring them back to England.

An offer of assistance came from an unexpected source via a phone call from Lady Cunard, who wanted to meet with him regarding an urgent matter. Bliss had never met Lady Cunard and so he was as curious as he was hopeful. He went to see her that very day. After some uneasy preliminaries, she got to the point. It seemed that England's celebrated conductor, Sir Thomas Beecham, was in America and had become, as she said, "emotionally involved." It was important, she said, for him to return to England. Bliss knew nothing about Beecham's private life and had no interest in it. He began to wonder what Beecham's personal problems had to do with him.

Lady Cunard cut to the chase. Her plan was for Bliss to urge the Director-General of the BBC to invite Beecham to come to England and replace Bliss as the music director. In exchange, Lady Cunard would use her influence to make sure that Bliss could get back to America to rejoin his family.

At first Bliss fought the impulse to laugh at the thought of the dapper, distinguished Beecham in the mundane position of running the BBC music staff. Then he got angry at the presumption that he would step down for the sake of getting Beecham out of a romantic entanglement. Controlling his temper, Bliss suggested that Lady Cunard take her plan straight to the Director-General. Their parting was less than cordial.

Arthur Bliss–later Sir Arthur Bliss–had hung onto his job and his professional pride, but at a cost. Two-and-a-half years would pass before he would see his family again.

May 3rd

How to Beat a Deadline

Sooner or later every composer has to deal with a deadline. Gioacchino Rossini shared some of his trade secrets in a letter that shows his boisterous sense of humor:

Wait until the evening before the performance. Nothing stirs up a person's enthusiasm so much as pure necessity, a copyist waiting for your work and the pleadings of an impresario at the end of his rope, tearing out his hair by the handful. In my day in Italy all impresarios were bald by the age of 30.

I wrote the overture to Otello *in a little room in the Palazzo Barbaja where the baldest and fiercest of the directors had shut me in by force with nothing but a plateful of macaroni, vowing not to let me out until I had written the last note.*

I wrote the overture to La Gazza Ladra *on the very day of the premiere, beneath the roof of La Scala, where I had been imprisoned by the director and put under guard by four stage carpenters who were under orders to throw my manuscript out the window, page by page to the copyists, who were down below waiting to copy it out. If the pages of music failed to come out, their orders were to throw* me *out.*

For The Barber of Seville *I did better. I didn't write any overture at all. I just borrowed one I had designated for a semi-serious opera called* Elisabetta. *The public was perfectly satisfied. I wrote the overture to* Le Compte Ory *while standing with my feet in the water, fishing, in the company of Signor Aguado, who was talking about Spanish finance. I wrote the* William Tell Overture *under similar circumstances. For* Mosé *I didn't write one at all.*

May 4th
The Judas Biographer

On May 4, 1908, 64-year-old Nikolai Rimsky-Korsakov told a friend about a music treatise he had begun and laid aside. They spoke about the details of composing but, as the evening progressed, the composer and his friend became increasingly reflective.

As a rule, Rimsky-Korsakov said, it must always be remembered that a melody in octaves should be scored for instruments of the same timber, otherwise the octaves will not sound good. "And yet," he continued, "a melody in octaves given to the top register of the flutes and the bottom register of the oboes and violins doesn't sound bad."

It was after midnight by the time the evening of music talk came to an end. His friend moved solemnly toward Rimsky-Korsakov and said, "And now accept this kiss from me—the kiss of Judas, according to Oscar Wilde. For I am your future biographer, and in Wilde's opinion, the biography of a great man is always written by a Judas."

"Don't believe him, my dear friend," Rimsky-Korsakov replied. "They're all fools."

Less than a month later Rimsky-Korsakov was dead. His friend's biography, in the form of journal entries, began publication in 1917. But only about a quarter of the memoir had seen print when the Russian Revolution cut it short. It was not until 1959 that the entire biography finally was published.

Ironically, the only issue on which Rimsky-Korsakov and his friend had not seen eye-to-eye was the politics of revolution. In 1905 Rimsky-Korsakov had sided with the students and workers opposing the Czar's policies. His friend had been a moderate, while Rimsky-Korsakov came to describe his own politics as "vivid red."

May 5th

Winning Over the Master

When the young American composer Daniel Gregory Mason came to Boston to interview the great pianist and composer Ignacy Jan Paderweski, there was trouble from the start.

Because of a misunderstanding, Mason was two-and-a-half hours late for his meeting with the great pianist. Mason was waiting in the hotel lobby while Paderweski was upstairs, getting more and more aggravated by Mason's tardiness. Finally Mason went up to see Paderewski and found him cordial enough, but Paderweski's wife was cold and standoffish. Mason felt awkward and self-conscious. He complimented Paderewski on his "Variations and Fugue on an Original Theme." Then he added: "Just so you don't think that's empty flattery, I'll tell you frankly that I do not care so much for some of your early pieces."

Paderewski's wife gave Mason a stony look. "What pieces? What do you not care for?"

Mason got in deeper. "Well, for example, I do not care so much for the A Minor Concerto."

Her gaze was unwavering. "The concerto is one of my favorites among my husband's compositions. I love it more and more."

Valiantly, Mason complimented Paderewski's use of French impressionism.

Now Paderewski himself spoke. "I utterly repudiate any debt to French impressionism. I do not believe in the modern French school, because it is not founded in tradition. It is erratic, bizarre, wayward."

At last Mason ventured to show Paderewski a movement of his new violin sonata. Paderewski shook hands with him about eight times as he read through the sonata, singing the melody and exclaiming "beautiful!" Finally, with his music, Daniel Gregory Mason had won over the master.

May 6th

Chopin in Vienna

In 1831 a young pianist and composer named Frédéric Chopin left his native land, Poland, in order to establish himself in European musical circles. He was a popular success as a concert performer, but at times he was lonely in a crowd. In Vienna, in the spring of 1831, Chopin wrote in his journal:

Today it was beautiful on the thoroughfare. Crowds of people but I had nothing to do with them. I admired the foliage. The spring aromas and that innocence of nature brought back the feelings of my childhood. A storm was looming so I went in, but no storm developed–except for melancholy.

Why? I don't even care about music today. It's late but I'm not sleepy. I don't know what's wrong with me. And I've begun my third decade! The papers and posters have announced my concert. It's in two days, and it's as if there were no such thing. It just doesn't seem to matter to me. I don't even listen to the compliments. They seem more and more stupid. I'd wish I were dead, except that I would like to see my parents.

Her image stands before my eyes. I think I don't love her anymore, and yet I can't get her out of my head. Everything I have seen abroad so far seems old and hateful to me and just makes me sigh for home, for those blessed moments that I undervalued. What used to seem magnificent today seems common. What I used to think common is now incomparable, too great, too lofty. The people here are not my people. They're kind, but kind from habit. They do everything too formally, flatly, moderately. I have no desire whatsoever to think about moderation.

I'm confused. I'm melancholy. I don't know what to do with myself. I wish I weren't alone!

At age 21, Chopin was soon to meet the great musicians of the day–Rossini, Liszt, Cherubini, and many others. He would never return to Poland.

May 7th
The Money Back Guarantee

The following letter to Giuseppe Verdi shows that to be a composer is to expose oneself to criticism from anyone and everyone:

May 7th, 1872. Much Honored Signor Verdi, on the second of this month I went to Padua, lured by the sensation caused by your opera Aida. *I was so intrigued that I was in my seat—number 120—half an hour before the performance began. I admired the sets. I enjoyed hearing the excellent singers, and I did everything I could not to let a single thing slip by me.*

When the opera ended I asked myself if I was satisfied and the answer was no! I started back toward Reggio and listened in the railroad car to the opinions about Aida. *Just about everyone agreed that it was a first-rate work.*

I was struck by the idea of hearing it again, and on the fourth I went back. Because the crowd was so huge, I went through unprecedented efforts to get a reserved seat. I had to throw away five lire to see the performance in comfort.

I came to this conclusion: It's an opera that has nothing to stir up any enthusiasm or excitement, and if it didn't have the pomp and spectacle, the public wouldn't sit through it to the end. After it has filled the house for a night or two it will be consigned to the dust of the archives. So you can imagine, dear Signor Verdi, my regret at having twice spent thirty-two lire! Add to that the aggravation of depending upon my family and that this money troubles my sleep like a frightful ghost, and I sincerely address you so that you may send me that amount.

Enclosed was an itemized bill for train fare, opera tickets, and a "detestable supper."

Verdi arranged to send the plaintiff a refund, minus five lire for the supper.

May 8th

Richard Strauss and the Yanks

May 8, 1945–V.E. Day. Germany surrendered to the Allies, ending World War II in Europe. Composer Richard Strauss was among the many who were glad that the war was over regardless of who had won. He and his family had been suffering under the Nazi regime while living near the village of Garmisch in the Bavarian Alps.

Strauss was 81 years old. He and his wife had wanted to go to Switzerland to restore their health at a spa near Zurich, but had been forbidden to do so by the highest authority–Hitler himself. There was an order to arrest Strauss' daughter-in-law, but she had dared to remain with her family. Refugees had been billeted with the Strausses–a cabaret worker and his two starving children.

Garmish had fallen to the Allies without a shot being fired., and on the morning of April 30 American tanks rolled into the meadow beside Strauss' house. The composer's grandson, 18-year-old Richard, reported, "No one believes me, but I swear that there was a GI sitting on a tank, whistling the *Don Juan* theme!" The American army was requisitioning villas for its use, giving the occupants 15 minutes to vacate. About eleven o'clock in the morning jeeps came up Strauss' driveway. Strauss' daughter-in-law began to pack food and valuables. Despite his family's protests, Strauss went out the front door to meet the Americans.

He spoke to a Major Kramer who sat in one of the jeeps. "I am Richard Strauss," he said, 'the composer of *Rosenkavalier* and *Salome*."

He had spoken to the right person. Major Kramer was a music-lover. He ordered his men to show respect for Strauss, and the composer returned the compliment by inviting several of the Americans in for wine and venison stew. A sign that said "Off Limits" protected the house. In the days that followed, many American soldiers wanted to meet the famous Richard Strauss, even though some of them were under the mistaken impression that he had written "On the Beautiful Blue Danube."

May 9th

Only You

Paris Opera director André Messager conducted the debut of Claude Debussy's opera *Pelléas and Mélisande*. Then he had to leave the country to fulfill other commitments. That left the direction of the opera to the second conductor, Henri-Paul Büsser. A despondent Debussy wrote to Messager on May 9, 1902:

Since you left I've been as gloomy as an abandoned road. I don't want to bore you with my lamentations though, so let's discuss Pelléas. *Last Thursday we had a quick pass at the opera, which Büsser needed. Just between you and me, the management should've given time for a full rehearsal. Büsser was nervous and seemed not to know how to come to terms with the entire score. Pelléas sang in a voice that seemed to come out of his umbrella! Mélisande refused to look at him, contending that she was accustomed to gazing upon a much more agreeable face, and there's plenty of truth to that. The result was blurred and muddy. There was no telling where it would go.*

On Friday a wonderful audience, very respectful. Büsser showed up looking like a gentleman who's dreading a cold bath. The orchestra was admirable, carrying him along and guiding him through the nuances. He paid no attention whatsoever to the singers, throwing chords at them with complete disregard for harmony.

Anyway, it all turned out passably, and after the fourth act there were three curtain calls to reward all of those deserving people for their efforts.

All in all, a pleasant evening during which only you were missing—and missing utterly. What I'm trying to say is that you managed to bring Pelléas *to musical life with a subtle tenderness that can never be repeated. Because, without doubt, the conductor who brings it forth tempers the inner rhythm of any composition, the same way that a word is colored by the lips the speak it.*

May 10th

Offenbach's Short Comeback

Eighteen-seventy-one. It was the end of an epoch in France. Years of opulence and gaiety had been blasted by the grim, disastrous Franco-Prussian War. One of the less obvious casualties was a musician huddled in an oversized coat. He was Jacques Offenbach, composer of buoyant operettas that must have seemed like relics from a bygone day.

Offenbach was attending a rehearsal for the revival of his operetta *The Brigands*. The chorus sang the drinking song at the end of the first act. They were drab and uninspired. During intermission they spoke not of the operetta but of their war experiences. Offenbach was sitting on the forestage, crippled with gout, shivering beneath a heavy coat although the day was warm. At first he told his friend, the librettist Ludovic Halévy, that he was too downhearted to interfere. Then suddenly he jumped to his feet, angrily shaking his walking stick, and shouted, "What do you think you're singing, ladies? Start all over again, the whole finale all over again from the beginning!"

He strode over to the conductor at the piano and took over, now full of strength and energy. He started singing and shouting. The singers dozing in the back row came to life. He flung away his overcoat and started counting the tempo with all his strength. He smacked the piano so hard that his walking stick broke in two. He swore, threw the stump on the floor, and grabbed the violin bow from the startled conductor. He went on beating the time with frightening force—no longer the same man. The players were no longer the same and neither were the singers. The finale of the operetta sparkled with gaiety and surged forth with a sweeping rhythm.

As the last note sounded, everyone applauded Offenbach enthusiastically. He sank back down in his seat, exhausted. "I've broken my stick," he said, "but I've saved my finale."

For a few minutes, Offenbach had also brought back the joy that Parisians had felt before the ravages of war.

May 11th
William Grant Still

It was the place for an artist to grow—Paris in the 1920's. The American melodist William Grant Still took an unlikely route to get there, and chose an unlikely teacher—the champion of electronic music, Edgar Varèse.

Still was born on a plantation near Woodville, Mississippi, on May 11, 1895. His parents were teachers with musical talent, and young William Grant showed a penchant for music early on. About 1912 the works of the Afro-English composer Samuel Coleridge-Taylor inspired Still to begin writing. But he spent most of his time playing in vaudeville bands and theater orchestras before entering the New England Conservatory in 1923. Then he became the recording manager for the Black Swan Phonograph Company—the first recording company owned and operated by blacks. The Black Swan roster of stars included classical singers, ballad and pop singers, and folk singers. As recording manager, Still made arrangements for recording artists and played the oboe and other instruments in the house orchestra.

One day, Still happened to look over the shoulder of the secretary of Black Swan owner Harry Pace, and noticed that she was writing a reply to a letter from the French composer Edgar Varèse. Varèse wanted to teach a black composer to write avant-garde music and was asking Pace to recommend someone. The secretary was responding that Pace had no one to recommend.

"Tear that up," Still cried. "I'll write to Mr. Varèse myself." It was the beginning of two years of study with the innovative composer. Still was able to write works that reflected the influence of Varèse, and he broadened his style during his two years of study. But he was too deeply rooted in melody and musical nationalism to develop into an avant-garde composer. And within a few years, William Grant Still would become famous throughout the western world via a work that celebrated American folk music and jazz in a classical setting—his *Afro-American Symphony*.

May 12th
The Unlikely Ally

The Frenchman Gabriel Fauré was inclined to write refined, soft-spoken music. In 1908 one of his staunchest supporters was a composer of outgoing, often dissonant pieces—the Spaniard Isaac Albéniz.

Fauré was born on May 12, 1845. He was 15 years Albéniz' senior, but Albéniz had been a dazzling child prodigy and a freewheeling world traveler by the age of 12. At age 63, Fauré was still having trouble getting recognition.

In 1908 Albéniz introduced Fauré into musical circles in Barcelona. The next year, Fauré was invited to conduct his *Requiem, Shylock,* and *Caligula* as well as his *Ballade for Piano and Orchestra*. According to the pianist, Marguerite Long, during one rehearsal of the Ballade, Fauré was conducting badly. He was eagerly awaiting a telegram telling him whether or not he had been elected to membership in an important musical organization—the Instutut.

"All through the rehearsal, Fauré kept looking at me," Marguite Long recalled, "not because of anything in the Ballade but out of desperation to know the result of the election. In that huge auditorium holding 7,000 people, I kept my eyes glued to the door. The rehearsal finished at midnight and still there was no word, so Fauré went off to find out what he could. At the post office we discovered there was a postal strike and nothing was getting through. Then, around dawn, just as we were all getting some much-needed sleep, Fauré banged on the door, waving the telegram. He'd been elected!"

There had been some resistance to Fauré's election to the Instutut, and it's likely that Albéniz used some of his powers of persuasion to Fauré's advantage. By the time of the election, though, Albéniz was seriously ill. He was staying in Paris, and Fauré and Paul Dukas went to see him often. On one occasion, he paid Fauré the ultimate compliment when he asked Marguerite Long, as a last favor, to play one of his favorite piano pieces, the second "Valse-Caprice" by Gabriel Fauré.

May 13th

Faces to Make One Miss Notes

New Orleans-born pianist and composer Louis Moreau Gottschalk toured the northern states during the Civil War. As he traveled through New York State, he was occasionally able to forget about the war and concentrate on the two great loves of his life—music and women. In May 1864, he wrote in his journal:

At Rochester I have seen some of the most charming types of women that have ever crossed the dreams of an old bachelor! Outside of my exceptional position of pianist and old bachelor, this is the element I dread the most in my concerts—it makes me absent-minded—the quick result being a wrong note! Suppose I have to reach a black key at the extremity of my keyboard. I take my measure well, but my finger is not well assured because my eyes are on my audience and D-sharp is ignominiously propelled into the depths of E natural. Much to the joy of those who sniff out defects and are hostile toward accomplishments.

They always sing the same song. "He does not play classical music." And when mere mortals applaud, he shrugs his shoulders. But, wretched man, be prudent then! The more you malign me, the more you bemire yourself in the dark mud in which your venomous impertinence stagnates.

I know an ass who, having devoted his pen for ten years to proving to the artistic world that my compositions were detestable, was advised, miserable wretch, to publish in an unlucky day, one of the offsprings of his pen and of his gall-filled brain.

I had thought myself killed by his attacks, but after having read this one, I consoled myself by borrowing from Voltaire: "Sir, I pardon your criticisms because nobody reads them. But I shall never pardon your compositions because I have been obliged to read them, and they are too bad for me ever to forget them."

May 14th
Toscanini & the Fascists

You might think that conducting an orchestra would be a safe profession, but, at times, a conductor can fall into a life-threatening situation. So it was with Arturo Toscanini in Bologna, Italy, on May 14, 1931.

Toscanini had accepted an invitation to conduct two concerts in Bologna. The purpose was to celebrate the 75th anniversary of the birth of composer Giuseppe Martucci, and Toscanini insisted on conducting for free. But a celebration of a different sort was also scheduled–a Fascist Party festival. The Deputy Mayor told Toscanini that two government officials would be attending the first concert and that he should, therefore, begin the performance with the royal march and the Fascist favorite "Giovinezza." Since the concert was supposed to consist entirely of music by Martucci, Toscanini declined to play the two anthems, not wanting to turn the concert into a political event.

When Toscanini arrived at the theater he found himself surrounded by Fascist youths. One of them asked him whether he would play "Giovinezza." When the conductor refused, the Fascist hit the 64-year-old conductor in the face and neck and shouted insults while the crowd added taunts of their own. Toscanini's wife and chauffeur and a friend managed to pull him into a car while the national police stood by in their plumed ceremonial hats. The Toscaninis sped back to their hotel.

When it was announced in the packed theater that the concert would be postponed because Toscanini was ill, there were shouts of "It's not true!" The black- shirted guards panicked and shut the exits, but as the surge of humanity became irresistible, they were ordered to reopen the doors, and the crowd poured out into the streets.

Toscanini sent a disgruntled telegram to Mussolini. Although Mussolini never replied directly, he reportedly said, "He conducts an orchestra of one hundred people; I have to conduct one of forty million, and they are not all virtuosi."

May 15th
Dangerous Disobedience

Vienna in 1787. It could be a risky place and time for a composer to make a living. And Antonio Salieri took a big risk. He disobeyed the Emperor.

Salieri had recently returned from Paris, where his opera *Tarare* had been produced. Emperor Joseph II ordered Salieri and his librettist, Lorenzo Da Ponte, to translate the French opera into Italian. But the work went badly and, despite the Emperor's order, Salieri suggested that they start from scratch. Occasionally Salieri would borrow a musical idea from the original French opera, but usually he found it necessary to alter it considerably. To save time, Salieri composed the scenes one by one as Da Ponte brought them.

Hearing that three acts of the opera were finished, the Emperor was eager to perform them at one of his afternoon concerts, and he got the parts from the copyist and assembled his musicians. Sitting at the pianoforte, he suggested that the singers follow the vocal parts of the new score while the instrumentalists played from the French original.

"Act One, Scene One," the Emperor announced. "Duet."

"The French opera begins with a prologue," someone said.

For two hours they tried to find something they could perform together, but in vain. The Emperor and his musicians found that the two versions of the opera had very little in common.

"This is enough to drive a person crazy," the Emperor declared. He sent for an explanation.

Salieri had been laid up with a rheumatic knee, but two days later he came to the palace to face the music. Bravely, he explained his reasons for disobeying the Emperor's order. The Emperor accepted the reasons, and once he heard the opera, he gave Salieri an imperial reward.

May 16th

Distractions

Composers of concert music have enough distractions to cope with. Composers of movie music have even more. Consider the case of Bernard Herrmann, one of America's leading writers of film music, when he was visiting Hollywood in 1943.

Herrmann and his wife were having a working lunch at the home of film star Joseph Cotton. Also attending were Alfred Hitchcock and his wife. At the time, Cotton was starring in Hitchcock's film *Shadow of a Doubt*. The movie-makers were dining on the terrace overlooking the Cottons' swimming pool. The business discussion was overshadowed by the sudden, unexpected arrival of two acquaintances—Orson Welles and Rita Hayworth.

Welles barged onto the terrace saying, "Don't let me interrupt your lunch. Rita and I just want to use your pool." The catch was that the interlopers hadn't brought bathing suits. Welles peeled off his trousers and went swimming in his boxer shorts.

Rita, who was soon to be Mrs. Orson Welles, was more ingenious. She went upstairs to Joseph Cotton's bedroom and helped herself to two designer ties, each worth about 50 dollars. One of them she draped around her neck and bosom and secured in the back. The other became the lower part of a bikini—somewhat before that form of swim apparel had become fashionable. Thus equipped, Rita Hayworth slid into the pool.

Speaking for the diners, Herrmann's wife later recalled, "It was very distracting to eat lunch and watch Orson and Rita swim."

A few months later, Bernard Herrmann left the distractions of Hollywood and the movies and went to New York to begin work on a less glitzy and less profitable project—an opera.

May 17th
The Meeting of Three Arts

Many fine works of art have resulted from the connection between music and painting. In his memoirs, British baritone George Henschel tells of an occasion when the two arts benefitted from a third.

In 1877, Henschel was attending a dinner part at the town house of Lord and Lady Airlie. The guests were awaiting the entrance of the most talked-about artist of the day—the American painter James McNeill Whistler. The American kept everyone in suspense as they sat there past the appointed time—and past the time for a fashionably late arrival.

Finally, after everyone had sat down to dinner, Whistler arrived with what Henschel thought was the loudest laugh he had ever heard. It reminded him of Mephisto's first appearance in Berlioz' *Faust*, "the zigzag flash of trombones...on the single fortissimo clash of the cymbals being no whit more effective than Whistler's Cyclopean laughter."

All through the evening Whistler kept the company entertained with "the dazzling fireworks of his wit."

After dinner Henschel sang a few songs and was flattered when Whistler invited him to one of his Sunday "breakfasts" at which he introduced the singer to buckwheat cakes with maple syrup, which Whistler was proud to have introduced to the British.

The painter introduced the singer to another American delicacy. After a chance encounter on London's Haymarket Street, Whistler told Henschel about an exciting discovery—a restaurant that imported especially sweet Blue-point oysters. The two walked arm in arm to the place and settled into a wooden booth. There, Henschel recalled, they had "a regular feast on the seductive bivalves to the accompaniment of I will not say how many pints of stout."

Music and painting mixed more smoothly when seasoned by the art of congenial dining.

May 18th

Liszt in the Lap of Luxury

In 1876 Franz Liszt was on his way from Hanover to Weimar, but he was making the trip in a leisurely, glamorous way. He stopped over at Loo Castle near Utrecht in Holland. On May 18, he wrote to a friend in Weimar:

I already asked you from Hanover to keep your quartet together on Friday, May 26. I'll arrive by the night train about ten hours before the first stroke of the bow; and the day after that we'll go to Altenburg. Please find out if some new railroad might make it possible for us to avoid going through Leipzig.

Loo Castle provides just as many pleasures as it did last year. The king is really very charmingly gracious when it comes to famous artists, painters, and musicians whom he has chosen to gather here. We're also expecting Thomas and Saint-Saëns.

No awkward moments in conversation. Always good form with great animation. Gerome, Cabanel, and Gevaert tell very witty stories. Everyone is driven by a strong desire to please the king, and he maintains his way of doing things without letting it become oppressive.

Twice a day, between fifteen and twenty members of the ugly sex appear at the table—at noon for lunch, at five o'clock for dinner. The menus and the wine are bountiful and excellent. At meals the fair sex is conspicuous by its absence, and only appears in the form of a few selected examples in the evening at the theater. There, the same fifteen or twenty guests gather to attend the daily auditions by His Majesty's pensioners.

The large medal that the king ordered to be struck as an award for one of his female pensioners has an intrinsic gold value of 800 florins. There are four or five young ladies who have the task of performing a few scenes from comedies, tragedies or operas every evening. Their costumes are magnificent and artistically designed.

May 19th

Telemann's Runaway Wife

Composer George Philip Telemann had lived a long productive life, but on the home front events had taken some unhappy turns and he consoled himself with two loves—poetry and plants.

Telemann's unfortunate home life was publicized by a theater scandal that broke in Hamburg. A play was being planned that would satirize three Hamburg celebrities, including Telemann. The satire was aimed particularly at Telemann because his wife had left him and run away with a Swedish officer. When news of the planned production leaked out, Hamburg authorities put a stop to it. But worse damage was to follow. Telemann's wife took his money and ran off with her lover, leaving Telemann in debt to the tune of 3,000 thalers—a huge sum of money in the 1750's.

Telemann was forced to rely on the charity of nearby friends, some of whom covered a good deal of the debt. Maintaining his sense of humor, Telemann wrote to one of them for aid:

> *My fate now gives me generous reprieve,*
> *Extravagance departed with my spouse.*
> *Can I my debts from time to time relieve*
> *And Paradise return to grace my house?*
> *True, Hamburg rallies 'round me in my need*
> *With open hand, and charity has done.*
> *Can friends beyond her walls perhaps be found?*
> *Consoled! I am meanwhile Thy Servant Telemann.*

Among the most consoling responses of his friends was a gift of exotic plants that Handel sent from England. Handel wrote: "I am sending you a present—a chest of flowers which botanical experts assure me are select and rare." But Telemann's greatest consolation must have been his music, which he wrote at a furious rate. In fact, according the *Guinness Book of World Records*, George Philip Telemann is probably the most prolific composer of all time.

May 20th
The Plow That Broke the Plains

The Great Depression was a difficult time for most Americans, including musicians. In 1936 Virgil Thomson was a 40-year-old composer struggling for recognition and cash. His friend, John Houseman, recommended Thomson to a documentary film maker named Pare Lorenz. Lorenz had already interviewed other composers, including Aaron Copland, by the time he talked to Thomson. Thomson's first concern was not aesthetics.

Lorenz explained that the film was a documentary about cattle raising, wheat growing, and dust storms on the Western plains. Lorenz asked Thomson if he could imagine writing music for it.

"How much money have you got?" Thomson asked.

Lorenz said that the costs of the orchestra, conductor, and recording left only about $500 for the composer.

"Well," Thomson said, "I can't take from any man more than he's got, though if you did have more, I would ask for it."

Lorenz hired him on the spot. "All those high-flyers," he said, "talk nothing but aesthetics. You talk about money; you're a professional."

Thomson set about acquainting himself with the film by watching it over and over in its uncut state. Lorenz had his mind set on telling the story of the landscape through the music of its people, so Thomson studied cowboy songs and settler folklore. When Lorenz finished cutting the film, he asked Thomson for 25 minutes of symphonic music–in one week. Thomson talked him into a two-week deadline and, working day and night with a copyist and a musical secretary, Thomson finished the composing on time. The result was an aesthetic triumph–a blend of images, words, and music that became a classic documentary film–*The Plow That Broke the Plains.*

May 21st
The Man I Was Looking For

He is generally thought of as a singularly English composer, but early in his career, Ralph Vaughan Williams had trouble developing his style in England. He needed the right teacher and he found him in an unexpected place.

One of Vaughan Williams' first teachers was Charles Villiers Stanford, who favored a neo-classical style with a clear outline. That kind of structure did not square with Vaughan Williams' more imaginative approach. "Stanford was a great teacher," Vaughan Williams later recalled. "But I believe I was unteachable. I made the great mistake of trying to fight my teacher. The way to get the best out of instruction is to put oneself entirely in the hands of one's instructor and try to find out all about his method regardless of one's own personality."

About 1900 Vaughan Williams asked Edward Elgar to give him lessons and received a polite refusal. So he studied Elgar's works on his own and essentially taught himself orchestration by trial and error, and he continued to attend performances of Elgar's works although Elgar never received him with any cordiality. In 1908 Vaughan Williams decided he would have to go elsewhere to learn technique while developing his style. He chose Paris. His friends suggested that he would do best with Maurice Ravel.

At first Vaughan Williams fell back into his mistake of trying to fight his teacher. He resisted Ravel's assignments to write exercises in the style of other composers. But from Ravel he learned to find new approaches to orchestration by experimenting with the piano. He wrote to a friend, "Ravel is exactly the man I was looking for. As far as I know my own faults, he hit on them exactly, and is telling me to do exactly what I half felt in my mind I ought to do." The promising English composer had found his style through an inspired teacher in France.

May 22nd

Bruckner's Clutter

He wrote vast dramatic symphonies, but Anton Bruckner led a life that tended to be prosaic and more than a little cluttered.

He didn't look like other musicians of the 1880's. He kept his hair cut so short that many people remembered him as being bald. He wore a short jacket and voluminous trousers that made some people think he was a peasant. A colored handkerchief hung from his pocket. Holding his hat in his hand, he walked so fast through the streets of Vienna that even his young pupils had trouble keeping up with him.

Bruckner's two-room apartment was in similar disarray. In the middle of one room stood a very old Bösendorfer grand piano, its white keys almost as dark as the black, thanks to the ravages of dust and snuff. Against one wall was an American cottage organ—a pedal harmonium. Against another was a bed with a large crucifix hanging over it. In front of the window was a little table used for writing and dining. The rest of the room contained nothing but the bare necessities of day-to-day living. The furniture was minimal.

On the piano was a tangle of clothing and scores by Bach, Beethoven, Schubert, and Wagner. Only two books were to be found in the entire apartment—the Bible and a biography of Napoleon. The second room had no furniture at all. Stacked in one corner were bundles of reviews, papers, and letters. Manuscripts of Bruckner's symphonies and Masses lay interspersed with newspaper articles and letters from conductors. One time, a quintet by Bruckner disappeared in the mound of paper. While searching for it a friend came across the only piano work Bruckner had ever written and the composer gave it to him. Appropriately, it was called "Souvenir."

At night, Bruckner lit his chaotic domain with just two tall candles, a habit that stemmed from his understandable fear of fire.

May 23rd
The Grocer Librettist

New York, 1805. The Italian, at age 56, was a little old to be starting a second career, as a grocer, but Lorenzo Da Ponte had a compelling reason for abandoning poetry and music and coming to the New World. He wanted to stay out of prison.

Even the brightest moments of his first career had been marred by scandal. At 20 he had taken holy orders largely for financial security. Still in his 20's, Da Ponte became a professor of literature. He wrote Latin and Italian poems, including one in praise of wine. In 1773, shortly after he had been ordained a priest, he went to Venice, where he fell in love with a noblewoman. He became professor of humanities in the seminary at Treviso, but, in 1776, his opinions on natural laws caused his dismissal. In 1779 he was banished from the city for 15 years because of adultery.

In 1780 he went to Dresden to learn the art of writing opera texts. Then he turned up in Vienna, where Antonio Salieri got him an audience with Emperor Joseph II, who appointed Da Ponte librettist for the newly founded theater. He wrote for an unwieldy trio of composers—Mozart, Salieri, and Martin y Soler, who had been the butt of one of Mozart's obscene songs. For Mozart, Da Ponte's successes included *The Marriage of Figaro* and *Cosi fan Tutte*. But within a few years he had again turned success into failure by antagonizing the Viennese with his haughtiness. The death of the emperor in 1792 left him without work, and he spent much of the 1790's in London trying to keep out of the poorhouse. By 1805 he was forced to flee his debts, but his New World ventures, including the grocery, came up short.

Finally, near the end of his life, Da Ponte struck one more high note. On May 23, 1826, an earlier collaboration paid off in New York with the celebrated American premiere of Mozart's *Don Giovanni*.

May 24th
D'Indy's Quest

In 1872, 22-year-old Vincent d'Indy went to Germany hoping to meet three of his musical idols–Franz Liszt, Richard Wagner, and Johannes Brahms. As a way to break the ice, he took with him a manuscript of a work called *Rédemption* by his mentor César Franck.

He found Liszt at work in a secluded cottage near Weimar, but as he entered the study, d'Indy startled Liszt, who quickly disappeared and then returned a few minutes later and greeted the young Frenchman warmly. It turned out that Liszt had just been inducted into a minor order of the Roman Catholic Church and was duty-bound not to receive any guests without being dressed in the long cassock of the order. Liszt seemed unimpressed with Franck's *Rédemption*. When he played it on the piano, he skipped over entire sections.

For 12 days d'Indy enjoyed morning coffee and conversation with Liszt, and when Liszt left Weimar, d'Indy went off to Bayreuth looking for Wagner.

Liszt's daughter Cosima, who was Wagner's wife, received d'Indy cordially but told him that Wagner was not to be disturbed. She did let d'Indy observe Wagner from a distance, though, as he paced in his study, nervously tossing sheets of paper into every corner of the room. The pages were the final part of the full orchestral score of Wagner's *Twilight of the Gods*.

D'Indy caught up with Brahms on the steps of a chalet near the village of Tutzing. The bear-like Brahms was not in a mood to receive visitors and was uninterested in the Franck manuscript. When d'Indy asked him to play some of his latest piano pieces, Brahms replied that he didn't play the piano. He said "auf Wiedersehen " and showed d'Indy the door.

Although his quest had not been a great social success, d'Indy always regarded his pilgrimage as an event that expanded his cultural horizons immeasurably.

May 25th
The Gruff Giant

At the age of 21 Felix Mendelssohn was already known as one of Europe's finest composers, and he came from a family that moved in high social circles. But young Mendelssohn was in awe and unsure of himself when he visited the 81-year-old literary giant, Johann Wolfgang von Goethe. On May 25, 1830, he wrote from Weimar to his family in Berlin:

Goethe is so friendly and congenial with me that I don't know how to thank him or how to be worthy of it. This morning he made me play the piano for him for about an hour, pieces by all the great composers, in chronological order, and explain to him how they had crafted them, while he sat in a dark corner like the god Jupiter with his old eyes flashing lightning.

He didn't want me to play any Beethoven. But I told him that I had to and so I played him the first movement of the C Minor Symphony. That had a strange effect on him. At first he said, "that's not the least bit moving. It's only stunning. It's overblown." And then he went on growling to himself until after a while he started again, saying, "that's very great, quite wild. It almost makes me afraid that the house will fall down. And just imagine when they're all playing at once!"

As you know, I dine with him every day now. He asks me very probing questions, and after the meal he's so cheerful and talkative that we usually sit on in the room for more than an hour while he talks continuously. It's absolutely wonderful the way he brings me etchings, for example, and explains them or gives his opinions on literature or the theater or pretty girls.

I inquired yesterday if I were really not coming too often. But he growled that he had hardly begun to talk to me.

May 26th
Wagner vs. the Londoners

It was not the best offer Richard Wagner had received—an invitation to conduct eight concerts for the London Philharmonic Society for a fee of 200 pounds. But Wagner was attracted to the chance of conducting a large and excellent orchestra, and so, in 1855, he came to London—and the center of a musical controversy.

Once he got to London, Wagner found out that the conductor of the orchestra, a Mr. Costa, had argued with the Philharmonic Society and refused to conduct their concerts. Apparently Costa had been bluffing, though, and was thoroughly disgusted when the society not only took him at his word, but also hired Wagner to replace him for the season. Costa did his best to alienate the orchestra from its guest conductor and, at the same time, a powerful critic with the *London Times* took a hostile attitude toward Wagner. Then Wagner discovered that he was limited to one rehearsal for each concert.

At the first concert, Wagner conducted Beethoven's Eroica Symphony, and members of the society were so impressed that they arranged for two rehearsals for the next concert and insisted that some of Wagner's own music be included on the program along with Beethoven's Choral Symphony. For the chorus, Wagner had to use an Italian Opera ensemble. It included a baritone of whom Wagner later said, "his English phlegm and Italian training drove me to despair." Nonetheless, the concert, in Wagner's words, "left nothing to be desired." Still the critic for the *Times* pounced upon it with contempt. Wagner considered backing out of the contract, and tensions grew right up to the eighth and final concert.

Made cautious by the errant conductor Costa and the consistently hostile reviews, the orchestra had kept their distance from their guest conductor. But at the end of the final concert they crowded around him and cheered as the audience pressed forward to shake the hand of Richard Wagner.

Wagner's London experience as he describes it in his autobiography, *My Life*.

May 27th

The Catastrophic Conductor

Louis Spohr was one of the first conductors to use a small stick–a baton–instead of a staff. The baton enabled Spohr to direct the orchestra in subtle ways, the staff was good for little more than beating time. But the conductor whom Spohr found dramatic and expressive–to a fault–was Beethoven.

Spohr had heard plenty about Beethoven's conducting and still was shocked when he saw it. Beethoven used all sorts of body motion to communicate with the orchestra. For emphasis, he would throw his arms wide apart, for a quiet passage he would bend down. The quieter the passage, the farther down Beethoven would go until he had all but crawled under the music desk. As the music got louder he would rise back up, slowly at first, then leap into the air, often shouting as he went.

During a performance of one of his piano concertos, Beethoven was the soloist, and he got so carried away with conducting that, at one point, he forgot to play the piano. He flung his arms wide and knocked the candlesticks off each side of the keyboard. The audience burst out laughing and Beethoven got so mad that he ordered the orchestra to start over again.

Two choirboys were enlisted to hold the candlesticks out of harm's way. One of them got increasingly intrigued by the piano score and came in closer and closer just as a loud passage broke forth. Out went Beethoven's arm, knocking the choirboy in the mouth and making him drop his candlestick. The other choirboy, having followed Beethoven's exertions more cautiously, ducked, to the complete delight of the audience.

Beethoven fell into such a rage that on the first chord of his solo he pounded the piano so forcefully that he broke half a dozen strings. Die-hard music lovers in the audience tried to restore order, but failed. After that debacle, Beethoven became increasingly reluctant to give concerts.

May 28th

Stravinsky Cheated

He was an extremely motivated student who would soon emerge as a world-class composer, but Igor Stravinsky had his own ideas about how his education should proceed. Respect for authority never got in his way and, in at least one instance, he passed an exam by cheating.

Stravinsky was never nostalgic about his early days. He once described his childhood as "a period of waiting for the moment when I could send everyone and everything connected with it to hell." He summarized one of his first teachers as "an excellent pianist and a blockhead." By which he meant that her "bad taste was impregnable" but her pianism "of a high order." From the same teacher he learned to play Mendelssohn and Clementi and Mozart, but she tried to discourage his interest in Wagner. Nevertheless, young Stravinsky got to know all of Wagner's works from the piano scores, and as soon as he had the money, he went out and bought the orchestral scores.

In grammar school, Stravinsky studied history, Latin, Greek, Russian and French literature and mathematics and later described himself as "a very bad pupil." At St. Petersburg University, he remained less than inspired. Attendance at lectures was optional, so Stravinsky opted rarely to attend. He studied criminal law and legal philosophy but spent most of his time with the family of composer Nikolai Rimsky-Korsakov.

In one instance, Stravinsky's brushes with authority could have turned into a disaster. During his last spring at the university, as everyone was cramming for exams, Stravinsky realized that he would never pass one of his subjects. He suggested to a friend that they take each other's exams since they were better in each other's subjects. Because their faces were unknown to the professors, the ruse worked, and with his unorthodox education behind him, Igor Stravinsky was soon able to devote his inventiveness full time to composing. Stravinsky's fellow student went on to take bigger risks. Shortly after passing Stravinsky's exam, he was killed in a duel.

May 29th
The Riot

The Champs Elysées Theater. May 29, 1913. One of the most notorious premieres in classical music is about to occur. Pierre Monteux is about to conduct the first performance of Igor Stravinsky's ballet, *The Rite of Spring*.

The wife of dancer and choreographer Vaslev Nijinksy has heard bits of the music during rehearsals, and she suspects that the audience will get restless, but at the opening notes of the overture, her worse fears are surpassed.

Part of the audience decides that Stravinksy's ballet is an attempt to destroy music as art. They make catcalls and snide suggestions as to how the performance should proceed. Monteux continues to conduct the orchestra, though they are rarely heard above the racket. A young man stands up to see better and begins to beat time with his fists–on the head of the man sitting in front of him. By now people are whistling and shouting. Monteux keeps his eyes on the score, dutifully keeping to the tempo Stravinsky has given him. The house lights are turned on, only to make the violence more visible. One elegantly dressed lady in an orchestra box stands up and slaps the face of a young man who is hissing in the next box. The young man and the lady's escort challenge each other to a duel. A society lady confronts one of the demonstrators and spits in his face.

A princess stalks out of her box saying, "I am 60 years old but this is the first time anyone has dared to make a fool of me."

The director, Serge Diaghilev, the color drained from his face, shouts, "Please! Let them finish the show!"

The police arrive. Monteux is determined to keep the orchestra together at any cost, and they play the ballet to its conclusion–in an empty theater. The night is over, but not the spectacle. There are to be five more Paris performances of *The Rite of Spring*–all prompting the same reaction.

May 30th
If Only

After a pleasant vacation, it can be hard to return to the home routine, at least it was for Joseph Haydn. On more than one occasion, he wrote longingly from Esterhás, his princely employer's country home, to a friend in Vienna. On May 30, 1790, he wrote to Maria Anna von Genzinger:

I beg your Grace not to be frightened away from consoling me occasionally with your enjoyable letters, for they comfort me in my wilderness, and are crucial for my heart, which is so often deeply hurt. Oh! If only I could be with your Grace for a quarter of an hour, to pour out all my troubles to you, and to hear all your comforting words. I have to put up with many irritations from the Court here, which I have to bear in silence.

The only consolation I have left is that I am—thank God—well and eager to work. I'm just sorry that even though I'm so eager, your Grace has had to wait so long for the symphony I promised. But this time it's simply a matter of sheer necessity, the result of my situation here and the current rise in the cost of living.

Your Grace therefore must not be angry with your Haydn, who can't go to Vienna, even for 24 hours, no matter how often the prince leaves Esterhás. It's hard to believe, and yet a refusal is always so polite that I don't have the heart to press for permission.

Oh well! Whatever God wills! This time will pass, and the day will come when I'll have the indescribable pleasure of sitting beside your Grace at the pianoforte, hearing Mozart's masterpieces, and kissing your hands for so many wonderful things.

Within a year, Haydn would have his wish. The death of Prince Nicholas Esterházy would free him to travel to Vienna and far beyond.

May 31st

The Ambulance Driver

When World War I swept across France, Maurice Ravel set aside composing and became an ambulance driver. He was an ambitious volunteer. But, at the age of 41, he discovered a problem that threatened to take him out of the service entirely. He wrote to a friend at the end of May, 1916:

You know–because you tried to talk me out of it–that ever since the war began, I had intended to join the Air Force. As soon as I joined this unit three months ago, I wrote to inform Captain L. that I was at the front and to remind him that I wanted to become a bomber pilot. I received no answer and, as it turned out, my work here quickly became so interesting that I forgot my Icarian dreams.

Until the day before yesterday, when I heard that the commander of the squadron had been killed, that the squadron had been disbanded, and that Captain L. was in this vicinity, and would soon be writing to me. That immediately revived my old yearning. I forgot how tired I was and asked to take the examination for my medical certificate.

The Major urged me not to fly. I have an enlarged heart. It's no big deal, nothing serious, they say I wouldn't give it a second thought if I'd had little heart flutters all my life, as most men do. But at the end of last year, when I had a complete examination, the doctors found nothing whatsoever, which means it's a recent occurrence, and now I understand that troublesome discomfort that I didn't notice while I was leading an adventuresome existence.

Now what can I do? If I'm looked at again by a more thorough doctor I'll be told I'm not fit for driving and pigeonholed into office work. So surely you will understand that I prefer to let the matter drop."

The patriotic composer signed his letter "Driver Ravel."

June 1st

Surviving a Russian Tour

Clara Schumann was one of the best-known pianists in the world. After a concert tour, she shared some of her impressions of Russia and Russian performers in a letter she wrote to Johannes Brahms from Düsseldorf on June 1, 1854:

We attended a grand festival in the Kremlin on Easter night and I'll remember it for the rest of my life. As far as my success in Russia is concerned I have to say that I'm perfectly satisfied given the current acute financial crisis there. I couldn't have done that well in Germany. It's true though that the stress was extreme. For example, the trip from St. Petersburg to Moscow lasted twenty hours. I got there at nine in the morning, had a rehearsal at eleven and a concert in the evening. Then I had three concerts on three successive days. When we returned from St. Petersburg straight to Berlin the journey took forty-four hours. It was murder on my poor back. But I survived it all in good shape even though I was never in great health in Russia since the weather and the water didn't exactly suit me.

In Moscow I heard Nikolai Rubinstein. The man has amazing technique even though his fingers are quite short and thick. Mostly he played drawing-room pieces and he pounds the piano in the latest fashion with gobs of pedaling and no emotion beyond the soft pedal. But he's a lovable soul despite his moral principles, which I detest. It's really a shame about those two brothers. They are so highly gifted but completely lacking in seriousness and respect for their art. Anton Rubinstein is coming to Baden for two months to work. For his sake I wish he would, but I suspect he'll just carry on again.

June 2nd
War in Laces

The frail, dark-eyed young woman was vying for the greatest accolade in music—
the hotly contested Prix de Rome for the year 1913. The field had been narrowed
to five composers whose cantatas were to be evaluated by a vote of 36 members of
the Académie des Beaux-Arts. One critic attending the final judging of the cantatas
contrasted contestant Lili Boulanger with the rest of the competitors:

*Perched over the piano like jockeys over the necks and withers of their
horses, the intrepid composers spurred on their accompanists and desperately
flailed away at the performers. Then the superiority of the eternal feminine
became apparent to the audience. Compared to her hot-blooded
colleagues—who apparently believed that "their hour had come" —the young
girl, who had just as much reason to be nervous and impatient, showed the
most perfect poise. She had a modest and unaffected attitude, her eyes lowered
to the score.*

Another witness reported that the three singers with the composer's sister Nadia
at the piano, were directed by Lili Boulanger, standing nearby, "a slender shadow in
a white dress, so simple, calm, serious and smiling as to be unforgettable."

But as far as the judging was concerned, the outcome was by no means a sure
thing. On the previous day, the preliminary vote by a panel of eight had given Lili
Boulanger's cantata a scant majority of five votes. Now it was up to the 36 to
decide. After considering the merits of the candidates and other prizes they had
won, the members voted. Of the 36, 31 voted in favor of Lili Boulanger and her
cantata on the basis of intelligence of subject, correctness of performance,
sensitivity and warmth, poetic feeling, and intelligent, colorful orchestration.

With her personality, her poise, and her cantata, Lili Boulanger had set a
precedent. In the 110-year history of the Prix de Rome, she was the first woman
to win.

June 3rd

Marriage on a Sour Note

The best-known picture of composer Thomas Arne shows him scowling as he plays the harpsichord. The scowl apparently was an expression Arne wore often. He was one of the finest composers in 18th century England. His "Ode in Honor of Great Britain"–better known as "Rule Britannia"–is one of the world's noblest anthems, but Thomas Arne himself was far less noble than his music, as his dealings with his wife demonstrate.

Cecilia Young was a capable soprano. She married Arne in 1736, despite her father's objections. For many years, Cecilia Arne traveled and performed with her husband and both enjoyed considerable popularity. Accounts of her singing suggest that Mrs. Arne's performances contributed a good deal to the success of her husband's music. But as the years went by, illness limited her performing more and more. Arne was not one to stand by in sickness and in health. In 1756 he left her.

Although the composer had permanent positions with two major London theaters, he resisted supporting the wife he had left behind. In 1770 Mrs. Arne sent her husband's lawyer a letter threatening legal proceedings, saying that what money he had sent her "fell greatly short of supplying her with common necessaries, and that even that small sum was in arrears." Arne replied that setbacks had left him with little money to spare, adding that any further annoyance might prompt him to cut off his support completely. About then Arne began falling out with some of his best friends–Charles Burney the music historian and David Garrick the actor. His work became second rate.

Then, in 1777, after more than 20 years of separation, husband and wife were reconciled when Arne agreed to see Cecilia again for the sake of his ten-year-old grand niece. Although it was happy, the reconciliation was short-lived because, within a year, Thomas Arne died.

June 4th

Paganini's Gratitude

Hector Berlioz and Niccolò Paganini. The passion, the extravagance, and the eccentricity of their music was a reflection of the way they lived. Berlioz wrote one of his greatest works, *Harold in Italy*, for Paganini, and it brought the two composers together in an extraordinary way.

Paganini was away when Berlioz completed *Harold in Italy*, so he heard it for the first time as a member of the audience. At the end of the concert, as Berlioz stood trembling and perspiring with exhaustion, in through the orchestra door came Paganini followed by his son Achilles. Because of a throat infection Paganini couldn't speak, but he was making wild gestures. He motioned to Achilles, who got up on a chair, put his ear next to his father's lips, and listened carefully. Then Achilles climbed back down and said to Berlioz. "My father wants me to assure you that never in his life has he been so powerfully affected by a concert. Your music has stirred him, and he says that if he didn't restrain himself, he would go down on his knees to thank you for it."

Berlioz was flattered but embarrassed. He tried to dismiss the praise with a wave of his hand, but Paganini took him by the arm and said in a hoarse voice, "Yes, yes!" He hauled Berlioz up onto the stage and, before a good number of musicians, he knelt down and kissed Berlioz' hand.

The next day, Achilles delivered a letter to Berlioz. When Berlioz' wife, Henrietta, entered the room and found the composer pale and dazed, she thought some disaster had struck.

"No, no, just the opposite," Berlioz told her. "Paganini—he has sent me twenty thousand francs."

Henrietta ran into the next room, where their son Louis was playing. "Come here," she cried, "come and thank God for what He has done for your father." With that, mother and child dropped to their knees, Henrietta praying in gratitude as the astonished little boy folded his hands beside her.

June 5th
That Useless Company

Sometimes even the greatest composers have to distinguish between just and unjust criticisms of their work. After a bad performance of his opera *Un Ballo in Maschera*, Giuseppe Verdi wrote to the producer on June 5, 1859:

You were wrong to defend Un Ballo in Maschera *against the attacks in the newspapers. You should do what I always do–don't read them, or let them sing whatever tune they want. Fact–an opera is either bad or good. If it's bad, the journalists are right to pan it. If it's good and they refuse to acknowledge it because of some prejudice, it's best to let them ramble on unheeded.*

Anyway, you've got to confess that if anyone needed defending during the Carnival season it was that useless company you stuck me with. Put your hand on your heart and admit that I was a paragon of restraint in not picking up the score and going away to look for dogs less prone to howling than the ones you foisted on me.

Forgive me, but I can't write to the publisher and ask him to lower his rates because I'm not in the habit of doing that kind of thing. Anyway, the price you're offering for Aroldo, Boccanegra, *and* Un Ballo in Maschera *seems to me–as little as the operas may be worth–to be too low. You need three operas? Well, here you go–*Nina Pazza *by Paisiello,* Armide *by Gluck, and* Alceste *by Lully In addition to the savings, you can be sure that with those operas you won't have to duke it out with the journalists or anyone else. The music is gorgeous and the composers are dead. Everyone has been saying nice things about them for a century–two centuries. And they'll keep on doing so if only for the sake of slandering those who have not yet been foolish enough to die.*

June 6th
The Shaky Accompanist

Modest Mussorgsky's physician had arranged a concert for the benefit of medical students, but he had good reason to fear that Mussorgsky was in no state to participate as the pianist.

Mussorgsky was to accompany the distinguished Italian tenor Ravelli. And when, on the day of the performance the singer asked to meet Mussorgsky, the physician found the composer reeling under the influence of alcohol. Mussorgsky told his friend that he wasn't up to meeting Ravelli at that particular moment, but assured the doctor that he would be just fine for the evening performance.

With that, Mussorgsky saw the doctor to the door and bowed with exaggerated politeness saying, "Well then, until tonight."

The doctor went back to the tenor and told him that he had been unable to find Mussorgsky. Then he asked a friend to keep an eye on Mussorgsky and see to it that he got to the concert on time.

Mussorgsky showed up punctually, but trouble soon reared its head again. The composer hung around the artists' green room long enough to sample every drink on a table there, and he became drunk all over again. In the meantime, the Italian tenor had done a little sampling himself. And, as if to make a bad situation worse, he decided that his voice was a little strained and said that he wanted to sing his entire program a half or perhaps a whole tone lower than usual.

Sensing a catastrophe, the doctor asked Mussorgsky if he could accommodate the tenor's need to take the songs down a step or two. "Why not?" the composer said with disturbing geniality. He suggested an informal rehearsal. Apparently he had never heard most of the music to be performed.

The result astonished the doctor—and delighted him. Mussorgsky completely charmed the tenor with an elegant performance that he could play in any key, and the grateful singer embraced him, saying over and over, "What an artist!"

June 7th
A Friend and a Liability

Composer Charles Gounod was handsome, talented, and charming. He needed to make some connections in opera circles. When he met Pauline Viardot he made connections quickly, but he paid for them.

In 1850 Madame Viardot was the talk of Paris music circles. Some thought she was ugly, some found her strangely attractive. All agreed that she was a fine singer, though not in the usual way. According to composer Camille Saint-Saëns, Madame Viardot's voice was neither velvet nor crystal, but harsh and powerful, with the "pungent flavor of a bitter orange."

She lived in an unusual household. It consisted of Pauline, her husband Louis, and her lover—the novelist Ivan Turgenev.

Enter Gounod, a young composer looking for a librettist and a theater for an opera he wanted to write. A mutual friend suggested that by dint of her considerable reputation as a singer, Pauline might be able to help. She and Gounod hit if off right away, intellectually and musically.

Pauline's interest in Gounod was apparently platonic and professional. She wasted little time in finding him a respected theater manager and a librettist for his opera. An important theater manager agreed to commission an opera from Gounod as long as it had a role for Madame Viardot. A well-known dramatist agreed to write a libretto for the opera as long as Madame Viardot was singing the lead role. The result was Gounod's first opera, *Sappho*.

The audience enjoyed the originality of Gounod's opera, but the critics were not so kind, largely because Madame Viardot had made some enemies in her climb to the top. They suggested that Pauline Viardot was over the hill and went on to condemn the opera itself. After only seven performances, *Sappho* folded—partly on its own merits and partly because of Pauline Viardot, the friend who had helped Charles Gounod to produce it.

June 8th

Favors

Pianist and composer Stephen Heller had gotten to know violinist Joseph Joachim during a concert tour in England. When a friend needed a favor, Heller wrote to the influential Joachim from Paris on June 8, 1862:

Besides the quiet sincerity and simple manners of the good men of the country I miss all the lush greenery that you get in the parks and squares and gardens of London. The heat is intense and I dread July and August. My new rooms are pretty and cool and comfortable. The only problem is a piano teacher who lives on the fourth floor and gives lessons all day long. Her demonic pupils obliterate any pleasure in music. I can't hear it so much in my study, but in my bedroom I am catapulted out of sweet dreams of Beethoven by wretched noodling.

And now I have a request. At the end of June a friend of mine will be returning to Hanover, his hometown, for a month. Years ago he played the cello in the orchestra there and later for twelve years in St. Petersburg where he gave composition and harmony lessons and was a close friend of Rubinstein and Henselt. Now he has settled in Paris where he gives lessons and has an excellent reputation. While he's in Hanover he'd like to play his Trio or his piano and cello sonata for the king, who saw him years ago and gave him a gold medal as a return favor for a dedication.

What do you think? Is he likely to be granted the favor of playing something for the king? And could you give him a letter from some influential person? I'll vouch for the Trio and the Cello Sonata as excellent works. They've been played at concerts here and were well received. Both of them are way better than works that have been accepted here.

June 9th

Elgar's Unfinished Plan

In 1901 Edward Elgar began a set of six marches. He never did complete all six. But by the time he had finished the first, he had achieved lasting fame.

In 1900 Elgar had been working on his buoyant, cheerful *Cockaigne Overture*, which contained a passage describing a military procession passing along the streets of London, so the transition to writing marches must have come easily. And he began very auspiciously. Elgar wrote to a friend, "In haste and joyful! Gosh, man! I've got a tune in my head!" A few months later, he called his friend Dorabella into his study and announced, "I've got a tune that will knock 'em—knock 'em flat." He then played for her his "Pomp and Circumstance March" No. 1.

Within three months he had completed the second march. Elgar conducted the two pieces in Liverpool, and a few months later they were performed again in London at a Queen's Hall Promenade Concert. Henry Wood was the conductor. Elgar wasn't present at what proved to be quite a spectacle.

Henry Wood later recalled that at the end of the first march "the people simply rose and yelled. I had to play it again—with the same result. In fact they refused to let me get on with the program. I went off and fetched Henry Dearth, who was supposed to sing 'Hiawatha's Vision,' but they would not listen. Merely to restore order I played the march a third time."

Of course, it was a difficult act to follow, and in 1910, Elgar was still trying. His wife Alice recorded in her diary: "E working on 'Pomp and Circumstance March'—not very well and rather depressed."

Elgar stopped with a total of five marches in 1930. But 29 years earlier, he had been more right than he had known when he had announced, "I've got a tune that will knock 'em—knock 'em flat."

June 10th

Chemistry versus Opera

Composer Alexander Borodin was a chemistry professor by profession, and so he had a slightly detached view of making music. He had to do justice to two careers—one for his students, the other for the public. He wrote to a friend on June 10, 1876:

As a composer trying to remain anonymous I am wary of discussing my musical activity. That makes sense enough. For others music is the mainstay of their life. For me it's a diversion, a hobby that distracts me from my primary occupation—my professorship. I love my profession and my science. I love the Academy and my students, male and female, because in order to direct the work of others a person has to be close to them at all times. I have the interests of the Academy in mind. On the other hand, if I want to finish my opera, I'm afraid of throwing myself into it too fervently and letting it overshadow my scientific work.

But ever since the performance of the chorus from Prince Igor, *everyone knows that I'm working on an opera. No longer is there anything to hide or be embarrassed about. I'm like the girl who has lost her innocence and has thus acquired a certain kind of freedom. Now, by hook or by crook, I've got to finish the work.*

In opera, as in decorative art, there is no place for details and minutiae, it's necessary to stick to the big picture. Everything has to be clear and straight-forward. The voices should be most prominent, followed by the orchestra.

It's odd the way everyone in our group agrees in their praise of my work. While we disagree about everything else, so far everyone likes Prince Igor. *Such is the story of my child Igor, whose time has yet to arrive.*

June 11th

More Than You Deserve

Ludwig van Beethoven was very dependent upon the good will of his publishers, but he was blunt by nature, and in a letter to Breitkopf and Härtel in June 1810, Beethoven minced no words:

Plenty to do, enjoying life a little, suddenly very busy, yet still unable to resist doing nothing from time to time—all of those situations have kept me from answering your letter. You can still have everything I offered you. And now I'm also going to give you the music to Goethe's Egmont, *which includes ten numbers, overture, entr'acte music and so on. For this work I am asking 400 silver gulden. I can't make any other deal without coming out a loser. I've cut my fee for your sake, even though you don't deserve that kind of a break from me. After all, your behavior is frequently so arbitrary that only a person prejudiced in your favor would go on working with you. I'd like to go on dealing with you in some capacity, but at the same time I can't end up a loser.*

When you write to me, please enclose another list of the works I've offered you in order to avoid any misunderstanding. But reply immediately so as not to tie me up any further, especially since Egmont *is to be performed in a few days and I'll be receiving offers for the music. I might add that the cost of living in Vienna has continued to go up, so that the amount of money a person needs to live on is frightful. From that point of view—or any other for that matter—my fee is certainly not too high. My four thousand gulden, on which I can no longer live, isn't worth even a thousand in today's prices.*

June 12th

The Rhapsody That Wouldn't Let Go

Composers have various reasons for writing—inspiration, pleasure, and money. In the case of Claude Debussy's Saxophone Rhapsody the motivation was provided by money and a persistent music-lover named Mrs. Elise Hall.

Mrs. Hall was a wealthy Boston matron who had taken up the saxophone. In 1895 she commissioned Debussy to compose a work for her instrument. As far as Debussy was concerned, Mrs. Hall's commission had a good side and a bad side. On the bad side was his lack of familiarity with the saxophone. On the good side was the payment enclosed. He accepted the commission. But he steadfastly avoided working on Mrs. Hall's composition. He went to work on his opera *Pélleas and Mélisande*. And a lot of other things—The *Prelude to the Afternoon of a Faun*, *Nocturnes*, and *La Mer* among them. Suddenly eight years had passed.

One day in 1903, who should turn up at Debussy's apartment but Mrs. Hall—the "femme saxophone" as Debussy called her. She wanted to know where her saxophone composition was.

Debussy was caught. He forced himself to get started on something for what he thought of as "that aquatic instrument." He still didn't know much about it. He started doing some homework. Was the saxophone capable of romantic tenderness like the clarinet, he asked a friend in the know. In 1904 he attended Mrs. Hall's Paris recital. Wearing a pink gown, she honked away at something by Vincent d'Indy—another of her commissions.

Another year went by. Debussy roughed out a draft of a piece and called it "Fantasie." But even the title was slow to come. He tried "Oriental Rhapsody" and "Moorish Rhapsody" before settling on plain old "Rhapsody." In 1911 he tried orchestrating it, but it was no go. He bundled up what he had and sent it incomplete to Mrs. Hall. Seven years later, Debussy finally escaped the project—he died. His colleague Jean Jules Roger-Ducasse took on the orchestration and the *Rhapsody for Saxophone* was performed at last in Paris in 1919.

June 13th
They Barely Understand Me

June 13, 1865. New Orleans-born pianist Louis Moreau Gottschalk was making a concert tour of the American West. Traveling through Nevada, he wrote in his journal:

The first rays of day light up our faces–dirty, dust-covered, our eyes swollen from lack of sleep, etc. We arrive at Dutch Flat, a pretty little town hidden at the bottom of a wooded gorge like a nest in a bush. The neat white houses are covered with splendid rosebushes whose flowers cover the trellises all the way up to the roofs. They are small frame houses, very neat, very small, etc.

Concert this evening. About one hundred seventy persons. Audience very quiet–very quiet because they do not applaud. It is true that they did not show their discontent in any other way. I greatly suspect that they regretted investing their dollar and a half. "Taken in," said one of them later, adding to console himself, "It is true that it is just one time." It will be the concert-givers after me who will experience their resentment.

It often crosses my mind when playing to glance at my audience. There are certain passages where I am so accustomed to see their faces light up that in civilized audiences I trend to consider it an inevitable thing like cause and effect. For example, the end of Aeolian Murmurs *or even* Last Hope *or the finale of* Creole Eyes. *Here I perceive that it is precisely as if I were speaking Chinese. They barely understand it, and curiously watch me exerting myself with that odd and vacant look which other ignoramuses, for instance, cast upon the hands of a telegraph operator.*

I have been sick for three days. I cannot recall in fifteen years of travels and vicissitudes having passed eleven days so sadly as here. I defy you to find in all of Europe a village where an artist of reputation would find himself as cut off as I have been here.

June 14th
Musical Diversions for the President

Eighteen fifty-nine. America was on the brink of Civil War, and the weary President of the United States needed music to divert him from the big troubles. The music in the White House of James Buchanan varied considerably.

One of the year's biggest hits was Ullman's Opera Troupe and its prima donna Marietta Piccolomini. The 20-year-old singer had just performed in Donizetti's *Don Pasquale* in Washington. She attended a White House reception at which she shared the spotlight with a delegation of Potawatomie Indians. Through an interpreter, the 67-year-old bachelor president engaged in small talk with the singer. One guest remarked that Buchanan "would probably have stayed till daylight did appear" if someone hadn't hinted that it was time to go.

A more unusual "star" performed at the White House later that year. He was the pianist Thomas Greene Bethune, a husky ten-year old black boy billed as "Blind Tom." An observer said that Tom's "sightless eyeballs seemed to be searching in the stars and the great opera ear seemed to be catching harmony from the celestial spheres...He claws the air with his hands, whistles through his teeth, capers about and see-saws up and down." Yet, it was said that Blind Tom could play the piano like Gottschalk, Mozart, or Beethoven. For President Buchanan, Blind Tom played a 20-page piece of music after hearing it just one time.

It is likely that the more eccentric part of Blind Tom's presentation was pure showmanship, coached by money-minded managers who had toured him through Europe claiming that his talent came from some magical source. The simple truth was that Bethune, who was born a slave in 1849, was a professional—a naturally gifted musician and a capable composer. Some saw beyond the ruse to his greater gifts. One of them was the American piano manufacturer who gave the boy a grand piano bearing the inscription: "A tribute to true genius."

June 15th

An Improviser Par Excellence

By 1740, when Carl Philip Emanuel Bach went to Potsdam to work for King Frederick the Great, his father, Johann Sebastian Bach, was famous throughout Europe, and King Frederick grew increasingly eager to meet the man known as "the Old Bach."

In 1747 Johann Sebastian Bach, age 62, finally left Leipzig and made the journey to Potsdam with his eldest son, Wilhelm Friedemann. The king was in the habit of holding private concerts every night, during which he would solo in the performance of flute concertos. One evening, as the king and his musicians were all ready to play, an officer of the court brought the king a list of guests. Flute in hand, the king scanned the list and turned excitedly to his musicians saying, "Gentlemen, old Bach has arrived."

The king set his flute down and sent a messenger to Wilhelm Friedemann's lodgings, summoning old Bach to the palace. The evening's concert was set aside for the sake of inviting Bach senior to play the king's forte-piano. The musicians followed Bach from room to room as he extemporized on each keyboard. After a while Bach asked the king to give him a theme for a fugue to be improvised on the spur of the moment.

After obliging and admiring the resulting fugue, the king asked for a fugue with six obbligato parts. But Bach found the king's theme not quite suitable for such rich harmonizing, He chose one of his own and developed it into a complex fugue that amazed everyone.

The next day, Bach worked his keyboard magic on every one of the organs in Potsdam.

When he got back home to Leipzig, he took the king's theme, added several complex pieces in canon form on the subject, and had the impressive collection engraved and dedicated to the king under the modest title *A Musical Offering*.

June 16th
The Dynamic Hugo Wolf

The Austrian composer Hugo Wolf was brilliant if erratic. A letter he wrote to a friend on June 16, 1890, shows that he was dynamic, whether he was talking about music or the weather:

The publisher skips over the proposal to share profits as if it were unimportant. He enlarges his first suggestion to say that after the sale of 300 copies of the twelve Selected Songs, *he could see his way clear to print the rest. I'll write to him today to say that I insist on sharing the profits, and that a complete volume must be issued if he expects us to close any kind of deal. He may still print the twelve alone in single editions.*

Liliencron writes that he doesn't have the nerve to adapt Shakespeare's Tempest. *He's offering me a tragedy which, of course, I'm turning down. He has nothing but admiration for my Mörike and Goethe songs. He became aware of my work through an article that he found extremely interesting, and through a piece in the newspaper. Furthermore, he paid me the questionable compliment of including me in his pantheon of favorites–Wagner, and the "giants," needless to say–Schubert, Schumann, Robert Franz, and Brahms. Brahms has also set two of his poems, Liliencron tells me.*

Other than that, all I have to report from here is that I'm miserably cold. Last night I bundled myself up in three blankets and an enormous feather comforter and still froze. I hope the awful weather will change soon, and grant me the pleasure of welcoming you all here.

Grohe disagrees with my Tempest *idea. He thinks there's too much opera in it. As an alternative he's trying to convince me to set to music a "Buddha" by Heckel, which I'll very likely not touch.*

June 17th

Satie the Ardent Suitor

Eric Satie is known for the eccentricity of his music. That eccentricity was only a reflection of the odd way in which the composer conducted his life–including his love life.

Satie is known to have had an affair with only one woman, and it is possible that he could not have survived–or had time for–more than one such affair. Satie was in his 20's when he was introduced to Suzanne Valadon. She was one year older than Satie, and was a painter educated in the street of Montmartre. She had been the mistress of Renoir, and of Degas, who had helped to arrange the first exhibition of her drawings.

Suzanne's fondness for variety led her next to a wealthy young banker who proposed marriage. She refused, but agreed to be his mistress. No sooner had he reluctantly agreed than Suzanne took on an additional lover–Eric Satie.

When he met Suzanne, Satie proposed to her, but the marriage was not to be. Suzanne, Satie, and the banker constituted a rather shaky triangle for two years. No doubt, Suzanne liked the banker for his stability, and liked Satie for his imagination. One evening, Satie took Suzanne and the banker to the theater and hired a pair of African boys to proceed them beating on drums.

But Satie's humor wore thin. When he pleaded with Suzanne to stop seeing the banker she laughed at him. Satie put a sign in the window denouncing her morals and generally proclaiming her uselessness to the universe. Shortly afterward they had a quarrel so violent that the neighbors talked about it for years. Suzanne moved out–but not far. She moved in with the banker–two doors down from Satie. She made a point of driving past Satie's apartment in an elegant carriage, accompanied by two wolf hounds and a parrot in a cage.

He wrote letters begging her to return–but it was hopeless. Deprived of Suzanne, he turned to a new love, mysticism, which would be a lifetime companion for the eccentric Eric Satie.

June 18th
Engrave This In Your Head

Vincenzo Bellini had strong ideas about what an opera should do. And he could be very forceful in trying to get his ideas across to others. For example, he wrote to a librettist in June 1834:

Don't forget to bring with you the piece you've roughed out so far, so that we can resolve the business of the first act. If you'll fortify yourself with plenty of patience, the act will emerge as an interesting, magnificent, worthwhile poem in music. That's in spite of you and all your absurd rules, which are useless except for generating unending palaver that will never sway a soul who has ever experienced the difficult art of drawing tears by means of song.

If my music proves beautiful and the opera pleases, you can write a million letters complaining about the misuse of poetry by composers and so on, without proving a thing. Engrave this in your head in brass letters: An opera has to draw tears, excite horror, and bring death, by means of song.

Poetry and music, to be effective, have to be true to nature—period. Anyone who forgets that is lost, and will wind up turning out a boring, plodding work that can please only the pedants. If he moves the heart, a composer will always be in the right. Will you or won't you comprehend that this is the goal? I implore you to understand it before starting the libretto.

And do you know why I tell you that good drama is unrelated to good sense? It's because I know all too well what stubborn beasts the literati are, and how silly they are with their sweeping rules about good sense. What I'm saying has been proven by the facts in the world of art by the near majority of your famous men who have gone astray in this regard.

June 19th

A Dangerous Homecoming

In 1866 Mily Balakirev was asked to go to Prague to arrange a production of Mikhail Glinka's opera *A Life for the Czar*. He was to have the greatest adventure of his life–getting home.

Balakirev set out in June and had just arrived in Prague when war broke out between Austria and Prussia. Balakirev wrote to a friend, "I had to stay whether I wanted to or not. All the next day I was on edge. Every hour they posted on street corners new bulletins from which you could determine nothing except that the Austrians were fighting doggedly against the Prussians."

He went to Vienna with the intention of returning to Russia, and wrote a letter commenting on the Austrian conduct of the war:

Emperor Franz Josef is behaving just like an Austrian hero–that is, he keeps retreating. Yesterday, I'm told, the all-wise Austrian state council met at the palace and decided, after great thought, not to defend Vienna, and to withdraw to Pest, where the Empress has already relocated herself. As you see, there's no chance of remaining in this area, and I have to hurry while the road is still open from Cracow to Russia. Fortunately I have found a traveling companion, a Russian bound for St. Petersburg, and we have decided to leave tomorrow. We'll travel through Pest by train as far as possible, and from there about 120 miles by horseback to Cracow.

You won't believe how agitated and shaky I am. Nervous and jumpy. But I am consoled by the thought that I'm not the only one who is sleeping badly. Franz Josef is also sleepless at night in the Schönbrunn Palace, and has already had attacks of fainting sickness. I can't wait to leave, and will feel calmer only when I've reached Russian territory.

Six months later, the war was over, won by Prussia, and Balakirev was in Prague again. Finally *A Life for the Czar* was performed, but Balakirev's ordeal in Prague was far from over, as we'll find out shortly....

June 20th
Too Political

The opera had been produced in his absence, and when he arrived in Prague, Balakirev saw a performance of it. He wrote to a friend in Russia, "What a horror it was! I haven't quite returned to my senses yet. The overture was passable, but then the curtain rose, and–oh, horror! What costumes! Peasants waving some kind of peaked caps, overcoats with white buttons. They had beards, but not Russian ones."

Balakirev wrote that conductor Bedřich Smetana had tried to sabotage the opera.

Thank goodness Smetana will not be training the chorus. A proper musician who appreciates Glinka's music is replacing him. The artists are very eager to sing Glinka's operas properly because they like them. They assure me that Smetana intentionally gave them the wrong tempi in performance in order to throw them off, and he sometimes succeeded.

They say that Smetana and a cohort are forming a large faction to hiss A Life for the Czar *off the stage, but another group is being formed to sabotage them. The main instigators in all these local plots are the Poles. They have already managed to form an entire anti-Russian coalition among the Czechs. Smetana and I are no longer on speaking terms. All we do is bow to one another. Clearly he knows that I know everything.*

Glinka's less political opera *Russlan and Ludmilla* was received with thunderous applause. But then came Balakirev's long-awaited performance of *A Life for the Czar*. It created such political tensions that, after a single performance, the Prague directors asked Balakirev to return to Russia.

June 21st

Saved By a Button

The *Water Music,* the *Royal Fireworks Music, Messiah*. It's possible that none of them would have been written if it hadn't been for a lucky encounter with a button.

In 1704 George Frederick Handel was a 19-year-old hothead who took his music-making very seriously. He was serving as harpsichordist in a Hamburg production of the opera *Cleopatra* by another young composer, Johann Mattheson. Mattheson was one of the stars of the production, playing the part of Antonius. After falling on his sword and going through his death scene, Mattheson was free to slip into the orchestra pit and pick up at the harpsichord. As the composer, he was within his rights to do so. The only problem—Handel refused to give up his place.

Despite their argument, somehow the show continued, although the musicians did their best to keep the feud going. And, once the curtain came down, tempers flared. At the stage door, egged on by a crowd of musicians and passers-by, Handel and Mattheson drew their swords and hacked away at each other in the open marketplace outside the theater. Mattheson gained the advantage and thrust his sword at Handel. The point struck one of Handel's broad metal coat buttons and shattered.

Temperamental as he was, Handel was able to put the quarrel behind him, and the relationship between the two proved more resilient than the sword. Within a month of the duel, mutual friends brought about a reconciliation between Handel and Mattheson. They celebrated with a meal, then attended the rehearsal of Handel's first opera, *Almira*. When the opera premiered, Johann Mattheson sang one of the leading roles.

Although Handel never again resorted to drawing his sword, he would run afoul of his friends for the rest of his life.

June 22nd

Mahler's Appointment with Freud

It was to be a meeting of minds. The great symphonist Gustav Mahler had an appointment with the founder of psychoanalysis, Sigmund Freud.

Although he initiated it, Mahler was clearly uneasy about the meeting. He canceled three times before finally coming face to face with Freud in 1910. By the time the session was finally arranged, Freud was vacationing on the Baltic coast.

After an exchange of telegrams, they met at a hotel in Leyden and spent four hours ambling through town as Freud delved into Mahler's mind. Although Mahler had no previous experience with psychoanalysis, Freud later said that he had never met anyone who seemed to understand it so quickly.

Mahler was particularly taken with a comment of Freud's. "I gather your mother was named Marie. So how did you come to marry someone with a different name—Alma—since your mother obviously played a dominant part in your life?"

Mahler answered that his wife's name was Alma Maria, but that he called her Marie. As the walk progressed, he suddenly said that he now understood why the most emotional passages of his music had blocked him from first-rate composing: Those passages, he explained, had always been ruined by the intrusion of some commonplace melody.

Freud got to the root of the problem. It seemed that Mahler's father had brutalized his mother. When Mahler was a young boy, there had been a particularly violent encounter between them, and Mahler had run from the house. As he reached the street, a hurdy-gurdy was cranking out "Ach, Du Lieber Augustin," and ever since, in Mahler's mind, high emotion and light music had been intertwined.

Result of the session: A rekindling of Mahler's relationship with Alma and, for the short time remaining to him, a composer more capable of reconciling his emotions with his music.

June 23rd
Bull of the Frontier

What he lacked in musical training, the Norwegian violinist Ole Bull made up for in power and enthusiasm.

In the mid-19th century, Bull spent a good deal of time in the United States. One day he was traveling down the Mississippi on a steamboat. As he sat reading a newspaper, a frontiersman approached him and offered him a drink of whiskey from a flask. Politely, the violinist declined. "Whiskey is like poison to me," he said.

The man's friends gathered around, saying, "If you can't drink, then you've got to fight. You look damned strong! Show us what you're good for!"

"A Norseman can fight as well as anybody when his blood is up," said Bull. "But I can't fight when my blood is cold and why should I?"

"You look like a strong fellow," was the response, "and damn it, you shall fight!"

Seeing that he had no choice, Bull said calmly, "Since you insist on testing my strength and I have no reason for fighting, I'll tell you what I'll do. Let any one of you take hold of me in any way he likes and I'll wager that in half a minute he shall lie on his back at my feet."

They chose a big man who stepped forward and grasped the violinist by the waist. Instantly Bull wrenched himself free and threw the challenger over his head and slammed him senseless to the deck. One of the challenger's friends pulled a Bowie knife and came forward. To Bull's relief, the man used the knife to open a flask, the contents of which he poured down the challenger's throat to revive him. Later, when a newspaper editor gave a bad review to one of the violinist's concerts, he was taken to task by Ole Bull's former adversary, who declared himself ready to fight for the strongest fiddler he had ever seen.

June 24th

At Odds with Interlochen

An inspired composer and performer does not necessarily make an inspired teacher, even at a great teaching facility. Percy Grainger was a square peg in a round hole during his years at the National Music Camp at Interlochen, Michigan.

Grainger had traveled far from his native Australia, gathering folk tunes and concertizing, by 1931, when he first visited Interlochen. By 1937, when he began teaching there, he was attracted to the quiet, and to the idea of not traveling, and he also found the salary appealing.

Grainger and his wife Ella lived in a cabin within earshot of the band shell. The days were long–private teaching from eight o'clock in the morning until 6:30 in the evening. Evening rehearsals until ten. Then Grainger would often practice until one or two in the morning. He was popular with the students, although the music he chose to teach was not. He remarked that he felt like "a lonely old crow on the bough." He complained of being unable to find a talented student. He was puzzled by the emphasis on developing piano technique–which came to him naturally. He told one student, "You can get more keyboard skill out of Bach's 48 Preludes and Fugues than out of a boatload of studies by tone-deaf nit-wits like Czerny."

Another student persisted in playing a piano passage faster than he was capable, explaining that he had heard Horowitz play it "like a blue streak in his recording." Grainger dismissed the phenomenon by saying, "There likely wasn't room on the recording at the right speed, so he had to hurry it up."

Finally, the teaching and rehearsing got to be too strenuous, and Grainger became increasingly disillusioned with the staff and students at Interlochen. It was simply not the place for him. After his last summer there, in 1944, he vowed, "I shall never teach again." His wife echoed his sentiments by commenting, "It would have been so nice there if it wasn't for all those horrible children."

June 25th

Scottish Novel, Italian Opera

The 38-year-old composer was gambling that his new opera would succeed where others were failing. Gaetano Donizetti was pinning his hopes on a hastily written opera based not on an Italian subject but on a Scottish novel.

By 1835 Donizetti believed that the state of opera in Naples was in a shambles. Rossini had retired. Bellini was dead. "Our theaters go from bad to worse," he said. "The operas fail, the public hisses, the attendance is poor. The crisis is at hand. The public has indigestion, the theater society is about to be dissolved, Vesuvius is smoking, and the eruption is near." The erruption he had in mind may have been an opera he had based on Sir Walter Scott's 1819 novel, *The Bride of Lammermoor*. Donizetti completed his opera *Lucia di Lammermoor* in just six weeks. The story was one of love and treachery, forced marriage and madness. Naples audiences loved it.

Three days after its premiere, Donizetti wrote to a friend, "It pleased and pleased a good deal if I am to believe the applause and compliments I received. I was called out many times, the singers even more often. On the second evening the king's brother was there and said the most flattering things to me. Every piece was listened to with religious silence and honored with spontaneous *vivas*."

The influence of *Lucia di Lammermoor* went beyond music and back into literature. In 1857, in Gustave Flaubert's novel *Madame Bovary*, Emma Bovary attends a performance of *Lucia* with her lover Leon, and in the scene of the lovers' farewell, she feels in the music her own love being reborn. Twenty years later, in Leo Tolstoy's novel *Anna Karenina*, the opera is the backdrop for Anna Karenina's defiance of social rules when she goes to a performance of *Lucia di Lammermoor* in search of her lover, Vronsky.

On the stage and in great novels Donizetti's opera became a symbol of ill-fated love destroyed by social conventions.

June 26th

Upstaged at the White House

The playing was some of the finest in the world. But on this particular occasion in 1986, Vladimir Horowitz was to be upstaged by the President and first lady of the United States.

The East Room of the White House was packed with musicians and political figures. Horowitz was being honored for his role in bridging the gap between the United States and the Soviet Union. The crowd included America's ambassador to the Soviet Union, Arthur Hartmann, who had arranged for Horowitz' triumphal return to Russia for the first time in 60 years. Secretary of State George Schultz was in attendance. And among the many from the music world—conductor Zubin Mehta, violinist Isaac Stern, and cellist Yo-Yo Ma.

Horowitz played supremely well, adding personal touches to the pieces and a delicacy and a precision that made the concert a standout. And yet the day after the concert, front-page headlines brayed about something that happened before Horowitz had begun playing.

While President Reagan was introducing Horowitz, describing the pianist's difficult life in revolution-torn Russia, Nancy Reagan absent-mindedly shifted the legs of her chair over the edge of the platform that served as the stage in the East Room. The first lady tumbled into the audience and came down at the feet of the former ambassador to Great Britain, Walter Annenberg. The audience let out a collective gasp and everyone surged forward to help. Mrs. Reagan laughingly assured everybody that she was unhurt and walked back onto the stage, where Horowitz embraced her.

"That's the reason I did this," Mrs. Reagan told the audience with a smile.

"Honey," the President said, "I told you to do it only if I didn't get any applause."

June 27th

The Gamble

In June 1907, Franz Lehár had a good reason to be nervous about the London debut of his operetta *The Merry Widow*. Too late, he had found out that the male lead couldn't sing.

The casting for the performance had been a gamble by London producer George Edwards, who had chosen a popular comic actor named Joe Coyne for the part of Danilo. During the rehearsals, Edwards had kept Coyne's inability to sing a secret from Lehár by saying that the actor had a bad cold and needed to preserve his voice for the performances. And so a skeptical Lehár had settled for hearing Coyne speak all of his songs.

Many in the audience were used to bold, handsome leading men. When the curtains parted they beheld a rather plain man ambling on stage. The expression on his round face ranged from blank to worried. The audience didn't know what to make of him. Lehár watched with a mixture of wonder and dread, mentally comparing this Danilo with the dark, dashing, exotic leading men he was accustomed to and concluded that they had nothing in common.

It was time for Coyne's first song—praise for the Parisian restaurant Maxim's. Lehár conducted, Coyne spoke. But he spoke in perfect time to the music and so effectively that the audience was charmed.

As the operetta went on, it became clear that there was something magical between the two lead characters, Coyne as Danilo and the alluring Lily Elsie as Sonia. The slow waltz they danced was such a hit that the two had to repeat it over and over. By the time Danilo finally spoke the long awaited "I love you," the crowd was completely won over, and the London debut of *The Merry Widow* was a triumph.

George Edwards' daring gamble had paid off, thanks to a trick, some showbiz magic, and the music of Franz Lehár.

June 28th

Always the Critic

"Who could not win the mistress wooed the maid." So said Alexander Pope, suggesting that critics are failed, envious artists. Henri Blanchard may well have been one of them. In the spring of 1841, writing for the influential Paris *Gazette*, Blanchard had this to say about a concert that included the 19-year-old Belgian composer César Franck:

Like the Roman emperors who bear his name, and who carry on their shoulders the great burdens of world government, Monsieur César-Auguste Franck was loaded down with almost the entire musical accountability of the concert. There were two trios by him, a solo, a quartet, and the last ensemble of the whole business. César-Auguste carried on manfully with all of it. He came, he saw, he conquered. Veni, vidi, vici.

The young man does indeed have talents but they are all mechanical. He hops all over the keyboard, on and on, ceaselessly. It's all very clear, tidy, and dry. But he has no inspiration as a pianist or a composer. He has knowledge but no feeling. No tricky phrase or passage interrupts his bland smile.

A few weeks later, Blanchard struck again when Franck performed at a benefit for the poor, suggesting that Franck had allied himself with charity to avoid criticism. Nearly a year after the first concert, when Franck performed at a piano salon, Blanchard couldn't resist a third strike:

Monsieur César-Auguste Franck has apparently forgotten the old proverb that if you chase after two hares you won't catch either because there he was pursuing a third one. He teaches the piano fairly successfully, plays the piano about as well, and now he hopes to be a successful composer. Would anyone else presume to take on such a threesome of challenges? I myself would not.

Had the barbs hit their mark? Within a month César Franck went back to Belgium.

June 29th

Villa-Lobos Plays the Guitar for Segovia

It was only natural that Brazilian composer Heitor Villa-Lobos would write for the guitar. And maybe it was inevitable that he would meet the world's greatest guitarist, Andrés Segovia. But exactly what happened at that first meeting is not so certain, because Villa-Lobos and Segovia gave sharply contrasting accounts of it.

It happened in Paris in 1924. They were at a party given by a mutual friend. According to Villa-Lobos, Segovia didn't recognize him at first and remarked that the composer wrote music that was at odds with the guitar since it required impossible techniques. Then, according to Villa-Lobos, the composer introduced himself and asked what Segovia meant. The embarrassed guitarist replied that classical guitarists didn't use the little finger. "Well, if it isn't used," Villa-Lobos snapped, "cut it off."

Then he asked Segovia for a guitar on which to demonstrate his techniques. When the virtuoso reluctantly complied, he was astonished by Villa-Lobos' ability. After the demonstration Segovia took his guitar and left, refusing to see the composer the following day, although he later commissioned an etude.

Segovia told it differently. According to him, he recognized Villa-Lobos at once, and when the composer borrowed the guitar, he had to try several times to begin playing it and finally gave up because his fingers had become clumsy from lack of practice. According to Segovia, despite the awkwardness of Villa-Lobos' playing, he knew at once that he was in the presence of a great musician because the chords were full of exciting dissonances and the melodic fragments were original. As for Villa-Lobos' unorthodox fingering, the guitarist found it ingenious. And above all, Segovia could tell that Villa-Lobs was "a true guitar lover."

Whatever exactly happened on that night in Paris in 1924, two of the century's great musicians had come together and made a moment of musical history.

June 30th
The Unexpected Debut

One of the greatest conducting careers in history began by accident. It came about when a 19-year-old cellist was called upon to lead a performance of *Aida*. The cellist was no ordinary musician though. He performed every opera by memory. His name–Arturo Toscanini.

In 1886 Toscanini was performing with an Italian orchestra touring South America and things were going badly. The conductor, a Brazilian, did not impress the Italians. He thought the Italians were out to get him. He quit and the assistant conductor, an Italian, replaced him.

On opening night, June 30, the audience stubbornly refused to hear the assistant conductor. The ballet master came out and told them to quiet down while a substitute conductor could be found.

Someone tried to conduct but it didn't work. The audience grew more restless. It occurred to Toscanini that no performance meant no pay–and no money for a ticket back to Italy. Then someone came up and pleaded, "Isn't there anyone in the orchestra who can conduct *Aida?*"

The second cellist pointed to Toscanini, and he ran on stage. He went to the podium, as he later recalled, "in a stunned state, as if I were drunk."

"My arms were used to playing the cello, not to conducting," Toscanini said later. "But as soon as the chorus entered, I conducted. I really conducted. I didn't have the technique for conducting. But I conducted. I got used to it."

The next morning, the Rio papers proclaimed his triumph. It was only the beginning. The conducting career of Arturo Toscanini would go on for another 68 years.

July 1st
A Difficult Living

He may have been one of America's first outstanding composers, but William Billings had to struggle just to make a living–with or without music.

Billings was born in Boston in 1746. When he was 14, the death of his father forced him to become apprenticed to a tanner. It is likely that he attended singing schools and participated in amateur singing societies. By studying the writings of English psalm-writers, Billings learned enough to become a music teacher. He began to support himself through his music. He married and bought a house.

It's unlikely that Billings' success came from his looks. A contemporary described him as "a singular man of moderate size, short of one leg, with one eye and an uncommon negligence of person." Another noted that Billings had a withered arm and a habit of taking large amounts of snuff.

To his credit, Billings had a powerful voice and proved an effective singing master. He taught in the most fashionable churches in Boston.

When the American Revolution broke out, Billings wanted to do what he could for the patriot cause. He was unable to serve in combat, apparently signed on as a wagon driver, and is said to have come up with words and music for new songs while driving a supply wagon over the hills of New York. Billings prospered for a while after the war, but by the late 1780's he had fallen on hard times, and resorted to taking a series of odd jobs–leather sealer, hog-tender, scavenger. In 1790 a public concert was arranged for his benefit with the assurance that "the distress is real." Billings had to mortgage his house and attempted to sell the rights to his music to a publisher, but the resulting deal was more charity than business.

Although Billings died poor, he left a rich store of music to the young American republic.

July 2nd

Stravinsky's Star-Spangled Banner

Igor Stravinsky had been living in the United States for two years and he wanted to make a patriotic gesture. But America didn't exactly appreciate Stravinsky's gift—an arrangement of "The Star-Spangled Banner."

Two things gave Stravinsky the idea of writing the arrangement. A composer who visited him twice a week "to have his works re-composed" suggested it. And since Stravinsky was obliged to begin all of his concerts with the National Anthem anyway, and didn't care for any of the existing arrangements, he set to work. He finished it in Los Angeles on July 4, 1941. Shortly afterward an orchestra and chorus performed it. Stravinsky sent the manuscript to Eleanor Roosevelt for a war-fund auction. The manuscript was returned with an apology. Stravinsky could only guess at the reason for its refusal. "My major seventh chord in the second strain of the piece, the part patriotic ladies like best, must have embarrassed some high official," he speculated.

In the winter of 1944, Stravinsky performed his arrangement with the Boston Symphony. He stood with his back to the orchestra, conducting an audience that refrained from singing. At the time, no one seemed to notice that Stravinsky's arrangement was different from the traditional ones, but the next day, he found out that someone had noticed. Just before a second concert a Boston police commissioner visited Stravinsky in his dressing room and informed him of a Massachusetts law against "tampering" with national property. The policeman said that officers had already been told to remove his arrangement from the music stands.

Stravinsky countered that if there was a definitive version of the "Star-Spangled Banner" it was not played very often in Massachusetts. But the argument fell on deaf ears, and so far as anyone knows, the Stravinsky arrangement of the National Anthem hasn't been played since.

"It ought to be," Stravinsky once said. "For it makes the linear and harmonic best of the material, and is certainly superior to any other version I have heard."

July 3rd
Sad Thoughts from Paris

In 1778, 22 year-old Wolfgang Amadeus Mozart had gone with his mother to Paris, hoping to enhance his international reputation. He had gone reluctantly, and once he got there, he found one obstacle after another. On July 3, he wrote to his father in Salzburg:

I have very painful and sad news to give you, which in fact accounts for my not having replied sooner to your letter. My dearest mother is very ill. They have bled her according to custom, which was indeed quite necessary and did her a lot of good. But a few days later she complained of shivering and feverishness.

As she became worse by the minute, could barely speak, and lost her hearing, we had to shout to her. Baron Grimm sent his doctor to see her. She is still very weak, still feverish and delirious. They do give me some hope, but I don't have much. I wavered from hope to fear day and night, but I'm completely reconciled to the will of God, and hope that you and my sister will be too....

Let us put aside these sad thoughts, and still hope, but not too much. I have written a symphony for the opening of the Concert Spirituel, which was performed to great applause on Corpus Christi day. I was very nervous during the rehearsal because in my whole life I've never heard anything go so badly. You can't imagine how they scraped and scurried through it twice. I was really very edgy, and would've been happy to have it rehearsed again, but there wasn't time. So I went to bed with an aching heart, dissatisfied and angry.

The next day I decided not to go to the concert at all, but the fair evening weather made me change my mind. I was nonetheless determined that if the performance proved as bad as the rehearsal, I would go into the orchestra, take the violin from the first violinist, and lead myself

Later that night, Mozart's mother died.

July 4th

A Versatile Tune

The song began humbly and rose to great heights over the course of 150 years. Our story begins in London, in 1780, with a social club named after a fun-loving Roman poet said to have died at 86 while choking on a grape seed.

Most of the members of the Anacreontic Society were amateur musicians, though a few of them were professionals. They met every two weeks at the Crown and Anchor Tavern in the Strand. The evening's entertainment consisted of a concert, dinner, and drinking songs. The society began each evening with a song tailor-made by two of their members. Poet Ralph Tomlinson provided lyrics and antiquarian and musicologist John Stafford Smith contributed a genteel melody. Their song "To Anacreon in Heaven" celebrated the mingling of love and wine.

Not everyone loved the society though. The Duchess of Devonshire made a habit of eavesdropping on the proceedings from a secret room in the tavern, and she was no lover of bawdy songs and ballads. No doubt the possibility that she might be listening in at any time had something to do with the demise of the Anacreontic Society in 1786.

For the next 28 years, its theme song floated from one side of the Atlantic to the other, and in 1814, it turned up in a setting that was anything but convivial.

During the War of 1812, as the British retreated from Washington, a well-known Washington lawyer and amateur poet was on a prisoner exchange ship in Baltimore Harbor. The lawyer, Francis Scott Key, spent a night nervously watching the British bombardment of nearby Fort McHenry. At sunrise, seeing the American flag still flying over the fort, Key was inspired to write the poem known as "The Star-Spangled Banner." Key later forwarded his poem to a Baltimore printer, coupling it with a slightly less singable arrangement of "To Anacreon in Heaven." In 1931, 150 years after its modest beginnings in a London tavern, the quaint old drinking tune became officially the national anthem of the United States.

July 5th

The Summer Job

In the 1920's, the most reliable way for a young composer to make money was to teach–without being too picky about the quality of the students. When 25 year-old Aaron Copland had a chance to make money by performing in a trio at a Pennsylvania summer resort, he took it.

Copland was working on a symphony. He imagined a perfect summer with leisurely mornings in which to compose, free meals, and playing easy pieces for afternoon teas and genteel dinners.

It was not to be.

The Milford Inn was running in the red and had so few guests that the dining room was deathly quiet. The proprietor, a Mr. DiLorenzo, decided that if his business was going to pick up, the dinner music would have to be chosen very carefully. He insisted that the bulk of the inn's music come from operas. He wanted the pieces played just as they had been played in southern Italy when he was a boy. He also required that all of the arias be as lively as possible. "What's the matter Don't you understand the word *vivace?*" he would ask the trio. "Play with life, with feeling, joy–*molto vivace!*"

On mornings when there were no "rehearsals" Copland attempted to compose in the empty dining room. But the kitchen crew invariably found mornings the best time to burst into song or to gossip as they worked. His piano playing seemed to be a signal for plumbers or carpenters to show up and begin banging and sawing. In desperation Copland took off for the local movie theater, where he paid to use the miserable house piano. The place reeked of stale cigarette smoke, but amid the debris of popcorn and ice-cream wrappers, far from the glamor that he had imagined, Aaron Copland found the quiet that he needed to compose his *Symphony for Organ and Orchestra.*

July 6th
Too Much of a Good Thing

Was it too much of a good thing? He was born with the best musical heritage imaginable and his talent was considerable, but Wilhelm Friedemann Bach fell short of everyone's expectations. He was the first-born son of Johann Sebastian Bach, and that in itself may have proved a handicap. Friedemann was his father's favorite among his four composer sons, and among the four it was Friedemann who wrote music most like his father's.

By the 1730's though, Friedemann found himself defending his and his father's harmony-rich music against those favoring a newer style that Friedemann disdained as mere "ear-tickling" and "bouncing melodies." Friedemann and his father went so far as to dismiss as "pretty little things" the keyboard sonatas of his brother, Carl Philipp Emmanuel.

Friedemann's academic approach to composing put him in the lonely position of writing music that was too newfangled for older listeners but too old-fashioned for the young. Even in the area of church music–a traditional haven for organists of the Bach family–Friedemann suffered an embarrassing setback when his job application was passed over in favor of one of his father's pupils.

In later years, Friedemann isolated himself further. He suddenly resigned from his position as a church organist, abandoned his wife and daughter, and became a vagabond–one soon in need of cash. He made what little he could from giving private lessons, and on several occasions he sold his father's compositions as his own.

When Wilhelm Friedemann Bach died in 1784 at the age of 74, an acquaintance remembered him as one whose friends had raised him out of the dust more than once. It was said that those friends remaining had, "lodged him decently and seen to his basic needs...but his stubbornness, his glaring pride, and his strong passion for drink caused him always to drop back into misery."

July 7th

John Bach & the Stage Coach Robbery

At the age of 27, Johann Christian Bach–the youngest son of Johann Sebastian Bach–settled in London, where he became known as John Bach. His music suited the tastes of the times, and the congenial Bach prospered, enjoying the patronage of the royal family. On one occasion, though, his attempts to stay close to the nobility put his life in danger.

In 1775 John Bach rented a house in Richmond to be near the British royal family's summer residence on the Thames River. There Bach took part in elegant evenings of chamber music and shipboard concerts, and he taught the four young princes. Bach's circle included the celebrated composer, Karl Friedrich Abel, and the famous painter, Thomas Gainsborough.

The road from London to Richmond was notorious for its robbers. Writer Horace Walpole complained, "You are held up every hundred yards."

On July 7, 1775, Abel, Gainsborough, and Bach were on their way from London to Richmond. Abel rode in one coach, Gainsborough and Bach followed in another. As evening darkened into night, Bach dozed off only to be awakened by someone yelling, "Your money or your watch!" The groggy Bach found himself face to face with a pair of highwaymen. For some reason, they had taken pity on Abel and let him pass, but Bach and Gainsborough were not to be so lucky. The robbers were fast and thorough. They took Bach's money and his gold watch, plus an expensive chain.

Since the holdup had endangered the lives of highly placed artists, it attracted considerable attention, and eventually the highwaymen were caught. Bach was called on to testify, but he was apparently not eager to prolong any kind of relationship with the robbers. He said that he was unable to identify any of them. Apparently, his pleasant evenings of music-making had enabled John Bach to put the incident behind him.

July 8th
The Family Tradition

In his autobiography, Carl Philipp Emanuel Bach states that, "In composition and keyboard playing I had no teacher other than my father." When the time came to carry on the family tradition of music-making, Emanuel Bach would face some challenges.

He probably began his keyboard lessons around 1720, at the age of six or seven, using a collection of keyboard pieces that his father, Johann Sebastian, had written for Emanuel's older brother, Wilhelm Friedemann. Years later, Emanuel recalled that all of his father's pupils had to begin immediately with "works that were by no means easy." From there, the young keyboard player progressed to his father's Inventions and Sinfonias and then to the *Well-Tempered Clavier*.

It is likely that, before long, Emanuel also played in public in Leipzig as a harpsichordist, at first providing accompaniment and then soloing in performances of his father's keyboard concertos. By the time he was 17, Emanuel Bach was a published composer and, though he was educated to be a lawyer, he went on to become a major composer, who influenced Haydn and a generation of composers to follow.

But when it came to the next generation of his family, Emanuel Bach was not so influential. He had three children. His first, Johann August, showed no particular musical talent, and eventually became a lawyer. His daughter, Anna Carolina Philippina, is said to have "occupied herself with domestic duties all her life." Emanuel put his greatest hope in his youngest child, optimistically named Johann Sebastian. According to one account, he declared that, through his young son, he would continue the family tradition and bequeath to the world all he had learned from his father and all that he had discovered himself.

Apparently, the keyboard lessons and musical tradition didn't turn out quite as well as Emanuel had hoped. But young Sebastian did have artistic talent. He became a painter.

July 9th

The Starving Artist

The starving artist. The phrase is a cliché, but it is also a literal description of composer Karl Goldmark as a young theater musician.

In 1851, at age 21, Goldmark was scraping out a living as a theater musician in Budapest. He and a friend rented a single room with a kitchen. They slept in the kitchen on a bag stuffed with straw. Their only other furniture was a chair and a piano. Goldmark practiced diligently, hoping to become a capable self-taught pianist so that he could supplement his income as an accompanist for singers. He also played for all-night dances, and he was not exactly prospering.

When the management of the theater in Budapest changed, Goldmark moved to Vienna, where he worked at major theaters for minor compensation. In his autobiography *Notes from the Life of a Viennese Composer*, Goldmark describes his steady decline:

The long years of starvation were not without serious consequences to my health. I had existed one winter simply on potatoes, without any bread, the next summer on curds and raw cucumbers and that kind of thing. I was anemic. My glands were swollen. My eyes were bloodshot. From sheer weakness I almost faded away completely. The two-mile walk from Alser Street where I lived, to the Carl Theater took me two hours. In those days there was no other way of getting around except in expensive carriages.

My brother's faithful old friend, Dr. Adolph Fischof, took me to a hospital. I was well fed and discharged after three weeks, pronounced cured. I was advised to take plenty of cold baths and to keep well nourished. The baths weren't difficult, the nourishment was very difficult.

And the theater did not always provide cultural nourishment. The fare consisted of farces, opera parodies, acrobats, and trained monkeys. But Goldmark later recalled, "To this long experience of the theater, with all its misery, poverty—and gaiety, I owe one valuable advantage: I came to know the theater thoroughly. It was because of this preparation that I was able to compose and to put my operas on the stage."

July 10th
The Ruins of Babylon

Greatness in ruins–it was a popular theme for poets and composers in the early 19th century. A little too popular as far as Beethoven was concerned. In July 1811, he found himself being upstaged, and he wrote to a Viennese theater director to do something about it.

Your Excellency–I hear that the actor Scholz will shortly be giving as a benefit for the Theater An der Wien the melodrama The Ruins of Babylon. *I wished to write an opera on the subject, as I have already announced to you. I cannot comprehend this complication! I dare say you know nothing about it? Whatever it may be, you can be sure that the melodrama given at the Wieden will fill the house five, maybe six times. The music for it is dreadful stuff. As an opera the story will become an enduring work, beyond compare, and will bring further monetary advantage to your theater.*

It's so hard to find a good book this year. Since last year I have returned at least twelve, maybe more. I've paid out of my own pocket and still couldn't get anything useful. Now, for the sake of an actor's assets, there will occur for me–and I assert it boldly–a deficit for your theater.

I hope, with your better judgement, that you will prevent the actor Scholz from giving this melodrama, since I have already informed you of my intention to treat it as an opera. I was so glad to have found this subject that I myself informed the Archduke of it, and many other men of intellect, and everyone thought is was excellent. I have even written to foreign language newspapers to have an announcement inserted to prevent the subject from being used for an opera elsewhere. And now I have to withdraw my plan? And for such a wretched reason?

I'm waiting to hear from you and beg you to send me an answer quickly, so that I'll know how I stand in this situation. Otherwise too much time will be lost.

Beethoven never wrote the opera.

July 11th
The Sunday Pianist

Franz Liszt was not only a masterful pianist and a world-class composer. He also fostered the talent of other composers. Alexander Borodin wrote of a formative encounter with Liszt in July 1877:

When I told him that I was only a Sunday pianist, he quipped, "but Sunday is always a feast day, and you are just the right person to preside."

After tea our hostess led us to the piano in the drawing room and handed Liszt one of his own rhapsodies, asking him to show us how certain passages ought to be played. Liszt laughed. "You want me to play it! All right, I will. But first I want to play Monsieur Borodin's symphony with him." He asked me, "Do you play treble or bass?" I flatly refused to play, but finally I convinced the baroness to play just the andante, which she did with Liszt playing the bass. It was a fascinating performance and I was the only listener.

Liszt, however, was not content. "The baroness is very kind, but I want to play it with you." He took my hand and made me sit down at the bass while he took the treble.

I wanted to argue but the baroness said, "Play or you'll irritate Liszt. I know him."

First we tackled the finale, then the scherzo, then the first movement. Then we played the entire symphony, including all the repeats. Liszt wouldn't let up. After every movement he turned the page, saying, "Let's continue."

Whenever I left something out or made a mistake, Liszt would say, "Why didn't you play that? It's so splendid." When we had finished, he repeated several passages, complimenting their originality. He critiqued my symphony in great detail, and said that the andante is a perfect masterpiece.

July 12th
Busoni in America

On July 12, 1911, composer Ferruccio Busoni was in Berlin. A few months earlier he had been in America, and a meeting with New York publisher Rudolph Schirmer set him to thinking about the United States as he wrote to his friend, pianist Egon Petri:

Last Friday we met up with Schirmer from New York and conductor Oskar Fried, for an economical aristocratic meal at the Kaiserhof Hotel. It was quite a memorable undissonant evening. Right off we were united in our devotion to Gustav Mahler. We three happened in fact to have been his true friends.

Fried has–in all likelihood–fulfilled his most heartfelt wish–America. From which you can see how human passions can be misled.

Schirmer has decided to buy up the complete works of Delius. On top of that there was further pleasure. A Gustav Mahler Foundation for the support of gifted musicians has been started. It was the wish of Frau Mahler herself that I be one of only three people who should serve as a sort of trustee. You were also a topic of the conversation with Schirmer. If you eventually go to America, I can guarantee a good friend in this Schirmer fellow.

My opinion of that country has again changed considerably. Not only do I put no stock in its cultural rise, but I also believe it has already passed its high point. What the Americans have done since crossing that line is leading to a moral desert. That is to say practical exploitation for its own sake and coarse indulgence in luxury. As other problems–moral, religious, and artistic questions are not being taken into account, America presents itself as the Middle Ages fitted up with machines and electricity. A great country! Yes, by God, and just as He created it, even if it does lack nightingales and wine. A person could be reconciled with the Americans if they weren't so impertinent.

July 13th
A Tune for Revolution & Revelry

The young captain of engineers in the French army was popular as a poet, violinist, and singer among his fellow officers in Strasbourg. He wrote a hymn to liberty and several plays but, above all, Claude-Joseph Rouget de Lisle is remembered for his war song for the army of the Rhine—better known as the *Marseillaise.*

France declared war on Austria in 1792, and on the night of April 25, Rouget de Lisle wrote hastily a rousing song vowing death to the enemy. The song was quickly arranged for a military review, and was snapped up by volunteers from Marseilles, who took part in a Paris insurrection a few months later. Known from then on as the *Marseillaise*, the tune became so popular that in 1795 it was declared a national song.

The politically-charged call to arms was banned in France under the Empire, only to be reinstated again in 1830, when Hector Berlioz orchestrated it with a dedication to the aging and indigent Rouget de Lisle.

In 1838 the tune was illegal in the Austrian capital, and Robert Schumann made a prank of hinting at it in his suite *Carnival Jest from Vienna.*

In 1879, under the Third Republic, the *Marseillaise* became the national anthem of France and, by the next year, when Tchaikovsky included it in his *1812 Overture*, the tune had come to symbolize France, both the Republic and the Empire.

But where did the tune come from in the first place? A tempting possibility arises in a piece of music completed in Vienna in December 1786, several years before Rouget de Lisle dashed off his marching song. The first movement of Mozart's Piano Concerto No. 25 in C alternates between martial and festive airs, including a recurring theme that sounds remarkably like the beginning of the *Marseillaise*. Is it possible that Rouget de Lisle picked his tune up from the very nation his song was attacking?

In any event, in short order, an inspired Rouget de Lisle created a song for the ages.

July 14th
Debussy's Love Triangle

A man leaving one woman for another. It happened every day in Paris in 1903, but this love triangle was different. It involved a wealthy society woman, a much younger lower-class woman–and one of France's great composers–Claude Debussy.

The scandal may have begun in 1901, when a young man named Raoul Bardac began studying composition with Debussy. Raoul's mother, Emma, was the wife of a wealthy banker, and was well-known in Paris society for her charm and her interest in the arts, music in particular. At first, Debussy and his wife Lily were dinner guests at the Bardic home, but Lily, coming from a lower-class background, was no match for the Bardacs intellectually. Increasingly she felt out of place at the dinners, and she urged Debussy to attend without her.

It was the beginning of the end for the marriage of Lily and Debussy. Emma Bardac, with her green eyes and red-gold hair, was a beautiful and brilliant conversationalist.

Lily, his wife of five years, was also beautiful. She had shown spirit and courage and poise during the dark moments of Debussy's career, had been able to divert him from his worries with a single funny word. But now that he was drawn to Emma, Debussy found that the sound of Lily's voice left him cold On July 14, 1903, Debussy went out for his morning walk and didn't come back. When Lily discovered that Debussy had moved in with Emma, she wrote a letter to Debussy. Then she shot herself.

Debussy returned in time to take Lily to the hospital. He sat in the waiting room until a doctor informed him that Lily would live. Then he thanked the doctor and left.

Friends of the Debussys sided with Lily and raised money to pay her hospital bills. Debussy found out who the contributors were and broke off relations with every one of them, including another of France's great composers, Maurice Ravel.

July 15th
The Stradella Scandal

Alessandro Stradella was one of the 17th century's finest composers—and one of its most threatened. An incident from the year 1677 is typical of Stradella's dangerous life.

The composer was living in Venice, having fled Rome because of a scandal that had arisen over his attempt to embezzle money from the Roman Catholic Church. For a time he contented himself with music-making. He played the lute and may have participated in the writing and performances of vocal works. He was well connected with many instrumentalists and singers in Venice.

Then he became too well-connected with a young woman named Agnese, the mistress or perhaps the fiancée, of Alvise Contarini, who was a member of one of the most wealthy and powerful families in Venice. Perhaps naively, Contarini had asked Stradella to be Agnese's music teacher. Exactly what happened next is unclear, but can be conjectured because soon afterward, Stradella and Agnese left Venice together.

Contarini cried foul, accusing the lovers of stealing a large sum of money from him—his inflated estimate of the value of jewelry and other gifts he had given Agnese. Stradella and Agnese, meanwhile, turned up in Turin, where Agnese took refuge in a convent. Contarini came to Turin and put pressure on her either to marry Stradella or become a nun. Stradella meanwhile was allowed to send her some basic necessities and music, but not direct communications, although he did attempt to sneak a letter to her in the form of a cantata.

Before long, Agnese became eager to leave the convent, and public opinion pushed Stradella into agreeing to marry her. But just after signing the marriage contract, Stradella walked out of the convent and was beaten senseless by two thugs hired by Contarini. Having taken his beating, Stradella apparently felt himself free of the whole affair. He took off for Genoa without ever again mentioning Agnese.

July 16th

Grieg's Rambunctious Move

Occasionally, an artist becomes too popular for his own good. In his autobiography, Edvard Grieg tells about trying to find a place to put up a hut where he could work undisturbed by his public.

He built on a secluded hill overlooking a fjord, to which there was no visible path, hoping to be free from intruders. But, unbeknownst to him, an old right-of-way path led right to it. So all winter long, if the weather wasn't too bad, Grieg heard people tiptoeing around the hut as he worked.

It also turned out that the hut was exposed to powerful winter storms, so that Grieg often thought that he and the hut would go flying into the sky together.

One day he couldn't take it anymore. He decided to move the hut to a secluded wooded area down by the fjord, and invited about 50 peasants to assist—their only reward being ale and aqua vitae and edible delicacies. With a loud hurrah, Grieg's helpers tugged the hut from its foundation. Then they rolled it on tree trunks and dragged it to its new foundation among the birches at the water's edge. Next, a suspiciously animated bunch came galloping up with the crated piano.

Those who were not too affected by the ale insisted on a concert in the crowded hut. Grieg obliged with a log dance while one listener nearly edged him off the stool and another talked with such gusto that he sprayed the piano keys. A third quickly declared that he had heard quite enough, and was literally kicked out of the hut. Grieg could hardly play for laughing.

The newly located hut provided Grieg the longed-for peace and quiet until summer, when tourists discovered it and began parking their boats under the window in order to get a free concert as Norway's most popular composer tried to work.

July 17th
The Theft

Musicians are never far from the possibility of a professional catastrophe. But when it became known that composer Heinrich Whilhelm Ernst suffered from an incurable illness, his friend, violinist Joseph Joachim, participated in a benefit concert for Ernst. Then came a second blow, which Ernst described in a letter to Joachim on July 17, 1862:

I've been somewhat better for the last few days. I'm in less pain and the weather is so splendid that I can go for an unbroken swim in the sea. I hope I'll get some relief, and build up enough strength to get me through the winter.

Not a thing has been said, but it looks more and more as if our servant is the culprit—now that it's too late. She left us almost a month ago and the police don't seem any too anxious to start a new investigation. In that regard I forgot to respond to the charming and intelligent remark that the robbery simply proved how soundly I slept.

My reply is that nothing like that would happen to a soldier of fortune—that it takes an unlucky clod like me to lie awake all night until a quarter past four and then, just as the thief is starting to get impatient, to roll over and fall asleep from sheer exhaustion and pain so as to allow his watch and other valuables to be stolen from his bedside table right there beside his very posterior.

If the thief was a professional it was probably very fortunate that I didn't roll over and face him just then. I can laugh about it now, because in life all unpleasant memories fade, thank God. But you can be sure that I didn't have a moment's peace during the night for a week after the unhappy incident.

July 18th
The Masterpiece

Peter Tchaikovsky had reservations about his fellow Russian composers, but great respect for a contemporary from France-George Bizet, the composer of *Carmen*. In a letter to his brother Modest, he wrote on July 18, 1880:

To refresh myself last night I played Carmen *from beginning to end and all my wonder and love for this wonderful opera flared up again. I even mapped out in my mind an article in which* Carmen, *in spite of its modest pretentions to be only an opéra comique and not grand opera, is shown as really one of–if not the most–prominent lyric-dramatic creations of our time…*

In my opinion Carmen *is an absolute masterpiece, i.e., a work that is very much a reflection of the musical taste and aspiration of a whole epoch. It seems to me that the epoch we live in differs from its predecessor by reason of this characteristic trait–that composers pursue what (Mozart, Beethoven, and Schubert never did) pretty, piquant musical effects.*

What, for example, is the new Russian school but a cult of spicy harmonizations, original orchestral combinations, and all sorts of superficial effects? The musical idea has been pushed into the background. It has become not the aim but only the means; that is, the reason for the invention of this or that combination of sounds. This, purely brainy process of musical reasoning makes contemporary music, however amusing, witty, curious, and even "tasty"…at the same time cold, not warmed by real inspiration. But suddenly a Frenchman appears (whom I can sincerely call a genius), whose piquancy and spiciness do not result from ingenuity but flow in an unhindered stream, to flatter your hearing, to excite, and to touch you at the same time. As if he means to say, "You do not want anything grand, mighty, and strong, but prettiness– here it is!" He has indeed given us an example of the element which is called the pretty. Bizet is an artist who, in spite of paying tribute to the decadent taste of this century, is nonetheless full of sincere feeling and inspiration.

July 19th

The Innovator

He was a major innovator in the insurance industry. He created the concept of estate planning, and introduced the idea of training schools for insurance agents. When it came to composing music, Charles Ives was also a mover and shaker, but followers were few.

In 1910 a business acquaintance talked the celebrated conductor Walter Damrosch into having the New York Symphony Orchestra play through parts of Ives' first symphony during a rehearsal. Although he had misgivings, Ives needed to hear his music performed, so he offered the second movement of his symphony for the exercise.

At first the playing went well. A pretty tune prompted Damrosch to call out "Charming!" But after a while the orchestra ran into trouble and ground to a halt. Damrosch changed some of the notes and the symphony continued. They soon bogged down again though, and again—each time with Damrosch "correcting" the composer's notes. At one passage Ives had put duple meter in one part and triple in another—a device used by Chopin, Schumann, and Brahms. Damrosch called out condescendingly, "You'll just have to make up your mind, young man! Which do you want, a rhythm of two or a rhythm of three?"

A few years later, another friend—the assistant concert master of the New York Symphony—brought some orchestra members to Ives' Manhattan apartment to play his piece *Washington's Birthday.* The musicians complained so much about one thing and another that Ives made cuts that included some of the best parts. The only receptive member of the group was the viola player, who suggested the piece for one of the orchestra's concerts—to which someone replied, "No, we must think of the audience." When another friend asked the composer why he didn't write music that people were sure to like, Ives answered, "I can't do it! I hear something else!"

July 20th
The Concert from Hell

Call it the concert from hell. In his autobiography, Louis Spohr tells of a performance that got off to a bad start and hit the skids to disaster.

It happened during a German tour in 1811. Before the concert, a wealthy amateur treated the musicians to a lavish evening of dinner and champagne. The musicians grew so merry that they forgot all about the concert and rushed to the hall at the last minute. The concert began with an overture by a composer named Romberg, who overreacted to criticism that he conducted too slowly. He conducted so fast that the orchestra couldn't keep up. Spohr and his wife Dorette were next with a sonata for violin and harp. The usually poised Dorette gave Spohr a worried look and whispered, "For heaven's sake, Louis, I can't remember which sonata we're supposed to play or how it begins." Spohr hummed the beginning and husband and wife got through their sonata with ample applause.

Now the soprano came on stage to sing her aria. Suddenly she ran into the wings. Dorette went after her and found her hastily loosening her clothes, which—after the big dinner—were so tight that the singer was short of breath. The clarinetist, proud of a new mouthpiece and emboldened by champagne, showed off with louder and louder notes, astounding the audience until he pushed a little too hard and let out an enormous squawk. The worst came last. The violist was unaware that he had broken his belt buckle. As he stood up to play his solo, his trousers started to fall. Not wanting to miss a single note, he pulled up his drooping pants only during the rests, much to audience's amusement. Then, during a virtuoso passage his breeches dropped decisively and the concert collapsed in laughter.

It may not have been the best music, but it wasn't bad comedy as described in the autobiography of Louis Spohr.

July 21st

Sibelius' Prank

Jean Sibelius enjoyed proving his musicianship, but he wasn't always receptive when others tried to prove theirs.

One day when Sibelius was a young musician living in Berlin, he was running short of cash and he made a bet with some fellow Finns that they could pass as popular musicians. Sibelius and his friends presented themselves to a theater manager as famous Finnish musicians. Sibelius said that the theater had a high reputation, and that he and his ensemble would enjoy playing for its customers.

The manager was convinced. He invited the trio to perform. Sibelius played the violin, his two countrymen, the piano and cello. They performed for an hour—exclusively Finnish music. The audience applauded. The manager paid the three about 40 dollars apiece for their concert and offered them a two-week engagement at the same rate. Somberly, Sibelius told the manager he would get back to him.

Once they were out on the street Sibelius laughed and said, "I told you we could do it." They might have been tempted to accept the engagement, too, if money from home hadn't arrived in the mail the next day.

Years later, when Sibelius really was a famous musician, he was in London, trying to finish his string quartet called "Intimate Voices." He asked an English friend to find a house for him—one that was quiet. When she called on the composer to see if his rooms were suitable, she found him fit to be tied and eager to move out.

Apparently, an elderly lady living in the room below his had been showing her solidarity with the composer by making music of her own—a personalized version of Beethoven's "Moonlight Sonata"—over and over again. Once the enthusiastic neighbor had been spoken to, Sibelius was able again to hear his "intimate voices" and to complete his quartet.

July 22nd
Sibyl

On a summer evening in 1887, Jules Massenet was about to escape from a tedious party, when a young American woman approached him. She would soon make her mark on his personal life and his career.

Her name was Sibyl Sanderson. She was a 22-year-old heiress from Sacramento, California, and extremely beautiful. She was eager to become an opera singer, and had studied with a prominent teacher. She asked if Massenet would be willing to hear her sing.

Never one to turn his back on beauty, Massenet agreed. He accompanied Sibyl as she sang the aria of the Queen of the Night from Mozart's opera *The Magic Flute*. Massenet found her voice thrilling. It ranged from lower to upper G, three octaves at both its loudest and softest. "I was thunderstruck," Massenet said later. "I was amazed, bedazzled, overwhelmed." He added, "I have to say that combined with such a rare voice I perceived intelligence, inspiration and personality reflected in her wonderful appearance—crucial qualities on the stage."

The morning after his encounter with Sibyl, Massenet's publisher asked him to write an opera for the upcoming Paris Exposition. After glancing at the libretto, Massenet declared that he had just the soprano to sing the lead role of Esclarmonde.

Massenet labored intensely on the opera for two years, determined to produce his best work for Sibyl. They were years of doubts and difficulties for Sibyl, for Massenet—and for his wife. But when the opera was finally finished, Massenet was so pleased with it that he asked Sibyl to add her signature to his on the last page of the manuscript.

The composer left nothing to chance and supervised every detail of the production. He gave 22 rehearsals with the singers and 57 rehearsals on stage. He suffered a nervous breakdown.

Partly because of the festive atmosphere of the Paris Exposition and partly because of the combined talents of Massenet and Sibyl Sanderson, *Esclarmonde* was a success. And, while critics found it a bewildering pastiche of styles from other composers, Massenet always steadfastly maintained that his favorite of all his operas was *Esclarmonde*.

July 23rd
Respect for a Master

By 1750, Francesco Geminiani had been in England off and on for more than 35 years. He had become known as one of Europe's finest composers and violinists. Running short of money, he decided to conduct a benefit concert at Covent Garden. Unfortunately, conducting was not his strong suit, but his reputation and sheer musicianship carried him through a looming disaster, as becomes apparent in an eyewitness account of the concert:

The singers not being perfect in the parts, the performance miscarried. The advertisements had drawn together a number of persons, sufficient to make what is called a very good house. The curtain drew up, revealing a numerous band with Geminiani at the head. By way of an overture was performed a Concerto of his in the key of D...in which is a fugue in triple time, perhaps one of the finest compositions of the kind ever heard. Then followed a very grand chorus, which, being performed by persons accustomed to sing Mr. Handel's oratorios, had justice done to it.

But when the women to whom were given the solo airs and duets rose to sing, they were not able to go on, and after a few bars the whole band had to stop. The audience, instead of expressing resentment in the usual way, seemed to sympathize with Geminiani in his distress and to consider him a man who had almost survived his faculties, but whose merits were too great to justify their slight.

They sat very silent till the scores were changed, when the performance was continued with compositions of the composer's own which, notwithstanding his advanced age, he performed in a manner that yet lives in the memories of many of the audience.

At age 63, Francesco Geminiani had long since earned the respect–and patience–of his audiences.

July 24th
The Boy Who Dared

The young soloist had made up his mind. He was going to play Beethoven's Violin Concerto with the New York Symphony—even though the conductor and the New York music critics scoffed at the idea. When push came to shove, they all gave way for Yehudi Menuhin.

The year was 1927. Walter Damrosch was America's best-known conductor. He tried to reason with the boy. "Now, Yehudi, you probably realize that Beethoven is to music what Shakespeare is to the stage. What is it, then, that makes you think you can play his concerto?"

"I don't know," Menuhin said. "I never thought about it. I just play. Maybe to speak on stage a person needs more than just instinct."

Damrosch had heard the boy play and said that he had no objection to his taking on the Beethoven, but he cautioned that a flawed performance would damage his career.

"I don't care about a career," Yehudi said, "I just want to have some fun playing with the orchestra."

The conductor of the concert, Fritz Busch, was not so accepting. He sat at the piano, smiling sarcastically, and began playing the last part of the concerto's orchestral introduction. Yehudi adjusted his violin, lifted his bow, and poured forth the opening measures—broken octaves known to strike fear into the hearts of violinists.

In his memoirs, Busch recalled, "Yehudi played so gloriously, and with such complete mastery that I was completely won over. That was perfection." He interrupted the music and threw his arms around the boy.

On the night of the Carnegie Hall Concert, Yehudi pointed to a fireman's hatchet hanging on the wall and asked a guard what it was.

"To chop the heads off the soloists who don't play well," the guard replied.

There was no need for it that night. Audience and doubting critics alike were won over by violinist Yehudi Menuhin, who had taken New York by storm at the age of 11.

July 25th
The Literary Critic

Peter Tchaikovsky had nothing but praise for the French music of his time. He valued George Bizet's opera *Carmen* above anything produced by the Russian national school, and he was so taken with Jules Massenet's drama *Marie-Magdeleine* that he wrote a duet based on words by Tolstoy to a tune inspired by it. But when it came to French literature, Tchaikovsky's opinions ran strongly counter to the trends of the day. In July 1880, he wrote to his brother Modest:

When it comes to your advice to read The Laughing Man, *I thank you, but facetiously. Don't you know about my relationship with Victor Hugo? I'll tell you how it ended. I started to read* Toilers of the Sea. *The more I read, the madder I got by the minute at all the affectations and scowling. Finally, after reading an entire row of meaningless noisy phrases full of exclamations, arguments, omissions, and so on, I flew into a rage and started spitting on the book. I tore it to tatters, stamped my foot on it, and finally threw it out the window.*

Ever since, I have been unable to look at a book with Hugo's name on it. And as far as reading one is concerned, you couldn't tempt me, not even with the tastiest little tidbit. And take it from me, your Zola is the only other actor in a new style. I'm not sick of him, as I am of Hugo, but I'm getting there. He disgusts me just like young women who pretend to be simple and natural but, in fact, are flirtatious and manipulative. I have to say that, as much as I like the latest French music, their literature and journalism disgust me.

As for French history, Tchaikovsky was anything but repelled. In the same letter he wrote of having completed an opera on a thoroughly French subject, Joan of Arc.

July 26th

Dvorak Goes to the Fair

In the summer of 1893, the great Bohemian composer, Antonin Dvořák, paid a celebrated visit to the Bohemian community of Spillville, Iowa. It was a peaceful sojourn during which Dvořák made a side trip to a vortex of chaos known as the World's Columbian Exposition Quadricentennial in Chicago.

The "white city," as it was known, rose up in Jackson Park on Lake Michigan, at the edge of the second biggest metropolis in the country. It had a Venetian theme of canals and gilded gondolas and palaces. Packed into its midway was a dizzying multitude of ethnic encampments—including miniature villages from China, Lapland, West Africa, and Ireland. There were marketplaces—Persian, Japanese and Indian wedged together cheek to jowl. Dominating the scene was a new marvel and the white city's main attraction—the 264-foot Ferris wheel.

The entertainment came from some of the most famous names of the day—actress Lillian Russell, Buffalo Bill's Wild West Show, an up-and-coming pianist named Scott Joplin, and showman Florenz Ziegfeld.

Enter Antonín Dvořák. As part of the exhibition's Bohemian Day celebration, 30,000 Czechs and Moravians paraded from downtown Chicago to the fairgrounds. The great American conductor, Theodore Thomas, and an entourage of local Czechs cordially welcomed Dvořák. Dvořák conducted his Eighth Symphony for an audience of 12,000.

Dvořák was later quoted as saying, "The Exhibition is enormous, and to describe it in writing would be a hopeless task. You would have to see it and see it often, and still you wouldn't know anything. There is so much and everything is so big, truly made in America."

On the darker side, another big American phenomenon was in the making in the summer of 1893—the financial panic that would threaten the solvency of Dvořák's American sponsor, and put the rest of his visit to the United States in jeopardy.

July 27th
Words You Can Understand

In the spring of 1561, the Santa Maria Maggiore church in Rome hired a new choirmaster. His name was Giovanni Perluigi da Palestrina, and his abilities as a composer of church music would become legendary.

Santa Maria Maggiore had a down-to-earth problem that persists in many church choirs today. It was summarized in a complaint by a bishop who informed church officials that after listening very closely to the choir, he had been unable to distinguish a single word they had sung.

There were other difficulties that the new choirmaster faced. Church composers had fallen into the habit of appropriating secular melodies for masses, and the masses were often casually referred to by the less-than-sacred names of the popular tunes. As if that indignity were not enough, non-sacred texts were often inserted into the mass.

The dispute between musicians and clergy over the trivializing of church music led Pope Pius himself to intervene. He placed the matter before the Council of Trent. At this point, the legend begins. According to one account, the dispute became so sharp that the churchmen proposed banning music from the mass altogether. The legend goes on to state that Palestrina stepped in and single handedly rescued church music by composing three masses so serenely beautiful that the Pope compared them to the heavenly music of the spheres.

In truth, the reform was much more logical and democratic. It was made by committee. Two Cardinals and eight papal singers met and agreed to ban masses with secular themes and to halt the interpolation of unauthorized text. But when one of the cardinals suggested that the words being sung should be intelligible, the singers said, "Impossible!" At which point the Cardinal pointed out several works in which the words most definitely *were* intelligible—all of them by Palestrina.

So while Palestrina did not "rescue church music" as the legend states, he did something more lasting by setting a direction that composers of church music would follow for hundreds of years. To be continued.....

July 28th

The Biggest Challenge

In the spring of 1565, composer Giovanni da Palestrina was nervous. He was facing the biggest challenge of his career–one that put his reputation and his livelihood at risk.

Cardinals at an ecumenical council had recommended a new approach to church music. Two of them had commissioned Palestrina to compose a mass to serve as a model for all writers of church music.

The cardinals wanted a mass that was reverent, simple, not too long, and free from all worldliness. The 40-year-old composer was honored but also worried. He was afraid that if he failed, Pope Pius IV would banish him from every chapel in the land. To quell his anxiety, Palestrina wrote three masses in the hope that one of them would satisfy the cardinals.

On a Sunday afternoon in 1565, the three masses were performed for the first time at the palace of one of the commissioning cardinals. Eight cardinals listened intently while Palestrina waited to see if his career would come to a screeching halt.

The cardinals were delighted with all three masses. They arranged for the Sistine Chapel singers to perform their favorite of the three for the new Pope, Marcellus II, who made a sacred occasion of the elaborate event. More than ever, Palestrina's career was on the line.

The mass moved the Pope to tears. He said, "surely these are the harmonies of the new song which the Apostle John heard in the Triumphant Jerusalem."

Just for Palestrina, the Pope created a lofty new position–special composer to the Pontifical Choir–the Pope's personal choir. On top of that honor, he made Palestrina the superior of all composers in Christendom.

Although the Pope died only two months later, Palestrina's position was secure. The next Pope kept Palestrina in his post as head of the pontifical choir–and so did six popes to follow.

July 29th
Amazing Speed

Although he was one of America's finest composers of piano music, Edward MacDowell was a reluctant performer. A long-time friend described MacDowell's playing:

As he never felt quite sure that what he was composing was worthwhile, so in the matter of playing in public he was so self-distrustful that when he came on the stage and sat down at the piano stool he hung his head and looked a good deal like a school boy detected in the act of doing something he ought not to do.

I never could persuade him to play for me. I once asked Paderewski to play for me his new set of songs, and he promptly did so. But MacDowell always was "out of practice" or had some other excuse, generally a witticism or a bit of sarcasm at his own expense.

A few years earlier, in 1888, MacDowell was described by a concertgoer as a virtuoso with an unusual trait:

The speed of his fingers was the most striking characteristic of his playing. He took to prestissimo like a duck to water. He could, in fact, play fast more easily than he could play slowly. One of his ever-present fears was that in performance his fingers would run away with him. And many hours were spent in endeavors to control such an embarrassing tendency. This extraordinary velocity...invariably set his listeners agape and was always one of the chief sensations at his concerts.

Despite his self-doubts, MacDowell was capable of far more than speed. In 1894, a New York critic referred to MacDowell's performance of his second piano concerto as "a success for both pianist and composer, such as no American musician has ever won before a metropolitan concert audience." The reviewer added, "again and again he had to get up and bow after every movement of his concerto. For once a prophet has had great honor in his own country. He played with that splendid kind of virtuosity which makes one forget the technique."

July 30th

The Crystal Palace

Violinist Joseph Joachim was one of the best, and he performed all over Europe. He learned where to play and where not to play, as he wrote in a letter to Clara Schumann from London at the end of July 1858:

I don't think it's very kind or trustful of you to suspect me of going on a tour for money which, no reputable artist would otherwise make. As rebuttal I inform you that Hallé, Piatti and your humble servant had planned to test the English people's solid and apparently growing taste for chamber music and to see how it would reward the artists.

In that regard, I don't have anything to complain about here. I might have earned more if I hadn't turned down all private engagements, which would no doubt have brought me more than another hundred pounds. I turned down other engagements too, for example, three at the Crystal Palace. I turned them down just because I don't see any reason why a foreigner should make an adjustment for English bad habits.

No matter how fine a place the Crystal Palace may be to visit, and no matter how much I may respect the English people for maintaining such an expensive wonder at their own cost and without any help from the government, as a place for music it is a monstrosity, unless you have several thousand people singing or playing there.

To perform as a soloist in that place is like declaring yourself the youngest in a swarm of gnats. But more than anything else in my life, that spectacular glass temple makes me regret that I'm not an organist. To hear Brahms play there on one of the many beautiful organs—particularly the big one in the middle of the building—would be outstanding.

July 31st
The Inconsiderate Duke

The year 1778 was a difficult one for Mozart. At age 22 he had gone to Paris to bolster his international reputation. During his stay in the French capital his mother died, and when he finally was able to turn back to business he found that his reputation as a child prodigy was getting in the way. On July 31, he wrote to his father in Salzburg:

Now two of my students are in the country, and the third—the Duke de Guines' daughter—is betrothed, and is not planning to continue her lessons, which so far as my finances are concerned doesn't particularly bother me. After all, the Duke only pays me what everyone else does.

But get this. I went to his house every day for two hours, being hired to give twenty-four lessons. It's the custom here to pay after each twelve lessons. They went to the country, and when they came back ten days later, I wasn't even informed of it, and found out by chance.

When I went to collect, the governess took out her purse and paid me for twelve lessons, explaining that she didn't have enough money to pay for more. Then she gave me three gold pieces and urged me to let her know if I was dissatisfied.

This thickheaded German was very far from being satisfied, so I refused the sum being offered. Since the Duke has now had a harp-and-flute concerto of mine for the past four months and hasn't paid me for it, I am only waiting until the wedding is over to go back to the governess and ask for my money.

What aggravates me most of all is that these stupid Frenchmen think I am still only seven years old, because that's how old I was when they first saw me. So I am treated here like a beginner, except by the musicians, who think very differently, but the majority opinion rules.

August 1st
The Most Musical

He's been described as the most musical of all U.S. presidents, and Harry S. Truman was as outspoken about his musical tastes and abilities as he was about everything else. Truman had always taken to music. With the encouragement of his mother, he took piano lessons from the time he was eight until 16 or so. He enjoyed practicing, saying that it was pleasure, not work. Truman quipped that he hadn't pursued a musical career only "because I was not good enough."

Truman was particularly fond of the music of Mozart, Chopin, Liszt, Mendelssohn, and Debussy, but he also liked Bach's *Well-Tempered Clavier* and Gershwin's *Rhapsody in Blue*. He sometimes surprised people who asked him about particular favorites. In private, the President from the "Show-Me State" said of the popular Missouri Waltz, "I don't give a damn about it."

He particularly liked the "Pilgrims' Chorus" from Wagner's *Tannhauser* and "Toreador" from Bizet's *Carmen*. But, in the same breath, he would add the World War I hit "Hinky Dinky Parlez–Vous" and a ditty called "Dirty Gertie from Bizerte."

One frequent visitor to the White House noted that Truman seemed to find it hard to pass a piano anywhere without sitting down and playing it, no matter who was around. He played for Stalin and Churchill, he played for movie stars, he even played for concert pianists.

And yet, during his two terms, Truman held only one concert series in the White House. He had a good reason though. The place was unsafe. The upper floor of the building was so shaky that the Steinway of his daughter Margaret cracked it. And when pianist Eugene List played in the East Room, in 1947, the seating omitted a large area beneath a crystal chandelier because of the danger that the fixture might fall and kill somebody.

As much as he enjoyed playing the piano, for Harry Truman singing was a different matter. "I never sing," he said one time, "I'm saddest when I sing and so are those that listen to me."

August 2nd
Fundamental Differences

In the 1930's composer Erich Wolfgang Korngold was best known for his popular Hollywood film scores. His friend, Arnold Schoenberg, was known– or notorious–for his avant garde musical experiments. Korngold's son, George, recalled one lively argument between the two.

Despite their differences, Korngold was always glad to see Schoenberg because he liked the challenge of a good debate. On one occasion, Schoenberg, Korngold, and conductor Otto Klemperer were talking about serial music. Korngold disagreed with Schoenberg's contention that a series of notes played in reverse had the same theme as the original series.

Growing impatient with Korngold's resistance, Schoenberg held up a pencil and asked, "Erich, what's this in my hand?"

Korngold replied, "Obviously it's a pencil."

Schoenberg turned it upside down so that the eraser was at the bottom. "Now what is it?"

Korngold saw the trap. "It's still a pencil," he said, "but now you can't write with it."

Despite their disagreements, though, Korngold was an informed debater. One time, an exasperated Schoenberg asked, "Erich, do you like *any* of my music?" Much to his surprise, Korngold replied by going to the piano and playing from memory a series of little pieces that Schoenberg had written perhaps 30 years before.

On another occasion, Schoenberg came to see Korngold, at the movie studio. Schoenberg sat at the piano to wait. After five or ten minutes he began to doodle on a piece of music paper. When 20 minutes had passed he got up and told Korngold's son, "I can't wait any longer." He handed the young man the piece of paper and said, "This is for you." When Korngold saw it, he grinned. Schoenberg had written a double fugue that could be played regardless of which end of the paper you started from.

Arnold Schoenberg and Erich Korngold might have had their differences, but their friendship had a solid base–in music.

August 3rd

The Concert Storm

In 1852 the American educator Lowell Mason was traveling through Europe observing and reporting on musical life there. On the third of August he attended a concert of orchestral and choral music in Düsseldorf. He reported that music had to wait for a more powerful force:

The rehearsal being closed, the dinner hour and the hours devoted to smoking, drinking and the like–in the garden–having passed away, the company began to flock in at about four o'clock to attend the concert. At a little before five, when the building was filled, one of the most severe showers of rain and hail arose that we ever witnessed. The rain poured down in torrents, the rattling hail beat upon the apparently frail building, in which thousands were assembled, the lightning flashed and blazed in one almost continuous stream of fire, and the deep thunder roared loud and terrific.

To add, if possible, to the sublime chorus of nature, at the moment when the storm was raging most violently, the powerful voices of two thousand men were heard in the loud "Hurrah! Hurrah! Hurrah!" The rain began to find its way through the roof, umbrellas were spread, cloaks and shawls were wrapped around the elegantly-dressed but trembling ladies, the chill cold quickly succeeded heat, while the rattling of glass broken by hail-stones seemed to indicate the crash of the whole building in one common ruin.

But all was safe. Quickly the rain ceased, the winds were hushed, and amidst the retiring roll of the more distant thunder, violins, clarinets, and the various orchestral instruments were heard, seeming like the rainbow of promise, to proclaim that Music's welcome sun should soon shine brightly upon the waiting multitude.

August 4th

Mendelssohn's Summer Cooler

On August 4, 1834, Felix Mendelssohn was affected by the summer weather. He wrote to his parents from Düsseldorf:

For the past week, during which we've had heavy storms and muggy air, I felt so drained that I was unable to do anything all day long. Worst of all, I can't compose, which irks me no end. I don't care about anything other than eating and sleeping, except maybe for bathing and riding. My horse is a favorite with everyone I know, and his good nature has earned their respect. But he's very jumpy and when I was riding him recently during a storm every flash made him flinch so wildly that I felt sorry for him.

Not long ago we went on a horseback excursion to celebrate a lady's birthday, which we celebrated with wreaths of flowers, fireworks, shooting, a ball and so on. The route was as charming as ever, though different from what it was in spring. The apple tree, which was blooming in the spring, was now loaded with unripe green apples. And sometimes I was able to ride across the stubble fields and get into a shady wood via a side path.

We met several public coaches at precisely the same places and some of the very same flocks of sheep, and the same boisterous life at the blacksmith's forge, and a man in town was shaving himself just the same.

The next day I rode to Werden, a charming, secluded spot, where I wanted to inquire about an organ. The whole party rode with me there. Cherry tarts were handed to us from the carriages. We dined in the open air. I played fantasies and pieces by Bach on the organ to my heart's content.

Then I bathed in the Ruhr, so cool in the evening breeze that it was a real luxury. First of all I picked a place close to the water with high grass, in which large cut stones lay as if put there by some sultan to shade himself and his clothes. Close to the shore the water came up to my chin and the evening sun illuminated the green hills across the water. The little stream flowed quietly along, wonderfully cool and shady.

August 5th

The Unappreciative Guest

Theirs was one of the great friendships in musical history. In July 1859, Clara Schumann wrote to Johannes Brahms about people she had encountered in her musical adventures:

At last I can find a quiet moment for you, dear Johannes. Two days ago, I spent all day with Hiller. He played a large portion of Saul, canons with violin, solfeggios for three women's voices and so on. I'm told that he's again caught up in writing a grand tragic opera. My only hope is that this time it won't be tragic for him. I always feel so sorry for him with his constant efforts and such little reward.

And on August 5, she wrote about an unappreciative guest:

A thousand thanks, dear Johannes, for the letters and the package. Since the package took an entire week to get here, I wasn't able to play the serenade with Fräulein Wagner because she had already left. But I almost preferred playing it alone for myself to playing it with an amateur since I can enjoy music only with people who feel the same way I do about it.

I played very little for her since she didn't ask me to, and I couldn't offer to play for her a second time after having done it once. I don't think that it means much to her, and under such circumstances my inspiration evaporates. If I'm going to enjoy playing for people I need eager listeners and often you can read eagerness in their eyes.

But she's a very refined girl. I think I've already told you that she once played something for me She told me about your lovely Marienlieder. What are the words like? Have you started working on the German Dances again? And what about he quartet? I heard that you played it with Reimers at Frau Peterson's.

August 6th
The Mangled Serenade

It was no ordinary singing club. Its members paraded through the streets accompanied by 50 to 100 bodyguards. The extra muscle was necessary. When rival clubs clashed, they did more than sing–they fought.

America was being pulled apart by sectionalism, and the 1856 presidential contest was a hot one. Like the rest of America, Pittsburgh was swept up in politics, and its musicians were in the thick of the dispute between presidential contenders. On August 6, 1856, Stephen Foster jumped into the free-for-all by helping to form the Allegheny Buchanan Glee Club. Foster was to select musicians and solicit subscriptions to the club's concerts. But he would soon find out that singing would be the easiest part of what they did.

Returning to Pittsburgh after a rally in nearby East Liberty, the Allegheny Buchanan Glee Club stopped in Lawrenceville to serenade at a house of Buchanan sympathizers. Singer Billy Hamilton began a Foster tune and was quickly joined by a stranger in the crowd who was mangling the melody. The annoyed Hamilton asked one of the bodyguards to persuade the man to limit himself to the choruses. The bodyguard did so–by knocking the man to the ground, twice. The firemen headquartered across the street supported Buchanan's rival. They rushed into the serenade with fists flying. Billy Hamilton described what happened next:

Our peaceful body of serenaders was transformed into a howling mob. Foster, his brother, myself, and other vocalists hastened out of the crowd. We were all too small and had no business around where any fighting was going on. None of us were hurt, and few of the members of the guard suffered, but the firemen were completely routed and driven back into their headquarters. They had tackled the wrong crowd that time.

For better or worse, music and politics were thoroughly intertwined. Stephen Foster's candidate managed to win that no-holds-barred election of 1856.

August 7th

The Opera War

For the 1883 American season music agent James Mapelson wanted to beat out a new competing opera company so he dared to bring together two of the most temperamental singers in the world. He would soon find out that his biggest problem was not his competitor, but his two divas.

Mapelson already had a big star, Adelina Patti. He kept her with his company by paying her more than $5,000 per performance and providing her with a private railway car that cost $60,000 and included a solid silver bathtub and a key of 18-carat gold. For the new season Mapelson brought in a singer sought by his upstart competitor. She was Etelka Gerster, whom he took to be "a most admirable singer, and a charming woman into the bargain."

The strife began in Baltimore when Gerster noticed a playbill with Patti's name in bigger print than her own and admission prices that were higher than hers. Gerster fled on a train for New York, where Mapelson finally tracked her down and agreed to all of her demands. Then, in Chicago, Mapelson boldly cast both prima donnas in the same opera, *The Huguenots*. Confusion over bouquets led to Patti receiving most of the floral tributes after an act in which Gerster had done most of the singing. The audience responded by rewarding Gerster with a wild ovation, convincing a hysterical Patti that Mapelson had plotted against her. In St. Louis, Missouri Governor Thomas Crittenden stole a kiss from Patti, of which Gerster said, "There is nothing wrong in a man kissing a woman old enough to be his mother."

Patti went on to San Francisco, where her performance as Violetta in Verdi's *La Traviata* caused such a stir that the entire police force had to be called out to protect the theater. A journalist noted, "I doubt if twenty women in the house heard the music in the ballroom scene. La Diva treated the house to a view of as many of her diamonds as she could carry without being brought in on trestles."

A few months later the opera war ended when Patti and her husband sailed for Europe, taking with them the comforting proceeds from the contentious American season-fees totaling $250,000. And a battered Mapelson took satisfaction in having trounced his competitor, the fledgling Metropolitan Opera.

August 8th

The Request

It began as a congenial summer evening, but it didn't end that way. Franz Schubert and some fellow musicians had walked over to a suburb of Vienna to taste a new wine that Schubert liked. They moved on to a tavern and afterwards to a coffeehouse where they whiled away the hours with hot punch and a lively discussion about music.

At about one o'clock in the morning, two well-known musicians from the Vienna Opera orchestra came into the coffeehouse and, seeing Schubert, hurried over to him. The composer broke off his musical discussion as the musicians shook hands with him and paid him all kinds of compliments. It soon became clear that they wanted Schubert to write a composition for them so that they could have prominent solos in an upcoming concert. They were confident that Schubert would cooperate.

After they had asked him several times, Schubert said suddenly, "No. For you I'll write nothing."

That caught them off guard. "Nothing for us?" one of them asked.

"No way," Schubert said.

"How come? We're artists too—the best in Vienna."

"Artists!" Schubert tossed back his glass of punch and stood up. "Musical hacks is what you are! Period. One of you bites the brass stem of a wooden stick, the other blows his cheeks out on the horn. You call that art? It's a craft, a skill." He went on to toot his own horn, concluding, "I am not just a composer of Ländler, as the stupid newspapers say and stupid people repeat. I am Schubert, Franz Schubert!"

The next morning one of Schubert's companions found him in bed asleep, still wearing his glasses. Schubert was embarrassed about the encounter of the previous night, but not entirely apologetic. "The rogues," he said, "I'll write them the solos they want and they'll keep right on pestering me. I know how they operate."

August 9th
A Simple & Private Wedding

The pianist and composer Percy Grainger liked to do things in a big way. He was a showman, an eccentric, maybe even a madman when it came to music—and his own wedding.

The Australian-born Grainger had been in the United States for some time when the Swedish poet and painter Ella Viola Ström agreed to marry him. Perhaps not knowing just how flamboyant Grainger could be, Ella left the wedding arrangements to the groom. She was expecting a simple wedding attended by a small group of friends and, knowing nothing of America, she readily agreed when Grainger suggested the wedding take place at a spot called the Hollywood Bowl.

Grainger was slated to perform and conduct four concerts at the Bowl and he chose the second of them—August 9, 1928—as the setting for the wedding. The program was ethnically diverse, including "In a Mission Garden" by Grainger's protégée Fanny Dillon, "Pavane" by Gabriel Fauré, and "A Negro Rhapsody" by Rubin Goldmark.

Perhaps in honor of his Swedish bride, Grainger included the *Nordic Symphony* by Howard Hanson and—last on the program—Grainger's own composition "To a Nordic Princess."

It soon became clear to the bride that this event was not going to be the intimate gathering she had imagined. The orchestra was the biggest ever to perform at the Hollywood Bowl—126 musicians. After the wedding ceremony, the "guests"— about 20,000 of them—were entertained by an a capella choir on a stage bracketed by the Stars and Stripes and the British Union Jack. Screen star Ramon Novarro, who had attended the ceremony, posed with the couple for photographers.

No doubt the bride was beginning to realize that her life with Percy Grainger would be short on privacy and long on spectacle.

August 10th

Christ Suffered More Than You

On August 10, 1842, Mikhail Glinka and a few friends passed a pleasant evening playing a first run-through of his opera *Russlan and Ludmilla.* When the full-scale debut took place, the experience was not so congenial–as Glinka reports in his memoirs.

During rehearsals it became clear that cuts would have to be made–plenty of them–to keep the action from bogging down. The sets left something to be desired. A castle looked more like a barracks. Flowers painted at the sides of the stage were ugly and dull and smeared over with gold leaf. A banquet table was represented by a sort of pulpit that jutted out of the stage. Beside it was something resembling a spindly gilded bush. The set had become a snare for the actors.

The singers were cool to Glinka after a newspaper article attributed scathing criticisms of them to him. Equally offended, some of the musicians played badly. At the end of one of the last rehearsals a friend of Glinka's remarked, "My dear boy, it's bad." Glinka made more cuts.

On the night of the premiere the lead soprano got sick and had to be replaced by a less capable understudy. Glinka felt sick too, as he usually did on opening night, but he remained hopeful. As the opera progressed though, the audience became less and less enthusiastic. Before it was over, the czar's family left the theater.

When the curtain finally came down, the applause was lukewarm and there was some hissing–mostly from the stage and the orchestra. Nonetheless, some were calling for Glinka to take a bow. He turned to a friend in the director's box and asked if he should go out.

"Go right ahead," his friend replied. "Christ suffered more than you."

Although it would not soon be free of its critics, on its better nights, *Russlan and Ludmilla* began to win audiences over, and within a few years it became one of the most popular of all Russian operas.

August 11th
Love via Violin

Niccoló Paganini was one of the greatest violinists the world had ever known. He also knew how to win friends and influence people with a good gimmick. This is his account of an incident that occurred in 1807:

A charming lady and I had an interest in each other–an interest intensified by secrecy.

One day I promised her a surprise at the next concert– a little musical trick that would refer to our relationship. In the meantime, I announced to the court an entertaining novelty called "Amorous Scene" Everyone's curiosity was thoroughly piqued by the time I appeared with my violin–from which I had removed the two inner strings, leaving only the E and G strings.

The E string, I explained, represented the woman and the G string, the man. Then I started a kind of dialogue representing little arguments and a reconciliation between my two lovers. The strings first scolded, then sighed, lisped, groaned, teased, rejoiced, and voiced their ecstasy. The scene ended with a reconciliation and the two lovers performed a pas de deux, concluding with a dazzling coda.

This love scene received enthusiastic applause. The lady for whom I had devised it rewarded me with most affectionate glances.

The princess was in the audience. She was very gracious and generous with her compliments. Then she said, "Since you've already performed something so lovely on two strings, couldn't you favor us with something on one?"

I responded with the "Napoleon Sonata" for the G string, which I played before the assembled court. I received so much applause that a Cimarosa Cantata played afterward was completely upstaged.

August 12th

Or Else!

In the 1930's, the Great Depression was taking its toll on Arthur Fiedler's cherished Esplanade concerts of the Boston Pops. Wealthy patrons withdrew their support, and Fiedler had to take on the task of coming up with ways to keep the concerts funded. At the Esplanade, he had contribution boxes set up to invite audience members to contribute during the concerts.

But while the concerts drew bigger and bigger crowds, from night to night the boxes had less and less money in them. Fiedler faced the danger that the concerts might come to a halt.

One night in 1935, Fiedler realized that, unless he did something drastic, the end would come soon. After a concert that had drawn an audience of 15,000, the collection boxes brought in a paltry $23. In that dark hour, Fiedler put his showmanship to the test.

During the next night's concert, before a near-capacity audience, Fiedler tried a trick similar to what Joseph Haydn had done 150 earlier, to call attention to his musicians' need for a vacation. In the middle of the performance, one of the light bulbs in the orchestra shell blinked out. One of the violinists stood up, tucked his fiddle under his arm, and left the stage. Then a second light went out, and another musician departed. One by one, as the lights went out, the musicians took their leave, until only Fiedler remained, in near darkness, facing a stage full of empty chairs and abandoned music stands. Finally, he turned slowly, took an exaggerated bow, and left the stage.

Then the stunned crowd heard a voice over the public address system, informing them that the continuation of the Esplanade concerts was in their hands. They got the message. The next night's take from the collection boxes jumped to $485, and from then on, the future of the series was secure.

August 13th
How Veracini Broke His Leg

Music-making was highly competitive in the Baroque era. We have two accounts of Francesco Maria Veracini's last days at the court in Dresden. Both of them spell disaster.

Veracini was a world-famous violinist. He had come from Florence hoping to get a high-paying position at the Dresden court. According to one story written 63 years after the fact, King August wanted to hear Veracini play a violin concerto. The court concertmaster, Johann Georg Pisandel, suggested that Veracini give his audition concerto to the accompanist for rehearsing. But the self-assured Italian supposedly had no confidence in German musicians, and when the performance for the king went badly, Veracini blamed them.

Then, according to the story, Pisandel asked the king for permission to perform the same concerto with the violin part played by a German. Pisandel had a trick up his sleeve. He called on one of his least important violinists to perform the work—a player with whom he had secretly rehearsed the concerto. The king and the unwitting audience much preferred the German's performance.

An account written only a month after the incident corroborates what happened next. The humiliated Veracini sulked in his room for several days. Then, on August 13, 1722, he jumped from his second-floor window, landing 40 feet below in a Dresden street, breaking his leg and his hip. Veracini also wound up with a "considerable scar" on his head, and a limp that resulted from a hasty treatment.

One of his contemporaries was afraid that the violinist might never regain his good sense and blamed the incident partly on lack of sleep and partly on Veracini's "all too great application to music." But Veracini wasn't finished. He went on to Prague and London, where he retained the reputation as the greatest violinist of his time.

August 14th

An Appeal from the Destitute

War had depleted the treasury of Saxony, and the finest musicians in the land were living from hand to mouth. On August 14, 1651, Heinrich Schütz wrote a letter to Prince Christian on behalf of his suffering ensemble:

Most gracious lord, even though I am reluctant to bother a celebrated Prince with my repeated letters and reminders, I am forced to by constant restlessness hour after hour, by loud cries of despair, by the misery and complaints of the entire company of poor, neglected musicians of the Chapel, who are living in misery such as would make a stone in the ground burst into tears.

As God is my witness, their misery and pitiable complaints are like a stab in my heart since I don't know what comfort or hope of relief I can give them.

In happier times I would hardly have thought this possible, but most members of the company have made up their minds that rather than discrediting their gracious Lord by begging for bread, they will, from sheer necessity, depart. It's impossible for them to stay on and continue to suffer any longer. They will leave their debts to be paid by anyone willing to do it. They've had their fill of insults. Nobody will extend them credit, not for a single penny.

It's my duty to call this matter to the attention of Your Princely Highness and to point out that it would be sad if a company assembled with such care and effort should be broken up and scattered this way.

Therefore I ask most humbly that Your Princely Highness request His Serene Highness, as your dearly beloved Father, to permit a single quarter's salary to be paid to the company so that they might be kept together.

If Your Princely Highness should be unable to make some helpful arrangement, it would be impossible for me to hold the musicians longer. But at least I will have done my best.

August 15th

The Frenchman

It was a well-to-do Russian household, but one inclined toward pessimism and boredom, and the young French visitor was just what the doctor ordered. But it took a while for the lady of the house to warm to Claude Debussy.

In 1880 Debussy's teacher wrote him a letter of recommendation for employment in the household of a widow named Nadezhda von Meck, who was already the patroness of Tchaikovsky, whom she had never met. In the summer of 1880, the 18-year-old Debussy joined the von Meck family for a European tour, and in May of the following year, von Meck wrote to Tchaikovsky from her Ukrainian estate: "My little Frenchman is very eager to come here. I won't have the heart to turn him down even though I already have a pianist."

Once he arrived at the von Meck household, Madame von Meck was slow to be won over by him. In a letter to Tchaikovsky she praised Debussy's sight-reading, adding that he was quite taken with the music of Tchaikovsky. She and Debussy played piano four hands versions of Tchaikovsky's Fourth Symphony and *Orchestral Suite No. 1.*

His personality had something to do with Debussy finding acceptance with the von Meck family. In August of 1882, Madame von Meck wrote again to Tchaikovsky: "Yesterday my favorite Achille Debussy arrived to my great joy. Now I'll have plenty of music, and he brightens up the whole house. He's a Parisian from top to toe, very witty, and mimics Gounod, Thomas, and others very amusingly. He is so good-natured and content with everything and entertains everyone so much."

Von Meck's son Nicholas referred to "the little Frenchman...dark, slender, and sarcastic," who gave everybody funny nicknames. He called the plump tutor "the little vacationing hippopotamus." In appreciation of his clowning, the family dubbed Debussy "Petrouchka."

The teenaged Claude Debussy had finally become a hit with his host family.

August 16th

Seeing Through the Quirks

Sometimes it takes a great student to recognize a great teacher. One such teacher was Alexander Glazunov. It took some doing, but Dmitri Shostakovich discovered that Glazunov had something special to offer.

Shostakovich was a student at the Moscow Conservatory when he encountered Glazunov—a bulky man who sat far away at his desk while his students played the piano and waited for his critiques. Glazunov never interrupted and never left his desk. Once the student had finished playing, Glazunov would mutter something incoherent.

The students were reluctant to ask him to repeat what he had said and uncomfortable about moving closer in order to understand him. So they would repeat the work from beginning to end, making changes that they thought Glazunov might want. After the modified performance, the sedentary Glazunov would mutter even more softly and indistinctly. Assuming the lesson was over, the bewildered students would get up and leave.

At first Shostakovich was annoyed by Glazunov's remoteness, but after a while he figured out what was behind it. He noticed that Glazunov would occasionally grunt, lean over his desk, remain bent over for a while, and then—with some effort—straighten back up. Shostakovich determined that his teacher was drinking alcohol through a rubber tube, fortifying himself to get through the lessons.

Shostakovich figured out that the best way to tap into Glazunov's knowledge was to meet with him as often as possible at concerts and in private homes as well as at the Conservatory.

Most of all, Shostakovich gained from Glazunov an appreciation for early music at a time when most teachers felt that music began with Mozart. Josquin des Pres, Orlando di Lasso, Giovanni di Palestrina, and Domenico Gabrieli—Shostakovich learned to appreciate them all because he took the effort to get past the quirks of a great teacher.

August 17th

Wagner's Undignified Entrance

They got off to a bad start. In 1877 Richard Wagner was in England as guest conductor for a series of ten concerts. A large orchestra—nearly 200 Englishmen and Germans—was to begin rehearsing. The music for this first rehearsal was to be *Das Rheingold*. The English members of the orchestra waited for their first glimpse of the great Wagner, even though their long-time leader, the highly respected Hans Richter, was expected to do most of the conducting.

Then an unfortunate accident occured. As he entered the hall, Wagner walked past some kind of overhang that crushed his hat. Apparently unaware of the mishap, he strutted up to the orchestra with a haughty demeanor, unintentionally creating a comical first impression for the English members of the orchestra. The musicians closest to Wagner seemed to be too in awe of him to suggest that he remove his hat and punch it back into shape.

Trying to ignore the mysterious mirth of the Englishmen, Wagner raised his baton and began to conduct long, rolling arpeggios evocative of the Rhine. He soon got so swept away that he forgot about the baton and tried to conduct with his fingertip. The music came to grief. "*Schlect*," Wagner said, pacing back and forth, "Bad!" The Englishmen had a good chuckle.

The German leader of the second violins jumped up and rapped his bow on his music stand, saying "Is no tink to laugh!" The ivory tip of the bow flew off and hit another German in the face, and Englishmen and foreigners alike laughed aloud. Wagner was furious. Hans Richter led him from the room, trying to calm him down as the musicians gave way to complete merriment.

Richter returned without Wagner. He had a baton in his hand and said just two words: "Now, boys!" And, as if it were all one instrument, the orchestra began playing the soaring measures of *Das Rheingold*.

August 18th
Bruch's Liverpool Battle

By the summer of 1882, the German composer Max Bruch had been the Director of the Liverpool Philharmonic Society for two years. It had not been an entirely happy experience for Bruch. He was at odds with musicians who were past their prime, and at least one member of the women's chorus made a habit of ridiculing Bruch's conducting in a voice that could be heard by the audience in the front row. Bruch also objected to the huge sums paid to guest artists, singers in particular.

Bruch hoped to alleviate his situation by working with artists he knew and respected.

Among them was the pianist Ferdinand Hiller. Bruch wanted him to play a Mozart piano concerto in the opening concert of the 1882-83 season and offered Hiller a modest 50 pounds for a fee, and then had to withdraw the offer altogether when fees paid to singer Emma Albani and other prima donnas created a deficit.

Forced to withdraw the offer, Bruch wrote Hiller an angry, embarrassed letter:

Now it has been shown that these people–who generally understand as much about music as a donkey does about lute playing–had something else planned and no power in Heaven or Hell will compel them to change their plans and adopt ours. There are too many cooks on the committee and I don't have to tell you that they very often put too much salt in the porridge. I was so annoyed by the stupidity of these wretched cotton-merchants that I was unable to write to you until several days after the Committee meeting.

Bruch pinned his hopes on a generous offer from Edinburgh to direct a new conservatory to be established there–an offer that would enable him to leave Liverpool. But the Scottish plan fell through for lack of money, and Bruch's association with Scotland was to remain imaginary, taking the form of music inspired by Scottish tunes–most notably the popular *Scottish Fantasy*.

August 19th
Purcell Upstaged

The theater music of Henry Purcell is rich with ornamentation. It had to be, if it was going to match the elaborate special effects that graced the stage in 17th century London. The stage directions for the 1691 production of *Dioclesion* show that Purcell's music was constantly in danger of being upstaged:

While a symphony is playing a machine descends, so large it fills all the space from the frontispiece of the stage to the farther end of the house, and fixes itself by two ladders of clouds to the floor. In it are several stages representing the palaces of two gods and two goddesses. The first is the Palace of Flora–the columns of red and white marble breaking through the clouds, the columns–fluted and wreathed about with all sorts of flowerage, the pedestals and flutings enriched with gold. The last is the Palace of the Sun. It is supported on either side by rows of Termes* the lower part white marble, the upper part gold.

The whole object is terminated with a glowing cloud on which is a Chair of State, all of gold, the sun breaking through the cloud and making glory about it. As this descends, there rises from under the stage a pleasant prospect of a noble garden consisting of fountains and orange trees set in large vases. The middle walk leads to a palace at great distance.

Then the actors came in–gods, goddesses, fauns, nymphs, shepherds and shepherdesses, as well as singers and dancers. And that was just the beginning. At one point in the drama the special effects included distant thunder created by a channel with steps through which cannon balls were rolled. Close thunder came from a closed box filled with rocks tipped from side to side. Wind came from a machine said to be so ingenious that its design has changed little from Purcell's time to our own. In Act Three, figures embroidered on tapestries stepped out and danced, then sat on chairs which, in turn, slipped out and joined in the dancing.

One other phenomenon occasionally overshadowed Purcell's music–the tendency of some audience members to climb on stage and participate in the plays.

* The god of boundaries

August 20th

Donizetti vs. the Dilettantes

Writing an opera may be the simplest step in its production—when the staging is left to a committee.

In 1834 Gaetano Donizetti signed a contract with the management of the Royal Theaters of Naples to write three operas. The theaters in Naples were under new management—a committee of aristocratic dilettantes who called themselves the Society of Industry and Fine Arts. According to the contract, the Society would choose the plots and librettists for the operas, with Donizetti's agreement. The Society would turn the completed librettos over to the censors for approval, and finally pass them on to Donizetti at least four months before each opera was to be produced.

For the first of the three operas, Donizetti chose a story based on Sir Walter Scott's 1819 novel *The Bride of Lammermoor*, to be produced in July 1835. Donizetti recommended poet Salvatore Cammarano as the librettist. Repeatedly. Time passed. At the end of May, the Society finally got around to approving Donizetti's choice. Donizetti met with his librettist at once and the two agreed immediately on the subject of the opera. Donizetti fired off an impatient letter telling the Society that if they didn't authorize the librettist to go to work at once, he would enforce the terms of the contract and cancel the whole arrangement.

The theater commission must have acted quickly for once because Donizetti and his librettist began working feverishly at the end of May and completed the entire opera by July 6. Donizetti wrote to a friend that he expected the opera to be produced by August 20. But August 20 came and went without so much as a rehearsal. The Society was in such a state of disarray that finally the King of Naples himself intervened, firing the directors and appointing new ones.

At the end of September, when the opera was performed at last, the composer had a chance to forget his frustrations with the Society. He enjoyed one of the finest triumphs the theater had ever seen. The audience was moved from tears to wild applause as they called Donizetti on stage time and again in honor of his greatest success, *Lucia di Lammermoor.*

August 21st

Keen Hearing

The farmer tramping over his grounds in Medfield, Massachusetts, had a keen ear for nature that served him well in his other job as one of America's leading composers.

Charles Martin Loeffler had come to America from Alsace in 1881 at the age of 20. For 20 years he played in the first violin section of the Boston Symphony, then devoted himself to composing and farming. One friend recounts that Loeffler's sense of nature was as keen as his ear for music. Walking through his woods immersed in conversation, the composer would break off in mid-sentence and whisper, "see that fox!" Or, passing a pond, take his companion by the arm and say, "watch that turtle raise his head."

Loeffler's friend recalled that on a hot summer day in 1914, the composer and his wife and friends were gathered around the dinner table when Loeffler jumped up and said, "Listen to that bird! She's in distress—it must be a snake!" A hasty investigation found the bird fluttering frantically at the front door, which was adorned with leafy vines that hid a nest full of young birds. One of Loeffler's helpers reached into the vine and pulled out a long black snake. Once the snake had been killed, the mother bird flew back to comfort her agitated brood.

On one occasion, however, Leffler's hearing was not so acute. Word had it that a band of gypsies had been stealing things in the neighborhood. Loeffler swore that he would shoot the first trespasser he encountered on his property. On a still and moonless night, he was awakened by the sound of hooves on the road that approached his house. Loeffler jumped from his bed, gun in hand, leaned out of the open window, and shouted at the unseen intruders, commanding them to respond at once and turn back or be shot. On cue, out of the darkness, came the reply—a long, familiar *moo*.

Maybe it was keen senses—plus a touch of imagination—that enabled Charles Martin Loeffler to become one of America's great composers.

August 22nd
Both Sides

Was it just the review or did something bigger break up a major musical friendship? One way or the other, in 1952, a music critic for the *New York Tribune* helped to widen the gap between the American composer John Cage and the French conductor and composer Pierre Boulez.

The reviewer, Peggy Glanville-Hicks, was a conservative composer, but after a Greenwich Village concert, she made a distinction between the avant-garde writing of Cage and the style of Boulez. She referred to "the real impression of the real poetry that Cage's scores create."

On the other hand, Glanville-Hicks described a sonata by Boulez as "chaos, organized, stabilized chaos," without the joy of life that's evident even in the most dissonant American pieces. She added that the works of Boulez and other European avant garde composers emphasized "acidity," as if it were their only aim.

Before the review, Boulez and Cage had been friends. After it, Boulez would have nothing further to do with Cage. But from the start, contrasting temperaments had put a strain in their relationship. Cage had been living on pennies ever since his arrival in New York, but tried to give his poverty a kind of gentility. As a visitor to New York, Boulez expected everything to be elegant and was annoyed when Cage's car ran out of gas during a return trip from Cape Cod. Cage took Boulez to a diner in Providence and Boulez complained about the food and the service and wanted to get up and walk out.

For his part, Boulez later dismissed Cage as "refreshing, but not very bright," adding, "his freshness came from an absence of knowledge."

The friendship between Pierre Boulez and John Cage, shaky from the start, never did recover from the review that favored the American over the Frenchman.

August 23rd
Chabrier the Dazzling Pianist

Emmanuel Chabrier wrote some of the 19th century's most colorful music. Intentionally or not, he was also one of the century's most colorful performers.

The composer's friend, Alfred Bruneau described him this way:

He played the piano as nobody had ever played it before or ever will play it. The sight of Chabrier in a drawing-room full of elegantly-dressed women, approaching the delicate instrument and then playing his "España" in a flash of broken strings, hammers reduced to pulp and shattered keys, was indescribably amusing, and a spectacle of genuinely epic splendor.

Another friend of Chabrier's was painter Auguste Renoir. Renoir's wife, Alice Charigot, was an amateur pianist and left this impression of Chabrier's piano playing:

One day Chabrier came and played his "España" for me. It sounded as if a hurricane had been turned loose. He pounded the keyboard relentlessly. While he was playing I chanced to look into the street. It was full of people and they were listening, enthralled. When Chabrier reached the last thundering chords, I vowed to myself that I would never touch the piano again. As for Chabrier, he had knocked the piano out of action.

At a Paris club, Chabrier was well known for his ability to improvise. Someone would show him a newspaper account of a crime or accident and Chabrier would start to sing it out at the piano, creating an atmosphere of suspense and terror, complete with the pursuit, apprehension, and punishment of the criminal.

Once when Chabrier's playing had drawn a street-side audience beneath his open window, someone declared, "if I were your landlord, I would be so proud that I would offer you your rooms rent-free."

Emmanuel Chabrier, who had more to give than the piano could take, won with his playing the affection of friends and strangers alike.

August 24th
The Traffic Victim

The six-year old had been hit by a car on a Manhattan street and dragged for a block. She was in a coma for 12 days. During her 23 days in the hospital, she wasn't expected to live. But she survived, determined to overcome any obstacle between her and what she wanted.

What she wanted was to become a singer–a great singer–and there were major obstacles in her way. The Depression had kept her Greek-born family unsettled. In eight years they had moved nine times in the Hell's Kitchen section of Manhattan. The girl's mother was ambitious, neurotic, and eager to find success through her talented daughter.

The girl loved classical records and made weekly pilgrimages to the public library to listen to them. At age eight she began taking singing lessons. By age nine she was the star of recitals at Public School 164. At ten she knew Bizet's Opera *Carmen* by heart and could point out errors in Metropolitan Opera broadcasts.

Only when she was singing did she feel loved, and she pursued her career with a passion. At 11, listening to Lily Pons performing at the Metropolitan she declared, "One day I'm going to be a star myself–a bigger one than she is."

It became true in more ways than one. She accepted food as a substitute for affection, and by the time she was a teenager, she stood five feet, eight inches tall and weighed 200 pounds. When she graduated from eighth grade, her parents separated and she moved to Athens with her mother and sister. She was two years too young for the prestigious Royal Academy of Music, but her size made it easy for her to lie about her age. Within five years she had made her professional debut as *Tosca*.

Soon she became world famous, but not by her long Greek name, Maria Kalogeropoulos. She had long since shortened it to Maria Callas.

August 25th

Mute Rebellion

Daniel François Esprit Auber was so shy that he couldn't conduct his own music and was known to flee upon hearing it. And yet he's credited with starting a revolution.

In 1828 Auber's opera *Masaniello* or *La Muette di Portici* was such a hit in Paris that its use of local color, crowd scenes, and revolution began an era of grand opera in France. The libretto by Eugène Scribe and Germaine Delavigne was based on history–the Neapolitan insurrection of 1647. The opera tells the story of the fisherman Masaniello whose mute sister Fanella has been imprisoned by her seducer, Alfonso, son of the Spanish ruler of Naples. Hearing of his sister's imprisonment, Masaniello swears vengeance against the Spanish oppressors, He leads a successful revolt and is offered the crown, but the story ends tragically with the deaths of Fanella and Masaniello.

When the opera, with its tale of oppression, captivity, and revolt was performed in Brussels on August 25, 1830, it literally took the country by storm.

For 15 years, Belgium had been forcefully united with the Netherlands, even though the two countries had contrasting traditions and religions and conflicting interests. Auber's opera was like a match to gunpowder. Riots led to insurrection. The military leader of the Belgians was Charles Rogier. Like Masaniello he became the political leader of the country after a successful revolution, although his tenure as prime minister was longer and happier. Within a year of the revolt, the Belgians wrote a constitution and elected Prince Leopold of Saxe-Coburg to be the first king of an independent Belgium.

Auber wrote at least one more grand opera on a historical theme, *Gustav III*, but he never equaled the daring spirit of *Masaniello*, and to this day the reputation of the shy composer rests mostly on his comic operas.

August 26th

Mahler in Vienna

They were an irresistible force and an immovable object. The innovative young conductor named Gustav Mahler and the tradition-bound musical establishment of Vienna.

Mahler assumed the directorship of the Vienna Philharmonic in 1898. He was dedicated to conducting music for the time in which he lived, and within a year his performances of Beethoven's Fifth and Ninth Symphonies were raising cries of treason from his critics. One of them wrote of Mahler's barbarism in re-orchestrating many passages in Beethoven's Ninth against the clearly expressed intention of the composer. Mahler persisted, presenting Beethoven's music as he thought Beethoven would want it played had he lived at the end of the 19th century. He led a performance of Beethoven's F Minor Quartet as played by the entire string section of the Vienna Philharmonic. To his vociferous critics, Mahler replied that the concert hall demanded a larger sound than a string quartet could provide. Then he turned the idea around and added that if he were conducting Wagner's Ring Cycle in a small room he would reduce the size of the orchestra.

The result of all the publicity? Mahler became the sensation of Vienna. He continued on his collision course with the musical establishment. He concluded that Beethoven's deafness and the limitations of early 19th century instruments had kept Beethoven from doing full justice to his visions. He wrote in response to his critics that not to use the best instruments available would be an outrage against Beethoven. In short, Mahler said that he was performing Beethoven as the composer would have intended had the Vienna Philharmonic been available in his day.

By now, even the orchestra wasn't sure what Mahler's intentions were. A final confrontation between Mahler and his critics seemed certain. But suddenly the conductor's health forced him to leave Vienna in mid-season. Mahler's letter of resignation was little more than a formality. This time the immovable object had prevailed. But Gustav Mahler would endure as the foremost symphonist of the 20th century, his works performed many times over by the great orchestras of the world, including the once contrary Vienna Philharmonic.

August 27th
Gustav Holst & Thomas Hardy

Although he's best remembered for his orchestral suite, *The Planets*, the English composer Gustav Holst liked nothing better than the down-to-earth pleasure of a long walking tour. In the summer of 1927, he took a train from London to Bristol, then set out on foot for Dorchester to visit the celebrated author Thomas Hardy.

Holst had admired Hardy for years. Twenty-five years earlier Holst had written settings of three poems by Hardy. In 1922 he had finally met Hardy for the first time, though not without comic effect. Holst had been on a two-day walking tour and wore an old Panama hat and his customary thick glasses. When he presented himself at Hardy's door the author's wife remarked, "Oh, Mr. Hardy never sees photographers."

Prior to the 1927 visit, Holst had written Hardy to tell him that he was working on an orchestral piece, *Egdon Heath*, inspired by repeated readings of the first chapter of Hardy's novel *The Return of the Native*. Holst added that the music was also a product of his walks over the Wessex countryside that Hardy described so effectively.

Four days after setting out from Bristol, Holst arrived in Dorchester. The next day they toured the surrounding heath land by car. Hardy professed to know nothing of music, so Holst was surprised to find that Hardy had heard *Egdon Heath* on gramophone records. He was even more surprised when he found out that the gramophone records belonged to another English author, one who had been stationed at Royal Tank Corps depot nearby. The author was T.E. Lawrance—better known as Lawrence of Arabia.

The visit had a lifelong impact on Holst. Years later, when he was lecturing on Haydn, he compared the character of Haydn with that of Thomas Hardy. "There was a wealth of experience of town and country," he said, "deep and controlled emotion, wisdom and humor, all clothed in perfect courtesy and kindliness."

August 28th
The Infamous Boléro

A composer's best-known work is not necessarily his personal favorite. Consider the case of Maurice Ravel and the infamous *Boléro*.

Boléro owes its existence to a disappointment. In the summer of 1928 Ravel was planning to orchestrate some of Isaac Albéniz' piano pieces from the suite *Ibéria*. His idea was to turn them into ballet music for the famous dancer Ida Rubinstein. A friend informed Ravel that Albéniz' pieces had already been orchestrated for a ballet. "My whole summer's ruined," Ravel declared. "Orchestrating *Ibéria* was going to be so much fun. What am I going to tell Ida? She'll be furious."

A few weeks later, Ravel wrote to his friend that he was working on something unusual. "No form in the true sense of the word," he wrote. "No development, barely any modulation." The piece was *Boléro*. Ravel was surprised and somewhat annoyed at the popularity of *Boléro*. He suspected that its obsessive quality and sexual undertones were responsible for the success. After the first performance, Ravel's brother Eduoard told the composer that he had seen an old lady in the audience, shouting above the applause, "Rubbish! Rubbish!" To which Ravel replied, "That old lady got the message."

Ravel didn't grow any fonder of the piece. It had already flopped as a ballet when Arturo Toscanini conducted it in a performance by the New York Philharmonic with a tempo much faster than Ravel's. The composer was so annoyed that he wouldn't even stand up when Toscanini tried to get him to take a bow. Ravel went backstage and told Toscanini, "It was too fast." To which the conductor replied, "It was the only way to save the work."

To composer Arthur Honegger, Ravel would later say, "I've written only one masterpiece–*Boléro*. Unfortunately it has no music in it." Sometime later conductor Paul Paray and Ravel were at the casino in Monte-Carlo and Paray asked Ravel if he'd like to try his hand at gambling. Ravel declined. "I wrote *Boléro* and won," he said. "I'll let it go at that."

To this day, Ravel's most popular piece is his much-maligned *Boléro*.

August 29th
A Glorious Secret

In 1792 Domenico Cimarosa's friend and patron, Emperor Leopold II of Austria, appointed him music director with a salary of about $450,000 and a princely apartment in the royal palace. Now he wanted Cimarosa to write a comic opera.

The Emperor put the court poet on the project and the result was a libretto based on an English play, *The Clandestine Marriage* by George Coleman the Elder and David Garrick. The librettist called his adaptation *Il Matrimonio Segreto*. Cimarosa took to the story right away, but because he was preoccupied with an international treaty, the Emperor wasn't able to attend the debut. At the second performance, though, he made up for lost time, as an eyewitness related:

When the Emperor attended an opera, it was customary for the audience to withhold their applause until the Emperor gave his sign of approval. At the end of Cimarosa's opera the Emperor stood up and said in a loud voice, "Bravo, Cimarosa! Bravissimo! Everything is wonderful, charming, captivating!" Then he said something that must have surprised everyone. "I'm not applauding because I don't want to forget a single note of this, your masterpiece. Now you have to do two things and you can't sleep until you've done both of them. The singers and instrumentalists have to come to my banqueting hall and you, Cimnarosa, must come and preside over the banquet prepared by my order."

Then he added the real surprise, saying, "After a short rest, you've got to do it all over again, an encore of the entire opera that you performed so well. And now I give you the applause you deserve."

The Emperor clapped his hands, setting off a barrage of bravos.

After the banquet, the Emperor presented Domenico Cimarosa with the equivalent of $75,000, and for a century, *Il Matrimonio Segreto* remained one of the most popular operas in the repertory.

August 30th
Victim of History

Composers are often involved in major historical events. In the case of Claude Goudimel, the historical event was fatal.

Goudimel was a well-known composer and music theorist of the 1550's and '60's. He was born in Besançon about 1510 and studied at the University of Paris, where he published a book of songs in 1551. During the next seven years, he published songs, psalms, motets, and masses.

In 1557 Goudimel's life took a turn. He moved to the city of Metz, which had a large population of Protestants—or Huguenots as they were known in France. During his ten years there, Goudimel converted to Protestantism. There he collaborated with the poet and dramatist Louis des Masures on a complete psalter—a setting of the Book of Psalms. His later psalm settings would become the basis of his lasting reputation. About 1567, Goudimel left Metz and eventually settled in Lyons. He began corresponding with the humanist poet Paul Schede. They would exchange letters for the rest of Goudimel's life.

The mid-1500's were a time of tension between French Roman Catholics and Protestants. In 1562 a civil war had begun between the two factions. It raged for eight years.

A treaty of 1570 granted the Huguenots freedom. But Catherine di Medicis, the mother of King Charles IX, initiated a plot to assassinate Protestant leaders. She convinced Charles that the Huguenots would attack the palace and might even kill him. The king is said to have replied, "Kill every one of them so that not a single one will be left to accuse me."

On August 24, 1572, the killings began in Paris. Clashes flared in cities across France. On August 23, Goudimel had written a letter to Paul Schede from Lyons. It would be his last. Sometime between August 27 and August 31, 1572, composer Claude Goudimel fell victim to what would become known as the St. Bartholomew's Day Massacre.

August 31st
Bartók's Medal

He became known for his turbulent modernism and became one of the most honored composers of the 20th century. But Béla Bartók was a modest, retiring man who was inclined to view honors with a sense of humor.

In the 1930's, as a member of the Congress of Humanistic Sciences, Bartók attended a meeting in Geneva. Included was a glittering dinner at the Hungarian ambassador's residence. Bartók took it in stride. He wrote:

There was only X-the Hungarian charge d'affairs, myself, and his wife–a detestable female. The ambassador's wife is American, speaks only American but makes a show of being Hungarian. There were such artfully crafted delicacies that I hardly remember eating anything like them. And yet the dinner was not enjoyable because, aside from the shrill shrieks of Mrs. X, these polished diplomats are artificial people, very unlike artists.

From Geneva, Bartók went to Mondsee to teach at a summer school–the Austrian-American Conservatory. The faculty was a distinguished group of musicians, but again the reality did not live up to the glamor of the place. Because of sloppy planning, most of the students didn't show up when the session started, and so the two women who had organized the school decided to study with Bartók. He wrote to his mother:

Now I have three regular pupils–three for piano, not bad, one for composition–passable, one only for harmony–all three girls, plus the old witches. A sixth wanted to study harmony with me, but didn't even know the scales well, and I said no to that!

At a reception for a visiting dignitary, faculty members were asked to wear their medals from the Legion of Honor. Bartók opened an old-fashioned coin purse, took out the decoration, and secretly offered it to a fellow faculty member. When asked why he was carrying the decoration in his coin purse, Bartók replied that his mother had put it there.

September 1st
The Symphonic Striptease

The Assyrian mural sculptures in the British Museum had a powerful hold on French composer Vincent d'Indy. They inspired him to write his most provocative work–a musical striptease called *Istar*.

D'Indy visited the museum in 1887 and became fascinated by the 2700-year-old carvings depicting Assyrian military campaigns and royal lion hunts. Delving further into Assyrian culture, he found the epic poem *Izdubar* and a story certain to appeal to concert goers. According to the ancient story, the goddess Istar–in order to win the release of her lover from the underworld–must remove one of her ornaments or garments as she comes to each of the seven doors of the Dark Abode. Finally, triumphant in her nakedness, she passes through the seventh door.

To tell the story, d'Indy employed a shrewd musical device. He wrote a theme and variations in reverse order, saving the bare statement of the basic theme for the end to represent the goddess in her nakedness. As she progresses through the seven doors, a rich impressionistic orchestration conjures the image of Istar provocatively adorned in emeralds and gold, with pearls in her hair.

The success of d'Indy's *Istar,* both as an orchestral piece in 1898 and later as ballet music, has raised questions about the composer and his times. Vincent d'Indy, after all, was considered a pillar of Roman Catholic conservatism at a time when traditional morality was being tested daily by French artists of all kinds. What would have prompted the respectable, prosperous composer to write such a scandalous piece of music?

A clue may lie in d'Indy's fondness for Gustave Flaubert's sensuous historical novel *Salammbo,* a literary reconstruction of ancient Carthage. Something about the cruel, barbaric civilizations of the ancient world appealed to the straight-laced d'Indy and many of his contemporaries, and with its dazzling orchestration and appeal to the repressed imagination, *Istar* might well have offered another welcome escape.

September 2nd
The English Musical Detectives

The two Englishmen were musical detectives. One of them, Sir George Grove, had taken a fancy to a rather obscure Viennese composer named Franz Schubert, and had conducted the few Schubert works that were in print, much to the delight of London audiences. A beautiful fragment of Schubert's music called *Rosamunde* fascinated Grove.

In 1867 Grove and a young friend set out for the Continent to look for the rest of the *Rosamunde* manuscript. Their search led them to Vienna to the publishing house run by a Herr Spina. Spina was a cordial host. He kept the two Englishmen well supplied with cigars, plus paper and pens for copying any manuscript that struck their fancy. He also gave them a letter of introduction to a relative of Schubert's, a doctor, in whose house they found a Schubert overture and two symphonies.

But the beautiful *Rosamunde* continued to elude them. Herr Spina turned the publishing house upside down, opening half-forgotten drawers and musty cupboards, stacking up bundles of old manuscripts without success. Discouraged, the Englishmen concluded that a complete score to *Rosamunde* might never have existed, or that Schubert had lost it. Reluctantly they decided to leave Vienna.

They went to say good-bye to the doctor. The subject of the elusive *Rosamunde* came up. The doctor thought that at one time he had owned a copy of the entire music. The young Englishman asked if he might go into the cupboard for one last search. The doctor said, "By all means, if you don't mind being choked with dust." As he dug into the farthest corner of the cupboard, the young man found a bundle of music books nearly two feet high and practically black from almost half a century of dust. It was the long-lost *Rosamunde*, wrapped up after the second performance in December 1823 and untouched since.

The discovery was a major accomplishment for the 25-year-old Englishman, but within a decade he would become far better known for something else—his collaborations with a poet named William S. Gilbert. And few would remember that the discoverer of Schubert masterpieces was Sir Arthur Sullivan.

September 3rd
The Casualty

On September 3, 1914, a German cavalry unit approached a French country estate. The owner of the estate, who had been working in his upstairs study, was not one to accept the encroachment without a struggle. He was a composer named Albéric Magnard and he was about to cross the line from civilian to combatant.

Magnard had never been one to bend easily. He grew up in wealth, comfort, and success—disdainful, aloof and humorless. At his father's expense, he traveled widely before settling down to attend law school. By the time he got his degree in 1887, though, Magnard had decided to devote his time to music even though he hadn't yet shown any particular musical aptitude. During a year at the Paris Conservatory, he studied composition with the distinguished opera composer Jules Massenet, who seems to have had no great effect upon him.

More influential were Vincent d'Indy, with whom Magnard studied for four years, and César Franck. During his years of apprenticeship, Magnard wrote two symphonies, had an opera performed in Brussels without acclaim, and composed a series of seven *Promenades* for piano that evoke a walking tour of Paris.

In 1894, when his father died, Magnard turned inward, concentrating not on pleasing an audience, but on pursuing his ideals of artistic truth and form. He published most of his works at his own expense and met with scant response, heightening his sense of artistic failure and his disillusionment with his surroundings.

That was the man who watched from an upstairs window as the German soldiers approached his country house. He shot, killing two of them. The Germans shot back, killing the composer, and then set the house on fire, destroying his latest work, a set of 12 songs.

The personality of the ill-fated Albéric Magnard might be best expressed in his chamber music, which has been described as "uniformly intense and severe."

September 4th

Granados' Food Fight

They were the most distinguished composers in Spain—Enrique Granados, Isaac Albéniz, Pablo de Sarasate, and Enrique Arbós. During summers in the 1890's, they met occasionally at a music shop in San Sebatián, where they engaged in small talk and put on informal concerts. One of the concerts turned out to be so informal that it degenerated into a food fight.

The trouble began with a suggestion by Granados. His idea was that he and his colleagues would form an orchestra in which each of them would play an instrument about which he knew nothing. The result—a famous singer became an extremely amateur violinist, Albeniz—best known as a pianist—grappled with a wind instrument. Granados played on comb and paper or conducted, depending upon his whim. The ungainly ensemble rehearsed on the open patio behind the music shop. And though they did their best to remain discrete, stories about the orchestra quickly circulated, so that before long the king himself had heard about it and asked about its progress.

The progress, apparently, was not encouraging. The residents of the area adjacent to the patio were mostly cooks and domestic servants. And one day, as Granados was conducting the group in a performance of a full-fledged symphony, the neighbors decided that they had heard enough. At first the orchestra may have thought they were feeling rain, but when they looked up, they saw a cloudless sky. As they played on, the blue sky opened up with a downpour of rotten fruit, eggs, vegetable peels and other household debris.

Granados kept right on conducting, despite the deluge and an increasing racket of shouts and catcalls and the banging of trays and kitchen utensils, and the battered orchestra stayed with him until, at last , he swept his arms in a final gesture. Then he bowed ceremoniously to the right and to the left and retired in a dignified manner although his clothes were caked with garbage and completely ruined.

It had been one of the less glamorous concert appearances of the eminent Spanish composer—and occasional conductor—Enrique Granados.

September 5th

Royal Concert

They made music for the most important personages in France, and François Couperin entered their circle of musicians by means of a simple deception.

Couperin came from a respected musical family, and he attained the highest possible musical positions in the French court in the time of King Louis XIV. Couperin gave harpsichord lessons to noble patrons and performed every Sunday for the King, either as a soloist or as a member of the most prestigious ensembles in France.

Music was such a part of King Louis' court that concerts by the same group of performers were a part of the daily routine. A typical concert would include two performers who, like Couperin, were also composers, Robert de Visée as lutenist and Jean-Féry Rebel playing the violin. Two of the best flutists of the day rounded out the group.

An account from the summer of 1702 describes how King Louis enjoyed music after a day largely given over to wolf-hunting.

Supper was served at seven o'clock. When it was over, two ladies, one of them Couperin's niece, performed music from operas while the composer accompanied on the spinet. After the nobles had played a game of cards, a distinguished instrumental ensemble performed, and the party broke up at midnight, when the King retired.

For the next day's concert, the two ladies sang a motet, again accompanied by Couperin. Dinner was served at one o'clock, after which the musicians played until ten, when a supper including many delicacies was served on two large tables. After supper, the musicians played again while Couperin again accompanied his niece's performance of recitatives from early operas.

François Couperin helped to define the sound of French music, even though he had first gained attention at the court of King Louis through a series of sonatas that he had written under a fashionable *Italian* name.

September 6th

The Apprentice Murderer

Even a masterpiece isn't finished until the "customer" is satisfied–as a poet named Carlo Goldoni relates in an account from 1735:

Antonio Vivaldi was desperate for a poet to revise–murder actually–a drama so that he could include the arias that his pupil had sung on other occasions and, being assigned the task by a noble patron, I introduced myself to him.

Vivaldi received me rather coldly. He took me for a novice, which I was, and judging me incapable of wrecking dramas, made it clear that he wanted me to get lost. When I all but begged him to give me a chance he smiled sympathetically and showed me a libretto.

"See this?" he said. "This opera is first-rate. The part for the leading lady couldn't be better, but certain changes have to be made. If you know the rules–but how could you know them? Here for example, after this tender scene, there's a cantabile aria, but since the leading lady doesn't like this kind of aria she couldn't sing it, so we need an action aria to express passion."

"I see," I said. "Well, I'll try to satisfy you. Please give me the libretto."

"I need it back," Vivaldi said. "How soon can you return it?"

"Right away," I said, "please just give me a piece of paper and an inkstand."

"What?" he said. "You think an opera aria is as simple as one in an intermezzo?"

I was starting to get a little hot under the collar. "Look, just let me have the ink well," I said, taking a letter from my pocket and tearing off a piece of it.

Vivaldi softened. "Please don't be offended. Here, sit down at this desk and take as much time as you need."'

The result made Vivaldi so happy that he embraced Goldoni and hired him to "murder" other dramas for the sake of operatic success.

September 7th
Bizet, Citizen Soldier

Composer Georges Bizet was a patriot. But the Franco-Prussian War and the occupation of Paris by Prussian troops put his patriotism to the test. It was 1871, and France was on the brink of civil war. In a letter to his uncle, Bizet summarized the situation:

Thirty thousand men in Montmartre, Belleville, et cetera. Twenty-five thousand of whom gave up at the first gunfire. In Paris, three hundred thousand men, a disgrace never to be forgotten, three hundred thousand cowards. I should say two hundred and ninety-five thousand because about five thousand men—I was among them—went to offer their services to the government. Despite our small numbers, despite our defective weapons, despite the lack of ammunition, we would have gone into action—insane as that sounds.

They kept us waiting for eighteen hours. We saw not one superior officer, were not given a single order. At midnight some kind of staff officer showed up and advised us to go home.

Yesterday two of the Montmartre men called out to me, "Hey there, citizen, everything's hunky-dory. Liquidate the reactionaries and save the social order."

I said, "My lambs, have you thought of the Prussians?"

"What Prussians?"

"Why the Prussians from Prussia, for pity's sake. They'll be on our necks."

"No — this time we'll boot 'em out for you!"

I looked the fellow right in the eye and said, "Yes, but this time you'd better not turn tail and run." The expression on his face said that he knew I had him pegged.

A few weeks later, Bizet and his wife would flee the city.

September 8th

Behind the Scenes at Bayreuth

The Ring Cycle is one of the most massive undertakings in all of opera. Wagner's masterpiece requires complicated logistics on stage and behind the scenes, and its first performances at Bayreuth were not as dignified as the composer intended.

In August and September 1876, the Ring Cycle was performed three times in three weeks at Bayreuth. Wagner's final words of advice to the singers were posted in a notice backstage:

"Clarity! The big notes will take care of themselves. The small notes and their text are the main thing. Never address the audience directly. In monologues always look either up or down, never straight-ahead. Last wish—be kind to me, dear people!"

Despite the best efforts of the singers, the first performance of the first opera in the cycle, *Das Rheingold* was cursed by bad luck. Franz Betz—as Wotan—lost the all-important ring. During the first scene change a stagehand raised the backdrop too soon, revealing the back wall of the theater and people standing around in their shirt sleeves, much to the embarrassment of the singers.

At first Wagner was very upset, but the arrival of an important visitor soon put him in good spirits. It was Dom Pedro II, Emperor of Brazil, perhaps the only princely visitor to Bayreuth—other than Wagner's patron, King Ludwig—who was there for purely artistic, rather than social, reasons. But even Dom Pedro's experience at Bayreuth was a little awkward. Arriving in town unannounced, he was not given the appropriate accommodations at Ludwig's palace. Instead he had to put up at a local hotel, where—just like any other guest—he was asked to sign the register. After a slight pause, he dutifully listed his occupation as "emperor."

Meanwhile some of the most important composers of the day, including Saint-Saëns, Bruckner, Grieg and Tchaikovsky, were complaining about the wretched train service, price-gouging by the local innkeepers, and the difficulty of getting a meal in Bayreuth's crowded hotels and restaurants.

But by the end of third performance, King Ludwig was so taken with The Ring Cycle that he personally led the audience in a round of applause while Wagner bowed to all sides.

September 9th

From Dream to Nightmare

It was to be Edward Elgar's crowning work, but his oratorio *The Dream of Gerontius* gradually developed into a nightmare.

Preparations for the oratorio's premiere at the Birmingham Festival of 1900 went on for months with only occasional hints of disaster. The first warning sign came with the death of the choral director. His hastily chosen replacement was 70-year-old W.C. Stockley, called out of retirement to train the choir.

After attending a London orchestral rehearsal of the work, Elgar wrote that he was "ashamed of myself as author of *Gerontius*," and wondered if he would have the courage to attend that first performance.

Four days before the premiere, Elgar was invited to address the choir, but by now he was so tense that, instead of encouraging the singers, he accused them of turning his oratorio into a drawing-room ballad.

Three days before the premiere, he realized that he had underestimated the complexity of the score. He took the highly unusual step of calling another rehearsal—one that lasted six hours and left the chorus confused, tired, and frazzled.

One concertgoer described the resulting performance as "hideously out of tune." Eleven days later a publisher friend of Elgar's wrote that Stockley, the choral conductor, ought to have been "boiled and served on toast for having had the audience in purgatory for two hours." Nonetheless, his belief in the inherent beauty of Elgar's *Dream of Gerontius* never faltered.

September 10th

Anton Rubinstein's Reward

The virtuoso pianist Anton Rubinstein had heard plenty about the extremes of performing in America. In 1872 he decided to find out for himself. He knew the Americans liked showmanship, but Rubinstein vowed to avoid spectacle. He would give the Americans serious, straightforward music without gimmicks. He almost succeeded.

He came with violinist Henri Wieniawski, arriving in New York on a hot, hazy September day. Their host was piano manufacturer William Steinway, and Rubinstein was pleased with both the new Steinway Hall and the piano he was to use. On the night of Rubinstein's American debut, the hall was packed. People had come from as far as California for the performance. They stood on the stairs and on the steps that led to the street.

When Rubinstein hammered out the first notes of his *Piano Concerto in D Minor* the audience stood up and shouted. By the time he got to the middle of the concerto, the furor had died down but another problem arose. Rubinstein was trying to play a soft passage when, through the open window on the east side of the hall, there came an awful howling. At the same time, from the west, there was a repeated pounding and splintering. Rubinstein turned to the wings and looked at William Steinway beseechingly.

Steinway hurried outside and found the source of the pounding–a man chopping kindling. The howling was coming from another man's efforts to teach his dog to jump rope. Steinway bribed both men to lay off until after the concert.

At the close of the concert the audience went wild with praise. Rubinstein was presented with massive bouquets of roses and a silver wreath on a satin cushion. But, still annoyed by the dog-and-kindling incident, he remained remote and unsmiling. The next day, when he discovered another aspect of performing in America, he, no doubt, was smiling again.

He came to see Steinway. Lugging in a large, heavy canvas bag. he asked, "What am I going to do with all this money?" America had paid Anton Rubinstein generously in silver and gold.

September 11th

The Captive Composer

The trail goes from Cairo, Egypt, to Winston-Salem, North Carolina, to Montgomery County, Pennsylvania. It leads to one of America's most intriguing composers. His name was John Antes.

Antes spent his early years—the 1740's—near Philadelphia, and received his education in a Moravian boys' school in Bethlehem, Pennsylvania. In 1759 he built a violin—possibly the first made in America. He also crafted a viola and cello that may be the earliest of their kind made in America. In 1764, Antes went to Europe to serve the Moravian Church, which sent him to Egypt as a missionary.

His existence in Egypt might best be described as life-threatening. It resulted in a flogging and imprisonment ordered by a Turkish strongman who was trying to extort money from Antes. Perhaps as a distraction from that crippling experience, Antes began to write music—three string trios that were published in London in the 1780's after Antes settled there. The trios, published as Opus 3—there is no Opus 1 or 2—attracted the attention of Haydn during his stay in England in the early 1790's.

Although he composed about 25 short anthems for chorus, winds, strings and organ, Antes had long been a watchmaker by trade, and he set his mechanical aptitudes to the service of music. He produced a device to improve violin tuning. He developed a better keyboard hammer and violin bow. He invented a machine that could turn music pages for a performer.

Once he got out of Egypt, Antes spent the rest of his life in London, where he died in 1811 at the age of 71. But all of his manuscripts are in the archives of the Moravian Church at Bethlehem, Pennsylvania, and in Winston-Salem, North Carolina. His trios lay forgotten until the 1940's. And though he never returned to his native land and wrote his trios in Cairo, John Antes is credited with writing the first chamber works by an American-born composer.

September 12th

Admiration and Disdain

They were the three greatest Czech composers, and the relationship between two of them was less than friendly.

Leoš Janáček, the youngest of the three, admired one of the other two. He was drawn to the earthy, sensual, popular qualities of the music written by Antonín Dvořák. He also liked the classical basis of Dvořák's compositions and the purely musical, rather than literary, basis of his music.

As a young man, Janáček remarked that he had such an affinity for Dvořák that the older composer seemed to be taking the words from his mouth. Janáček's *Suite for String Orchestra* and *Idyll for String Orchestra* show the influence of Dvořák. Janáček sent the first draft of his opera *Sàrka* to Dvořák and made a revision based on Dvořák's criticism. He dedicated the opera and two other works to Dvořák.

While giving a lecture on Czech folk song, Janáček declared, "I am convinced that we have in Antonín Dvořák our one and only Czech composer."

Janáček's admiration for Dvořák had a dark side—a disdain for the other great Czech composer, Bedřich Smetana.

During the years when Janáček was director of the music school in Brno, the works of Smetana were rarely performed there. In 1882, when the school was invited to commemorate the hundredth performance of Smetana's celebrated opera *The Bartered Bride*, the school committee declined. Two years later Smetana died, but another two years passed before the school in Brno got around to putting on a memorial concert, which Janáček suggested should be low key, featuring only a chorus and a string quartet by Smetana.

Strong as it was, young Janáček's disdain for Smetana wasn't personal. Although he later had positive things to say about Smetana, Janáček simply felt that the older composer's music dramas, comic operas and symphonic poems were too artificial—and more German than they were Czech.

September 13th

Desperate Measures

San Francisco, 1865. Louis Moreau Gottschalk had an unusual problem. He had promised a concert featuring 14 pianists playing Wagner's march from *Tannhäuser*. One of them had gotten sick, and Gottschalk was hard-pressed to find a replacement. For his unusual problem he resorted to desperate measures.

The proprietor of the concert hall was sympathetic. He offered the services of his son. Gottschalk suggested a rehearsal, but the young man said it would he unnecessary since the march was so easy. He sat down at the piano, executed a noisy flourish, and launched into a horrific rendition of the piece. Gottschalk was appalled.

His piano tuner came up with a plan. The newcomer's piano was a vertical and the tuner removed its entire interior mechanism. "The keyboard remains," he told Gottschalk, "but I assure you there will be no more false notes."

Just before the concert, the young pianist requested a prominent position on stage. Gottschalk obligingly had the magic piano moved to center stage. He instructed his 14 pianists not to play the pianos before the first note of the concert, so as not to spoil the effect for the audience.

The *Tannhäuser* march began. Fourteen sets of hands went to the keys, producing a great crescendo of Wagner. The novice pianist was pouring everything he had into it, sweating conspicuosly as he impressed his friends in the audience, some of whom applauded and called out his name.

The audience demanded an encore, and this time the novice couldn't resist a few preliminary flourishes. No sound came out. He tried to get Gottschalk's attention. Hastily, Gottschalk gave the other pianists the downbeat.

In order to save appearances, the novice faked his way through the entire piece, although now there seemed to be some anger in his piano pounding.

At the end of the encore Gottschalk remarked wryly, "Very well done, gentlemen, but the effect was less than the first time."

September 14th
Old Borax

Bringing the great composer Antonín Dvořák to New York in the 1890's was one thing. Keeping him entertained once he was there was something else again, as critic James Huneker found out.

Mrs. Jeanette Thurber, the wife of a prominent New York greengrocer, brought Dvořák to America to direct her newly founded National Conservatory of Music. For after-hours amusements she turned Dvořák over to Huneker, who invited Dvořák to experience the American drink called the whiskey cocktail. Huneker observed that in reply Dvořák "nodded his head, that of an angry-looking bulldog with a beard. He scared me with his fierce Slavonic eyes." Huneker added, "but he was as mild-mannered a man as ever scuttled a pupil's counterpoint." Among themselves, the Americans referred to the composer as "Old Borax."

Huneker thought that the hard American liquor might agitate Dvořák's nerves, but the two set out on a tour of the "huge circle through the great thirst belt of central New York." Not being a heavy drinker, Huneker ordered a beer every time Dvořák had a cocktail. They spoke in German, Huneker taking comfort in finding a man whose accent and grammar were worse than his own.

As Dvořák was drinking his nineteenth cocktail, Huneker suggested that it might be time to get something to eat. Dvořák suggested instead that they go to the East Houston Street Bohemian Café and drink something called a Slivovich. "It warms you after much beer," he said.

Huneker begged off and never did get around to joining Dvořák at the café. "Such a man is as dangerous to a moderate drinker as a false beacon is to a shipwrecked sailor," he said later. "And he could drink as much in spirits as I could in the amber brew." Huneker told Mrs. Thurber that he was through piloting the composer around. The next time he encountered Old Borax at a Bohemian resort on the East Side, the American was careful to avoid him. Dvořák's American adventures continue....

September 15th

It's Very Strange Here

The Czech composer Antonín Dvořák wrote some of his best music during a stay in Spillville, Iowa. Part of his inspiration may have come from the excitement of new surroundings. He wrote to a friend in Bohemia on September 15, 1893:

The three months here in Spillville will be a happy memory for the rest of our lives. We enjoyed being here and were very happy, although the three months of heat were somewhat tedious. We were compensated, though, by being among our own people, our fellow Czechs, and that was a great joy. If it hadn't been for them, we wouldn't have come here in the first place.

Spillville is a completely Czech community, founded by a Bavarian German named Spielman, who dubbed the place Spillville. He died four years ago, and in the morning on my way to church I passed his grave, and odd ideas fill my head when I see the graves of so many Czechs who sleep their final sleep here. These people came here about forty years ago, the poorest of the poor, and after great suffering and striving they are quite well off here. I liked to mingle with the people and they like me too.

It's very strange here. Not many people and plenty of room. A farmer's nearest neighbor might be four miles away, especially on the prairies—I call them the Sahara. The only thing to see is acres and acres of fields and meadows. You don't encounter a soul. Everyone gets around on horseback. It's good to see the vast herds of cattle, which are out in the fields in summer and winter. Men go into the woods and meadows where the cows graze to milk them. So it's very wild here and sometimes very sad—sad to the point of desolation.

We recently took a trip to Omaha in the State of Nebraska. Omaha is 400 miles from here, and then we went to visit—guess who—Father Rynd whom I met on Czech Day in Chicago—and would you believe where—in the State of Minnesota, in the town of St. Paul, which is 400 miles from Nebraska.

September 16th

A Joke on Prokofiev

Sergei Prokofiev was known for his stubbornness. When he found himself at loggerheads with a strong-willed choreographer, something had to give.

In 1939 Prokofiev was attending rehearsals of his ballet *Romeo and Juliet*. He and the choreographer, L.M. Lavrovsky, were not seeing eye to eye. Lavrovsky wanted an opening dance for the ballet, and he asked Prokofiev to provide something but the composer refused. "You have to make do with what you've got," he said.

Lavrovsky could see by Prokofiev's face that it would be pointless to argue. So he hit on a plan. After the rehearsal, he went to a music store, searched through a stack of Prokofiev scores, and came up with Prokofiev's Second Piano Sonata. He began to use the scherzo in rehearsals, calling it "Morning Dance."

A few days later, knowing nothing of Lavrovsky's plan, Prokofiev walked into the theater and heard his Scherzo being used as dance music. "You have no right to do that!" he shouted. "I won't orchestrate it!"

"Then we'll have to play it on two pianos," Lavrovsky replied calmly.

Prokofiev got up and walked out. Several days passed. Lavrovsky began to think that he had gone too far, had offended the composer beyond repair. But finally Prokofiev showed up at the theater again. For a long time he watched the dancing without comment. Then suddenly he asked, "What did you do with that number—that piece you had the gall to call 'Morning Dance?'"

"I'm working hard on it," Lavrovsky told him.

"I'd like to see it performed," Prokofiev said.

Lavrovsky had his dancers go through it. Prokofiev sat down and played it on the piano. Then he got up, saying nothing. Lavrovsky, watching nervously, observed that he was making notes in a little book he always carried. The next day he received, without explanation, a copy of "Morning Dance" freshly scored for orchestra. The confrontation of two stubborn artists had resulted in a victory—for audiences of *Romeo and Juliet*.

September 17th

Berlioz vs. Cherubini

It was the meeting of two great composers—and it's a wonder no one got hurt.

In his memoirs, Hector Berlioz relates that Luigi Cherubini issued an order instructing men and women to enter the Paris Conservatory from opposite ends of the building. Unaware of the order, Berlioz went to the library one morning and entered the courtyard through the newly designated female door. Suddenly he found himself face to face with a servant who commanded him to turn back and enter through the other door. Instead Berlioz continued on to the library.

Cherubini came into the room trembling with rage. "So you are the man who dares to come in by the door I have forbidden you to enter," he said.

Berlioz explained that he was unaware of the order and would obey it next time.

"Next time! Next time!" Cherubini flared. "What are you doing here?"

"As you can see, sir, I'm studying Gluck's scores."

"And what are Gluck's scores to you, and who allows you to enter the library?"

Berlioz was starting to lose his temper. "Gluck's music is the most magnificent I know, and I need no one's permission to come here and study."

"I–I forbid you to come here."

"Well, I will anyway."

"What–what is your name?"

Berlioz was by now red with rage. "Sir, maybe you'll hear my name someday—but you won't hear it now."

"Seize him," Cherubini commanded his servant. "Seize him and take him away to prison!"

Then, to everyone's amazement, Cherubini and his servant chased Berlioz around the table—knocking over stools and reading desks. But Berlioz broke free and ran off, calling out, "You shall have neither me nor my name, and I'll soon be back to study Gluck's scores again!" It was a meeting of composers, yes, but a meeting of minds it was not.

September 18th
Robert & Clara

Twenty-seven-year-old Robert Schumann was a gifted composer. But the father of his 18-year-old fiancée, Clara Wieck, was unimpressed. Clara's father steadfastly refused permission for his daughter to marry. Schumann tried everything he could think of to make the marriage take place—including a meeting with Clara's father. On September 18, 1837, He wrote to Clara:

My meeting with your father was awful. Such coldness. Such ill will. Such spite. He has a new way of destroying a person. He sticks the knife into your heart up to the hilt.

You'll have to be very strong, stronger than you can imagine, because your father gave me the terrible feeling that nothing will move him. You must fear everything from him. He will overpower you by force if not by trickery. So fear everything!

Today I feel so dead, so humiliated, that it's all I can do to take hold of one beautiful thought. Even your image eludes me, so that I can barely remember your eyes. I haven't become so disheartened that I'm able to give you up, but I feel so bitter and so violated to have my most sacred sentiments reduced to the level of the commonplace.

I try to find some excuse for your father because I've always taken him for an honorable, kind man. Vainly I try to see in his refusal some finer, deeper motive—such as being afraid that your art will suffer if you are engaged too soon, that you are altogether too young and so on.

But it's nothing like that—believe me. He'll throw you to the first suitor who has enough money and status. His highest goal is giving concerts and traveling. His oppression of you breaks my desire to bring beautiful things into the world. He laughs at all your tears.

September 19th

First Meeting

In the fall of 1913, when Robert Nichols was in his first term at Oxford, a friend said, "there's a chap in the house you ought to know. An extraordinary chap–plays the pianola, the piano and all that. In fact, I think he's a what-d'you call it– a musician."

Nichols was eager to meet someone his own age that shared his interest in music. He wanted to see the student at once, but his friend warned, "He might not be in the right mood." Nichols was not to be put off though, so even though his friend warned Nichols that the musician was a bit peculiar, they went to see him. They found him behind the sofa, looking downhearted.

"Go away," said the musician, whose name was Peter Heseltine. "I don't want to see you. Go away." Nichols saw a manuscript on the piano, settings of poetry by William Butler Yeats. He remarked proudly that he, too, was a poet.

Heseltine got up and asked him if he'd ever heard of Frederick Delius. "No," was the answer. "Who's he?"

"The greatest living composer," replied Heseltine, tucking away his manuscript while getting into a discussion about the merits of Delius. Nichols cajoled Heseltine into playing something by him and praised the harmonies as pleasantly unexpected.

"Well, Delius has developed all that," Heseltine said. He described the way Delius made one chord melt into another. Their conversation moved along nicely until a look of despair crossed Heseltine's face. Nichols asked what was the matter and learned that Heseltine was in the throes of unrequited love. Nichols confessed that he, too, was in love–with a musician.

"At least she's an artist," Heseltine said, approving of Nichols' attachment all the more when he discovered that she was beautiful and played brilliantly.

Nichols would find that his first bumpy encounter with Philip Heseltine was typical of the man who would become well known as composer Peter Warlock.

September 20th

Too Much Partying

John Dowland probably thought that he had it made. He was at the height of his reputation as one of England's greatest lutenists, and he had just been appointed as lutenist to the Court of Christian IV of Denmark. But coming from service to the reserved Queen Elizabeth, Dowland was shocked by the partying at the Danish court. He described it in a letter in 1598:

I have been well nigh overwhelmed with carousel and sports of all kinds. We had women and, indeed, wine too, of such plenty as would have astonished any sober beholder. Our feasts were magnificent and the two royal guests did most lovingly embrace each other at table. I think the Dane hath strangely wrought on our good English Nobles, for those, whom I never could get to taste good liquor, now follow the fashion and wallow in beastly delights.

The ladies abandon their sobriety, and are seen to roll about in intoxication. There hath been no lack of good living, shows, sights and banquetings from morn to eve.

One day a great feast was held, and after dinner the representation of Solomon, his Temple, and the coming of the Queen of Sheba was made, or as I may better say, was meant to have been made, before their Majesties...but alas! The lady who did play the Queen's part did carry most precious gifts to both the Majesties, but forgetting the steps arising to the canopy, overset her baskets into his Danish Majesty's lap and fell at his feet, though I rather think it was in his face.

Much was the hurry and confusion. Cloths and napkins were at hand to make all clean. His Majesty then got up and would dance with the Queen of Sheba, but he fell down and humbled himself before her and was carried to an inner chamber and laid on a bed of state....

It's unlikely that the lute music of John Dowland was fully appreciated by his new royal patrons.

September 21st

Schubert's Vision of War

Franz Schubert wrote many songs celebrating the beauty of nature, but his letters reveal that his response to nature went far beyond mere sightseeing.

In September 1825, Schubert was traveling through the Tyrolese Alps with his friend, the singer Michael Vogl. It was a time when much of Europe was still recovering from the ravages of the Napoleonic wars. Tyrolese resistance fighters continued to struggle against Bavarian domination. On September 21, Schubert wrote to his brother Ferdinand of the beauty–and the terror–that he saw in the mountains:

After a few hours we came to Hallein, which truly is a spectacular town, but extremely dirty and sinister. I couldn't persuade Vogl to visit the Salzburg area with all of its salt mines.... So we drove on past Golling, where we saw the first high, impassable mountains whose frightening gorges the Lueg Pass cuts through.

We clambered up a tall mountain with other awesome mountains towering before our noses on either side as if the world had planks nailed all over it in this vicinity. When we finally reached the summit, we found ourselves looking down into a terrifying gorge that set our hearts to fluttering.

Amid this terrifying scenery, mankind has tried to perpetuate his even more terrible beastliness. For it was here, where the frothy Salzach–far, far below– blocks the Bavarians on one side and the Tyrolese on the other–that the terrible slaughter occurred. The Tyrolese, concealed among the rocky peaks, fired down with fiendish yells of exultation at the Bavarians who were trying to capture the pass, and those who were hit went tumbling into the chasm without ever knowing where the shots had come from.

A chapel on the Bavarian side and a red cross in the cliffs on the Tyrolese side commemorate this disgraceful event, which went on for days and weeks. Oh, glorious Christ, how many infamous deeds must be done in your name!

September 22nd
The Society for Private Musical Performance

Nineteen eighteen was a difficult time to be making a living writing music in Vienna, especially if that music was avant-garde. Nonetheless, Arnold Schoenberg, Alban Berg, and Anton Webern decided to create a Society for Private Musical Performances in Vienna.

The purpose of the society was to give new compositions their due by providing unlimited rehearsal time and frequent performances of important pieces. Membership fees were charged according to the member's ability to pay. The fees were intended not to support the society so much as to demonstrate the member's sincere interest in new music.

The founders of the Society banned the press from performances, discouraged guests, and did not even announce the evening's music in advance. The limited resources of the Society forced it into a curious logic. Symphonic works usually had to be played in the form of reductions for one or two pianos. The rationalization was that these stripped-down performances would be more effective in exposing the composition's basic worth—or worthlessness.

The composer whose music was performed more than any other was hardly avant-garde—Max Reger. Second was Claude Debussy. Then Béla Bartók. More than a year passed before Schoenberg allowed one of his own pieces to be included.

But a composer who was the antithesis of the avant-garde—Johann Strauss—received the most intensive preparations for a gala evening of music. In 1921 the Society poured twenty-five hours of rehearsal time into a gala waltz evening—more than twice the preparation time usually allotted for symphony orchestras.

For the big evening, Schoenberg, Berg, and Webern arranged Strauss waltzes for string quintet, piano, and harmonium with the idea of auctioning off the manuscripts to support the Society. The result was a charming perspective on some of the best-known pieces of the Waltz King. But six months later, the Society for Private Musical Performances passed into music history.

September 23rd
The Bellini Legend

A legend about composer Vincenzo Bellini would have made a fine plot for one of his operas.

The story begins about 1820 when Bellini was a student at the Conservatory of Music in Naples. He and a beautiful singing student named Maddalena fell hopelessly in love.

Once Bellini's first opera had been produced successfully he gathered up his courage and asked for permission to marry Maddalena. Her parents not only refused the request, they ordered Bellini never to visit the house again. The distraught lovers vowed to be true to each other forever.

"Before I've written ten operas, your parents will gladly give me permission to marry you," Bellini declared.

"It takes a long time to write ten operas," the disheartened Maddalena said.

"Only a few years. We're young. We can wait," Bellini told her.

"Then let's pledge to be united after your tenth opera–dead or alive," Maddalena replied.

Bellini made the pledge. His second and third operas made Bellini the talk of Italy. By the time he wrote his seventh, *La Somnambula*, he was known throughout Europe. Bellini received a letter from Maddalena saying that her father had consented to their marriage.

Was it success or the distraction of a nearby soprano that had cooled Bellini's ardor for Maddalena? He wrote her a polite reply saying that as soon as he finished his opera *Norma* he would return to Naples so they could talk about their marriage.

He never returned. And Maddalena, soon to die of a broken heart, wrote a letter reminding him of their vow to be united after his tenth opera, in life or death.

Her death and that final letter threw Bellini into a state of melancholy from which he never recovered. Many in Italy believed him to be haunted by poor Maddalena, who had taken the form of a white dove that fluttered through his bedroom every night.

One element of the legend is known to be true. On September 23, 1835, shortly after Bellini finished his tenth opera, *I Puritani*, he died at the age of 33.

September 24th

The Shocking Conductor

At orchestra concerts today we take for granted the conductor directing the music with a baton. According to Louis Spohr, things were done very differently in 1820, when he went to London to conduct a Philharmonic concert:

In those days it was customary there that when symphonies and overtures were performed, the pianist had the score in front of him, not to conduct from it so much as to play with the orchestra as he saw fit, which sounded awful. The actual conductor was the first violinist, who gave the tempi—and every so often, when the orchestra began to waver—indicated the beat with his violin bow. An orchestra that big, spread out like the Philharmonic, couldn't possibly play together no matter how good the individual players were.

Fortunately, at the morning rehearsal on the day of the concert, Mr. Ferdinand Ries, the pianist, willingly handed over the score and agreed to sit out the performance. Then I took my music stand with the score to a separate music desk in front of the orchestra, drew my baton from my coat pocket and signaled the orchestra to begin.

The novelty startled some of the orchestra directors but I talked them into giving it a try and they settled down. I knew the symphonies and overtures so well from conducting them in Germany that I could give the tempi very emphatically, plus indicate all the entrances for the winds and horns, which gave them a confidence they had never known. And when the execution didn't quite suit me I politely pointed out my criticisms, which Mr. Ries interpreted for the orchestra. This unusually close attention and the visual indication of the tempo caused them to play with a previously unknown accuracy and spirit.

The result in the evening was even more brilliant than I had hoped, and the triumph of the baton as a time-giver was decisive.

September 25th
It Happens to the Greatest of Them

Nowadays world class guest soloists usually rehearse a familiar concerto at least once with an orchestra. But before the middle of the 20th century great soloists frequently didn't rehearse familiar works at all—and occasionally experienced some uncomfortable surprises.

In his book *"Gentlemen, More Dolce Please!"*, longtime Boston Symphony associate Harry Ellis Dickson relates two such incidents. The sophisticated French violinist Jacques Thibaud had played the Beethoven Violin Concerto with the Boston Symphony so many times that on one occasion he didn't arrive at Symphony Hall until the day of the concert, a few minutes before his performance was to begin. Thibaud walked on stage, tuned his violin, and relaxed as he waited for the long orchestral introduction that was to lead to his entrance. The conductor seemed perplexed at Thibaud's casual stance. He nodded to Thibaud. Thibaud nodded back. They repeated the awkward acknowledgment a time or two, each waiting for the other.

Then the conductor began. But the concerto wasn't Beethoven's. It was Mendelssohn's, which gave the soloist a scant bar and a half introduction. Thibaud jerked his violin to his chin and asked, "Why didn't you tell me it was the Mendelssohn?"

"Why didn't you ask me?" shot back the conductor as they launched into what proved a perfect performance.

The great Dutch pianist, Egon Petri, had a similar experience. At a rehearsal of Beethoven's Fourth Piano Concerto he skipped the opening four bars, which is a piano solo, and at the concert he forgot that he was supposed to begin the concerto. After he and the conductor nodded back and forth for a while, Petri realized that he was supposed to start but he couldn't remember the beginning of the concerto. So he had to leave the piano, walk to the podium, and take a peek at the score to get the nudge he needed.

September 26th

Mussorgsky's Mysticism

Mysticism came easily to Modest Mussorgsky. A little too easily, according to a letter Mussorgsky wrote to his fellow composer Mily Balakirev, on September 26, 1860:

I think you will be interested in how I spent my time in the Moscow country-side. My illness dragged on almost until August so that I could devote myself to music only for short periods of time. All the same I gathered some materials that I'll need later. Oedipus and the little sonata have progressed somewhat. The sonata is just about ready. Something has to be tidied up in the middle section but the finale works. Oedipus has had two choruses added to it—an andante in B-flat minor and an allegro in E-flat to be used in the introduction.

Aside from those, I've received a very interesting work, which I have to prepare for next summer. It's an entire act that takes place on Bald Mountain from Mengden's drama The Witches' Sabbath, individual episodes of sorcerers, a solemn march for all this wickedness, and finale—the glorification of the Sabbath in which the playwright introduces the commandant of the entire orgy on Bald Mountain. The libretto is quite good. I already have some material for it.

It may prove a very good thing.

Mily, you would be delighted at the change I've undergone, and no doubt it is strongly reflected in my music. My brain has become stronger and has turned toward realities. The fires of youth have cooled down. Everything has evened out, and of mysticism for now there isn't even half a word. My last mystic thing is this andante in B-flat minor—a chorus—from the introduction to Oedipus I've completely recovered, Mily, thank God!

Despite his attempts to fend off mysticism, Mussorgsky's very mystical *Night on Bald Mountain* would become the cornerstone of his reputation.

September 27th

You're Under Arrest!

Karl Ditters von Dittersdorf was one of the most respected composers of the 18th century. In his early years, though, he made a professional error that resulted in his arrest. Dittersdorf tells the story in the autobiography that he dictated to his son.

Dittersdorf had a respectable job composing for a prince in Vienna, but he fell in with the wrong crowd and soon was spending more than he earned. A count from Prague who was visiting Vienna admired Dittersdorf's music and offered him a job that paid better. Out of loyalty to the prince, Dittersdorf turned down the offer.

But Dittersdorf continued to go into debt, and so he fled to Prague to take the higher-paying job. He was shocked to find that the count had left for a long stay in Paris. It would be weeks before Dittersdorf could even exchange letters with him, and, as usual, Dittersdorf was running out of money.

Through an oboist friend, he found temporary work with another count, who commissioned six symphonies and two oboe concertos. With his earnings from them, Dittersdorf dutifully sent some of the money he owed to his landlord back in Vienna.

Just as things were beginning to look up, a policeman arrived to arrest Dittersdorf. The composer admitted his guilt at once and was hauled back to Vienna, where he was placed under house arrest with a diet of bread and water every fourth day. Dittersdorf was overwhelmed with gratitude not to receive a worse punishment. Moved by Dittersdorf's remorse, the prince declared, "Go! Live a decent life! Then I shall forget the shame which you have brought on both of us."

The prince was more than kind, instructing members of the household to nurse Dittersdorf through an ensuing illness and forbidding any of them to scold the errant composer for running away. As for Dittersdorf, he settled down and worked hard at performance and composition and regained the trust of his prince.

September 28th
An Extraordinary Private Concert

It was a private performance by one of Europe's great violinists. Unfortunately, Eugène Ysaÿe wasn't playing the piece as it was written and his young visitor dared to tell him so.

In the early years of the 20th century, the young violinist Arthur Hartmann and a friend visited Ysaÿe in his hotel room. The celebrity was wearing a voluminous dressing gown, smoking his pipe and fiddling fervently. Ysaÿe was brushing up on Lalo's Concerto in F for an upcoming concert in Glasgow. Hartmann was thrilled because he knew the concerto well, although he had never heard it played.

Ysaÿe dazzled his young visitor with the beauty of his tone and his graceful bowing. But gradually Hartmann realized that Ysaÿe was playing "scarcely two consecutive measures as they had been written."

After a while, Ysaÿe lowered his violin, winked, and asked, "Well, piggy, not bad, huh?" When Hartmann hesitated, Ysaÿe laughed. "So say something. It went well, didn't it? What do you think?"

Hartmann blurted out that it was marvelous but not quite accurate. Ysaye roared like a wounded bull, put down his violin and his pipe and grabbed at his long hair.

Hartmann mustered his best French in an effort to apologize, but the virtuoso wasn't hearing him. He insisted that Hartmann play the concerto for him.

Hartmann begged to be forgiven, to be allowed to run from the room, but swearing and thrusting the violin and bow at him, Ysaÿe demanded that Hartmann play the concerto. He sat down, straddling a chair and smoking his pipe as the nervous Hartmann began to play.

When Hartmann came to the passage in question, the great Ysaÿe put up his hand and told him to play it again more slowly. At the end of the first movement, after more repetitions, he turned to Hartmann's friend and said, "*Eh bien*, he is right. I've got to look through the score a bit after lunch."

September 29th

The Disaster Concerto

It was a promising beginning. The American virtuoso Jascha Heifetz asking English composer William Walton to write a violin concerto for him. But before it would be performed, the concerto would have to survive many perils, including a tarantula, bombs, and torpedoes.

The success of Walton's Viola Concerto inspired Heifetz to commission a concerto for the violin. Delighted, Walton retreated to a seaside Italian villa to write the work. Almost immediately he received a more lucrative offer to write music to the film *Pygmalion.* Walton knew that writing for Heifetz was a gamble, but he turned down the film offer anyway, telling a friend, "It all boils down to whether I am to become a film composer or a real composer."

Then Walton began to feel that the concerto was too soft-spoken and not sufficiently virtuosic. Walton worried that if the concerto fell flat in America it would be a long time before he'd be able to have another work performed there.

Then a tarantula bit him. It was a painful experience, but in a wry way Walton celebrated the occasion by making the second movement of the concerto a Tarantella–a Neapolitan dance once believed to cure the spider's bite. The concerto was turning into something decidedly unorthodox.

Early in 1939, Walton took a chance and sent the still-incomplete score to Heifetz for approval. A month later came the reply: "Accept enthusiastically."

But the concerto was to have two more close calls. During a bomb scare the manuscript of the concerto was lost. Heifetz' copy of the score was later lost in the Atlantic, sunk during a convoy crossing. When the concerto finally was performed in Cleveland, Walton was unable to attend. He was too busy picking up the pieces. During an air raid, a bomb had flattened his house.

September 30th
The Perplexing Symphony

Taking on a new work by a major composer can be a daunting task, even for a seasoned conductor. On September 30, 1887, conductor Hermann Levi was starting to panic as he faced the debut of Anton Bruckner's Eighth Symphony. Levi wrote to Bruckner disciple Josef Schalk in desperation:

I'm at a complete loss and I'm appealing to you for advice and help! In short, I am completely flummoxed by Bruckner's Eighth Symphony and I don't have the nerve to conduct it.

No doubt my refusal would meet vociferous opposition among the orchestra and the public. That wouldn't make any difference to me if I were fascinated by it, as I was by the Seventh, if I could say to the orchestra, as I did then, "By the fifth rehearsal you'll come to like it." But I'm awfully disappointed! I've studied the work for days on end and I just don't get it. Maybe I'm too dense or too old but I find the instrumentation impossible, and what really shocks me is its resemblance to the Seventh Symphony—practically to the point of mechanical copying. The opening passage of the first movement is splendid but the development leaves me cold.

As for the last movement—it's a closed book to me.

What to do? I tremble at the thought of what this news will do to our friend! I can't write to him. Should I suggest that he come here to listen to a rehearsal? In my despair I showed the score to a musical friend of mine and he agreed that it's impossible to perform. So please write back to me at once and tell me how to approach Bruckner. If it were only a matter of him thinking I'm an idiot or a traitor, I'd make the best of it. But I'm afraid of something worse. I'm afraid the disappointment may wreck his courage.

By any chance do you know the symphony well? Can you make head or tail of it? I really don't know what to do!

Bruckner revised the symphony, which remained unperformed for another five years.

October 1st

Chopin in Scotland

In the fall of 1848, the Polish-born composer Fréderíc Chopin was in Scotland at the invitation of an admirer, Jane Stirling. Although he welcomed the retreat from the war raging in Europe, Chopin was ill at ease among his hosts. On October 1 he wrote to a friend:

I'll soon forget all my Polish. I'll be speaking French with an English accent and learn to speak English like a Scot. I'll end up like old Jawerski who spoke five languages all at once.

As far as my future's concerned, I'm going from bad to worse. I'm getting weaker and weaker and compose nothing at all, not because I don't want to but because of practical problems. Each week I haul myself off to some new perch. What can I do? At least this way I'm saving a little money for the winter.

I've received a sheaf of invitations but I can't even go where I'd like—to the Duchess of Argyll's or to Lady Belhaven's for example—because it's already too late in the year for my health. All morning and until two o'clock I'm useless. Later, when I'm dressed, everything bears down on me and I gasp until dinner, after which I have to sit around the table with the men, observing what they say and listening while they drink.

As I sit there my thoughts are far away from them despite their kindness and snatches of French. Soon—overcome by tedium—I go to the drawing room, where I have to stir myself a little because they're eager to hear me. Then my good servant Daniel carries me up to my bedroom, undresses me, leaves me a candle, and there I am to gasp and dream until the same thing begins all over again.

No sooner do I get a little accustomed to a place than I have to move on because my Scotswomen can't leave me in peace. Either they come to fetch me or they take me around to see their families. In the end they'll smother me with their friendliness and I—equally friendly—will let them do it.

October 2nd

The Other Milton

John Milton's epic poem, *Paradise Lost,* is one of the major landmarks of English literature. Less well known is his more modest poem, *Ad patrem, which* illuminates a composer much admired by John Milton, his father.

John Milton the Elder grew up in Oxford and attended school there until his father disowned him for behavior inappropriate for a student. In 1585 he settled in London, where eventually he set up shop as a copyist or scrivener.

Apparently Milton developed into a capable composer. In 1600 England's foremost madrigalist, Thomas Morley, visited him with important news and an exciting proposition. He told Milton that Queen Elizabeth, at age 66, was beginning to desire more gentle entertainments, and Morley was proposing a cheerful tribute to the finest composers in the kingdom. He invited Milton to contribute madrigals to the collection, to be known as *The Triumph of Oriana.* The heroine of the collection, Oriana, would represent Queen Elizabeth, and each madrigal was to end with the line "then sang the shepherds and nymphs of Diana: Long live fair Oriana."

How could Milton refuse? And how could any other madrigalist in England? The collection soon burgeoned with contributions by the best known names in the land, including John Wilbye, Thomas Tomkins, and Thomas Weelkes.

Milton contributed a cheerful six-part madrigal that must have helped to brighten the queen's mood when the collection was performed in her presence. Morley supervised the printed edition that came out in 1603.

As for John Milton the Elder, he went on to live a long and prosperous life and is said to have been a major influence on the poetry of his famous son. He must have had a good number of outstanding madrigals to his credit before Morley came to visit him, but his only surviving madrigal is the one he contributed to *The Triumph of Oriana.*

October 3rd

The Romantic

Romanticism swept Europe in the early decades of the 19th century. Among its hallmarks was a fascination with the supernatural, a love of freedom, and the awareness of life's brevity. A letter Hector Berlioz wrote to a friend on October 3, 1841, shows that he was very much a romantic.

I have never led a more active life, or more preoccupied even in its inaction. As you may know, I am writing a grand opera in four acts on a libretto of Scribe called The Bloodthirsty Nun. *I think that this time no one should complain about lack of interest in the piece. It's based on the episode in* The Monk *by Matthew Gregory Lewis and has an extremely dramatic effect at the end.*

At the moment they are counting on me at the Opera next year, but Duperz is in such as state of vocal dilapidation that if I don't have another leading tenor, it would be madness on my part to perform my work. I was—and still am—in line for Habeneck's post at the Opera. It would be a musical dictatorship of which I would hope to make much in the interests of art.

You have no doubt heard of the immediate success of my Requiem in St. Petersburg, performed by the combined forces of all the opera houses, the czar's chapel, and the choruses of the two regiments of the Imperial Guard. Thanks to the magnificence of the Russian nobility, the admirable Bomberg, who conducted, made a profit of five thousand francs. When it comes to art, give me a despotic government! In Paris, to put on the whole work, I would have to be mad or prepared to lose what Bomberg made.

I feel myself going downhill very fast. The idea that life has an end, I notice, occurs to me often. So I find myself snatching—instead of selecting—the flowers on the stony path.

October 4th

Special Delivery

John Bull was one of the great keyboard players and composers of Elizabethan England, but on one occasion he had to make a special effort to maintain his reputation.

One day the Countess of Pembroke–patroness of many musicians, dramatists and poets of the time–was visiting Hereford and went to the Cathedral just to hear Bull play the organ. She and a glittering group of important people settled into their places and waited. The only problem–John Bull was nowhere to be seen–or heard.

A friend of Bull's slipped out and went looking for him. He found the organist in his room, hunched over a piece of music paper, copying parts. He had completely lost track of the time.

Bull threw on his gown, clapped his cap on his head and rushed off to perform. He arrived just as the countess was getting up to go, saying that a musician should keep better time.

At the organ, Bull improvised a brilliant performance based on the theme he had been working on. The audience was completely won over by his playing, by the breadth and depth of its emotion. The countess was greatly moved by his playing and asked to meet him, but when he emerged from the seclusion of the organ, she burst out laughing. Bull had left his copying in such a hurry that he was still smeared with ink and his clothes were all askew. Bull's attempts at a dignified departure made the countess laugh all the more.

To set things right, Bull composed a piece just for the countess, but by the time he finished it, the house where she was staying was dark except for one upper window. Impulsively, Bull threw the manuscript through the window. It landed at the countess' feet as she was getting ready to go to bed. She was so charmed by the music and its special delivery that she put in a good word for John Bull at the court of Queen Elizabeth.

October 5th

Log Cabin Composer at the White House

He was the first composer to champion the cause of American music, but Anthony Philip Heinrich had his limits.

The man who became known as "the Beethoven of America" and the "Log Cabin Composer of Kentucky" was born in Bohemia in 1781 and, though he played a fine Cremona violin, Heinrich didn't take to writing music until he was 40. And though his compositions drew their sound from the wilds of America, Heinrich believed in refinement. That's why he came to grief during a visit to President John Tyler.

A companion, John Hill Hewitt, described the occasion:

At a proper hour we visited the President's mansion. We were shown into the parlor. The composer labored hard to give full effect to his weird production; his bald pate bobbed from side to side and shone like a bubble on the surface of a calm lake. At times his shoulders would be raised to the line of his ears, and his knees went up to the keyboard, while the perspiration rolled in large drops down his wrinkled cheeks.

The inspired composer had got about halfway through his wonderful production, when Mr. Tyler arose from his chair, and placing his hand gently on Heinrich's shoulder, said, "That may all be very fine, sir, but can't you play us a good old Virginia reel?"

Had a thunderbolt fallen at the feet of the musician, he could not have been more astonished. He arose from the piano, rolled up his manuscript, and taking his hat and cane, bolted toward the door, exclaiming,

"No, sir. I never play dance music!"

I joined him in the vestibule. As we proceeded along Pennsylvania Avenue, Heinrich grasped my arm convulsively, and exclaimed, "Mein Gott in himmel! De peebles vot made Yohn Tyler Bresident ought to be hung! He knows no more about music than an oyshter!"

October 6th

Beethoven's Testament

On October 6, 1802, Beethoven wrote one of the most powerful and mysterious letters in all of music history–his so-called Heiligenstadt Testament. Even the intended destination is puzzling, the letter being addressed "to my brothers," yet only Beethoven's brother Carl is mentioned by name, the name of his brother Johann having been omitted or removed. Beethoven wrote:

From childhood onward my heart and mind prompted me to be kind and tender, and I was always inclined to accomplish great deeds. But consider that in the last six years I have been in a wretched condition, made worse by unintelligent physicians. Deceived from year to year with hopes of improvement and then finally forced to the prospect of lasting infamy that may go on for years or even be totally incurable. Born with a fiery, active temperament, and susceptible to the diversions of society, I had to retire from this world to live a solitary life.

At times even I tried to forget all this, but how harshly I was driven back by the redoubled experience of my bad hearing. Yet it is impossible for me to say, "Speak louder, shout, for I am deaf!" How could I declare the weakness of a sense which in me ought to be more acute than in others–a sense which formerly I possessed in highest perfection, a perfection such as few in my profession enjoy or ever have enjoyed; no I cannot do it. Forgive, therefore, if you see me withdraw, when I would gladly mix with you.

How humiliating it was when someone standing close to me heard a distant flute and I heard nothing, or a shepherd singing and again I heard nothing. Such incidents almost drove me to despair; at times I was on the point of putting an end to my life. Art alone restrained my hand. It seemed I could not quit this earth until I had produced all I felt within me....

October 7th

Wagner's Rescuer

In his autobiography *My Life*, Richard Wagner wrote extensively about his early efforts to survive as a composer. In 1841, the 28-year-old composer and his wife, Minna, were living in the Paris suburb of Meudon and having a hard time of it.

Our lack of funds began to make itself felt with a severity that was very discouraging. We felt it all the more keenly when my sister Cecilia and her husband moved to a place quite near us. They weren't wealthy, but they were fairly well to do. They came to see us every day, but we never wanted to let them know how terribly hard up we were

One day it all came to a head. Being absolutely without money, I started out early in the morning to walk to Paris. I walked because I didn't have enough money for the railway fare. And I made up my mind to wander around all day, trudging from street to street on into the late afternoon, in the hope of raising a five-franc piece. But my mission proved utterly fruitless, and I had to walk all the way back to Meudon again.

Minna came to meet me, and when I told her of my failure, she informed me that one of our friends had returned so hungry that she had given him the last of the bread. Finally our lodger also returned, soaked with perspiration and exhausted, driven home by the craving for a meal, which he had been unable to get in town. He begged most piteously for a piece of bread.

That outcome inspired my wife with heroic resolve because she felt it her duty to appease at least the hunger of her menfolk. For the first time during her stay on French soil, she persuaded the baker, the butcher, and the wine-merchant, by plausible arguments, to supply her with life's necessities without immediate cash payment, and Minna's eyes beamed when, an hour later, she was able to put before us an excellent meal.

October 8th

Takemitsu

For some reason, the classical music of his native land did not appeal to the young man. Toru Takemitsu was more attracted to music from the distant West. But it was a bad time to develop a taste for western things. Toru Takemitsu grew up in Japan during World War II.

Takemitsu was born on October 8, 1930. His formal education ended when he was 14 and drafted into the depleted Japanese military. Toward the end of the war, as American forces prepared to invade Japan, Takemitsu was put to work constructing defensive bases in the mountains. It was a bitter experience that drove him even further from any appreciation of classical Japanese music.

One day, an officer led a group of young servicemen to the back of the barracks, where he had a record player. Using a carefully trimmed piece of bamboo for a stylus, he played them a record of Josephine Baker singing "Parlez-moi d'amour." It was a moment of revelation. Young Takemitsu thought the music was splendid.

A year after the war ended, the 16-year-old Takemitsu set his mind on becoming a composer. Rejecting any further formal education, he went straight to work and began to write compositions that were influenced by French composers– Claude Debussy and Olivier Messiaen. By the 1950's, when Takemitsu's music was being recorded and sold in the West, he was surprised and dismayed to find that it was being packaged in a jacket with a picture of Mount Fuji and a Geisha girl.

It was not until he was in his 30's that Takemitsu finally confronted–and appreciated–Japanese music. The confrontation came at an unlikely place–a puppet show. It was the tone quality and timbre of the samisen–the long-necked banjo-like instrument–that he found particularly moving.

From that point on, Takemitsu systematically studied his country's traditional music in order to bring out the sensibilities of Japanese music that had always been within him.

The result was music neither western nor Japanese, but a synthesis of many influences that was uniquely his own.

October 9th

A Devil of a Career

With more than 80 recordings to his credit, Samuel Ramey is the most recorded bass in history. His performances range from the title role in Arrigo Boitó's *Mefistofele* to 1930's Americana. But like many a low male voice, his has become most associated with satanic villains and, like the devils he plays, his spectacular career seems to have materialized from thin air.

Ramey was born in Colby, a farming town of 6,000 in the wheat country of northwestern Kansas known as "the oasis on the plains." His musical talent probably came from his mother, who had a pleasant singing voice. His father, a meat cutter, didn't see a great future in Ramey's musical inclinations, but was glad to see the young man go to a local college with the intention of becoming a teacher.

Ramey's college voice teacher suggested that he study Figaro's mocking aria "Non piú andrai" in Mozart's *Marriage of Figaro*, so Ramey bought a vintage recording of bass Ezio Pinza singing that and other arias and became intrigued.

A few years later he heard about a summer festival program at Central City Opera in Colorado, and, on a whim, Ramey went to a radio station, recorded some arias, and sent in the tape with his application. "Lo and behold, they accepted me," Ramey said later. The production was *Don Giovanni* with Norman Treigle in the title role, who influenced Ramey "tremendously."

Ramey transferred to Wichita State University, which had a strong music program, and, after graduation, went to New York, where he wrote advertising copy for a book publishing company, all the while auditioning for agents and opera companies. After a few auditions, the City Opera hired him; he had his debut as the officer Zuniga in *Carmen* in 1972 and, within a year, had become one of the company's top celebrities.

He went on to become one of the best known opera singers worldwide, even though, as Ramey noted of his Colorado debut: "I had never seen an opera before I was involved in one that summer."

October 10th

Perhaps It Was Fate

Giuseppe Verdi was one of the most inspired composers of all time. But when circumstances overwhelmed him, he needed help from a strong-willed friend—and fate.

Verdi was born on October 10, 1813. He was not yet 27 when he was overwhelmed by a triple tragedy—the deaths of his young son, daughter, and wife within a short period of time.

Verdi had been under contract to write an opera, but he wanted to turn away from art altogether. He begged theater manager Bartholomew Merelli to release him from his contract. Merelli's response was a strange mix of firmness and sympathy.

"Listen, Verdi," he said, "I can't force you to write. My confidence in you is undiminished. Who knows? Maybe one day you'll pick up your pen again. If you do, just give me two months notice before the beginning of the season and I promise you the opera you deliver me will be put on stage."

Some months later Mereilli showed Verdi a libretto.

"So fine a subject," he said. "Take it, read it."

"What the devil do you expect me to do with it?" Verdi asked. "I have no wish to compose."

"Well, it won't hurt you to read it. Just have a look at it and bring it back."

When he returned to his room the still-grieving Verdi tossed the manuscript onto a table. The pages fell open to a verse that began *Va pensiero*—"Go, my thought, on gilded wings." Despite himself, Verdi read the entire libretto over and over again until he had all but memorized it.

Nonetheless, when he went to return the libretto, he refused to set it to music.

Merelli stuffed the libretto into the pocket of Verdi's overcoat, pushed Verdi out of his office, shut the door in his face, and locked himself in.

Verdi went home and began writing, note by note, until at last he had written his great opera *Nabucco*. To be continued....

October 11th

The Rabble Rouser

"With this opera it is fair to say my artistic career began." So wrote Giuseppe Verdi of *Nabucco*, a masterpiece that also did much to launch his reputation as a political rabble-rouser.

The opera is based on the story of Nebuchadnezzar–given the more musical name Nabucco–who defeats the Jews at Jerusalem and has them carried off to Babylon as captives. It includes prayers by practically every character, a mad scene, warlike choruses and laments and a dead march as the Jews are nearly executed.

The story had political punch. In the 1840's, Austria controlled much of Italy, and a story about Jews in captivity was bound to be taken as a parallel to 19th century Italy. But on musical terms alone, *Nabucco* was so talked about during rehearsals that it was already a success before the curtain came up on opening night. When the debut came at La Scala in Milan in 1842, *Nabucco* lived up to its reputation and then some. The audience was so vociferous in their response to Act One that at first Verdi suspected that they were being insincere.

In Act Three came a clarion call for freedom, the Chorus of the Hebrew Slaves. It had a simple tune sung by all the massed voices of the chorus–a tune anyone could sing–and the audience demanded that it be repeated. The police patrolling the opera house grew uneasy. Repeats were against the law because of the danger that they would spark demonstrations against the Austrian officials and nobility looking down from their box seats. The police were no doubt relieved that *Nabucco* premiered late in the schedule so that there was time for only eight performances before the season ended.

If so, their relief was short-lived. Because when *Nabucco* reopened in the autumn, it had 57 performances–a record for one season–and it is said that the Chorus of the Hebrew Slaves was repeated at every one of them.

October 12th

Monteverdi & the Highwaymen

The highwayman leveling his firearm at a kneeling traveler was thinking only of the moment. He had no idea that the man trembling before him would be revered centuries later as a great composer.

The madrigalist Claudio Monteverdi had been traveling from Cremona to Venice when three bandits waylaid him and his companions. In a letter of October 12, 1613, he described the trauma.

One of the scoundrels, dark-haired with a sparse beard and of medium height, carrying a long musket with the trigger cocked, suddenly came forward and another approached and threatened me with his musket, while the third grasped the bridle of my horse, which continued on obliviously as he led it into a field. I was quickly dismounted and forced to go down on my knees while one of the two armed men demanded my purse and the other moved in on the courier and demanded his bag, which he handed out of the carriage.

They opened it and one of them packed up everything he could lay his hands on.

As for me, I remained on my knees the whole time, pinned down by the one with the firearm. Then both of them grabbed up as much as they could while the third kept a lookout along the road. When they had completely ransacked all of our possessions the man who had searched the courier came over to me and commanded me to undress so that he could see if I had any more money. I vowed that I had none, so he went over to my maidservant and demanded the same of her, but she resisted with such prayers, pleading and tears that he left her alone.

Finally they crammed everything into a huge bundle, hoisted it onto their backs and took off with it. Then we packed up what was left and went to the inn.

October 13th

The Flight of the Swallow

Would the third time be the charm? Late in his distinguished career composer Giacomo Puccini had a particularly nettlesome project on his hands–his opera *La Rondine*. The title means "The Swallow" and this one was having a hard time getting off the ground.

After the opera's favorable 1917 debut in Monte Carlo, its audiences had been polite at best. Puccini didn't like the way it was being performed, and the critics didn't like the way it was written. It seemed that there wasn't much left to work with but Puccini kept doggedly at it. After a lackluster performance in Vienna in October 1920, Puccini wrote to a friend:

I'm going to rewrite La Rondine *for the third time! I don't particularly like the second edition. I prefer the first, the one that was performed in Monte Carlo. But the third is going to be the first one with changes in the libretto.*

Puccini had referred to the libretto as "vapid," but the librettist responded that he had been working under difficult conditions–the disruptive environment of World War I, which had made it impossible for the librettist to keep in touch with Puccini regarding the development of the opera. He suggested that Puccini go back to the original version of the opera and touch that up rather than trying to revamp the work completely.

Eventually Puccini did just that, returning to the 1917 version, which he had always liked best of the three anyway. His decision was nudged along by the expense of engraving a third version–a daunting obstacle during times of tight money in postwar Italy.

He might also have realized that the problems with *La Rondine* had mostly to do with the politics of his critics and the fact that an opera set in the genteel 19th century was at odds with popular tastes during the burgeoning jazz age.

In the case of *La Rondine* the *first* time had been the charm.

October 14th

Brahms' Ingratitude

He was a 20-year-old who spent long nights playing the piano in Hamburg's tawdry taverns. Among the first to promote his career as a composer was Franz Liszt, but, on one occasion, the young pianist accepted Liszt's help less than graciously.

The American pianist William Mason tells the story this way:

One evening in 1853 Liszt sent us word to come up to his place the next morning as he expected a visit from a young man who was said to have great talent as a pianist and composer, and whose name was Johannes Brahms.

After some general conversation Liszt turned to Brahms and said, "We are interested to hear some of your compositions whenever you are ready and feel inclined to play them."

Brahms, who was evidently very nervous, protested that it was quite impossible for him to play while in such a disconcerted state. Liszt, seeing that no progress was being made, went over to the table, and taking up the first piece at hand–Brahms' illegible Scherzo in E-Flat–*said, "Well, I shall have to play," and placed the manuscript on the piano desk.*

He read it off in such a marvelous way–at the same time carrying on a running accompaniment of audible criticism of the music–that Brahms was amazed and delighted. A little later someone asked Liszt to play his own sonata, a work which was quite recent at that time, and of which he was very fond. Without hesitation, he sat down and began playing. As he progressed he came to a very expressive part of the sonata, which he always imbued with extreme pathos, and in which he looked for the special interest and sympathy of his listeners. Casting a glance at Brahms, Liszt saw that the young composer was dozing in his chair.

No stranger to the strenuous life himself, Liszt apparently was unfazed by the slight, because during the next 35 years, he continued to champion the music of Johannes Brahms.

October 15th

Mozart's Three Careers

In 1778, Wolfgang Amadeus Mozart, at age 22, was trying to cope with a three-fold career–that of court musician, performer, and composer. On October 15, he wrote from Strassburg to his father Leopold in Salzburg:

Dearest father! I assure you that if it weren't for the joy of embracing you so soon I would certainly not return to Salzburg. For you alone, dear father, can sweeten for me the bitterness of Salzbuzg. But I have to confess that I would arrive in Salzburg more cheerfully if I weren't in the service of the Court–a thought I find unbearable.

Put yourself in my place. At Salzburg I never know where I stand. I'm supposed to be everything and yet–sometimes–nothing! In every other place I would know what my duties were.

Everywhere else, whoever takes up the violin sticks with it. The same for the clavier and so on. But no doubt all of that can be arranged.

Things here are in a bad way but the day after tomorrow I'm giving a subscription concert all by myself–for the sake of economy, to gratify some friends, amateurs, and connoisseurs. If I hired an orchestra it would cost me–including the lighting–more than I might earn.

Apparently my sonatas haven't been engraved yet even though they were promised for the end of September. That's what happens if you can't take care of something yourself. It's likely they'll be fraught with mistakes because I haven't been able to revise them myself but have had to get someone else to do it. And I'll probably have to go to Munich without them.

Seemingly trivial matters like these can often bring success, honor, and wealth or–on the other hand–disgrace.

Well, so long. I embrace my dearest sister with all my heart and you, my most beloved father. I remain your most obedient son.

October 16th
Casals' Double Discovery

It was a day of double discovery for the young cellist, Pablo Casals. Years later, he would remember it as a turning point in his career.

Young Casals told his father that he needed new solo music to perform in a café. The two went off to look for some. Casals would remember that afternoon for two reasons. First his father bought him his first full-sized cello. Then they stopped at an old music shop. Casals began reading through a bundle of music scores. Suddenly he found a handful of pages that were crumbling and discolored with age. They were the *Six Suites for Violoncello Solo* by Johann Sebastian Bach. In the title alone, Casals saw magic and mystery.

He had never heard of them. Not even his teachers had ever mentioned the existence of the suites. Casals rushed home clasping the suites as if they were crown jewels. When he got to his room he read them over and over.

In the course of his long life Casals became world-renowned not only as a cellist but also as a conductor and a composer. Yet he never outgrew his fascination with the cello suites of Bach. In a 1970 interview, he looked back 80 years at the continuing effect the suites had on his career, saying that they had opened an entirely new world to him. He studied and worked on them every day for 12 years before he felt capable of performing them in public. Until then no violinist or cellist had ever played one of the Bach suites all the way through. The suites had been thought of as academic works, cold and mechanical. But to Pablo Casals they were the very essence of Bach, and Bach was the essence of music.

And just as the Bach cello suites had an effect on Pablo Casals, he, in turn, had an effect on them—leading the way for their entry into the repertory of the world's great performers.

October 17th

Rough Crossing

In October 1907, composer Edward German was on his way from England to New York for the American debut of his comic opera *Tom Jones*. He was soon to get caught up in a dangerous competition that had little to do with music.

The composer sailed for America on a new turbine ship of the Cunard Line. Her owners were eager to surpass the record set by a rival vessel, the *Deutschland*. Within a day of its departure, the English ship ran into rough weather. The queasy composer ate lightly. The next day, he woke up to find the ship rolling so much that the light fixture in his cabin was dangling at a strange angle. The main deck was closed because of waves washing over it.

But when the seas finally settled, German felt a sense of exhilaration. He later described a beautifully clear morning and huge, dark-blue, white-capped waves that came "like a tireless army and hurled themselves against the boat."

Some Metropolitan Opera stars, sailing on another boat, the *Kaiser Wilhelm*, had an even rougher time of it in the autumn storms. Their ship also was trying to make the Atlantic transit in record time and, in the process, the ship's rudder had come off. They arrived in New York so banged up that they were unable to perform in the ship's concert. Backers of the *Kaiser Wilhelm* published reports that the rival English boat was actually designed as a troopship built to land a British expeditionary force in Europe, and was being sailed by British Navy reservists.

When the English ship did break the record, getting a blue ribbon for speed, there was a concert to celebrate and German said, "Everybody seemed to feel that they personally had something to do with this record-breaking. I know I did."

Although German's transit was a success, the celebrating for the ship would be short-lived. Eight years later it would be one of the most notorious casualties of World War I—and Edward German would be glad indeed that he had not been aboard for that later voyage of the *Lusitania*.

October 18th
The Shipboard Romance

About the year 1770, during a voyage from Venice to Trieste, 30-year-old Karl Ditters von Dittersdorf fell in love with a pretty 18-year-old ballerina. The dark-eyed Italian beauty had a charming face, a slender and well-proportioned figure, an irresistible sense of humor, and a bewitching accent.

When they arrived in Trieste, they continued their shipboard romance, dining together day and night. They continued the romance in Vienna, where the ballerina's debut in a new work proved a sensation. Dittersdorf noticed that she beguiled sophisticated old men as well as young dandies, and it gave him great pride and satisfaction to think that the charming beauty was as taken with him as he was with her.

Dittersdorf tried to keep the liaison secret, but couldn't resist confiding in a close friend. The friend's reaction startled him.

"Shame on you!" he said, "a man of 30 without a second to lose in your artistic career! And yet you hang onto a girl–and a girl like that–at the risk of your future, your health, and your honor! Take my advice. Be a man. Tear yourself away from the arms of that wicked enchantress. Shake yourself free from a degrading passion. Choose any court you want where you can make a living and stay there. Then marry a virtuous girl and have children. If you don't, we part company."

When he had calmed down, Dittersdorf decided to stop seeing the ballerina. A year and a half later, he learned that she had had an affair with a wealthy count and had left him almost penniless. And when the Empress heard of the scandal, she had the ballerina arrested and carted bag and baggage to the Italian border.

Karl Ditters von Dittersdorf went on to become a major composer, and was forever glad that he had ended his shipboard romance.

October 19th

The Substitute

No performer has a more thankless task than the substitute. During a performance of *La Gioconda* at New York's Metropolitan Opera House in October 1982, tenor Placido Domingo was scheduled to sing the role of Enzo. He felt a cold coming on and thought about canceling. The management asked Carlo Bini–who was slated to take over the role in a few days–to prepare himself.

Domingo decided to go on, relying on his technique to carry him through the performance, so Bini relaxed and sat down among the audience to enjoy the opera. During the first intermission though, Bini was hit with the news that Domingo's cold was getting worse and that the great tenor felt that pushing his performance further would harm his voice. Domingo was supposed to sing three performances of *Tosca* the following week and he felt that he had to bow out for the remainder of *La Gioconda*.

Bini put on the unfamiliar costume and stepped into Act Two without the benefit of a stage rehearsal. He was unsure of where he was supposed to be from one moment to the next. When his first key aria came, the unpracticed Bini was at the mercy of the crowd, some of whom could barely contain their amusement. Mignon Dunn–the soprano lead–attempted to help Bini with his stage nerves by holding his hands firmly in hers during their scene together. When his hands slipped a little too low on her body some of the audience laughed out loud. Fistfights erupted between detractors and supporters of the performance.

Finally the conductor, Giuseppe Patanè, turned and implored the audience at least to have some respect for the composer. Things quieted down. But by the third act, Maestro Patanè's blood pressure was so erratic that he, too, had to withdraw from the performance. So a stand-in, staff conductor Eugene Kohon, stepped forward, bravely facing the groans of the audience as he took on the task of bringing the opera to a close.

One can only surmise that heaven holds a special place for that most maligned performer–the substitute.

October 20th

Rubinstein Meets Stravinsky

Arthur Rubinstein was a world famous pianist. But his London concerts were losing audience to the ballets of Igor Stravinsky.

Rubinstein decided to investigate. He attended a performance of Stravinsky's *Petrouchka* during which the ballet received thunderous applause. After a few curtain calls, a small man came onstage and took a bow. He received a long ovation. Rubinstein realized that the man was Stravinsky. Eager to meet him, the 27-year-old Rubinstein hurried backstage. Stravinsky was still taking bows. Rubinstein asked a stagehand to introduce him.

"This is Rubinstein," the stagehand said vaguely after the last curtain call. Stravinsky waited for his young visitor to say something.

"I've studied your *Rite of Spring* carefully," Rubinstein said at last, "and I'm eager to find out if my conception of that great work is right or wrong. Could you spare me a few moments to exchange ideas on the subject?" Stravinsky replied that he could spare half an hour at breakfast.

At breakfast, Rubinstein admitted that *The Rite of Spring* had caught him off-guard at first. Then he added, "After a long study of the score I came to the conclusion that your basic idea was to evoke the evolution of sound at the birth of nature rather than to illustrate some tribal rites of sacrifice of a maiden in order to pacify the gods."

Stravinsky was impressed but said that *The Rite of Spring* was essentially an effort to infuse new blood into music. That led to a far-ranging conversation about art.

They lunched with friends of Rubinstein's. Seeing a concert grand, Stravinsky dismissed the piano as a percussion instrument. A friend of Rubinstein's replied, "but if you had heard Arthur play your *Firebird* or *Petrouchka* you would have changed your opinion about the piano."

"Rubinstein is a pianist?" Stravinsky asked with astonishment. Everyone laughed, thinking Stravinsky was joking, except for Rubinstein, who realized that he had never mentioned his profession to the composer.

October 21st

Chabrier's Spanish Fling

French composer Emmanuel Chabrier's most famous work is Spanish-inspired. But Chabrier's *España* isn't his only writing inspired by Spain. The composer wrote some of his most colorful letters from south of the Pyrenees. On October 21, 1882 he wrote from Seville:

Eh bien, mes enfants! *What an eyeful we're getting of Andalusian derrieres shimmying like cavorting snakes! Every night we end up at the Basilos Flamencos surrounded by toreros in lounge suits, black felt hats creased down the middle, jackets crimped at the waist and tight trousers revealing sinewy legs and well-turned thighs. And all around, the gypsy women singing their malagueñas or dancing the tango, and the Manzanilla passing from hand to hand, everyone being forced to drink.*

Flashing eyes, flowers in their lovely hair, shawls knotted at the waist, feet tapping out an unending variety of rhythms, arms and hands trembling, rippling bodies in constant motion and that admirable derriere moving in every direction while the rest of the body remains motionless. And the whole time, cries of Ole! Ole!

At the same time, two somber guitarists puffing their cigarettes, keep on strumming anything in three-four time. The cries of the women excite the dancer who, when her turn comes to an end, becomes literally intoxicated with her body. It's truly fantastic!

Last night a couple of painters came with us and sketched while I was taking notes on the music. All the dancers surrounded us. The singers repeated their songs for me and then retired after cordially shaking our hands! Then we all had to drink out of the same glass—so hygienic! Anyway, none of us were any the worse for wear in the morning.

But to think that we'll be carrying on like this for a month after passing through Málaga, Cádiz, Granada and Valencia! Oh, my poor nerves!"

October 22nd

A Little Murder Mystery

France owed a good deal to Jean-Marie Léclair. He was one of the most distinguished champions of French music. He had risen through the ranks of the musical world, first as a dancer and ballet master, then as a violinist and composer. Then he had gone on to become a member of the royal chamber of musicians. He had developed a distinctly French style of violin playing.

But someone wanted him dead.

Léclair had accomplished much in his later years. At the age of 50 he had written his first opera, which proved a success of the season. At 51 he had become music director for the private theater orchestra of his former pupil, the Duke of Gramont.

And yet Leclair's more recent years had been clouded with distrust and despair. About 1758, he and his wife had separated. It was a double blow because Madame Léclair had also been the engraver of many of his works. Léclair had bought a small house in a dangerous part of Paris. Late in the evening of October 22, 1764, as the 67-year-old composer was entering his house, he was stabbed three times and died at his door. Because all three wounds were in the front part of his body, the police concluded that Léclair knew his assailant.

But who was it?

An investigation came up with three suspects. First, the gardener who found the body.

Second, Léclair's nephew, with whom the composer had quarreled. According to one account, the evidence in the French National Archives is so overwhelming against the nephew that the only mystery is why he was never brought to trial.

But according to another point of view, the most probable suspect is Madame Léclair.

To this day, no one knows who murdered Jean-Marie Léclair. Clear and precise as his music is, the details of composer's final moments are likely to remain veiled in mystery.

October 23rd

Satie's Prank

Erik Satie was a first-class eccentric, and when it came to publicizing his apocalyptic ballet *Uspud* he was more than true to form.

The ballet was the talk of Paris in 1892. Some declared it a masterpiece, others called it a shameful hoax. Satie vowed that he would go to the Paris Opera and insist on a performance that would prove his detractors wrong. Soon afterward Satie and a friend strode into the Paris Opera and asked to see the director, Eugene Bertrand. They were all but thrown out. Satie wrote to Bertrand, demanding a meeting within a week.

The week passed. Satie wrote Bertrand an insulting letter. Another week passed. Satie fired off another note, this time challenging Bertrand to a duel. He sent two friends to visit the director and arrange terms. Bertrand was not home. Several days later, Satie received a letter from Bertrand, who requested a meeting.

Satie and his friend returned. The director offered to look at Satie's manuscript. Satie was convinced that Bertrand was trying to brush him off.

"Monsieur," he said seriously, "the work we're offering is art of the highest order and we thought the opera would make it a point of honor to produce it with all due care and magnificence."

Bertrand stated emphatically that his budget would not allow such an outlay. Satie kept at him. "Furthermore, a work like ours cannot be appreciated without the support of the most highly qualified practitioners. So I have to insist on the appointment of a jury of forty reviewers–half of them chosen by the education minister and you–and half of them by us."

Bertrand hit the ceiling. "Impossible! Impossible! The rules forbid it!"

"In that case," Satie said in an offended tone, "there is nothing left for us to do but take our leave." With that, the prankster and his friend beat a hasty retreat. The ballet *Uspud* may not have made its mark, but Satie had secured his reputation as an original.

October 24th
The Mighty Handful

They were called the Mighty Handful—Russian composers who formed a national school. They included Nikolai Rimsky-Korsakov, César Cui, Modest Mussorgsky, Mily Balakirev, and Alexander Borodin. They were not so close a group as the name implies, as Alexander Borodin wrote to his wife on October 24, 1871:

The estrangement of Mily, his blatant turning away from the circle, his harsh comments about many—Modest in particular—have significantly cooled sympathies toward Mily. If he continues this way he might well isolate himself, which—in his position—would result in a spiritual death.

I'm not the only one who feels sorry for Mily, but what's to be done? Modest is put off by Mily's unfair and arrogant comments about his opera Boris Godunov, *voiced bluntly and harshly in the presence of people who by no means should have heard them.*

Cui is also offended by Mili's indifference and lack of interest in what occurs in our musical circle. There can be no doubt that the chasm between him and us is growing wider and wider, which is very painful. Painful because the victim of it all will be Mily himself.

The other members of the circle get along better than ever, especially Modest and Rimsky-Korsakov since they started to share a room, have both developed considerably. They're exact opposites in musical qualities and methods. One seems to complement the other. Their influence on each other has been extremely useful. Modest has improved the recitative and declamatory aspects of Rimsky-Korsakov, who in turn has cleared up Modest's inclination toward awkward novelty and smoothed all his rough harmonic edges—his overblown orchestration and his illogical construction of musical form.

And among all the relationships within our circle there is not a hint of jealousy, conceit or selfishness. Each rejoices at the smallest success of the other. There are the most cordial relations, including Cui, who for example ran up to me just for the sake of hearing my finale.

October 25th

Something Ventured

In 1933, the young American composer Samuel Barber ventured to the island estate of Arturo Toscanini in an effort to meet the famous conductor. The unannounced visit proved worth the risk because Toscanini not only received Barber and his friend Gian-Carlo Menotti, he expressed an interest in conducting one of Barber's works.

It was a rare honor because Toscanini was known to avoid contemporary music and music by American composers. Barber didn't take Toscanini's interest lightly. More than three years passed before he produced something he thought worthy of sending to Toscanini. Early in 1938 Barber reported to a friend that he was working day and night to finish an orchestral piece, probably his *Essay for Orchestra*, which he sent to Toscanini.

With the Essay, Barber also sent an arrangement of the second movement of his *String Quartet in B Minor*–his *Adagio for Strings*. Toscanini returned both scores to Barber without comment.

Barber had planned to visit Toscanini again the following summer, but he was so annoyed by Toscanini's lack of response that he told Menotti to pay the visit without him. After the visit, Menotti related a conversation he had with Toscanini.

"Well, where's your friend Barber," Toscanini asked Menotti.

"Oh, he's not feeling very well," Menotti explained.

Toscanini replied, "I don't believe that. He's mad at me. Tell him not to be mad. I'm not going to play one of his pieces. I'm going to play *both*."

The decision was a turning point in Barber's career. And Toscanini's presentation of the two works via broadcast with the NBC Orchestra showed his belief that the two compositions were American works worthy of bringing to the attention of a national audience. Toscanini proved more than right. Samuel Barber's *Essay for Orchestra* and *Adagio for Strings* have been major titles in the repertory ever since.

October 26th

The Spiritualist

The 1921 American tour of English composer Cyril Scott was a financial and artistic success, but Scott declined an invitation to return. He explained that a second tour would interfere with his creative work. He didn't mention that he had been advised to stay away—by a spiritualist.

In the 1920's, spiritualism was a widespread phenomenon in England and America. One of Scott's close friends was a psychic named Mrs.Nelsa Chaplin. In 1921, just before Scott began his American tour, he had a jarring encounter with the spirit world.

He'd been living alone in a small house in London. A housekeeper came in every day for a few hours to cook his lunch and keep the place in order. One day Scott telephoned to tell her that he was on his way home. When he arrived, he found that the housekeeper had committed suicide. He found her wrapped up in a blanket with the gas-tube in her mouth. She had left an apologetic note and several pawn tickets. It turned out that she had gotten into financial difficulties and had pawned some of Scott's clothes.

Mrs. Chaplin put her talents as a medium to work, got in touch with the distraught spirit of the housekeeper, and put her at ease by telling her that Scott had forgiven her.

During his tour of the United States, Scott began to feel uneasy and sensed that his creativity was waning. When he returned to England, Mrs. Chaplin told him that he had a sort of film over his aura. Scott later recalled, "Not being aura-sighted, that conveyed little to me. I only knew that it took me quite a time before I could see any beauty or poetry in anything again."

The year 1921 would bring a turning point for Cyril Scott. He began to delve more deeply into spiritualism and married a novelist who also communicated with voices from beyond the grave.

October 27th

The Pianist Who Wasn't There

It was the strangest assignment ever handed the young conductor. In October 1924, concert sponsor Karl Russell said to Malcolm Sargent, "I want you to conduct a piano concerto with the solo part played by a roll on one of those new 'reproducer' pianos."

The idea was simple enough in theory. "All you have to do," Russell told Sargent, "is give the orchestra their beat and cue in the piano by an electric switch held in your left hand." The music was to be the famous *Piano Concerto in A Minor* by Edvard Grieg. The distinguished pianist, Myra Hess, had performed the concerto to acclaim nine months earlier, and had recorded a reproducer roll of the solo part of the first movement for demonstration purposes.

The rehearsal was not encouraging. The reproducer piano was rolled onto the stage and positioned to the left of the podium. One of its two electric leads connected to a socket behind the platform, the other to Sargent's music stand. The first item on the rehearsal schedule was Schubert's *Unfinished Symphony,* and the orchestra was playing the Andante when the piano launched into the cascade of chords that begins Grieg's concerto.

The orchestra screeched to a halt while Sargent fiddled with the switches in a vain attempt to stop the piano. It paused for a page and a half, as prescribed by the score, and then began again, the keys depressing at the behest of phantom fingers. Then, abruptly, the piano fell silent. Sargent later found out that an electrician backstage had thrown the wrong switch, nullifying the conductor's control of the cues.

At the concert, the piano was perfectly well behaved and the audience was amazed, although some expressed a preference for a visible pianist. At the end of the concert, a pleased–and relieved–Malcolm Sargent left the podium and went through the motions of shaking hands with the pianist who wasn't there.

October 28th

My Family Could Use the Work

Genius was not enough. Johann Sebastian Bach also needed respect and money and he wasn't getting enough of either.

As director of the St. Thomas School in Leipzig, he answered to the town council and the town council had little appreciation for Bach's music. The money wasn't quite what it was cracked up to be either, and on October 28, 1730, Bach wrote to an influential friend in Danzig enumerating the faults with his job and hoping to find a new one:

Number one: I find that the position here is not nearly as remunerative as it was supposed to be. Two: Many of the fringe benefits have eluded me. Three: It's very expensive here. Four: the supervisors are hard to please and don't particularly care about music.

So I have to put up with constant annoyances, envy and harassment, and it seems that I must, with your gracious help, look for my fortune somewhere else. If by chance you know of or hear of any secure position for an old and steadfast servant where you are, if you would be so gracious as to provide me with a recommendation, I would do my very best to justify your gracious testimonial and involvement.

My current position brings in about 700 thalers, and when there are more funerals than usual the bonuses increase too. On the other hand, when the air is healthy, they decrease and during this last year my usual bonuses for burials dropped by more than a hundred thalers.

In Thuringia I can make 400 thalers go further than twice as many around here can do because of the extremely high cost of living.

All of my children are born musicians and I can assure you that I can already form ensembles with my own family since my wife sings a very pretty soprano and my eldest daughter also joins in not badly.

Despite his efforts, Bach remained in Liepzig.

October 29th

McCormack's Ordeal

October 1907: The young Irish tenor was more than nervous. He was about to perform his opera debut at London's prestigious Covent Garden. John McCormack had failed twice in auditioning for a role, but now, at the age of 23, he had the lead in *Cavalleria Rusticana*. His career was on the line.

Singing in Covent Garden had long been McCormack's secret dream. Each time he heard an opera in the great hall he longed a little more for the day when he would perform there.

At last he had gotten up his nerve and auditioned for Covent Garden's main conductor. McCormack sang from beginning to end the tenor part of *Cavalleria Rusticana*. At the last note the conductor had said, "Hmmm. Lovely voice but I don't think you're ready for Covent Garden."

McCormack tried again, this time auditioning for a group of Covent Garden associates. The verdict–his voice was not robust enough for opera. In a third audition he had, at last, won a contract Now it was opening night and time to deliver.

"I was so nervous," McCormack later recalled, "that I had ceased to be nervous. I guess the nerves for that evening were thoroughly burned out."

He was glad that his first aria–a serenade–was to be sung behind the curtain before it was raised. The harpist began the introduction. For an instant, McCormack thought he would die. He looked at the harpist. His mouth was dry. Then he said to himself, "Old boy, you've got to!"

About a dozen measures into the serenade, McCormack's voice began to steady so that when he appeared onstage he was " as cold as ice." Many of his singer colleagues were in the audience. Some of them had given up paid engagements for the evening in order to attend his debut.

During the entire performance, McCormack's senses seemed heightened so that he was ready for every musical word and phrase, for every gesture well in advance. In less than an hour and a quarter, his ordeal was over and his triumph at Covent Garden had begun.

October 30th

Shostakovich Confronts Stalin

He had been condemned during the Stalinist purge of 1948, and now composer Dmitri Shostakovich was being asked to undergo an equally unpleasant experience. He was being asked to perform in America.

The Cold War was in full force, but a peace movement had begun in the west. Shostakovich was told to attend the Congress for World Peace in New York. He felt that it would be humiliating to be put on display as part of a public relations spectacle when his music had been banned in his own country. He refused to go.

Then Stalin himself called and asked Shostakovich why he was refusing to go.

Shostakovich said with a brave bluntness that in America he would have to explain why his music was no longer being played in the Soviet Union. "What could I say?" Shostakovich asked.

Stalin pretended to be surprised. "What do you mean it isn't being played? Why aren't they playing it?"

Shostakovich explained that the censors had made a decree, that he and other composers had been blacklisted.

"Who gave the orders'!" Stalin demanded.

"It must've been one of the leading comrades," Shostakovich replied innocently.

Referring to himself in the royal plural, Stalin replied, "No, we didn't give that order. We'll take care of that problem," he said at last.

Shostakovich began to think that it would make sense to go to America if it would restore the music of his Soviet colleagues—and his own.

He went to America, where his music was a stunning success. But all the while he worried that he might let slip some comment that would get him executed when he returned home.

It was completely like Stalin, Shostakovich reflected, to put a man face-to-face with death and then make him dance to his own tune.

October 31st

The Murderous Madrigalist

The madrigals of Prince Don Carlo Gesualdo reach up toward heaven, but the story of the composer's married life reads like a page from Dante's *Inferno*.

In 1586 he married Donna Maria d'Avalas. She was an attractive woman whose previous two husbands had died. Don Carlo had shown no interest in marrying until his only brother died, leaving him responsible for producing an heir. Donna Maria was especially worthy since she was Gesualdo's first cousin. They were married in Santo Dominico Maggiore in Naples, where a portrait of Donna Maria and her family still hangs. The palace of the newlyweds was across the street. It was not to be a happy place.

Gesualdo was as indifferent to his bride as he had been to marriage. Donna Maria sought consolation in the embrace of the young Duke of Andria. Gesualdo became suspicious and decided to set a trap. One October night in 1590 the trap snapped shut. He came home from a hunting trip and caught Donna Maria in the arms of her lover. At his command the lovers were stabbed to death.

Because the murders were so cold-blooded, Gesualdo found little sympathy in Naples and had ample reason to expect an attempt at revenge. He withdrew to his country castle 20 miles away and had the forests on the hills below it cut down in preparation for a siege–a siege that never came. Then, according to legend, he began to doubt the paternity of his infant son, who soon afterward died by suffocation.

Was Gesualdo as adroit at politics as he was at music and murder? Within a year, his father had died and Gesualdo–now Prince of Verona–returned to Naples without incident and began courting a highborn lady of Ferrara. In the winter of 1594, they were married. True to his first love–music–Gesualdo had in his lavish wedding entourage several of the country's most famous instrumentalists. And like his lifestyle, his madrigals were some of the most dynamic and daring of their day.

November 1st

The Brave Queen

The 17-year-old playing her spinet on the storm-tossed ship was a remarkable person. Charlotte had refinements and courage fit for a queen. In fact, she was on her way across the English Channel to marry King George III.

At home she was known as Princess Sophie-Charlotte of Mecklenburg-Strelitz. She had enjoyed a rich musical life because celebrated musicians were always welcome at her parents' court. Her music teacher was one of the best, Carl Philipp Emmanuel Bach. Despite its cultural wealth, though, her country was a small duchy, hardly an obvious choice for a marital alliance with the vast British Empire. Power plays and court intrigues in London had settled on Charlotte as a politically safe and suitable queen for the 22-year-old George.

The young king and queen were not well-matched otherwise. George was awkward, could scarcely read or write, and had strange mental lapses, while Charlotte was poised, articulate, and charismatic. Unlike George, she quickly won the hearts of her subjects.

She made a powerful first impression with a combination of musical training and courage while she was still on her way to England.

Charlotte's Channel crossing was stormy and lasted nine days instead of the usual three. Charlotte's traveling companions were terrified. As the ship tossed and the storm raged, she sat down at a spinet and played English folk songs and Lutheran chorales, leaving the cabin door open so that all could hear. As the storm began to slack off, she picked up her guitar and played "God Save the King."

For the wedding, as if prompted by word of Charlotte's courageous crossing, the composer who would become the queen's music-master wrote a commemorative work. Johann Christian Bach called his congratulatory cantata *Thanks Be to God Who Rules the Deep*. Apparently Charlotte liked it. A note in the score reads: "This volume belongs to the Queen."

November 2nd

Stumbling Blocks

At every promising turn in her musical life, Rebecca Clarke faced a stumbling block. In 1902, at the age of 14, she entered London's Royal Academy, where she studied the violin and began to compose songs. In her third year there, her harmony teacher proposed to her and her father forced her to drop out.

In 1907, after three years at the Royal College, Clarke quarreled with her father, who cut off all support. She made do as a violist in the college orchestra and in 1912 she joined the prestigious Queen's Hall Orchestra.

In 1919 she wrote a viola sonata for an American competition sponsored by Elizabeth Sprague Coolidge. Her sonata, which had been submitted under a pseudonym, tied for first place. Mrs. Coolidge broke the tie by voting for the competing piece, which was by Ernest Bloch. According to the rules, only the winner had to be identified, but the judges were so taken with the sonata by the runner-up that they insisted on knowing the composer's identity, saying that the first prize winner was the work of a philosopher, and the runner-up the work of a poet.

"You should've seen their faces," Mrs. Coolidge recalled, "when they saw it was by a woman."

Clarke became well known as a violist and a composer and toured extensively during the 1920's and '30's. She was in New York when World War II broke out in Europe, and while stranded there, she resumed her acquaintance with a school mate from the Royal College, pianist and teacher James Friskin, In 1944, at the age of 58, she married him. Soon afterward, she gave up her career as a violist and before long also abandoned composing.

In later years, as her name was beginning to become known to a new generation of performers, Rebecca Clarke reflected upon her years of obscurity, saying, "I never was much good at blowing my own horn."

November 3rd

The Fate of La Scala

The opera house was the pride of Milan and its fate was about to be decided by war.

La Scala had been the focus of Milanese culture since it first opened in 1778. Now, in 1943, its very existence was in doubt. During an air raid on Milan, bombs had ripped a large gash in the roof and damaged the auditorium. Flying shell fragments had torn holes in the boxes on all four levels of the theater. The stalls and part of the stage had been hit, and the inadequate efforts of men wielding fire hoses had added water damage to the disaster.

One Milanese visiting the burned-out theater was struck by the sight of huge lengths of charred timber that had supported the ceiling for 150 years. But even more affecting was the harsh light that poured through the roof.

Despite the violence done the opera house, few Milanese were in a position to be concerned about it. Their lives and homes were still in danger. Some went so far as to say that after the war, Milan could do without an opera house—even the celebrated La Scala.

Those who still had a sense of humor observed that the city center had become too congested anyway and suggested that the bombing had provided an opportunity to expand the plaza surrounding La Scala, which might now accommodate a much-needed parking garage.

But the defenders of La Scala were quick to point out that Milan had always had an opera house and that whenever the opera house had been destroyed in the past, it had always been rebuilt without delay.

La Scala survived the war and was restored. At a grand re-opening in 1946, Arturo Toscanini conducted a concert of Italian music. Pristine white had replaced the golden tones of the walls of the theater, and a new generation of opera-goers was ready to start La Scala on its new life.

November 4th

Faure's Tough Teacher

Gabriel Fauré was nine years old when he arrived at École Niedermeyer–a new school in Paris with an unusual approach to teaching music.

The founder of the school–a Swiss named Louis Niedermeyer–had dedicated his life to the rediscovery of 16th and 17th century music. He opened his school in 1853 and hand picked his students, who were taught history, geography, literature, and Latin by clergy members. Musical education consisted of Gregorian chant, the sacred music of Palestrina, and the organ works of Bach.

Young Fauré found the curriculum "excessively rigorous." He recalled, "we were not allowed to play Schumann or Chopin. Niedermeyer didn't consider it appropriate music for young people."

Fauré won many prizes during his 11 years at the school. A solfeggio prize, a harmony prize, a prize for piano distinction and another for composition. He learned organ, counterpoint, and fugue.

Harmony was taught with more imagination at Niedermeyer's school than it was at the much-touted Paris Conservatory. And music-making there was often enriched with some of the more exotic modes, rather than a strict adherence to major and minor.

Difficult as the discipline was, Fauré flourished there. He learned to work under adverse circumstances. The school was short of space, so several pianists had to practice at the same time in the same room.

He also learned how to work with unwieldy instrumental combinations. Fauré and three friends assembled an orchestra with the instruments and performers available, namely four pianos, two violins, several pairs of tongs, some shovels, coal buckets, and a stove lid.

In 1861 the character of the school changed markedly when Louis Niedermeyer died. But Fauré received an important consolation in the appointment of a new piano teacher who became a lifelong friend–and one of France's great composers– Camille Saint-Saëns.

November 5th

The Bankrupt King's Musician

Henry Lawes had a position that was the envy of many a musician: He worked for the King of England. But the job had its disadvantages.

In 1626 Lawes became a gentleman of the Chapel Royal in the court of Charles I. Charles had been king for only a year. He laid down new rules for each member of his court, including the musicians:

Our chapel shall be all the year through kept both morning and evening with solemn music like a collegiate church, unless it be at such times in the summer or other times when We are pleased to spare it.

The king, however, was a devoted attendee at his chapel, so that even when he went hunting early in the morning he required pre-dawn services. His Majesty paid close attention to his music, too, often choosing the chapel service and the anthems to go with it. Occasionally he even joined in with the musicians, playing his part, it is said, "exactly and well on the bass-viol."

King Charles' attention also extended to the conduct, diet, and dress of his musicians. A household book prescribed the rules precisely.

The gentlemen of the chapel were to report promptly at service each morning and evening, appropriately clad. They were to chant the *amens* in a loud voice. Failing any of these rules, they were penalized, especially if they came in late, wore boots or spurs, failed to pay attention or rushed out before the final *amen*.

For his part as a musician, Lawes received clothing, loaves, fish, beer, wine and ale, plus a modest salary and occasional gifts from bishops and government officials.

Unfortunately though, King Charles was pressed for cash, and Lawes' pay came sporadically. But worse woes were to befall Henry Lawes and the court of King Charles I. To be continued....

November 6th

The Further Adventures of Henry Lawes

Henry Lawes had an enviable position as court composer to England's King Charles I. Although the job came with status, rich food and fine clothing, it had definite drawbacks.

A salary supposedly came with the position of gentleman of the Chapel Royal, but the king's financial problems often pinched off payments to members of the court. In 1627, the year after Lawes came to the court, it was rumored that the members of the king's household had gone unpaid for three years.

Then came the murder of the Duke of Buckingham, the king's best friend. The death cast a pall over the court. Even when the official period of mourning had passed, the king insisted that his music be melancholy. Songs of those unhappy times included "O let me groan one word into thine Ear" and "I rise and grieve, I walk and see my sorrow."

In those difficult times Lawes lived well. He was promoted to The King's Private Music. His new post brought him a higher salary–at least in theory, a billowy gown and doublet of black velvet, and a fine damask jacket. He dined on beef, mutton, fish, fowl, cheese, loaves, ale, and special dishes from the king's table.

His position required him to produce and perform in court masques. The king became increasingly fond of lavish pageants, perhaps because they provided a diversion from his debts, his dissatisfied subjects, and opposition from the increasingly powerful Puritans.

Lawes and his fellow musicians had the responsibility of creating a pleasant, fanciful world filled with cupids, shepherds, nymphs, gods and allegorical personages. The illusion–created with the help of ingenious stagecraft–lasted for nearly two decades before civil war toppled Charles from the throne and cost him his head.

The musician proved more durable than the monarch. In 1660, 11 years after the execution of Charles I, Henry Lawes became court musician to King Charles II.

November 7th
Tchaikovsky in Germany

On November 7, 1884, Peter Tchaikovsky was in Germany. He wrote to the wife of his brother Anatol:

Time in Berlin went pleasantly, and I saw Oberon. *I have always been told that it is boring but I liked it very much. In some places the music is charming; although the plot is silly It is a bit like* The Magic Flute *and quite amusing; and in the scene where the entire corps de ballet falls on the ground in convulsions, at the sound of an enchanted horn I laughed like a madman. Oberon's music is delightful, and whenever he appears the music is inspired and poetic. What I like about Berlin is that everything starts at seven p.m. There are very few breaks and everything was finished by 9:30.*

One evening in Berlin I met an acquaintance in a beer hall and begged him not to mention me to Anton Rubinstein (who prepares some horrid stuff of his own for an extraordinary concert)...Went to the home of Bilse and listened to the Andante *of my Quartet. Why always the* Andante? *They don't seem to want or know about anything else! On the day I left I saw that my* Andante *would be played again in another concert.*

Every day at dinner I was struck by the enormous quantities of food the Germans devour, much more than the Russians. I find all these dinner-times very congenial for one can keep silent and no one tries to talk.

As usual I've been out of luck at the theaters. Yesterday there was a performance of Gluck's Armida *but today it is* Carmen, *which obtrudes everywhere. Tomorrow it's* Posse mit Gesang, *whatever that might be and also tomorrow* Die Meistersinger. *Alas! I shall not be able to stay until then....*

November 8th

Down & Out in New York

In 1942 avant-garde composer John Cage was not prospering. He and his wife arrived in New York on the bus from Chicago with 25 cents between them. Cage would find New York rich in culture and poor in paying jobs.

The couple had come at the invitation of sculptor and painter Max Ernst, who welcomed them to stay in the apartment he shared with Peggy Guggenheim. Guggenheim had even suggested that Cage direct a concert of percussion music to celebrate the opening of her new gallery. In return, Guggenheim would pay the transportation costs for bringing the necessary instruments to New York.

At first Cage had the time of his life. "Somebody famous was dropping in every two minutes it seemed," he said later. He also succeeded in arranging a percussion concert at the Museum of Modern Art.

Then his luck turned sour. A meeting with avant-garde composer Edgar Varèse ended abruptly when Varèse's wife compared Cage's music to the work of a cartoonist.

Cage thought dance producer Martha Graham had invited him to work with her company as an accompanist or perhaps even as a composer. When he met her though, he found her cold and remote and completely uninterested in any kind of collaboration whatsoever.

Then Peggy Guggenheim found out about the performance that Cage had arranged at the Museum of Modern Art. She flew into a rage, canceled the performance at *her* gallery, and refused to pay for the transportation of the instruments. She also made it clear that Cage and his wife were welcome at the apartment only temporarily.

Cage wrote to friends and asked for money. He received about 50 dollars.

One artistic friend was both prosperous and generous. John Steinbeck treated the composer and his wife to lunch at the celebrated 21 Club on 52nd Street. The destitute John Cage was later stunned to discover that the cost of the lunch had been $100.

November 9th
Vivaldi's Biggest Crime

He was a distinguished composer with an international reputation but Antonio Vivaldi's opera *Siroe* was a disaster of the 1738 season at Ferrara. Writing to his patron on November 9, Vivaldi rushed to defend himself:

"Excellency," he wrote, "If the unhappy have no protection from the great patrons of the arts, they become desperate, and that's just the wretched state I'm in now if Your Excellency, my indulgent patron, doesn't come to my defense. My reputation in Ferrara is savaged to the point that they're refusing to stage my next opera."

Vivaldi went on to say that the biggest "crime" he was accused of was writing recitatives that were impossible to sing. But he stood by his reputation as a composer known throughout Europe, a composer of 94 operas, and refused to accept the accusations. Then he placed the blame squarely on the first harpsichordist, saying that, despite assurances that he was a competent artist and an honorable man, he proved to be "a reckless blockhead." "Even after the first rehearsals," Vivaldi wrote, "I heard that when accompanying the recitative he had no idea what he was doing, that he had the gall to meddle with my recitatives, ruining them with his incompetence."

"In fact," he continued, "they are the same recitatives that were played note for note in Ancona, and Your Excellency knows how highly applauded they were, even some entire scenes applauded just because of the recitatives. The main thing is that in my originals not one note was taken out, either with a knife or with a pen."

"Excellency," he concluded, "I am desperate. I can't stand having an ignoramus make his fortune on the destruction of my poor name. I humbly beg you not to forsake me, because I swear to Your Excellency, if my reputation is at stake, I shall take action to defend my honor, for he who takes my honor from me takes my life. The highest protection of Your Excellency is my only consolation in that case, and–kissing your hand with tearful eyes–I remain resigned to my fate."

November 10th

Love Letters from London

Hector Berlioz is considered a romantic composer. His letters reveal that he was also a romantic man. For example, here's one he wrote from London to a fellow musician on November 10, 1847:

Would you believe that in St. Petersburg I fell in love, truly and absurdly, with a member of your chorus? You can laugh here, to a full orchestral accompaniment in a major key. All right now, don't be put off. I continue. I am in love poetically, completely, and altogether innocently—interpret that any way you want—with a young girl—not all that young, who said to me, "I'll write to you," and who, referring to her mother's obsession with getting her married, added, "It's a bore!"

How many walks we took together in the outskirts of St. Petersburg and out into the countryside, between nine and eleven o'clock at night! What bitter tears I shed when, like Marguerite in Faust, she said, "For heaven's sake, I don't know what you see in me. I'm only a poor young girl beneath your class. There's no way you can love me like this," etcetera, etcetera.

But it's not only possible, it's true, and I thought I would die of dispair when I passed the Grand Theater on the coach out of St. Petersburg. And finding no letter from her in Berlin made me downright sick. She promised that she would write to me. And in Paris, too, no news. I've written, but no reply. Now that's a bore!

I know you have a kind heart, so stop laughing. I'm crying genuine tears as I write this. Kindly pass on to her the enclosed note, and I'll tell her, too, how unhappy her silence is making me. No doubt she's married by now.

Oh! God, I see us still on the banks of the Neva at sunset! What a burst of passion!

November 11th

Composer in the Trenches

George Butterworth had enjoyed significant success as a composer, but he found a cause that led him to abandon music. He enlisted as a soldier in World War I.

Like many composers, Butterworth planned a career in law. But he inherited a love for music from his mother, who was a singer. He learned to play the organ at school in Yorkshire and studied piano at Eton, where he began to show considerable talent as a musician. He wrote a barcarolle that was performed by the Eton orchestra in 1903, when he was 18.

The next year, he went on to Trinity College, Oxford, where music took up more and more of his time, particularly after he met composer Ralph Vaughan Williams. Butterworth left Oxford after less than a year and became involved with the English Folk Dance and Song Society. He went with Vaughan Williams on many expeditions into the countryside to gather folk tunes. He collected Morris dances from Oxfordshire and folk songs in Sussex.

The collaboration between the two went further. Butterworth suggested the idea for what became Vaughan Williams' great *London Symphony*. When the score was lost, he helped reconstruct it and wrote the program notes for the first performance.

He undertook projects of his own. Between 1911 and 1914, he wrote several significant works, including *The Banks of Green Willow, Six Songs from* A Shropshire Lad, and *Cherry Tree*, an orchestral prelude.

Despite all the activity, though, Butterworth found himself increasingly restless and haunted by a feeling of purposelessness. In 1914, when war broke out, he thought that he had at last found a cause. He enlisted in the Duke of Cornwell's Light Infantry, destroyed all of his manuscripts that he deemed unworthy, and went to the front.

During the Battle of Pozières in 1916, George Butterworth died defending a trench. He was awarded posthumously a medal and the dedication of the work he had helped to save, *A London Symphony*.

November 12th

Mozart's Mannheim Hopes

On November 12, 1778, Wolfgang Amadeus Mozart wrote to his father
in Salzburg:

*Mannheim loves me as much as I love Mannheim. And I'm not absolutely
sure, but I think that I may yet win an appointment here. Here, not in Munich.
Because my hunch is that the Elector will be happy to relocate his residence in
Mannheim since he won't be able to put up with the insolence of those
Bavarian gentry.*

*You know that the Mannheim company is here.Well, the Bavarians have
already hissed the two best Mannheim actresses, and there was such a
commotion that the Elector himself leaned out from his box and called out
Shhh! And, when nobody paid the least attention, he sent someone down to
put and end to it, and the go-between was told by the noisemakers that they
had paid to come in and would take orders from no one.*

*Now for something important. I have a crack at making forty gold louis here!
Of course, I'd have to stay six weeks or at most two months in Mannheim. The
manager of the Seyler company refuses to let me go until I have composed a
duodrama for him. You know of course that there is no singing in it, only
recitation to which the music is a sort of constant accompaniment. Now and
then the words are spoken while the music continues and the effect is quite
nice. You can imagine my delight at getting to compose precisely the kind of
work I have desired!*

*Do you know what that blasted scoundrel Seeau has been saying here'? That
my opera buffa was hissed from the stage in Munich! Too bad for him that he
said it in a place where I'm very well known! But what irks me is his nerve,
because when people go to Munich they'll hear the exact opposite!*

November 13th

Caruso's Big Audition

The 24-year old tenor was determined to have the part of Rodolfo in *La Bohème*. To get it, he went to see the composer, Giacomo Puccini.

He had volunteered to play the part for living expenses, a mere 15 lire a day instead of the thousand being offered established singers. But the theater manager had hedged, thinking that a better-known singer might bring the production more success. So the tenor boarded a train and headed for the rolling hills of Tuscany and Puccini's villa.

"Who is he?" the composer demanded when his handyman reported a stubborn visitor at the door. "Who is this Caruso?"

"He speaks like a Neapolitan and calls himself a singer," the handyman said gruffly. "A sawed-off little person with a petite mustache. Wears his hat cocked to one side."

"Another urchin from Naples," Puccini scoffed. He turned his attention back to a table piled high with musical scores and notebooks. "Tell him I'm busy."

The handyman replied that the singer was refusing to go away.

Puccini went to the door of his studio and barked, "Who are you?"

Caruso replied nervously with Rodolfo's lines from *La Bohème*. "Who am I? I am a poet."

Puccini laughed heartily and ushered Caruso into the studio. He sat down at an upright piano and asked him to sing "Che gelida manina" from the opera. When Caruso obliged, Puccini swung around and asked, "Who has sent you to me—God?" He offered to recommend Caruso for the part.

Caruso confessed that he still had trouble with the high C at the end of the aria.

Puccini shrugged. "You don't need it. Too many singers make a mess of the aria in order to save themselves for that high C. It's better to take it half a note lower than to wreck the song."

When opening night came, Enrico Caruso gave a spectacular performance as Rodolfo—including the high C.

November 14th

The Best Customer

One of the many young Americans pouring into Paris after World War I was composer Aaron Copland. He was born on November 14, 1900, and was not yet 21 when he arrived in the French capital to study and to take a place in the exciting cultural world there. He had a head start that many aspiring composers did not have–a publisher.

Soon after arriving in Paris, Copland signed a publishing contract for his piano piece "Le Chat et la Souris"–"The Cat and the Mouse." The biggest music publishing firm in Paris offered him 500 francs–the equivalent of about $300 in today's money–and Copland was delighted. He felt that he had made a beginning as a professional composer. And he wrote proudly to his parents in New York about the upcoming publication.

He ended the letter, "So we have a composer in the Copland family it seems. Who says there are no more miracles?"

While Copland was planning how to spend the 500 francs and looking forward to sending copies of his first published work to the United States before his 21stt birthday, reality set in.

As Copland waited for the publication, weeks dragged into months, and 1921 became 1922. Copland was learning his first lesson about the idiosyncracies of the music business and eventually vowed never again to announce the publication of a piece of music in advance.

One enthusiastic customer was particularly inconvenienced by the delay. He had ordered 25 copies of "The Cat and the Mouse." And although the composer was never sure what the would-be buyer was going to do with them all, through his long life, Aaron Copland remembered fondly that his first big customer was his father.

He tells the story in his autobiography, *Copland,* published in 1984.

November 15th

Snubbed

They were two of the greatest composers of the day, and at times they worked in the same vicinity. But one of them seems to have gone out of his way to avoid the other.

George Frederick Handel and Johann Sebastian Bach had plenty in common. Both were born in 1685 in Germany. Both produced vast amounts of first-rate music, sacred and secular. Both were virtuoso keyboard players.

By 1719, Handel had been living in England for several years. In that year he returned to Germany to recruit singers for a new academy in London. His mission brought him to Düsseldorf and Dresden. Handel spent eight months in the area but not once did he try to call on Bach. An intermediary, Count Flemming, attempted several times to meet with Handel, but was unsuccessful. He was always told that Handel was away or ill. Even the most impartial acquaintances of the two thought it strange that Handel made no effort to see Bach.

While Handel apparently found Bach's music uninteresting, Bach admired Handel's compositions and, with his wife's help, had even copied out some of Handel's works.

When Bach heard that Handel was only 20 miles away, in Hallé, he borrowed a horse from his employer, Prince Leopold, and went to see him, but when he arrived at Hallé he was told that Handel had left for England. It became clear that Handel was avoiding Bach—but why?

A key to the mystery may be Count Flemming, who had recently arranged a keyboard competition between Bach and a French performer named Louis Marchand. Apparently Marchand had sneaked a preview of Bach's playing and was so impressed that he quickly skipped town. Was Handel afraid of a similar match with Bach?

Many prominent musicians of his day were close friends of Johann Sebastian Bach, but George Frederick Handel was never to be among them.

November 16th

A Musical Revolution

On November 16, 1777, Christoph Willibald von Gluck was steeped in operatic intrigues launched by his rivals. He wrote to the Countess van Fries.

Never had a more terrible and hotly contested battle been waged than the one I began with my opera Armide. *The conspiracies against* Iphigenee, Orfeo, *and* Alceste *were no more than little cavalry skirmishes by comparison. The Neopolitan Ambassador, to ensure great success for Piccinni's opera, is doggedly intriguing against me at court and among the nobility.*

He has gotten Marmontel, La Harpe, and several members of the Academy to write against my system of music and my style of composing. The Abbé Arnaud and several others have come to my defense and the quarrel has grown so heated that the insults would have turned to blows had not friends from both sides brought them to order. The daily Paris Journal *is full of it. The dispute is making the editor a fortune.*

That's the musical revolution in France, amid the most glittering pomp. Enthusiasts tell me I'm lucky to be enjoying the persecution—an honor experienced by every great genius. The devil take them and their fine speeches. The fact is, the opera—which is said to have fallen on its face—brought in 3,700 livres in seven performances, not counting the boxes rented for the year and the subscribers.

Yesterday, at the eighth performance, they took in another 5,767 livres. The pit was so jam-packed that when a man was asked to take his hat off by the attendant, he replied, "Come and take it off yourself because I can't move my arms," which aroused great laughter.

I've seen people coming out with their hair bedraggled and their clothes as drenched as if they had fallen into a stream. Only Frenchman would pay so much for that kind of pleasure. There are passages in the opera that crack up the audience and cause them to lose their dignity. Come yourself, Madame, to behold the chaos. It will entertain you as much as the opera.

November 17th

Malcolm Arnold's Musical Jokes

Whimsy and humor run through much of the music of Malcolm Arnold—not surprisingly since the English composer always enjoyed a good joke.

As a student at the Royal Academy of Music, Arnold got attention, if not approval, by stuffing fish down the organ pipes in the Great Hall.

Although his parents were respectable and religious, a sense of the outrageous seems to have run in the family. The composer's elder sister Ruth was invited to leave the Slade School of Fine Art after she rode naked on a carnival float.

On one occasion Arnold, too, left school suddenly. In 1938, when he was 17, his studies at the academy became too intense and so he fled London with a beautiful redhead from the Royal College of Art. The couple went to Plymouth, where Arnold swore off music, but eventually got a job as a trumpeter in a dance band. He was completely happy until he was discovered by private detectives hired by his embarrassed parents.

After he returned to the academy, Arnold met flutist Richard Adeney, who had a similar sense of humor. The two arranged a concert at Town Hall for which Arnold wrote most of the music under various pseudonyms. One work, for example, was listed in the program as "Sonate poor flute, by A. Youngman"—the French word *pour* deliberately misspelled "p-o-o-r."

Since the local newspaper had no music critic, Adeney took a pen name and wrote a review of it himself in which he panned the concert and his own playing in particular. Friends who had been in the audience were so outraged that one of them thought Adeney should sue the newspaper.

The friendship of Malcolm Arnold and Richard Adeney, founded on a strong sense of humor, was built to last a lifetime.

November 18th

A Celebrity in America

By November 1891, when the Polish virtuoso Ignacy Jan Paderewski paid his first visit to America, he had all the stuff of a world celebrity–brilliant technique, abundant energy, and the ability to charm his American hosts.

Paderewski was renowned as a composer and a performer by the time he played his first American concert in New York. He was welcomed with unusual acclaim–and he was more than up to the lifestyle it demanded. By one count, during a 117-day sojourn in America, Paderweski played 107 concerts and attended 86 dinner parties.

Even before he had perfected his English, Paderewski was well-known for his wit. Conductor Walter Damrosch recalled a party at the home of the celebrated polo player John E. Cowdin. Admiring their host's handsome silver trophies, Damrosch told Paderewski, "You see, the difference between you and Johnny is that he wins his prizes playing polo while you win yours in playing solo."

Without hesitation, Paderweski went him one better, replying, "Zat is not all ze difference! I am a poor Pole playing solo, but Johnny is a dear soul playing polo."

Paderewski obliged so many of his American friends requesting a lock of his thick hair that his valet expressed concern that he would soon go bald. "Not I," Paderewski confided, "my dog."

During a second tour of America, Paderewski began a fantasy on "Yankee Doodle," which he offered to dedicate to pianist William Mason. Somewhat to his regret, Mason replied that Anton Rubinstein had already dedicated a set of "Yankee Doodle" variations to him and went on to explain that the tune was written to make fun of America. Paderewski never did finish the fantasy. But he did play some of it for Mason, who found it the best treatment of the theme he had ever heard.

November 19th

Father Mozart Fires Back

Wolfgang Amadeus Mozart had written to his father Leopold in Salzburg, enthusiastic about works he planned to compose for performers in Mannheim. Young Mozart reported that he might even be appointed to an important position. Leopold replied in a pointed letter on November 19, 1778:

Really, I simply don't know what to say to you. I'm going to go mad or shrivel up and die. Just remembering all of the projects you've dreamed up since you left Salzburg is enough to drive me crazy. All of them have amounted to proposals, empty words, resulting in nothing whatsoever.

During your stay in Nancy you were using your money for skipping stones, when–instead of squandering it away–you might have invested it in transportation of your own and getting to Strasbourg more quickly. Then you plunked down in Strasbourg until the heavy rains came, even though I had already told you that–if there was no profit to be made–you should depart right away and not waste your money. You yourself had told me that things there were in a sorry state and that you would depart immediately after the little concert you were giving on the seventeenth.

But people praised you! And that was enough for you! There you sat, not writing me so much as a line. Had you left Strasbourg on the 19th or 20th, you would have arrived in Augsburg before the floods, relieving us of our anxiety, with the wasted money still in your pocket

The main thing is that you must now return to Salzburg. I do not want to hear another word about the forty gold pieces that you might earn Your entire purpose seems to be to ruin me, just to go on building your castles in the air.

November 20th

The Widow Spy

Benjamin Britten's popular work *The Young Person's Guide to the Orchestra* of 1945 takes its theme from Henry Purcell's music for the play *Abdelazar, or the Moor's Revenge*, produced in 1695. The play was the work of a remarkable woman named Aphra Behn.

Much of Aphra Behn's life remains mysterious, partly because her own accounts of it are so fanciful. We do know that she wrote 15 plays plus a number of novels—and that she was a spy.

In 1666—a time when England and Holland were at war—Behn was a 36-year-old widow sent to gather military intelligence by the government of Charles II. Her instructions were to make contact with a Colonel William Scott, a political exile in Holland and an officer in the regiment of parliamentary soldiers in the service of the Dutch government.

Scott was eager for a pardon that would enable him to return to England, and in order to get it, he was willing to spy on his fellow refugees and to forward any information he could get about the plans and actions of the Dutch.

Aphra Behn wasted no time. She met Colonel Scott in the neutral city of Antwerp and, during a carriage ride, confirmed his willingness to spy for England. But Behn's success was gradually hampered as she began to run out of money. She wrote repeatedly to England asking for funds. She received no reply. As fall passed to winter, she was forced to borrow enough money to return to England.

When she finally returned to London, Aphra Behn was in for a double shock. In her absence, much of the city had burned to the ground, leaving many of its inhabitants homeless and starving, and Behn was soon one of them. She found herself in debtors' prison.

Eventually the forsaken spy was released from prison. And the resilient Aphra Behn turned her imagination to fantastic and exotic tales such as the one she told in *Abdelazar, or the Moor's Revenge*.

November 21st

Take It Away!

In the fall of 1920, Darius Milhaud had reason to be proud. His symphonic suite *Protée* was to be performed at an important concert. It had been chosen by the conductor, Gabriel Pierné, to share the program with a new work by Arthur Honegger.

The 28 year-old Milhaud had his misgivings though. The two compositions were lumped together under the heading of "Polytonality," which Milhaud thought was an arbitrary label that might put the audience on edge. His fears were well-founded.

Pierné devoted more than the usual amount of rehearsal time to Milhaud's and Honegger's pieces. Milhaud invited his parents to Paris for the big event, little expecting just what was in store for them. Even before the overture of his suite was finished, some in the audience were shouting, "Take it away!" Others made animal sounds.

A backlash arose with bravos and clapping–a show of support that just did more to drown out the music. When the orchestra got to a particularly innovative fugue in the suite, a battle erupted during which one audience member–a composer– slapped another–an organist–in the face. The police arrived and started clearing out troublemakers. With some satisfaction, Milhaud saw two policemen eject a prominent music critic

Pierné made a speech defending his choice of music for the concert and the crowd settled down– briefly. But before long they were at it again and drowned out the entire third part of Milhaud's suite. Sitting with him in a corner box, Milhaud's parents were horrified, not because they doubted the value of his music, but because they feared for his career.

The uproar had a surprising effect on Milhaud. In his autobiography, *My Happy Life*, he recalled that he was extremely proud, adding that "the sincere, sponta-neous, violent response gave me limitless confidence." The way he saw it, both noisy enthusiasm and vociferous protests are proof that a composer's work is alive.

November 22nd

Deliver Us from It Soon!

A great piece of music can fall flat unless it has a worthy place for performances, as Bedřich Smetana wrote in a newspaper column of 1864:

Boosters declare, "Thank God we have a provisional theater!" But let's pray to God to deliver us from it soon! How on earth can we present an opera in a house as small as ours? In Meyerbeer's opera The Hugenots *the armies add up to all of eight on a side, which makes the audience laugh.*

Smetana noted that the singers were squashed together so tightly that everyone had to take care not to hurt his neighbor when he turned around. As for the chorus, he continued, they had to stand either in a straight line in the footlights or in a semicircle at the back of the stage, packed so closely that they had to sing their parts without moving their arms or legs for fear of injuring the next person over.

"The acoustics are very different from those in our larger houses," he added, "and once an artist has gotten used to a small stage area it takes many tiring hours and many mistakes before he adjusts to a larger one."

He wrote that a particular terror was the orchestra pit—"a space that's hardly worthy of the name!" He asked, "Who in the world can hear the strings when there are hardly enough to make a chamber sound, let alone garden music!" He added up the musicians—four first violins, four seconds, two violas, two cellos, and only one double bass. "Never can we hear the musicians play as a group or in their proper proportions," he complained. "The brass and winds drown out the strings completely!"

"Under such conditions," he concluded, "it's hard to speak of higher artistic standards. If we're going to develop Czech opera we've got to build a theater that's suitable for opera—and the sooner the better."

November 23rd

The Premonition

Karl Ditters von Dittersdorf was not superstitious but he had no way to account for the strange touch that saved his life when he was 21 years old. In his autobiography he tells the story, which comes from 1759.

One snowy winter Dittersdorf had been giving violin lessons to a young courtier and, in exchange, a couple of times a week the young man drove Dittersdorf in a sleigh to a popular inn about a half mile out of town. One day the young man told Dittersdorf to expect a coach driver and groom to pick him up and take him to a grand ball given for a festive occasion. Dittersdorf accepted the invitation, put on his best clothes and went out to watch for the coach.

Just after Dittersdorf left his room, though, he was seized by a sense of panic as if an icy hand were passing down his back. Suddenly he had no desire whatsoever to go to the ball. When Dittersdorf's young friend stopped by, Dittersdorf told him he had changed his mind but couldn't give any reason. After pleading with him, the friend went away pouting. He made the groom take Dittersdorf's place on the sleigh so that the weight would be balanced. Dittersdorf watched through the window as the young man drove off toward the town gate.

Dittersdorf dismissed the matter and went over to his brother's place for an evening of coffee and smoking, reading and music-making.

They were just tuning for a new quartet when someone rushed up with the news that the sleigh had hit a stone, overturned, and thrown the groom headfirst at the town gate, killing him instantly. As for the young courtier, he had said that his one consolation in the disaster was that Dittersdorf had not gone on the fatal ride, since he would surely have been injured—or killed—the same way.

Ditteersdorf's young friend was put under house arrest for four months because of his reckless driving. As for Karl Ditters von Dittersdorf, he always believed that he owed his life to an inexplicable feeling of dread that seized him on that winter afternoon.

November 24th

An Immortal Dinner

The home of Anna and Adolf Brodsky was no ordinary place. One day when Johannes Brahms was paying a visit, practicing the piano, the doorbell rang and who should be there but a second guest, Peter Tchaikovsky. Apparently, Tchaikovsky didn not particularly like the music he was hearing and he was nervous about seeing Brahms, whom he had never met.

The two composers were about as different as they could be. The noble-born Tchaikovsky was elegant and courteous. Brahms was blunt and stocky and energetic and no respecter of manners. "Am I interrupting?" Tchaikovsky asked.

"Not at all, "Brahms said hoarsely. "But why are you going to hear this? It's not the least bit interesting."

Tchaikovsky sat down and listened, getting increasingly restless. Brahms paused, giving him an opportunity to comment. It passed. The situation became awkward and then the bell signaled the arrival of new guests—Edvard Grieg and his wife, Nina. They knew Brahms but had never met Tchaikovsky. The shy, sensitive Russian loved Grieg's music and took an immediate liking to the Griegs, who put him at ease.

At dinner Nina started out sitting between Tchaikovsky and Brahms, but after a few minutes she said, "I can't sit between these two. It makes me too nervous."

Grieg jumped up, saying, "I have the courage." And so the three great composers sat side by side— Grieg, Tchaikovsky, and Brahms, all of them in good spirits. After a while the dinner resembled a children's party. Brahms grabbed a dish of strawberry jam, saying that nobody else could have any. And after dinner, over cigars and coffee, Adolf Brodsky got out a magic set and began performing tricks, much to everyone's delight. The gruff Brahms was particularly taken with the show and demanded an explanation of the secret behind each trick.

But the real magic was in the gathering of three great composers—Brahms, Tchaikovsky, and Grieg.

November 25th

The Street Singers

At what point does a songwriter's work become public property? Stephen Foster found out that people very quickly got their own ideas about how one of his songs should sound.

In November 1858, Foster, his wife, his daughter, and his niece left Pittsburgh on the steamboat *Ida May*, bound for Cincinnati, where Foster was looking forward to some "recreation and variety" as he put it in a letter to his brother Morrison.

On a chilly evening Foster and his friend Billy Hamilton were walking back to the steamboat after a visit to the editor of the *Commercial Gazette*. From a distance they heard a party of young men singing a "strangely familiar melody" that turned out to be a badly bungled rendition of Foster's song "Come Where My Love Lies Dreaming." As they approached the ensemble, Foster and Hamilton couldn't resist joining in the singing. The serenaders got through the song and then scolded the songwriter and his friend in no uncertain terms, demanding to know what right they had to interfere.

Hamilton asked if they knew the song's composer. The young men replied, "Stephen C. Foster," adding that they did not know him personally. Hamilton tried to introduce them to Foster. The singers accused the two of being imposters.

"The situation began to grow alarming," Hamilton said later, "and we were in danger of having a lively set-to." Just in time it occurred to him to ask the agitated young men if they knew the editor of the *Commercial Gazette*. They said they did. Hamilton convinced them to visit the newspaperman's office. When the editor vouched for the identities of Foster and Hamilton, "suddenly nothing was too good for us," Hamilton recalled, "and we spent the balance of the evening in their company serenading."

And on that chilly November night, they might even have sung Foster's songs the way he intended them.

November 26th

Debussy's Parsifal

In the 1890's many French composers had a love-hate relationship with the music of Wagner. Among them was Claude Debussy. In 1892 he took time out from writing his opera *Pelléas and Mélissande* in order to perform his piano transcription of Wagner's *Parsifal*. A friend described Debussy's performance:

Debussy played the first act of Parsifal. *It came off very nicely and I think the audience liked it, although some of them said they couldn't hear the words. I'm not surprised! You know how he articulates. We count ourselves lucky if he sings anything other than* tra ra ra la la. Parsifal *is quite beautiful, particularly the religious parts. But poor Debussy came to the end of his rope. I thought he'd never follow through with it. As soon as it was over I took him aside in a back room and gave him something warm to drink. I thought he'd fall over. He sings with such energy!*

He assured me that if I hadn't been there turning the pages for him, at one point he would have clapped the score shut and taken off. The next time there will be time for a cigarette break in the middle of the second act, and then everybody will be happy.

Our good Debussy does this playing for the same reason that a man totes a trunk—to earn a few pennies. But I think he's happy at the thought that we were able to get about a thousand francs for him.

The following year, Debussy's friend, Eugène Ysaÿe, was hoping to arrange a performance of *Pelléas and Mélissande* in Brussels. For the sake of economy, he suggested a concert performance of certain parts of the opera. Claude Debussy respectfully declined to perform.

November 27th

Salieri & the Poisoning of Mozart

He taught great composers–Beethoven, Hummel, Schubert, Liszt–and many others. But today, Antonio Salieri is best remembered for something he probably *didn't* do–poisoning Mozart.

Peter Shaffer's play and Milos Forman's film *Amadeus* treat the poisoning story metaphorically, suggesting that the mediocre, jealous Salieri conspired to break the childlike genius Mozart physically and emotionally. Yet the rumor that Salieri literally poisoned Mozart persisted in Salieri's time and long after.

The first reports of Mozart's death speculated that he had been poisoned but did not mention Salieri, though as early as 1803 Carl Maria von Weber learned of the accusations when he visited Salieri. From then on, Weber–who was related to Mozart's wife–avoided all contact with Salieri. In the summer of 1822, when Rossini visited Vienna, he discussed the rumors jokingly with Salieri.

The next year, Salieri's health took a turn for the worse, and with it, his reputation. Salieri suffered a physical and mental breakdown in the autumn of 1823, was admitted to the Vienna general hospital, and in a deranged state of mind, accused himself of having killed Mozart. Quickly rumors spread throughout Vienna. References to them appear in Beethoven's conversation books of the time.

In a lucid moment, Salieri defended himself against the rumors, saying to composer Ignaz Moscheles: "Although this is my final illness, I can say in good faith that there is no truth to the absurd rumor that I poisoned Mozart. It's nothing but spite to tell the world that."

Nonetheless, the poisoning rumor quickly got its biggest boost–in Russia. In 1830, five years after Salieri's death, Alexander Pushkin wrote a miniature tragedy called *Mozart and Salieri* in which Salieri openly slips poison into Mozart's glass. In 1898 Nikolai Rimsky-Korsakov used Pushkin's drama as the basis for an opera of the same name. All the while, Mozart's reputation continued to rise, while Salieri fell into obscurity. When Salieri's music finally began to be performed again, it was inevitably linked with a legend that had gotten too big to stop. In the long run, it was not Mozart, but Antonio Salieri who had been poisoned.

November 28th

The Master Twice Over

The fortunes of the young French composer were worthy of an adventure novel by Henry Fielding. François-André Danican-Philidor got through some tough times by dint of his buoyant cheerfulness, hard work, and two talents.

In 1745, when he was 19 years old, Philidor was known in Paris as a capable musician. He was invited to accompany a dazzling 13-year-old Italian harpsichordist and her father during a Dutch concert tour that would include the distinguished violinist Francesco Geminiani.

The plan went awry from the start. Just as she was to leave Paris for Holland, the girl fell ill. As soon as she recovered, she was to go on to Holland to join her father, Philidor, and Geminiani. When Philidor and the girl's father arrived in Rotterdam, though, they received word that the girl had died. Suddenly, Philidor was alone in a foreign city with no money and no plan.

But the young Frenchman rose to the challenge. He made money by becoming a master at checkers and by serving as a mentor to some of the many Dutchmen who played the game in the city's coffeehouses. In Amsterdam and The Hague he sharpened his skills as a chess champion, and included a prince among his patrons. He went to England, where he became a chess celebrity, then became the chess master of central and northern Europe. He won two chess games simultaneously—while blindfolded.

After several years in England, Philidor applied for the position of court composer at Versailles but was passed over because his music was considered too Italian. So he began a successful career as a composer of theater music and opera. He is still considered the most skilled of the early writers of opera with spoken dialogue known as *opéra comique*.

But the work of François-André Danican Philidor that has remained the most popular—in more than 100 editions—is his *Analysis of the Game of Chess*.

November 29th
The Comeback

During World War I, violinist Fritz Kreisler had spent a few weeks serving in the Austrian army. After the war, when he tried to resume concertizing in the United States, he found that anti-German feelings still ran high.

Kreisler waited a year before returning to the United States. But while he waited, an operetta named *Blossom Time* that Kreisler had co-authored was a great success in New York in the fall of 1919, and Kreisler thought it had paved the way for his return. But concerts in Massachusetts ran into trouble. In Lawrence, the American Legion asked Kreisler not to play any German music and then withdrew its request. In Lynn the mayor demanded that Kreisler's program consist entirely of religious music and arranged for Kreisler's arrest if he didn't comply. The violinist declined to perform.

In Grand Rapids and Battle Creek, Michigan, Kreisler faced similar opposition. In Louisville, Kentucky, he postponed "indefinitely." A planned New York concert fell through. In Ithaca, New York, the mayor issued a proclamation urging people to boycott Kreisler's performance, but Kreisler went ahead with the concert. Members of the American Legion tried to force their way into the concert, and when they failed, they cut the electricity to the building, throwing performer and audience into darkness.

Kreisler played for 40 minutes, ignoring taunts of "Hun! Hun!" that came from outside while the audience responded with raucous cheers.

Kreisler persisted. By the time he gave concerts in Worcester, Massachusetts, and Boston, reaction had begun to reverse itself. And a performance at New York's Metropolitan Opera House resulted in a stunning ovation. *The New York Times* reported that "wave after wave of applause swept from floor to galleries as Kreisler bowed." He would still have occasional difficult moments, but for the most part, Fritz Kreisler had finally won back his American public.

November 30th

The Most Powerful Critic

November 1836. The most important supporter of Mikhail Glinka's opera *Ivan Susanin* was also his most powerful critic—not one to be argued with. Glinka explains in his memoirs:

Maybe because I had gone swimming in the sea on my last visit to Peterhof in the summer, I felt tremors around my heart and I began to suffer terribly. First it was my nerves along with an intolerable numbness in my entire body. After a while I developed a fever, accompanied by nosebleeds in the morning and burning sensations at night, so that pretty soon I found myself wasting away. Fortunately I already knew something about homeopathic remedies, and one dose of ipecac put a stop to my fever.

Glinka's illness forced him to remain at home, but when he felt a bit better, he started going to the rehearsals again.

Shortly before one of the rehearsals, the Czar stopped by. "Petrov and Vorobieva sang the E Major duet," Glinka recalled, "and naturally they did a lovely job." The Czar came up and asked him if he was satisfied with the performance. "Especially with their intensity and enthusiasm," the composer replied. The answer pleased the Czar and he passed it on to the actors. Through the theater director, Glinka was granted permission to dedicate his opera to the Czar and from then on, instead of *Ivan Susanin*, it was called *A Life for the Czar*.

Then Glinka's illness forced him to miss the final rehearsal—an absence he would regret.

The opera proved a thorough success. After the curtain came down, the Czar summoned Glinka to his box and thanked him for the opera, but then expressed his displeasure that the protagonist had been killed onstage. Mikhail Glinka was in no position to argue. He could only explain that the decision to place the death onstage had been made without his knowledge at the final rehearsal.

December 1st

The Clairvoyant Composer

Although she had no formal education, she composed 77 songs, blending words and music so well that they are still being sung eight centuries later. Hildegard of Bingen's inspiration came from a remarkable source—her visions.

Hildegard was born in the German duchy of Franconia in 1098. Before she was three years old, she had begun to have visions accompanied by a great light. When she was eight, her parents entrusted her to a prioress named Jutta at a Benedictine monastery. Although she had no teacher, Hildegard did benefit from a lifelong relationship with a monk named Volmar who served as her advisor. She learned Latin, which enabled her to read the writings of the church fathers and other authors of the times. As the years passed, she used her reading as the basis of her own brilliant, highly creative writings.

As she passed into adulthood and took the vows of a nun, Hildegard continued to experience her visions, which she described this way:

"I see these things not with external eyes and hear them not with external ears; I see them only in my soul with my bodily eyes open, so that I never lose consciousness of the ecstasy."

At the age of 43, Hildegard was inspired to write down a series of 26 visions in a detailed work called *Scivias* or "Know the Way," which has been described as part theology, part anthropology, and part cosmology.

When the work was done, the Pope thought so highly of it that he read portions of it to an assembly of cardinals, bishops, priests, and theologians. From then on Hildegard corresponded continually with the Pope and his advisors. She became known throughout Europe.

Hildegard's charisma comes through in her songs, which use Gregorian chant as a departure point but include a broader range of tone, soaring intervals, and rich melodic embellishment. Above all, they show the freshness and innovation of a composer whose creativity came from beyond the rules and confines of her time.

December 2nd

The Lives of the Bolshoi

The Bolshoi Theater in Moscow is a monument to Russian music–and Russian determination.

The story of the Bolshoi begins in 1776 when Prince Urusov, a devotee of dramatic art, secured a ten-year government monopoly on all theatrical performances in Moscow. At first, Urusov's troupe gave all of its performances in the mansion of Prince Vorontsov. Urusov then invited English impresario Michael Maddox to become the troupe's director.

According to the terms of Urusov's monopoly, he was to build, within five years, a stone theater "with such exterior decoration that it might serve as an ornament to the city." A site on Petrovka Street was selected for the new theater. But before the new theater was begun, a fire destroyed the theater at Prince Vorontsov's mansion.

Urusov suffered heavy financial losses. He sold his share of the monopoly to Maddox, who threw his efforts into building the promised theater, which became known as the Petrovsky Theater or simply the Opera House. For 25 years the Opera House served as the scene for operatic, ballet, and dramatic performances.

Then, in 1805, it too burned to the ground. The following year the troupe was given a magnificent place on Arbat Street–a building known as the "big" theater–or in Russian–Bolshoi. The Bolshoi Theater was ringed with columns and flanked by porches and galleries. But the new theater was to be short-lived. In the fires that erupted as Napoleon's armies retreated from Moscow in 1812, it was destroyed.

Eight years passed before another theater was begun at the original Petrovska Street location. Finally, in December 1824, the new Petrovska Bolshoi Theater was finished.

One more disaster lay ahead though. In 1851 a fire gutted the new Bolshoi. But this time there was a silver lining, because the replacement Bolshoi that opened in 1856–the theater that stands today–is said to be visually and acoustically the best of all.

December 3rd

The Broken Friendship

In the 1890's, Ernest Chausson and Claude Debussy were two of France's most important composers. They had in common the cause of music that was distinctively French. Then they had a falling-out.

It's not certain when Chausson and Debussy first met, although their names were first linked publicly in 1889 when both of them attended performances of Wagnerian operas at Bayreuth. In 1890 Chausson and a wealthy businessman financed a limited and deluxe edition of Debussy's Five Poems of Baudelaire. And the following year Debussy dedicated his song "The Sea is More Beautiful" to Chausson.

The two corresponded cordially from 1893 to 1894 and then something happened.

Early in 1894, Debussy announced his engagement to Thérèse Roger, a singer who was a friend of the Chausson family. A month later, when Debussy mysteriously broke off the engagement, Chausson was displeased, and the letters between him and Debussy stopped abruptly.

Then there was the matter of money. Chausson had arranged for Debussy to give a series of lecture-demonstrations on the music of Wagner at the home of Chausson's mother-in-law. But Debussy delivered only five of the lectures, forcing Chausson to refund half of the subscription fees.

The broken engagement with Thérèse Roger and the abortive lecture series might have been enough to cause a rift between Debussy and Chausson. But a third cause may have made the break permanent—jealousy. In the early years of their relationship, Chausson had been the "big brother," offering financial help and criticism of Debussy's nascent style. As Debussy found his distinctive musical voice and won more and more recognition as a composer, Debussy became increasingly critical of Chausson's' music and Chausson in turn expressed doubts about some of the compositions that were making Debussy the more famous of the two.

Five years later, the friendship was lost forever when Ernest Chausson died in a bicycle accident at the age of 44.

December 4th
Dueling Harpsichordists

Thomas Roseingrave was one the best harpsichordists in Ireland. In December 1709 he received permission from St. Patrick's Cathedral in Dublin to travel to Italy to expand his musicianship. But in Venice his career nearly ground to a halt when he encountered a keyboard phenomenon the likes of which he had never seen. The story comes from the English traveler and musicologist Charles Burney:

He was invited as a stranger and a virtuoso to the house of a nobleman where, among others, he was requested to sit down at the harpsichord and favor the company with a toccata as a specimen of his virtuosity. And says he, "Finding myself rather better in courage and finger than usual, I exerted myself and fancied by the applause I received that my performance had made some impression on the company."

After a cantata had been sung by a young woman, a grave young man dressed in black and in a black wig, who had stood in one corner of the room very quiet and attentive while Roseingrave played, was asked to sit down at the harpsichord, which he began to play. "Rosy" thought ten hundred devils had been in the instrument. He had never heard such passages of execution and effect before.

The performance so far surpassed his own—and every degree of perfection to which he thought it possible he should ever arrive—that, if he had been in sight of any implement with which to have done the deed, he should have cut off his own fingers. Upon inquiring the name of this extraordinary performer, he was told that it was Domenico Scarlatti, son of the celebrated composer Alessandro Scarlatti.

Roseingrave declared that he did not touch an instrument for a month after the encounter. However, he became very intimate with the young Scarlatti, followed him to Rome and Naples, and hardly ever quitted him while he remained in Italy.

December 5th

Indisposed

When a soloist is removed from a concert program with the vague explanation that he or she is "indisposed," the word covers—or covers up—a variety of situations. In the autumn of 1910, Nikolai Medtner had good reason to take issue with that word "indisposed."

Medtner was to solo in performances of Beethoven's Fourth Piano Concerto in St. Petersburg and Moscow under the renowned Dutch conductor Willem Mengelberg. Medtner took particular pride in the engagement because he was to perform his own cadenzas in the outer movements of the concerto.

But when Medtner met Mengelberg, things went awry right away. As far as Medtner was concerned, Mengelberg conducted the first movement way too fast. Mengelberg was patronizing. "Just play, young man, everything will be all right." The second movement was all right, but when they came to the finale, the tempo dragged. Medtner stopped the orchestra and asked for a faster pace. The conductor ignored him and kept on as before. And then, according to one account, Medtner slammed the piano shut and refused to have anything else to do with the performance.

The concerto was pulled from the concert, Beethoven's First Symphony substituted, and an announcement made that the intended soloist was "indisposed."

A day later, Medtner fired off his side of the story in a letter that turned up in the newspapers, saying that his supposed illness was nothing but a charade.

He referred to Mengelberg's "overbearing manner," "school teacher reprimands," and "megalomania." Medtner added that he had left the rehearsal because their disagreement had led to the final movement being played with two different tempi—one for the soloist and one for the orchestra. Then he played a trump card, saying that he was a Russian artist who had been insulted by a visiting foreigner.

The result was an immediate scandal that brought Nikolai Medtner the complete support of his fellow Russians. In the second of the two promised concerts, Medtner played and Mengelberg was replaced—without any explanation that he was "indisposed."

December 6th

The Phantom Concerto

On December 6, 1937, at Carnegie Hall in New York, Yehudi Menuhin gave the first American performance of a violin concerto by Robert Schumann. The performance might well have been forgotten after a few weeks except for some remarkable circumstances. Menuhin had wanted to give the world premiere of the concerto, but several people had blocked him from doing so—and some of them were dead.

The Schumann work was known as "the lost concerto" although its existence and whereabouts had been known ever since Schumann had written it in 1853. Schumann had written the concerto for the great—and particular—violinist Joseph Joachim, who had never played it, and left instructions in his will that no one should play the concerto until 100 years after Schumann's death in 1856.

But in the summer of 1937 it was announced that Yehudi Menuhin, who had called attention to the concerto, had obtained performance rights for the work and would give its world debut in America. Suddenly the plot thickened. English newspapers claimed that the rights to the concerto belonged to Jelly d'Aranyi, the grandniece of Joachim and herself a world-class violinist.

Then the German government stepped in and authorized Georg Kulenkampff to perform the work with the Berlin Philharmonic conducted by Karl Boehm.

Adding to the confusion, a book published that summer claimed that d'Aranyi had "discovered" the concerto through a series of seances in which she heard from both Joachim and Schumann, who ordered her to obtain the manuscript and play the concerto. Although the spirit messages had come in English and bad German, many accepted the story as true.

But the spirits were not to have their way. The Berlin premiere took place on November 26 before an audience that included Adolf Hitler and Joseph Goebbels.

Menuhin had to wait 10 days for his performance and settled for giving the American premiere of Schumann's *Violin Concerto in D Minor.*

December 7th

An Offer Too Good To Accept

Many young composers would have found the offer irresistible: An excellent salary, little responsibility, and plenty of time to write music. And Arthur Honegger received the offer from a very reliable source—his father.

Years later, in 1951, Honegger reflected that several career paths are open to a composer: A professorship, a civil service position, virtuosity, or writing for the movies. If the composer plays the piano like Rachmaninoff, the violin, like Enesco, or the organ like Marcel Dupré—he is "saved." Or, Honegger reasoned, if he has won a solid reputation in operetta—it's not impossible that some producer might add spark to his next film by listing the composer in the credits for dashing off a couple of tangos or some waltz tunes.

Then Honegger added, "there's the theoretical possibility of a guaranteed family fortune. A father who's an industrialist, a businessman or merchant, who just might help his son to pursue a profession that might bring him success—but not a living."

In that instance, Honegger was referring to himself. His father was the manager for a large coffee—importing firm in Le Havre. When young Honegger finished school his father told him, "You are entering the firm. You'll have very little to do. In the morning you'll spend two hours at the Exchange. In the afternoon you'll sign your correspondence. And the rest of the time you can compose music."

Honegger turned him down. "I was young," he said later, "full of enthusiasm and ridiculously conceited. I said to myself, 'Schubert, Mozart or Wagner would never have accepted such an offer. Sell coffee and compose "Der Erlkönig," *The Magic Flute,* or *Parsifal?* They don't belong together!'"

His parents graciously accepted his decision, which proved right on two counts. First, World War I ruined the coffee merchants of Le Havre. And instead of grinding out a living as a second violin in Le Havre's "Folies-Bergères," Arthur Honegger succeeded as one of the 20th century's leading composers.

December 8th

Performing for Tolstoy

In December 1909, a young Italian musician named Alfredo Casella was among a group of travelers who went to perform for the great Russian novelist Leo Tolstoy. Casella describes the visit in his memoirs:

After a half-hour sleigh ride through snowy woods, we arrived at the house of the grand old man.

We entered the foyer and found Tolstoy in his customary peasant's blouse and boots. In perfect French he told us that he had already heard our music in a dream the night before. He was sure that the real thing would be even more beautiful. We got down to work and played for about two hours. He couldn't get enough and constantly asked for something new.

After lunch and tea Tolstoy climbed onto his horse and went to ride in the woods for two hours. He was 80 years old, but still exercised every day.

Casella relates that after supper the musicians performed again. The ensemble played old music. He played piano pieces and accompanied string bass virtuoso Serge Koussevitzky in various solos. Word of the concert spread through the neighborhood and a fair number of peasants had slipped into the next room to listen. Casella continues:

When Tolstoy found out about them, he invited all the rustics into the room and personally offered seats to the women. At eleven o'clock—the hour at which he inevitably retired—all of us stood up with him. In a voice that I can still hear resounding he said, "I am infinitely grateful to you for your musical gift. I wish you all the best and hope to see you again in this world or in the next," adding with a peculiar smile, "if there is a next world."

Alfredo Casella was puzzled by Tolstoy's musical taste. The novelist didn't understand Bach and thought of him as too learned. He loved Beethoven and cherished Chopin, but he found Wagner incomprehensible, and he had no use for any modern composer except Mussorgsky.

December 9th

Bali

At the onset of a northern winter, many dream of warmer climates. In 1934, the Canadian-born composer Colin McPhee did more than dream. He set out for the island of Bali.

In his book *A House in Bali*, McPhee describes how he first gained insight into the essence of Balinese music. For about a month, he had been working on transcribing a complete score to a Balinese play he had seen. It seemed impossible that so much beauty could be achieved with a scale of only five tones.

But the distinctive embellishments of the music eluded him. A young household helper and his friend decided to assist. One morning they set two objects next to McPhee's piano. They were gangas—metal keyed instruments. The two boys played them in what struck McPhee as "a fast duet in Morse code."

At last the composer had found the key to Balinese music. "Wait!" McPhee would call out from the piano as the boys flew along, "Stop! Please! That bit once more."

Patiently the boys would stop and begin again. But soon they were flying again, faster than ever, amazing McPhee with their memory and precision. Sometimes the patterns repeated, sometimes they opened up into something new. Then, suddenly, the whole duet would fly apart and the boys would burst out laughing, breaking the spell.

Although Colin McPhee left the island in 1939, he remained spellbound by Balinese music. And its rich, distinctive sound would color many of the compositions he would write for the next quarter century.

December 10th

Puccini of the Golden West

Most of the thousands who made their fortunes from the California gold fields were miners. One was an opera composer. His name—Giacomo Puccini.

Puccini struck his gold without so much as lifting a shovel. He had been down on his luck. In 1904 his opera *Madama Butterfly* had premiered at La Scala in Milan. The audience responded with "roars, laughter, bellowing, and guffaws." It was almost impossible to hear the music, and shouts and jeers drowned any applause out. Puccini himself described the premiere as "a real lynching,"

During a visit to New York in 1907, he saw a play by David Belasco, set in the rough-and-tumble of the California gold rush. It told the story of Minnie and her devotion to the outlaw Johnson, whom she saves from hanging when she appeals to the miners to free him.

Puccini had his doubts about the play, but he was drawn to the subject of the American West. In 1890 Buffalo Bill Cody had brought his Wild West Show to Italy, and Puccini had joined the throngs eager to see rope-throwing cowboys and hard-riding Indians. Their splendid sharpshooting and authentic scenes of the frontier particularly impressed the composer.

Puccini set his doubts aside and based his new opera on Belasco's play—*The Girl of the Golden West*. But finding a librettist took some doing. Puccini began with Carlo Zangarini, who was fluent in English but not particularly poetic. Puccini had to resort to an attorney to convince Zangarini to work with a collaborator, poet, Guelio Civinnini. In the long run, Puccini wound up doing most of the writing himself.

It worked. One witness to the New York premiere of December 10, 1907, reported that the audience clapped, stomped, shouted, and called for encores. Puccini counted 55 curtain calls, about 30 of which seemed to be for him personally, as he stood onstage surrounded by the cast and joined by conductor Arturo Toscanini.

In addition to showering him with accolades, the opera made Puccini rich. According to a phrase common at the time, *The Girl of the Golden West* turned out to be Puccini's California gold mine.

December 11th

Mendelssohn on Music

A letter Felix Mendelssohn wrote from Leipzig to his mother in Berlin on December 11, 1842, shows that his thoughts were never far from music:

On the 21st and 23rd, we are to give a concert here for the king, who has vowed death and destruction to all the hares in the vicinity. In this concert we mean to sing for his benefit (how touching!) the partridge and hare hunt from Haydn's oratorio The Seasons. *My "Witches' Sabbath" is to appear again in the second part of the concert in a slightly different form than before, which was a little overdone in the trombone department and kind of deficient in the vocal parts.*

But to bring off the change, I've had to rewrite the whole thing from A to Z, and to add two new arias, not to mention the rest of the snipping and trimming. If I don't like it now, I solemnly swear to give it up for the rest of my life!

I wished for you the other day at a subscription concert. I don't think I ever played Beethoven's C Major piano concerto so well—my old war-horse—the first cadenza in particular. A new return to the solo really pleased me—and apparently pleased the audience even more.

What you write to me about the repertory of your Berlin concerts doesn't make me want to hear any more about them. The arrangement of Invitation to the Dance *and the compositions of English ambassadors—those are valuable things? If experiments are to be made and listened to, it would be advisable to be a little more generous with the works of our Fatherland.*

You'll say again that I'm cynical, but many of my ideas are so closely connected to my life and views of art that you have to bear with me when it comes to them.

December 12th
The Quick Study

In the mid-1890's, the German-American conductor Walter Damrosch was struggling toward success with his new opera company. Every setback was a potential calamity, and whenever a spectacular singer stepped forth to save the day, he was grateful. In the case of one singer, he was also amazed.

During the second season of the Damrosch Opera Company, a St. Louis performance of Wagner's *Die Meistersinger* was in jeopardy because bass Emil Fischer had been summoned to New York by a telegram stating that his wife was dying, requiring Damrosch to plan a last-minute substitution–single acts from various other operas.

The day before the planned performance, Damrosch received a visit from a young singer named Gerhardt Stehmann, who had been stranded in St. Louis the previous year and had continued to live there, acting in occasional German plays and teaching Latin to support himself. Stehmann asked to join Damrosch's company and volunteered to learn the third act of *Die Meistersinger* overnight. After the St. Louis success, Damrosch hired him as a permanent member of the company and found that the singer could learn an entire role in a few hours.

But Stehmann's greatest feat came during a New York performance of an opera by Xavier Scharwenka. Damrosch had awarded the tenor lead to a rather conceited singer named Ernest Krauss, who backed out the day before the performance. Stehmann said to the composer, "Give me the part and I will learn it for tomorrow night."

"But this is a tenor part and you're a bass baritone," Scharwenka replied.

"Give it to me," the singer insisted. I think I can transpose a few of the high notes and can at least save the performance.

The overjoyed composer gave him the part, and a night later, Stehmann sang and acted it without making a single mistake.

December 13th

One Woe Treads on Another's Heel

One woe doth tread upon another's heel, so fast they follow." Shakespeare's words would have rung true to the Norwegian composer Johan Svendsen in 1885 and '86.

The problems that plagued Svendsen the most were women and money—too many of the former, too little of the latter. Then there was the difficulty of his nationality. Svendsen had been hired to head the Danish Royal Theater orchestra, and some in the organization resisted the innovations of the foreigner. His fellow Norwegian, composer Edvard Grieg, said of Svendsen, "He's such a complex person that he will always be a mystery to me. He's at odds with just about all of the musicians here, so we don't see him at our post-concert get-togethers. We often have dinner together at the hotel though, and he often comes over to tell my wife Nina about his woes when I'm in my study."

Svendsen had plenty of women woes to report. His marriage was disintegrating, and he had become infatuated with a 19-year-old ballerina named Juliette Haase. But that relationship took a backseat to a romantic entanglement with the 32-year-old Danish pianist Golla Hammerich. Not long after they met, the two decided to run away together, although they seem not to have had any particular destination in mind. They stopped in the city of Aarhus, where they quickly ran out of cash. Embarrassed and disillusioned, the couple had to return to Copenhagen.

Svendsen did his best to put the debacle out of his mind by throwing himself into his work, but he never forgot Golla Hammerich. He wrote a small piano piece called "Album Leaf," which he dedicated to her, and long after he had married the ballet dancer, Juliette Haase, he secretly kept a letter from Golla. In 1911, when Johan Svendsen died, he discreetly asked two close friends to see to it that the letter was buried with him.

December 14th

Gershwin Finds His Calling

Nine-year-old George Gershwin was playing ball outside New York's Public School 25 when he discovered his passion for music.

Through an open window, he heard a violinist playing Antonín Dvořák's "Humoresque." The performer was a classmate of Gershwin's–an eight-year-old prodigy named Maxie Rosenzweig, who was playing in a school program.

Years later, Gershwin described the music as "a flashing revelation of beauty." He decided then and there to get acquainted with the violinist. He waited outside the school for an hour and a half, hoping to see him.

"It was pouring cats and dogs," Gershwin recalled, "and I got soaked to the skin." Somehow he had missed the young violinist. He found out where Maxie lived and trekked dripping wet to his house, where he introduced himself as an admirer. Maxie had already been home and left, but his parents were so charmed that they arranged for Gershwin to meet him.

The two became best friends although their houses were a hundred blocks apart. Maxie introduced Gershwin to the music of the great composers and explained to him the elements of a musical composition. Gershwin began experimenting on the piano at a friend's house on Seventh Street, trying to recreate familiar tunes with his right hand while improvising a harmonic background with his left. Then he tried making up his own tunes.

Two years later, Gershwin's mother bought a piano for his older brother Ira to play, but Ira quickly gave up on the dry exercises that his teacher assigned, and from then on the piano belonged to George.

December 15th
The Overbearing Teacher

She taught many of the 20th century's great composers. Nadia Boulanger had an extraordinary ability to assess and nurture the work of her students. In a way, she was too effective for her own good.

During a teaching career that centered in Paris and spanned the years from the 1920's through the 1970's, Boulanger's students included Aaron Copland, Elliott Carter, Jean Françaix, Darius Milhaud, Walter Piston, Virgil Thornson, and Roy Harris.

She could see immediately how a student's composition fit into musical tradition. Boulanger could analyze a piece of music down to the smallest detail and show how other composers had handled similar compositional problems. Whether evaluating a simple harmony exercise or a complex symphony, she could make comparisons by drawing from the vast store of music she had memorized.

She would occasionally play her students' work on the piano and change one element—often the bass line—to see if the aspiring composer noticed. If the student raised no objection to the alteration, Boulanger would scold him for a lack of artistic integrity.

When she complimented a student outright, it was an event worthy of celebration.

Effective as her teaching was though, it had a way of backfiring. The case of Roy Harris was typical. In 1929, the 31-year-old American broke with Boulanger, complaining that she had become incapable of letting him run his own life—artistic or personal. After Harris had separated from his wife, Boulanger had played the matchmaker, going so far as to convince one of her unmarried students to accompany Harris to Switzerland for a weekend in the hope that he would marry her.

In his farewell letter to his teacher, Harris thanked Boulanger for her rigorous harmony and counterpoint and analysis lessons and blamed himself for his need to be independent.

Like Roy Harris, sooner or later almost all of Boulanger's long-term students rebelled. But they never disputed her enormous influence on 20th-century music.

December 16th

Beethoven's Charitable Works

More than any other month, December is associated with charity. In December 1811, Ludwig van Beethoven wrote to acquaintance Joseph von Garena in Graz in response to a request for music that could he performed to benefit the poor.

From my earliest childhood my enthusiasm to serve our poor suffering humanity in any way possible through my art has been unaccompanied by any baser motive. Or rather, the only reward I have asked for is the feeling of inner happiness that always results from such actions.

Therefore you are receiving herewith an oratorio which takes half an evening to perform, an overture, and fantasy with chorus. If the institutions for the poor in Graz have a warehouse for such goods, then deposit these three works there as an expression of my sympathy for the poor in Graz, as the property of the promoter of concerts for the poor.

Additionally you will he receiving the overture to The Ruins of Athens; *the score of which I'm having copied as quickly as possible. Also—a grand overture to* Hungary's First Benefactor. *Both movements belong to two works that I have composed for the Hungarians for the opening of their new theater.*

You will have the grand overture as soon as I get it back from Hungary, which will surely be in a few days. Maybe the amateur pianist in Graz will be able to perform the engraved fantasia with chorus.

In one chorus the publishers have changed the words, completely disregarding the expression. Therefore the words written in pencil should be sung. If you can use this oratorio I can also send you the parts written out so that the costs would he less burdensome for the poor.

December 17th

Milhaud's Daring Debut

In 1922 French composer Darius Milhaud was eager to see America. Once he made arrangements for enough concerts as a conductor to justify the journey, only one problem remained—delivering. Although he had no experience beyond conducting his own works, Milhaud would soon find himself expected to lead one of the greatest orchestras in the world.

A few weeks before leaving France, Milhaud received a telegram from his manager telling him that he was to conduct a concert in Philadelphia. The program was to be half-classical and half-modern. Clearly, Milhaud was going to have to broaden his repertory quickly.

When he arrived in Philadelphia, the fledgling conductor was in for a bigger shock. Leopold Stokowski, the conductor of the Philadelphia Orchestra, had left for a European trip, designating as his interim replacements Georges Enesco, Alfredo Casella—and Darius Milhaud. The young Frenchman was now expected to make his debut as a stand-in for one of the most important conductors in the world.

Milhaud remarked later with typical nonchalance, "I was not too nervous. Since I had to begin some time, it was all for the best that it should be with the finest symphony orchestra in the world."

The contemporary works gave him less trouble than the others did, Milhaud said later. "I studied the scores very thoroughly and the rehearsals didn't go so badly. The orchestra must have found me clumsy but they were very kind."

Two friends who had helped arrange Milhaud's American tour came from New York for the concert, expecting to see the novice conductor in a sweat half an hour before the performance, but instead found him sitting calmly at the dinner table eating a dessert.

"I tried to conduct with simplicity and precision," Milhaud said of the big debut, "and that was my salvation. I even had the satisfaction of reading in one newspaper that I was a good conductor but a lousy composer." He added, "But I still tremble when I think of my gall—or innocence—back then. Ignorance is bliss."

December 18th

Mozart the Optimist

During much of his 23rd year, Wolfgang Amadeus Mozart was traveling, hoping to find a reliable patron or at least a well-paid position. His letters to his father Leopold in Salzburg were full of cheerful optimism that was not shared by his disapproving parent. Young Mozart had just left Mannheim when he wrote from Kaysersheim on December 18, 1778:

Not only I but all my closest friends, the Cannabichs especially, were in the most pitiable distress during the final days before my departure. We really believed it would be impossible for us to part. I left at half past eight in the morning but Madame Cannabich didn't get up. She simply would not and could not say goobye. For my part, I didn't want to upset her, so I left the house without seeing her.

Dearest Father, I assure you she is one of my best and truest friends. For the only people I call friends are friends in every situation, who day and night think only of how they can best serve the interests of their friend, and who employ their influential acquaintances and work hard themselves to ensure his happiness. Well, that's an accurate portrait of Madame Cannabich.

Of course, there may be some self-interest in this, but how does anything happen, how can anything be done in this world without some self-interest! And what I like best about Madame Cannabich is that she never tries to deny it.

Well, I'll feel very embarrassed if I get to Munich without my violin sonata. I cannot understand the delay. It's the most irritating thing I've ever run into. Think of it. I know that my sonatas were published at the beginning of November, and I—the composer—have not yet received them, and so I can't present them to the Electress to whom they are dedicated.

December 19th

The King of Lahore

The opera *The King of Lahore* is not the best remembered work by Jules Massenet. But the composer associated it with one of the best years of his life. In his memoir *My Recollections*, Massenet wrote of the excitement, amusement, and promise that accompanied the productions of the opera.

Early in 1878, the opera was doing well in Paris when Massenet learned that it was to be produced in Turin. The performance was an honor since, at the time, the only works translated into Italian and performed in Italy were the works of the great masters, which had to wait years for such a distinction, and yet Massenet's opera was to be performed there not long after its Paris debut.

During rehearsals the conductor said often to Massenet. "Are you satisfied?! I am extremely!"

The production was not without its amusing moments. One of the leads was a famous singer of the time, a Signor Fanselli. He tended to spread his arms wide in front of him with his fingers fanned out–an unpleasant mannerism that was all too common among singers trying to express emotion. Fanselli's finger flinging earned him the nickname "Five and five make ten."

The success of *The King of Lahore* and other works made Massenet well known in Italy. In the year of its Italian performances, he had an audience with the new Pope, Leo XIII. He was introduced to the queen, who asked him to play opera motifs on the piano. He met the son of Italy's great unifier, Garibaldi.

But the crowning success of the year came just after Massenet returned from Italy. He had an invitation from Ambroise Thomas to be professor of counterpoint at the Paris Conservatory.

Jules Massenet summarized in his memoirs. "What a contrast to the months of congenial frivolity and acclaim in Italy! Although I thought I had been forgotten in France, the truth was the exact opposite."

December 20th
The Helpful Trick

In Paris in the 1850's, many a young composer hoped for a helping hand from the great Rossini. After writing nearly 40 operas, Rossini had retired from public life at the age of 37 and settled into a life of relaxation and socializing. To his well-furnished apartment came one aspiring composer after another, hoping for advice—or better still—an endorsement from the master.

Rossini's wife served as hostess to the celebrities that crowded the drawing room and waited on the stairway. Rossini held forth in the dining room, reserving himself for conversation with a chosen few. Rossini had a mischievous wit, and, on one occasion, he used it to nudge the reputation of a promising young composer.

One evening in 1858, the visitors to Rossini's apartment included a 23-year-old named Camille Saint-Saëns. Rossini greeted Saint-Saëns without any special enthusiasm, but a few weeks later he invited Saint-Saëns to come back for a morning visit. Rossini had determined that Saint-Saëns was a cut above most of the musicians who packed into the apartment, and the two of them sat down to a serious discussion about modern music.

Not long afterwards, Rossini arranged for a home performance of Saint-Saëns' "Tarantella" for flute and clarinet. He gave the impression that he had written the "Tarantella." After an encore, Rossini took Saint-Saëns by the hand and led him into the dining room. In came the crush of admirers with no end of compliments, and when each admirer had poured on the praise, Rossini said casually, "I agree completely. But I didn't write it—this gentleman here is the composer."

During the next several years Rossini occasionally asked Saint-Saëns to stand in for him in performances of his entertaining piano pieces in the collection known as "Sins of My Old Age."

Thanks to a simple ruse, the two musicians, old and young, had forged a firm friendship.

December 21st

Nadja

Some critics have suggested that her media image is contrived, but world-renowned violinist Nadja Salerno-Sonnenberg showed temperament, flair, and a passion for music before publicity became a part of her life.

Already a virtuoso at the age of 17, she moved from Philadelphia to New York to attend the Juilliard School full-time and suddenly felt free–too free. "I cut classes," she recalled, "fell in love, snuck into Yankee Stadium. It was a year full of wonder. I learned an enormous amount about life, but nothing about playing the violin." For seven months she stopped playing the violin entirely, stopped bringing her violin to her lessons, preferring just to talk with her teacher, the distinguished Dorothy DeLay.

Then DeLay issued an ultimatum: Take the violin seriously or get another teacher. Salerno-Sonnenberg set her sites on winning the prestigious Walter W. Naumberg International Violin Competition, which gave her just three months to overcome seven months of inactivity. She practiced 13 hours a day. She won first prize in the competition.

By her mid 20's she had become a celebrity, first praised and then disparaged by critics because of her informal concert attire and tough demeanor. By the early '90's she was beginning to burn out, and she considered quitting the concert stage.

Then, in 1994, while chopping an onion for a Christmas dinner, she cut off the end of her left little finger. The accident and her painstaking recovery from it forced her to focus on what she wanted to do with her life. "In retrospect," she said later, "the accident was a blessing...I started to play again, and that's how I realized how much I loved to play. Now everything is a joy. Things I wouldn't have even considered doing professionally, I jump right in."

December 22nd
Too Much of a Powerful Thing

Composer and critic Johann Friedrich Reichardt attended one of the most important concerts in music history, but he didn't know it at the time. The program included the first performances of several major works by Beethoven. A few days later, he wrote about an event, which took place in Vienna on the evening of December 22, 1808:

"In that freezing cold theater we stuck it out from 6:30 to 10:30 and found out again that it's easy to have too much of a good thing—not to mention a powerful thing."

The box of his host, Prince Lobkowitz, was quite close to the stage where Beethoven was conducting the orchestra, and neither Reichardt nor the prince felt comfortable leaving before the concert was over, even though many a bad performance tested their patience.

After the Pastoral Symphony, a singer performing the aria "Ah Perfido!" seemed to shiver rather than sing, not surprisingly to Reichardt since he and the prince were shaking with cold, wrapped in furs in their closed-up box. According to Reichardt, a Gloria from the Mass in C, came off badly. For him the highlight was the Fourth Piano Concerto. Beethoven himself was the soloist and played with dazzling speed. During the Adagio, which Reichardt described as a masterpiece of beautiful, continuous melody, Beethoven made the piano sing out with a deep, overwhelming melancholy.

Reichardt described what followed as "huge, complicated, and overlong." It was Beethoven's Fifth Symphony. The Sanctus from the Mass in C followed, also badly performed. Then Beethoven played a long fantasy, and finally there was, as Reichardt saw it, another disastrous performance–the Choral Fantasy, during which "the orchestra dissolved into such confusion that Beethoven, roused by the creative flame, forgot all about the audience and shouted, 'Stop there and take it from the beginning!'" The fiasco made Reichardt so embarrassed for Beethoven that he regretted not leaving earlier.

The power of Beethoven was more than a distracted audience could absorb on that cold night of December 22, 1808.

December 23rd

Exile for Music

Most composers make sacrifices for their music. But few have had to give up their country for it. One who did was Arvo Pärt.

Pärt was born in 1935 in Estonia, one of the three Baltic states wedged in between powerful neighbors—Germany to the west and Russia to the east. Pärt felt that his musical education was western, emphasizing the great European composers, while his spiritual upbringing was eastern, influenced by the Russian Orthodox Church.

From the age of about seven Pärt attended a children's music school where he received instruction in piano, music theory, and literature.

His musical talent began to manifest itself. One fellow student recalled that Pärt just seemed to "shake his sleeve and the notes would fall out."

He entered the Tallinn Conservatory and studied with Estonia's great composer Heino Eller, who wrote conservative music, but allowed his students to explore the new ideas coming in from the West. But recognition as a composer still required Pärt to write within the traditional guidelines that persisted in the post-Stalinist Soviet Union.

In 1968 the eastern influence began to show in Pärt's music when he wrote his *Credo* for piano, chorus and orchestra. The *Credo's* overtly religious nature was frowned upon by Soviet authorities, and the work also sparked a creative crisis and physical collapse for the composer. In 1972 he joined the Russian Orthodox Church, his health returned, and he began studying early music, which led Pärt to a new tonal style.

By 1979 the strictures placed on Pärt by the Soviet government made it impossible for him to function as a composer. So early in 1980, Paärt and his family left Estonia to take up a new life in Berlin, where Arvo Pärt became known as one of the most innovative—and popular composers in the world.

December 24th

The First Radio Concert

The first radio concert was a brilliant success but, like many live broadcasts today, it required not only high technology, but artistry, fast thinking and improvisation.

The Canadian inventor Reginald Fessenden, who had worked for both Thomas Edison and George Westinghouse, was working on the problem of transmitting the human voice, and he succeeded on December 23, 1900, by sending a wireless message a between two 50-foot towers on Cobb Island in the Potomac River–the first time that intelligible speech had been transmitted by electromagnetic waves. The message for the great occasion was rather prosaic: "One, two, three, four. Is it snowing where you are, Mr. Thiessen? If it is, telegraph back and let me know."

Within a few years, Fessenden was making voice transmissions across the Atlantic, from Brant Rock, Massachusetts, to Machrihanish, Scotland. By December 24, 1906, Fessenden was ready to broadcast a full-fledged concert The audience was to be the crews aboard ships of the United Fruit Company for whom Fessenden had recently installed wireless stations. At 9:00 p.m. he began beaming his Christmas concert from the 400-foot towers at Brant Rock.

He began with a series of dots and dashes–"CQ, CQ, CQ"–a general call to stations within range. Then Fessenden stepped up to a microphone and announced the concert to follow. Next an operator turned on an Edison phonograph and played a vocal rendition of Handel's "Largo" from the opera *Xerxes*. Mr. Stein, an assistant, also had a first that night–the first case of mike fright. When he backed away, Fessenden snatched up his violin and fiddled and sang his way through "O Holy Night." Fessenden's wife Helen and his secretary, Miss Bent, nervously read a Biblical passage–"Glory to God in the highest and on earth peace to men of good will." Fessendem then returned to the microphone to wish his listeners a Merry Christmas.

That first broadcast concert was more successful than Fessenden had imagined. Responses poured in not just from vessels of the United Fruit Company, but from the astonished crews of ships all over the Atlantic Ocean.

December 25th

The Christmas Pledge

Christmas Eve, 1870. Richard Wagner and his wife, Cosima, had agreed not to give each other Christmas presents. They were simply too poor. But Wagner was planning a surprise gift.

For more than two months, he had been crafting a piece of music to be performed outside Cosima's bedroom door on Christmas morning. He had based it on themes later to be used in his opera *Siegfried*, plus a little nursery song he had written for their children two years earlier. He completed the *Siegfried Idyll* three weeks before Christmas and arranged for conductor Hans Richter to recruit the members of the small orchestra. Richter conducted secret rehearsals, first in Zurich, then at a hotel in Lucerne.

Wagner invited philosopher Friedrich Nietzsche to the final rehearsal on Christmas Eve at the Hotel du Lac and they arrived together at the Wagners' home in the village of Trihschen. There they found Cosima decorating the Christmas tree and preparing presents for the children

At seven o'clock on Christmas morning, the musicians arrived and quietly arranged themselves on the stairs outside Cosima's room. They began to play.

"As I awoke to the light of dawn," Cosima said later, "my mind passed from one dream into another. Familiar sounds from *Siegfried* came to my ears. It was as if the house—or more accurately—our entire being, were rising up in music and going up to heaven. Sacred memories, birdsong and sunrise, interwoven with music from *Siegfried*, soothed my heart and I came to realize that I was not dreaming, and yet was experiencing the most sublime of all dreams.

"Now at last I understood all of Richard's writing in secret."

And yet Wagner had kept his pledge not to buy his wife a Christmas present. December 25 was Cosima's birthday.

December 26th

Friendly Deception

The composing career of Albert Roussel got off to a wayward start, and received one of its biggest boosts from a lie.

Roussel was orphaned at the age of eight and went to live with his grandfather. He built on the music he had learned from his mother, entertaining himself by reading through the family music collection and playing operatic selections and popular songs on the piano.

Three years later, Roussel's grandfather died, and his mother's sister took him in. Her husband arranged for young Albert to take piano lessons. Summer vacations at a Belgian seaside resort added a second love to his life–the sea. He studied to be a naval cadet, but still made time to study music.

In the French Navy, while he was stationed on a cruiser based at Cherbourg, he and two friends found the time to play the piano trios of Beethoven and other composers. Roussel also began composing. At the Church of the Trinity in Cherbourg on Christmas Day, 1892, he had his debut as a composer with the performance of his *Andante* for string trio and organ.

That success encouraged Roussel to write a wedding march, and one of his fellow naval officers offered to show it to a prominent conductor, Edouard Colonne. When Roussel's friend returned with the manuscript, he reported that Colonne had advised Roussel to give up his naval career and devote his life to music.

Not long afterward, at the age of 25, Roussel did just that. He applied the self-discipline, conciseness, and spirituality that he had developed in the navy to his composing and became a major force in 20th century French music. As for Eduoard Colonne's inspiring advice that Roussel devote his life to music–Roussel's navy friend later admitted that he had made it up and that he had never even shown Roussel's manuscript to the conductor.

December 27th

The Kiss

He had money problems, his hearing was failing, and he was at odds with his wife. Bedřich Smetana needed something to cheer him up and he found it in his opera *The Kiss*.

In 1875, at the urging of his librettist, Smetana began work on the opera, and he quickly became enthusiastic about it. The woman employed as the librettist reported, in fact, that sometimes Smetana became a little too enthusiastic. She wrote:

He didn't realize how loud his voice was, and embarrassed me by stopping me on the street and shouting how happy he was that I had given him The Kiss, *which caused many a passer-by to give me strange looks. I pointed out the ambiguity, but to no effect.*

While he was writing the charming work he seemed to have a new lease on life. He would stand in my room in front of the mirror, laughing and pointing menacingly at his reflection, saying, "That gray-haired old badger looking at me from the mirror—that supposedly is me. Don't you believe it! That mirror's no good! I feel like a boy of seventeen, not like that bearded bespectacled old grandfather!"

Despite his enthusiasm, many months passed before Smetana finally finished the opera. But the first performance in Prague late in 1876 was well worth the wait. One audience member recalled the audience's lively response.

The artists accepted flowers and homage. Finally Smetana himself appeared, small, pale and self-conscious. Laurel wreaths flew from the beams to his feet, bouquets came down from all sides. The shouts and applause seemed endless. But Smetana heard none of it. Then scarves began to wave, the audience gave a standing ovation, and Smetana waved gently to the audience.

When he needed it most, Smetana had been given a new lease on life by *The Kiss*.

December 28th
Father Mozart's Demand

It was as if they were playing cat and mouse. In mid-December 1778, Wolfgang Amadeus Mozart had written to his father Leopold from Keysersheim explaining why—contrary to his father's wishes—he had not yet come home to Salzburg. On December 28, an outraged Leopold wrote hack:

I thought you would have been guided by your common sense and that you would put more stock in your father's judgement—which you know to he sound—than in your own fruitless wishes. So I had no doubt that by the New Year at the latest you would be home in Salzburg.

But what is the use of saying anything? If you will disregard all of your cheerful dreams, you will have to concede that I am right. And it is hardly necessary for me to bother to justify my opinion to you. All the more because I an sick to death of composing these long letters, and for the past fifteen months have practically written myself blind!

You left Paris on September 26th. If you had come straight to Salzburg, I could have paid off a large portion of our debts. So I command you to leave right away since your behavior is disgraceful and I'm thoroughly embarrassed by having assured everyone that you would positively be home by the New Year at the very latest. Good God! How many times you've made a liar of me!

I think I have made myself completely clear. Or do I have to take the mail coach myself and go get you? Surely my son won't let things come to such a pass.

Everybody sends greetings to you. Your sister and I kiss you several hundred thousand times and I remain your father who is still waiting for you.

December 29th

Enesco's Favorite

Composers and their public often disagree about which works have the most merit. The favorite work of the Romanian composer Georges Enesco is one rarely heard today-his *Romanian Poem*.

It was the *Romanian Poem* that launched his career as a composer. It was his first published work, written in 1897 when Enesco was only 16. The work is in two parts. The first evokes a summer evening, with the sound of distant church bells, the modal singing of priests, and a shepherd playing a slow, melancholy Romanian song. In the second, a storm breaks and then moves away. A cock crows and a country festival begins with a series of dances. The orchestral poem concludes with the Romanian national anthem.

During an interview a third of a century later, Enesco recalled that the most emotional moment of his life had been the first performance of the *Romanian Poem* in in Paris.

The debut was a major success. It won enthusiastic reviews, two of them by composer Paul Dukas, who remarked upon the certainty of the writing, the skillful instrumentation, and "the extraordinary grasp of rhythmical effects and contrasts of timbre."

Not surprisingly, the reception of the *Romanian Poem* in Bucharest was even more enthusiastic. Suddenly Enesco was famous all around Romania. A committee was established to buy him a violin worthy of his talents as a soloist. Public contributions and matching funds from his father enabled the teenaged phenomenon to buy a cherished Stradivarius.

Two years later, Georges Enesco would become internationally famous with his two *Romanian Rhapsodies*, which–to his chagrin–would eclipse everything else he wrote, including his favorite, the *Romanian Poem*.

December 30th

More Than Just Music

December 30, 1905. Franz Lehár had come through some tough times getting his operetta *The Merry Widow* to opening night. But it would take more than music to spark enthusiasm for the show. It would also take time, work—and marketing.

Lehár had worked hard to make *The Merry Widow* something fresh and original. In telling the story of diplomatic and amorous intrigue, he had used rich orchestral coloring hitherto employed only by classical composers, including Debussy, Richard Strauss, and Mahler.

When the final curtain came down at the end of the first performance, though, Lehár received the customary applause but had no "impression of a big success" —even when his friend Oscar Straus congratulated him and predicted worldwide acclaim. The reviews of the operetta were mixed, ranging from "magnificent" to "the most distasteful I have ever seen in a theater." Subsequent performances played to nearly empty houses.

Enter Emil Steininger, a Viennese official with a bent for music and marketing. He distributed free tickets until *The Merry Widow* began to develop an audience and a reputation in Vienna. The operetta stuck it out until April when the theater season ended, by which time it had received 119 performances. Theater manager Wilhelm Karczag, an optimist and gambler by nature, transferred the show to a theater in the Vienna suburbs for the summer. At the same time, tunes from *The Merry Widow* were being popularized in various garden, park and café concerts.

By mid-September, when the operetta returned to Vienna, it was playing in sold-out theaters.

Within a year, *The Merry Widow* had swept Vienna, Berlin, London, and New York. Soon it was playing all over the world. It became so popular that in the 60 years following its lackluster debut it was performed an estimated half a million times.

Franz Lehár wrote operettas for the next 30 years, but never again did he approach the runaway success of *The Merry Widow*.

December 31st
An End & a Beginning

Ottorino Respighi had accepted the offer, but he was beginning to have misgivings. The director of Steinway and Company in New York had signed him for a concert tour of America for the 1925-26 season, and as the time approached, Respighi looked for any excuse not to go.

He was to begin the tour–and his American debut–on New Year's Eve, performing his *Piano Concerto in the Mixalydian Mode* in Carnegie Hall with the New York Philharmonic conducted by Willem Mengelberg. And as the time approached, he became more and more convinced that the tour would be a failure, to the point of imagining a disabling pain in his hand. During the ocean crossing from Naples to New York, the December weather was fair and sunny, but Respighi became ncreasingly worried about the tour and the details of their arrival–customs, passports, and other red tape.

Two hours before the liner was due to dock, his worst fears began to take form as a tugboat pulled alongside and disgorged a dozen reporters and photographers who hounded him with questions and blinded him with flashbulbs. He had come completely unprepared to face the press, became flustered by the encounter, and threw off increasingly outrageous answers to their persistent interrogation.

The reporters were equally rattled when Respighi told them that he had prepared no interviews, statements, or photographs, let alone accounts of important or amusing events that would give them an angle for their stories.

But after Respighi had been ashore for an hour or two, the city's lofty skyscrapers and the cordial reception of Mengelberg and the orchestra members began to rouse Respighi's enthusiasm. From the first rehearsal things went smoothly, and on the big night, December 31, 1925, Ottorino Respighi put an end to his fears of failure with a performance that was a brilliant beginning to a dazzling American tour.

Afterword

Now that we've arrived at the end of the year, we have
scores of unfinished stories, and it would take volumes
to bring them all to an end, but here are a few:.
Mozart did finally make in back to Salzburg, early in 1779.
Gottschalk left the United States in 1865 and never returned.
Berlioz continued to suffer romantic setbacks and he
found solace in music.
The marriage of Robert and Clara Schumann, although tragic,
remains one of music history's great love stories.
Through their art, all of these composers and performers
achieved a measure of immortality.

Bibliography

Abraham, Gerald: *Rimsky-Korsakov.*
London: Duckworth, 1949.

Allen, George: *The Life of Philidor; Musician and Chess-Player.*
New York: Da Capo Press, 1971.

Angoff, Charles: *Palestrina, Savior of Church Music.*
New York: B. Ackerman, Incorporated, 1944.

Antheil, George: *Bad Boy of Music.*
Garden City, N.Y.: Doubleday, Doran and Company, 1945

Arditi, Luigi: *My Reminiscences.*
Ed. and comp by the Baroness von Zedlitz.
New York: Dodd, Mead and Company, 1896.

Arnold, Elliott: *Finlandia; the Story of Sibelius.*
Illustrated by Lolita Granahan.
New York: H. Holt and Company, 1941.

Ashbrook, William: *Donizetti.*
London: Cassell, 1965.

Attwood, William G.: *Fryderyk Chopin: Pianist from Warsaw.*
New York: Columbia University Press, 1987.

Auer, Leopold: *My Long Life in Music.*
New York: Frederick A. Stokes Company, 1923.

Barnum, P. T.: *Struggles and Triumphs: or, Forty Years' Recollections of P.T. Barnum.*
Buffalo, N.Y. : Warren, Johnson, 1874.

Beatty-Kingston, W.: *Music and Manners; Personal Reminiscences and Sketches of Character.*
London: Chapman and Hall, 1887.

Beaussant, Philippe: *François Couperin.*
>Translated by Alexandra Land.
>Portland, Or.: Amadeus Press, c1990.

Beethoven, Ludwig van: *Letters, Journals, and Conversations.*
>Edited, translated, and introduced by Michael Hamburger.
>New York: Pantheon Books, 1952.

Beethoven, Ludwig van: *Beethoven's Letters / a Critical Edition.*
>Translated by J.S. Shedlock.
>London: J.M. Dent; New York: E.P. Dutton, 1909.

Beethoven, Ludwig van: *The Letters of Beethoven.*
>Collected, translated and edited by Emily Anderson.
>New York : W.W. Norton, 1985.

Behn, Aphra: *The Works of Aphra Behn.*
>Edited by Montague Summers.
>London: W. Heinemann, 1915.

Bellasis, Edward: *Cherubini: Memorials Illustrative of His Life.*
>London: Burns and Oates, 1874.

Berlioz, Hector: *Hector Belioz: Selections from His Letters, and Aesthetic, Humorous, and Satirical Writings.*
>Translated by William F. Apthorp.
>New York: Holt, 1879.

Berlioz, Hector: *Lettres intimes.*
>Paris: Calmann-Lévy, 1882.

Berlioz, Hector: *Correspondance inédite de Hector Berlioz*
>Paris: Calmann Levy, 1879.

Berlioz, Hector: *Memoirs of Hector Berlioz from 1803 to 1865, Comprising His Travels in Germany, Italy, Russia, and England.*
>Translated by Rachel (Scott Russell) Holmes and Eleanor Holmes; annotated, and the translation revised, by Ernest Newman.
>[New ed.] New York: Tudor Publishing Co., 1935.

Biancolli, Amy: *Fritz Kreisler: Love's Sorrow, Love's Joy.*
>Portland, Or.: Amadeus Press, 1998.

Bierley, Paul E. John Philip Sousa; *American Phenomenon.*
    New York: Appleton-Century-Crofts, 1973.

Bird, John: *Percy Grainger.*
    London: Faber and Faber, 1982.

Bliss, Arthur, Sir: *As I Remember.*
    London: Faber, 1970.

Borodin, Alexander: P*is'ma A.P. Borodina.*
    Edited by S.A. Dianina.
    Moscow: Gosizd-vo, Muzykal'nyi sektor, 1927.

Bowen, Catherine Drinker: *"Free artist"; the story of Anton and Nicholas Rubinstein.*
    New York: Random House, 1939.

Boyd, Malcolm: *Domenico Scarlatti: Master of Music.*
    New York: Schirmer Books, 1987.

Bowers, Faubion: *The New Scriabin; Enigma and Answers.*
    New York: St. Martin's Press, 1973.

Braunbehrens, Volkmar: *Maligned Master: The Real Story of Antonio Salieri.*
    Translated by Eveline L. Kanes.
    New York: Fromm International Pub. Corp., 1992.

Brown, David: *Thomas Weelkes: a Biographical and Critical Study.*
    London: Faber, 1969.

Bull, Sara Chapman Thorp: *Ole Bull, A Memoir.*
    Boston: Houghton, Mifflin and Company, 1883.

Bülow, Marie von: Hans von Bülow: *Briefe und Schriften.*
    Leipzig: Breitkopf & Härtel, 1908.

Burney, Charles: *An Eighteenth-Century Musical Tour in Central Europe and the Netherlands; Being Dr. Charles Burney's Account of His Musical Experiences.*
    Edited by Percy A.Scholes.
    London; New York: Oxford University Press, 1959.

Burney, Charles: *The Present State of music in Germany, the Netherlands, and United Provinces. Or, The Journal of a Tour through Those Countries, Undertaken to Collect Materials for a General History of Music.*
London: T. Becket and Co. [etc.], 1773.

Burton, Humphrey: *Leonard Bernstein.*
New York: Doubleday, 1996.

Burton-Page, Piers: *Philharmonic Concerto: the Life and Music of Sir Malcolm Arnold.*
London: Methuen, 1994.

Busoni, Ferruccio: *Selected Letters.*
Translated and edited by Antony Beaumont.
New York: Columbia University Press, 1987.

Busoni, Ferruccio: *Brief an Henri, Katharina und Egon Petri.*
Wilhelmshaven: F. Noetzel, 1999.

Campbell, Margaret: *Henry Purcell: Glory of His Age.*
London: Hutchinson, 1993.

Careri, Enrico: *Francesco Geminiani (1687-1762).*
Oxford [England]: Clarendon Press ; New York: Oxford University Press, 1993.

Carroll, Brendan G: *The Last Prodigy: a Biography of Erich Wolfgang Korngold.*
Portland, Or.: Amadeus Press, 1997.

Casella, Alfredo: *Music in My Time; The Memoirs of Alfredo Casella.*
Translated and edited by Spencer Norton.
[1st English ed.] Norman: University of Oklahoma Press, 1955.

Chiapusso, Jan: *Bach's World.*
Bloomington: Indiana University Press, 1968.

Chopin, Frédéric: *Letters.*
Collected by Henryk Opie'nski.
Translated by E. L. Voynich.
New York: Vienna House, 1971.

Chopin, Frédéric, *Friedrich Chopins gesammelte briefe, zum erstenmal hrsg und getreu ins deutsch.*
Leipzig: Breitkopf and Härtel, 1911.

Cone, John Frederick: *Adelina Patti: Queen of Hearts*.
　　　Portland: Amadeus Press, 1993.

Copland, Aaron: *Copland: 1900 through 1942*.
　　　New York: St. Martin's Press/Marek, [1984].

Courcy, G. I. C. de (Geraldine I. C.): *Paganini, the Genoese*.
　　　Norman: University of Oklahoma Press [1957].

Cowell, Henry: *Charles Ives and His Music*.
　　　New York, Oxford University Press, 1955.

Curtiss, Mina Kirstein: *Bizet and His World*.
　　　New York, Knopf, 1958.

David, Hans T. and Arthur Mandel: *The Bach Reader*.
　　　New York: W.W. Norton, 1972.

Davies, Lawrence: *César Franck and His Circle*.
　　　London: Barrie and Jenkins, 1970.

Deane, Basil: *Albert Roussel*.
　　　London: Barrie and Rockliff, 1961.

Debussy, Claude: *Lettres*.
　　　Collected and edited by FranÁois Lesure.
　　　Paris: Hermann, 1980.

De-la-Noy, Michael: *Elgar: the Man*.
　　　London: A. Lane, 1983.

Dickinson, A. E. F. (Alan Edgar Frederic): *Vaughan Williams*.
　　　London: Faber and Faber, 1963.

Dickson, Harry Ellis: *"Gentlemen, more dolce, please!" (Second movement)
　　　An irreverent memoir of thirty-five years in the Boston Symphony
　　　Orchestra*.
　　　Boston: Beacon Press, 1974.

Dittersdorf, Karl Ditters von: *The Autobiography of Karl von Dittersdorf*.
　　　London: R. Bentley and Son, 1896.

Dobrin, Arnold: *Aaron Copland, His Life and Times.*
New York: Thomas Y. Crowell Co., 1967.

Emerson, Ken: *Doo-dah!: Stephen Foster and the Rise of American Popular Culture*
New York: Simon and Schuster, 1997.

Evans, Willa McClung: *Henry Lawes, Musician and Friend of Poets.*
New York: The Modern Language Association of America; London, Oxford
University Press, 1941.

Ewen, David: *George Gershwin, His Journey to Greatness.*
Englewood Cliffs, N.J.: Prentice-Hall [1970].

Fifield, Christopher: *Max Bruch: His Life and Works.*
New York: G. Braziller,1988.

Finck, Henry Theophilus: *Grieg and His Music.*
New York: J. Lane company, 1910.

Flanagan, Sabina: *Hildegard of Bingen, 1098-1179: a Visionary Life.*
London; New York: Routledge, 1989.

Flower, Newman, Sir: *George Frideric Handel; His Personality and His Times.*
London, New York: Cassell and Company Ltd., 1923.

Forkel, Johann Nikolaus: Johann Sebastian Bach: *His Life, Art, and Work.*
Translated from the German of Johann Nikolaus Forkel.
New York: Vienna House, 1974.

Fry, Mervyn C.: *"Radio's First Voice...Canadian!"*
Electric Radio, January 2001, pp. 3, 35-37.
Reprinted from *The Cat's Whisker*, March 1973.

Gal, Hans, ed.: *The Musician's World: Letters of the Great Commposers.*
London: Thames and Hudson, 1965.

Garden, Edward: *Balakirev; a Critical Study of His Life and Music.*
New York: St. Martin's Press, 1967.

Gartenberg, Egon: Mahler: *the Man and His Music.*
New York: Schirmer Books, 1978.

Garrtner, Heinz: John Christian Bach : *Mozart's Friend and Mentor.*
   Translated by Reinhard G. Pauly.
   Portland, Or: Amadeus Press, 1994.

Geiringer, Karl: *Johann Sebastian Bach; the Culmination of an Era.*
   New York: Oxford University Press, 1966.

Gianturco, Carolyn: *Alessandro Stradella, 1639-1682: His Life and Music.*
   Oxford: Clarendon Press; New York: Oxford University Press, 1994.

Gilman, Lawrence: *Edward MacDowell.*
   London: J. Lane; New York: J. Lane Company, 1906.

Glinka, Mikhail Ivanovich: *Memoirs.*
   Translated from the Russian by Richard B. Mudge.
   Norman: University of Oklahoma Press, 1963.

Gluck, Christoph Willibald, Ritter von: *Lettres de Gluck et de Weber.*
   Traduites par Guy de Charnacé.
   Paris: H. Plon, 1870.

Goldmark, Carl: *Notes from the Life of a Viennese Composer.*
   Translated by Alice Brandeis.
   New York: A. and C. Boni, 1927.

Goss, Madeleine: *Bolero; the Life of Maurice Ravel.*
   New York: Henry Holt, 1940.

Gottschalk, Louis Moreau: *Notes of a Pianist.*
   London: J.B. Lippincott, 1881.

Gray, Cecil: Peter Warlock: *A Memoir of Philip Heseltine.*
   London: J. Cape, 1934.

Grechaninov, Aleksandr Tikhonovich: *My Life.*
   Translation by Nicolas Slonimsky.
   New York: Coleman-Ross Co., 1952.

Grover, Ralph Scott: *Ernest Chausson, the Man and His Music.*
   Lewisburg: Bucknell University Press, 1979.

Grun, Bernard: *Gold and Silver; The Life and Times of Franz Lehár.*
   New York: D. McKay Co., 1970.

Habets, Alfred: *Borodin and Liszt.*
    Tanslated with a preface by Rosa Newmarch.
    London: Digby, Long and Co., 1895.

Hanson, Lawrence: *Prokofiev, a Biography in Three Movements.*
    New York: Random House, 1964.

Harding, James: *Erik Satie.*
    New York: Praeger, 1975.

Harding, James: *Gounod.*
    London: Allen and Unwin, 1973.

Harding, James: *Massenet.*
    New York: St. Martin's Press, 1971.

Harding, James: *Offenbach: a Biography.*
    London: J. Calder ; New York: Riverrun Press, 1980.

Harding, James: *Saint-Saëns and His Circle.*
    London: Chapman and Hall, 1965.

Haydn, Joseph: *Joseph Haydn gesammelte Briefe und Aufzeichnungen.*
    Unter Benützung der Quellensammlung von H. C. Robbins Landon;
    Herausgeben. und erläutert von Dénes Bartha.
    Kassel, New York: Bärenreiter, 1965.

Henry, Leigh: *Dr. John Bull.*
    London: H. Joseph, in conjunction with the Globe-Mermaid Association,
    1937.

Henschel, George, Sir: *Musings and Memories of a Musician.*
    New York: The Macmillan Company, 1919.

Heyman, Barbara B: *Samuel Barber: the Composer and His Music.*
    New York: Oxford University Press, 1992.

Hill, John Walter: *The Life and Works of Francesco Maria Veracini.*
    Ann Arbor, Mich : UMI Research Press, 1975.

Hillier, Paul: *Arvo Pärt.*
    Oxford; New York : Oxford University Press, 1997.

Holländer, Hans: *Leoš Janáček; His Life and Work.*
    Translated by Paul Hamburger.
    New York: St. Martin's Press, 1963.

Holst: *Gustav Holst, Letters to W. G. Whittaker.*
    Edited by Michael Short;
    Glasgow : University of Glasgow Press, 1974.

Honegger, Arthur: *I Am a Composer.*
    Translated by Wilson O. Clough in collaboration with Allan Arthur Willman.
    New York: St. Martin's Press, 1966.

Howard, Patricia, Gluck: *An Eighteenth-Century Portrait in Letters and Documents.*
    Oxford ; New York: Clarendon Press, 1995.

Huneker, James: *Steeplejack.*
    New York: C. Scribner's Sons,1920.

Hutchings, Arthur: *Delius.*
    London: Macmillan, 1948.

Jackson, Stanley: *Caruso.*
    London, New York: W. H. Allen, 1972.

Jacob, Heinrich Eduard: *Johann Strauss, Father and Son; a Century of Light Music.*
    Translated by Marguerite Wolff.
    New York: The Greystone Press, 1940.

Jacobs, Arthur: *Arthur Sullivan, a Victorian Musician.*
    Oxford ; New York: Oxford University Press, 1984.

Jeffery, Brian: *Fernando Sor: Composer and Guitarist.*
    London: Preachers' Court, Charterhouse, EC1M 6AS: Tecla Editions, 1977.

Joachim, Joseph: *Letters from and to Joseph Joachim.*
    Selected and translated by Nora Bickley,
    London: Macmillan 1914.

Johansen, David Monrad: *Edvard Grieg.*
Translated from the Norwegian by Madge Robertson.
New York: Tudor Publishing. Co., 1945.

Kamhi de Rodrigo, Victoria: *Hand in Hand with Joaquin Rodrigo: My Life at the Maestro's Side.*
Translation by Ellen Wilkerson.
Pittsburgh, Pa : Latin American Literary Review Press, 1992.

Keates, Jonathan: *Handel, the Man and His Music.*
New York: St. Martin's Press, 1985.

Kirk, Elise K.: *Musical Highlights from the White House.*
Malabar, Fla: Krieger Publishing Company, n.d.

Kirkpatrick, Ralph: *Domenico Scarlatti.*
Princeton, N.J.: Princeton University Press, 1983.

Knight, Ellen E: *Charles Martin Loeffler: a Life Apart in American Music.*
Urbana: University of Illinois Press, 1992.

Kracauer, Siegfried: *Offenbach and the Paris of His Time.*
London: Constable, 1937.

Landon, H. C. Robbins: *Vivaldi: Voice of the Baroque.*
New York: Thames and Hudson, 1993.

Langley, Hubert: *Doctor Arne.*
Cambridge [Eng.] The University Press, 1938.

Large, Brian: *Smetana.*
London, Duckworth, 1970.

Leyda, Jay, ed.: *The Musorgsky Reader; a Life of Modest Petrovich Musorgsky in Letters and Documents.*
[1st ed.] New York: W.W. Norton, 1947.

Lebrecht, Norman: *The Book of Musical Anecdotes.*
New York: The Free Press, 1985.

Leibnitz, Thomas: *Die Bruder Schalk und Anton Bruckner.*
Tutzing: Hans Schneider, 1988.

Leyda, Jay and Bertensson, Sergei, ed.: *The Mussorgsky Reader.*
New York: W.W. Norton, 1947.

Liszt, Franz: *The Letters of Franz Liszt to Olga von Meyendorff, 1871-1886.*
Translated by William R. Tyler.
Washington: Dumbarton Oaks, Trustees for Harvard University ;
Cambridge, Mass: Harvard University Press, 1979.

Lochner, Louis Paul: *Fritz Kreisler.*
New York, Macmillan, 1950.

Lockspeiser, Edward: *Debussy; His Life and Mind.*
London, Cassell [1962-65].

Lotti, Giorgio and Radice, Raul: *La Scala.*
New York, William and Morrow, 1977.

Macdonald, Hugh, ed: *Selected letters of Berlioz.*
Edited and translated by Roger Nichols.
New York: W.W. Norton, 1995.

Macqueen-Pope, and D. L. Murray: *Fortune's Favourite: The Life and Times of Franz Lehár.*
London: Hutchinson, 1953.

Magidoff, Robert: *Yehudi Menuhin; the Story of the Man and the Musician.*
Garden City, N.Y.: Doubleday, 1955.

Malcolm, Noel: *George Enescu: His Life and Music.*
London: Toccata Press, 1990.

Mapleson, James Henry: *The Mapleson Memoirs; The Career of an Operatic Impresario, 1858-1888.*
Edited and annotated by Harold Rosenthal.
New York, Appleton-Century [1966].

Martin, George: *Verdi at the Golden Gate.*
Berkeley, Los Angeles; Oxford: University of California Press,1993.

Martin, George Whitney: *Verdi; His Music, Life and Times.*
New York: Dodd, Mead, 1963.

Martyn, Barrie: *Nicolas Medtner: His Life and Music.*
>Adershot, Hants, England: Scolar Press; Brookfield, Vt.: Ashgate
>Pub.,1995.

Mason, Daniel Gregory: *Music in My Time, and Other Reminiscences.*
>New York: The Macmillan Company, 1938.

Mason, Lowell: *Musical Letters from Abroad.*
>New York: Da Capo Press, 1967

Mason, William: *Memories of a Musical Life, by William Mason.*
>New York: Century Co. 1901.

Massenet, Jules: *My Recollections.*
>Translation by H. Villiers Barnett.
>Westport, Conn.: Greenwood Press, 1970.

McCormack, John: *John McCormack; His Own Life Story.*
>Transcribed by Pierre V. R. Key. Edited by John Scarry.
>New York: Vienna House, 1973.

McKay, David Phares: *William Billings of Boston: Eighteenth-Century Composer.*
>Princeton, N.J.: Princeton University Press, 1975.

McPhee, Colin: *A House in Bali.*
>New York: The John Day Company, 1946.

Mendelssohn-Bartholdy, Felix: *Letters of Felix Mendelssohn Bartholdy, from 1833 to 1847.*
>Edited by Paul Mendelssohn-Bartholdy and Carl Mendelssohn-Bartholdy.
>Compiled by Julius Rietz. Translated by Lady Wallace.
>London: Longman, Green, Longman, Roberts, and Green, 1863.

Mendelssohn-Bartholdy, Felix: *Letters.*
>Edited by G. Selden-Goth.
>New York: Pantheon, 1945.

Meyerbeer, Giacomo: *The Diaries of Giacomo Meyerbeer.*
>Translated, edited, and annotated by Robert Ignatius Letellier.
>Madison, N.J.: Fairleigh Dickinson University Press ; London ; Cranbury,
>NJ: Associated University Presses, 1999.

Milhaud, Darius: *My Happy Life*.
    Translated from the French by Donald Evans, George Hall and
    Christopher Palmer.
    London; New York: M. Boyars, 1995.

Mirsky, D. S., Prince: *Pushkin*.
    London, G. Routledge and Sons, Ltd.;
    New York: E.P. Dutton and Co., 1926

Monson, Karen: *Alban Berg*.
    Boston: Houghton Mifflin Co., 1979.

Moore, Gerald: *Am I Too Loud? Memoirs of an Accompanist*.
    London: H. Hamilton, 1962.

Moser, Hans Joachim: *Heinrich Schütz; His Life and Work*.
    Translated from the 2d rev. ed. by Carl F. Pfatteicher.
    Saint Louis: Concordia Pub. House, 1959.

Mozart, Wolfgang Amadeus: *Die briefe W. A. Mozarts und seiner familie*.
    München und Leipzig, G. Miller, 1914.

Mozart, Wolfgang Amadeus: *Mozart's Letters, Mozart's Life: Selected Letters*.
    Translated and edited by Robert Spaethling.
    New York: Norton, 2000.

Mozart, Wolfgang Amadeus: *The Letters of Mozart and His Family*.
    Translated and edited by Emily Anderson; with extracts from the letters of
    Constanze Mozart to Johann Anton André translated and edited by C. B.
    Oldman.
    London, Macmillan and Co., Limited, 1938.

Mussorgsky, Modest: *Pis'ma*.
    Moscow: Muzika, 1981.

Myers, Rollo H: *Emmanuel Chabrier and His Circle*.
    London, Dent, 1969.

Nectoux, Jean Michel: *Gabriel Fauré: a Musical Life*.
    Translated by Roger Nichols.
    Cambridge [England] ; New York: Cambridge University Press, 1991.

Newman, Ernest: *Richard Strauss*.

London; New York: J. Lane, 1908.

Nichols, Roger: *Ravel Remembered*.
New York: W. W. Norton, 1988.

Nijinsky, Romola de Pulszky: *Nijinsky*.
New York, Simon and Schuster, 1934.

Orledge, Robert: *Gabriel Fauré*.
London: Eulenberg Books, 1979.

Orledge, Robert: *Satie Remembered*.
Translation by Roger Nichols.
Portland, Oregon: Amadeus Press, 1995.

Ohtake, Noriko: *Creative Sources for the Music of Toru Takemitsu*.
Aldershot, Hants, England: Scolar Press; Brookfield, Vt.: Ashgate Pub.
Co., 1993.

Paderewski, Ignace Jan, and Mary Lawton: *The Paderewski Memoirs*.
New York: C. Scribner's Sons, 1938.

Pahissa, Jaime: *Manuel de Falla, His Life and Works*.
Translated from the Spanish by Jean Wagstaff.
London: Museum Press, 1954.

Petzoldt, Richard: *Georg Philipp Telemann*.
Translated from the German by Horace Fitzpatrick.
London: E. Benn, 1974.

Peyser, Joan: *Boulez*.
New York: Schirmer Books, 1976.

Pincherle, Marc: *Corelli: His Life, His Work*.
New York, W.W. Norton, 1956.

Pokrovsky, Boris A. and Grigorovich, Yuri N.: *The Bolshoi*.
Park Lane, NewYork., 1976.

Pougin, Arthur: V*erdi: an Anecdotic History of His Life and Works*.
Translated from the French by James E. Matthew.
New York: Scribner and Welford, 1887.
Poulton, Diana: *John Dowland; His Life and Works*.

Berkeley: University of California Press, 1972.

Puccini, Giacomo: *Letters of Giacomo Puccini.*
Edited by Giuseppe Adami; translated from the Italian and edited for the English edition by Ena Makin.
Philadelphia; London, J. B. Lippincott Co.,1931.

Pyne, Zoë Kendrick: *Giovanni Pierluigi da Palestrina, His Life and Times.*
New York: Dodd, 1922.

Ravel, Maurice: *A Ravel Reader: Correspondence, Articles, Interviews.*
Compiled and edited by Arbie Orenstein.
New York: Columbia University Press, 1990.

Redlich, Hans Ferdinand: *Claudio Monteverdi, Life and Works.*
London; New York: Oxford University Press, 1952.

Reed, William H.: *Elgar As I Knew Him.*
London: V. Gollancz Ltd., 1936.

Rees, Brian: *A Musical Peacemaker: the Life and Work of Sir Edward German.*
Abbotsbrook, Bourne End, Buckinghamshire: Kensal Press,1986.

Reid, Charles: *Malcolm Sargent.*
London: Hamish Hamilton, 1968.

Respighi, Elsa: *Ottorino Respighi.*
Translated by Gwyn Morris.
London, Ricordi, 1962.

Revill, David: *The Roaring Silence: John Cage, a Life.*
New York: Arcade Pub., 1992.

Riesemann, Oskar von: *Moussorgsky.*
Translated from the German by Paul England.
New York: AMS Press, 1970.

Rognoni, Luigi: *Rossini.*
Parma, Guanda, 1956.

Rosenberg, Deena and Rosenberg, Bernard: *The Music Makers.*
New York, Columbia University Press, 1979.

Rosenberg, H.C.: *Jenny Lind in America.*
New York: Stringer and Townsend, 1851.

Rosenstiel, Léonie: *The Life and Works of Lili Boulanger.*
Rutherford, N.J.: Fairleigh Dickinson University Press, 1978.

Rosenstiel, Léonie: *Nadia Boulanger: A Life in Music.*
First ed, New York : W.W. Norton, 1982.

Rossi, Nick: *Domenico Cimarosa: His Life and His Operas.*
Westport, Conn.: Greenwood Press, 1999.

Rousseau, Jean-Jacques: *The Confessions; and, Correspondence, including the
Letters to Malesherbes.*
Edited by Christopher Kelly, Roger D. Masters, and Peter G. Stillman;
translated by Christopher Kelly.
Hanover: University Press of New England [for] Dartmouth College, 1995.

Rubinstein, Artur: *My Many Years.*
New York: Knopf : distributed by Random House, 1980.

Ruttencutter, Helen Drees: *Previn.*
New York, St. Martin's Press, 1985.

Sachs, Harvey: *Reflections on Toscanini.*
New York: Grove Weidenfeld, 1990.

Saussine, Renée de: *Paganini.*
Translated by Marjorie Laurie.
New York: McGraw-Hill Book Co., 1954.

Sayers, W. C. Berwick (William Charles Berwick): *Samuel Coleridge-Taylor,
Musician; His Life and Letters.*
London: Augener Ltd., 1927.

Schonberg, Harold C.: *Horowitz: His Life and Music.*
New York : Simon and Schuster, 1992.

Schubert, Franz: *Franz Schubert's Letters and Other Writings.*
Edited by Otto Erich Deutsch and translated by Venetia Savile.
New York: A. A. Knopf, 1928.

Schumann, Robert: *On Music and Musicians.*
New York: Pantheon, 1946.

Schumann, Clara: *Letters of Clara Schumann and Johannes Brahms, 1853-1896.*
Edited by Dr. Berthold Litzmann.
New York: Longmans, Green and Co.; London: E. Arnold and Co., 1927.

Schumann, Robert: *The Letters of Robert Schumann.*
Selected and edited by Dr. Karl Storck, translated by Hannah Bryant.
London: J. Murray, 1907.

Schütz, Heinrich: *Gesammelte Briefe und Schriften.*
Edited by Erich Hermann Miller.
Hildesheim; Georg Olms, 1976.

Scott, Cyril: *Bone of Contention; Life Story and Confessions.*
New York: Arco Pub. Co., 1969.

Searle, Muriel V: *John Ireland, the Man and His Music.*
Tunbridge Wells: Midas Books, 1979.

Seroff, Victor Ilyitch: *Debussy; Musician of France.*
London: Calder, 1957.

Short, Michael: *Gustav Holst: the Man and His Music.*
Oxford: Clarendon Press; New York: Oxford University Press, 1990.

Shostakovich, Dmitrii Dmitrievich: *Testimony: The Memoirs of Dmitri Shostakovich.*
Edited. by Solomon Volkov;
translated from the Russian by Antonina W. Bouis.
New York: Harper and Row, 1979.

Skelton, Geoffrey: *Richard and Cosima Wagner: Biography of a Marriage.*
Boston: Houghton Mifflin, 1982.

Slattery, Thomas C.: *Percy Grainger: the Inveterate Innovator.*
Evanston, Ill: Instrumentalist Co., 1974.

Smith, Ronald: *Alkan.*
London: Kahn and Averill, 1976.

Smith, Steven C.: *A Heart at Fire's Center: the Life and Music of Bernard Herrmann.*
    Berkeley: University of California Press, 1991.

Smith, William Ander: *The Mystery of Leopold Stokowski.*
    London; Toronto; Associated University Presses.

Snowman, Daniel: *The World of Plácido Domingo.*
    New York: McGraw-Hill, 1985.

Sourek, Otakar: *Antonín Dvořák: Letters and Reminiscences.*
    Translated from the Czech by Roberta Finlayson Samsour.
    Prague: Artia, 1954.

Spohr, Louis: *Autobiography.*
    Translated from the German.
    New York: Da Capo Press, 1969.

Spohr, Louis: *The Musical Journeys.*
    Translated and edited by Henry Pleasants.
    Norman: University of Oklahoma Press, 1961.

Stebbins, Lucy Poate: *Enchanted Wanderer; the Life of Carl Maria von Weber.*
    New York: G. P. Putnam's Sons, 1940.

Stendhal: *Life of Rossini.*
    Translated by Richard N. Coe.
    New York: Criterion Books, 1957.

Stevens, Halsey: *The Life and Music of Béla Bartók.*
    New York: Oxford University Press, 1953.

Stravinsky, Igor: *Memories and Commentaries.*
    Igor Stravinsky and Robert Craft.
    London: Faber and Faber, 1960.

Suarès, André: *Debussy.*
    Paris: Émile-Paul Frères, 1949.

Talbot, Michael: *Vivaldi.*
    London Dent, 1978.

Tarasti, Eero: *Heitor Villa-Lobos: the Life and Works.*
    Jefferson, N.C.: McFarland, 1995.

Tchaikovsky, Modest Il'ich: *The Life and Letters of Peter Ilich Tchailkovsky.*
    Edited from the Russian by Rosa Newmarch.
    New York: Haskell House Publishers, 1970.

Tchaikovsky, Peter Ilyich: *Letters to His Family: An Autobiography.*
    Translated by Galena von Meck.
    New York: Cooper Square Press, 2000.

Thomson, Andrew: *Vincent D'Indy and His World.*
    Oxford: Clarendon Press; New York: Oxford University Press, 1996.

Thomson, Virgil: *Virgil Thomson.*
    New York: A.A. Knopf, 1966.

Threlfall, Robert: *Sergei Rachmaninoff; His Life and Music.*
    London: Boosey and Hawkes, 1973.

Tibbets, John C., ed: *Dvořák in America, 1892-1895.*
    Portland: Amadeus Press, 1993.

Trotter, William R.: *Priest of Music: The Life of Dimitri Mitropoulos.*
    Portland: Amadeus Press, 1995.

Vallas, Léon: *César Franck.*
    Translated by Hubert Foss.
    London: Harrap, 1951.

Varèse, Louise: *Varese: A Looking Glass Diary.*
    New York: W.W. Norton, 1972.

Verdi, Giuseppe: *Verdi, The Man in His Letters.*
    Edited and selected by Franz Werfel and Paul Stefan;
    translated by Edward Downes.
    New York: L.B. Fischer, 1942.

Verdi, Giuseppe: *Letters of Giuseppe Verdi.*
    Selected, translated and edited by Charles Osborne.
    London: Gollancz, 1971.

Wagner, Richard: *My Life.*
>Authorized translation from the German.
>New York: Dodd, Mead and Company, 1911.

Walton, Susana: *William Walton: Behind the Façade.*
>Oxford; New York: Oxford University Press, 1988.

Waters, Edward Neighbor: *Victor Herbert; A Life in Music.*
>New York: Macmillan, 1955.

Weaver, William and Puccini, Simonetta, ed.: *The Puccini Companion.*
>New York: W.W. Norton, 1994.

Weber, Carl Maria von: *Briefe.*
>Christophoph Worbs.
>Frankfurt am Main: Christoph Worbs, Fischer Taschenbuch, 1982.

Weinstock, Herbert: *Donizetti and the World of Opera in Italy, Paris and Vienna in the First Half of the Nineteenth Century.*
>New York: Pantheon Books, 1963.

Wilhelm, Kurt: *Richard Strauss: an Intimate Portrait.*
>Translated by Mary Whittall.
>New York: Rizzoli, 1989.

Williams, Adrian: *Portrait of Liszt: by Himself and His Contemporaries.*
>Oxford: Clarendon Press ; New York : Oxford University Press, 1990.

Wolf, Hugo: *Briefe an Melanie Köchert.*
>Franz Grasberger, Tutzing: H. Schneider, 1964.

Wolff, Werner: *Anton Bruckner, Rustic Genius.*
>New York, E. P. Dutton and Co., Inc., 1942.

Ysaÿe, Antoine: *Ysaÿe: His Life, Work and Influence.*
>London: W. Heinemann, 1947.

Index

Abel, Karl Friedrich 189
Adeney, Richard 322
Adler, Larry 14
Albéniz, Isaac 42, 133, 241, 248
Alboni, Marietta 5
Alkan, Charles Valentin 89
Annenberg, Walter 178
Antes, John 255
Antheil, George 71
Anthes, George d' 41
Aranyi, Jelly d' 341
Arbós, Enrique 248
Arditi, Luigi 5
Arne, Cecilia 155
Arne, Thomas 155
Arnold, Malcolm 322
Arnold, Ruth 322
Assiere, Mikhail Andreevich (Misha) 2
Auber, Daniel François Esprit 238
Auer, Leopold 104
August, King 226
Avalas, Donna Maria d' 305
Avenarius, Cecilia Wagner 281
Bach, Anna Carolina Philippina 190
Bach, Carl Philipp Emmanuel. 167,
    188, 190, 306
Bach, Johann August 190
Bach, Johann Christian 53, 189, 306
Bach, Johann Sebastian 38, 46-47,
    143, 167, 188, 190, 214, 290,
    302, 309, 320, 343
Bach, Johann Sebastian (son of Carl
    Philipp Emmanuel) 190
Bach, Maria Barbara 47
Bach, Wilhelm Friedemann 167, 188,
    190

Baker, Josephine 282
Balakirev, Mily 171-172, 270, 298
Barber, Samuel 299
Bardac, Emma 196
Bardac, Raoul 196
Barnum, P.T. 94
Bartók, Béla 244, 266
Beecham, Thomas 57, 123
Beethoven, Carl van 280
Beethoven, Johann van 280
Beethoven, Ludwig van 7, 20, 22, 39,
    63, 84, 99, 115, 143, 146, 148,
    163, 166,192, 206, 239, 269,
    280, 332, 340, 343, 346, 351,
    357, 361
Behn, Aphra 325
Belasco, David 345
Bellini, Vincenzo 93, 170, 267
Berg, Alban 266
Berlin, Irving 76
Berlioz, Hector 37, 93, 138, 156,
    195, 261, 277, 315
Berlioz, Henrietta 156
Berlioz, Louis 156
Berner, Friedrich Wilhelm 11
Bernstein, Leonard 22
Bertha, Alexandre de 89
Bertrand, Eugène 297
Bethune, Thomas 166
Betz, Franz 252
Billings, William 183
Bilse, Benjamin 312
Bini, Carlo 293
Bishop, Anna Rivière 9
Bishop, Henry 9
Bizet, Georges 200, 207, 214, 251

Blakely, David 111
Blanchard, Henri 180
Bliss, Arthur 123
Bloch, Ernest 307
Boccherini, Luigi 15
Bochsa, Nicholas 9
Boehm, Karl 341
Boito, Arrigo 283
Bolshoi Theater 337
Bonaparte, Napoleon 90, 143, 337
Bordoni, Faustina 12
Borge, Victor 3
Borodin, Alexander 162, 193, 298
Boulanger, Nadia 350
Boulanger, Lili 154
Boulez, Pierre 235
Brahms, Johannes 72, 145, 153, 212, 218, 288, 329
Bridge, Frank 101
Britten, Benjamin 325
Brodsky, Adolf 329
Brodsky, Anna 329
Bruch, Max 231
Bruckner, Anton 35, 143, 252, 274
Bruneau, Alfred 236
Buchanan, James 166, 219
Buck Dudley 34
Bull, John 278
Bull, Ole 175
Bullock, Seth 15
Bülow, Hans von 58, 98
Burney, Charles 21, 62, 103, 155, 338
Busch, Fritz 206
Busoni, Ferruccio 31, 194
Butterworth, George 316
Buxtehude, Dietrich 47
Cage, John 235, 313
Callas, Maria 237
Cammarano, Salvatore 233
Cannabich, Madam 353

Capone, Al 14
Carter, Elliott 350
Carusi, Gaetano 79
Caruso, Enrique 318
Casals, Pablo 15, 290
Casella, Alfredo 22, 343, 352
Catherine di Médicis 243
Chabor, Duc de 122
Chabor, Duchesse de 122
Chabrier, Emmanuel 236, 295
Chaplin, Nelsa 300
Charigot, Alice 236
Charles II, King 311, 325
Charles IX, King 243
Charles I, King 310-311
Charlotte, Queen 306
Chausson, Ernest 338
Cherubini, Luigi 90, 127, 261
Chopin, Frédéric 26, 39, 87, 127, 214, 275, 309, 343
Christian, John 53
Christian, Prince 227
Churchill, Winston 214
Cimarosa, Domenico 242
Civinnini, Guelio 345
Clark, Melville 86
Clarke, Rebecca 307
Clementi, Muzio 77, 149
Cody, William F. ("Buffalo Bill") 208, 345
Coleman, George the Elder 242
Coleridge-Taylor, Samuel 68, 132
Colonne, Edouard 361
Coolidge, Elizabeth Sprague 307
Copland, Aaron 141, 187, 319, 350
Corelli, Archangelo 62
Cotton, Joseph 137
Couperin, Francois 249
Cowdin, John E. 323
Coyne, Joe 179
Crittenden, Thomas 220

Cui, César 75, 100, 298
Cunard, Lady 123
Custis, Patcy 53
Custis, Jack 53
Cuzzoni, Francesca 12
Czerny, Carl 72, 115, 176
Da Ponte, Lorenzo 136, 144
Damrosch, Walter 36, 201, 206, 323, 347
Dearth, Henry 161
Debussy, Claude 130, 164, 196, 214, 228, 266, 282, 331, 338, 365
Debussy, Rosalie (Lily) 196
Degas, Edgar 169
Delavigne, Germaine 238
DeLay, Dorothy 356
Delius, Frederick 28, 263
des Prez, Josquin 229
Diaghilev, Serge 29, 150
Dickson, Harry Ellis 269
Dillon, Fanny 222
Dittersdorf, Karl Ditters von 271, 292, 328
Dom Pedro II, Emperor 252
Domingo, Placido 293
Donizetti, Gaetano 166, 177, 233
Dowland, John 264
Dukas, Paul 364
Dunhill, Thomas 101
Dupre, Marcel 342
Dvořák, Antonín 43, 208, 256, 258-259, 349
Edison, Mina Miller 113
Edison, Thomas 359
Edwards, George 179
Elgar, Edward 83, 142, 161, 253
Elizabeth I, Queen 264, 276, 278
Ella, John 115
Eller, Heino 358
Elsie, Lily 179
Enesco, Georges 352, 364

Ernst Heinrich Wilhelm 199
Esterházy, Prince Nicholas 151
Falla, Manuel de 29
Fanselli, Signor 354
Fauré, Gabriel 133, 222, 309
Ferrand, Humbert 37
Fessenden, Reginald 359
Fiedler, Arthur 225
Fischer, Emil 347
Fischof, Adolph 191
Field, John 26, 38, 77
Flaubert, Gustave 177, 245
Flynn, Errol 105
Forman, Milos 332
Foster, Morrison 330
Foster, Stephen 219, 330
Françaix, Jean 350
Franck, César 54, 78, 119, 145, 180
Franklin, Benjamin 53
Franz Josef, Emperor 171
Frederick II ("the Great"), King of Prussia 167
Frederick III, King of Prussia 25
Frederick, Prince of Wales 55
Freud, Sigmund 174
Fried, Oskar 194
Friskin, James 307
Gabrieli, Domenico 229
Gainsborough, Thomas 189
Garrick, David 155, 242
Gay, John 12
Geminiani, Francesco 205, 333
Genzinger, Maria Anna von 40, 151
George III, King 306
George II, King 55, 118
German, Edward 291
Gershwin, Ira 349
Gershwin, George 76, 214, 349
Gerster, Etelka 220
Gesualdo, Don Carlo 305
Geyersbach 46

Gilels, Emil 103
Glanville-Hicks, Peggy 235
Glazunov, Alexander 229
Glinka, Mikhail 38, 171-172, 223, 335
Gluck, Christoph Willibald von 61, 157, 261, 312, 321
Gluck, Maria Anna 61
Goebbels, Joseph 341
Goethe, Johann Wolfgang von 146, 168
Goldmark, Karl 72, 191
Goldmark, Rubin 76, 222
Goldoni, Carlo 250
Gossec, François Joseph 63, 96
Gottschalk, Louis Moreau 4, 81, 134, 165, 166, 257
Goudimel, Claude 243
Gounod, Charles 159, 220
Goupy 56
Graham, Martha 313
Grimm, Baron Friedrich Melchior 96
Grainger, Ella 176, 222
Grainger, Percy 176, 222
Granados, Enrique 248
Gretchaninoff, Alexander 114
Grieg, Nina 329
Grieg, Edvard 48, 121, 198, 252, 301, 329, 348
Grove, George 246
Guggenheim, Peggy 313
Halévy, Ludovic 131
Hall, Elise 164
Hallé, Charles 32
Hamilton, Billy 219, 330
Hammerich, Golla 348
Handel, George Frederick 12, 55-56, 118, 140, 173, 320, 359
Hanson, Howard 222
Hardy, Thomas 240
Harris, Roy 350

Hartmann, Arthur (ambassador) 178
Hartmann, Arthur (violinist) 272
Hasse, Juliette 348
Haydn, Joseph 1, 40, 53, 74, 110, 151, 225, 255, 346
Hayworth, Rita 137
Heifetz, Jascha 273
Heinrich, Anthony Philip 279
Heller, Stephen 160
Henschel, George 138
Herbert, Victor 36
Herod, King 23
Herrmann, Bernard 137
Hess, Myra 301
Hewitt, John Hill 279
Hildegard of Bingen 336
Hiller, Ferdinand 63, 80, 231
Hitchcock, Alfred 137
Hitler, Adolf 71, 341
Holmes, Augusta 54, 119
Holst, Gustav 240
Honauer, Leontzi 97
Honegger, Arthur 241, 326, 342
Hopkinson, Francis 53
Horowitz, Vladimir 176, 178
Houseman, John 141
Hugo, Victor, 207
Hummel, Johann Nepomuk 38, 332
Huneker, James 258
Illica, Luigi 67
Indy, Vincent d' 54, 78, 119, 145, 245, 247
Ireland, John 83
Ives, Charles 201
Janáček, Leoš 256
Jefferson, Thomas 79
Joachim, Joseph 160, 199, 212, 341
John the Baptist 23
Jolson, Al 76
Joplin, Scott 208
Joseph II, Emperor 136

Kabalevsky, Dmitri 102
Karczag, Wilhelm 365
Kennedy, John F. 15
Key, Francis Scott 186
Khrushchev, Nikita 102
Kind, Friedrich 70
Klemperer, Otto 215
Kohner, Robert 105
Kohon, Eugene 293
Kondrashin, Kiril 102
Korngold, Erich Wolfgang 105, 215
Koussevitzky, Serge 343
Kreisler, Fritz 35, 334
Kulenkampff, Georg 341
La Scala, opera house 284, 308, 345
Lanier, Sidney 34
Lasso, Orlando di 229
Lavrovsky, L.M. 260
Lawes, Henry 310-311
Lawrence, T.E. 240
Leclair, Jean-Marie 63, 296
Leclair, Louise Roussel 296
Lehár, Franz 179, 365
Leopold II, Emperor 242
Levant, Oscar 108
Levi, Hermann 274
Lewis, Matthew Gregory 277
Liadov, Anatol 69
Lind, Jenny 94
List, Eugene 214
Liszt, Franz 8, 24, 38, 48, 80, 117,
    121 127, 139, 145, 193, 214,
    288, 332
Lobkowitz, Prince Joseph Franz
    Maximilian 357
Loeffler, Charles 234
Long, Marguerite 133
Lorenz, Pare 141
Louis XIV, King 82, 249
Ludwig II, King 252
Lully, Jean-Baptist 82, 157

Ma, Yo-Yo 178
MacDowell, Edward 211
Maddox 337
Magnard, Albéric 247
Mahler, Alma 194
Mahler, Gustav 174, 194, 239, 365
Mannlich, Johann Christian 61
Mapelson, James Henry 18, 220
Marchand, Louis 320
Maria, Queen 112
Marie Antoinette, Queen 67
Marolier 16
Martin y Soler, Vicente 144
Martucci, Giuseppe 135
Mason, Daniel Gregory 126
Mason, Lowell 216
Mason, William 288, 323
Massenet, Jules 204, 207, 247, 354
Mattheson, Johann 173
Maxwell Davies, Peter 110
Mayer, Charles 38
McCormack, John 76, 303
McPhee, Colin 344
Meck, Nadezhda von 228
Medtner, Nikolai 340
Mehta, Zubin 178
Mendelssohn, Felix 17, 25, 80, 116,
    146, 149, 214, 217, 269, 341,
    346
Mendès, Catulle 54
Mengelberg, Willem 340, 366
Menotti, Gian-Carlo 299
Menuhin, Yehudi 206, 341
Merelli, Bartholomew 284
Messager, André 130
Messiaen, Olivier, 282
Meyerbeer, Giacomo 327
Milhaud, Darius 44, 326, 350, 352
Milton, John 276
Milton, John the Elder 276
Mitchell, Howard 108

Mitropoulos, Dimitri 22
Monteux, Pierre 150
Monteverdi, Claudio 286
Moore, Gerald 101
Mops, dog 35
Mörike, Eduard Friedrich 168
Morley, Thomas 276
Moscheles, Ignaz 332
Mozart, Anna Maria 185
Mozart, Leopold 49-50, 96-97, 122,
    185, 213, 289, 317, 324, 353,
    363
Mozart, Maria Anna (Nannerl) 27
Mozart, Wolfgang Amadeus 27, 49-
    50, 64, 96-97, 122, 144, 149,
    166, 185, 195, 204, 213, 229,
    283, 289, 317, 324, 332, 342,
    353, 363
Mussolini, Benito 135
Mussorgsky, Modest 100, 158, 270,
    298, 343
Nicholas I, Czar 331
Nicholas II, Czar 66
Nichols, Robert 263
Niedermeyer, Louis 309
Nijinsky, Vaslav 150
Novarro, Ramon 222
Offenbach, Jacques 73, 131
Pace, Harry 132
Pacini, Giovanni 17
Paderewski, Ignacy Jan 58, 64, 126,
    323
Paër, Ferdinando 90
Paganini, Achilles 156
Paganini, Niccoló 32, 92, 156, 224
Paisiello, Giovanni 74, 90, 157
Palestrina, Giovanni Pierluigi da,
    209-210, 229, 309
Paray, Paul 241
Pärt, Arvo 358
Patanè, Giuseppe 293

Patti, Adelina 220
Pembroke, Countess of 278
Petri, Egon 31, 194, 269
Philidor, François-André Danican
    333
Philipp, Isidore 89
Philips, Ambrose 12
Piave, Francesco Maria 39
Piccolomini, Marietta 166
Pierné, Gabriel 326
Pinza, Ezio 283
Pisandel, Johann Georg 226
Piston, Walter 350
Pleyel, Ignaz Joseph 53
Pons, Lily 237
Pope, Alexander 180
Popper, David 15
Previn, Andre 110
Prokofiev, Sergei 106-107, 260
Puccini, Giacomo 52, 67, 287, 318,
    345
Punto, Giovanni [Jan Vaclav Stich]
    20
Purcell, Henry 22, 232, 325
Pushkin, Nathalie 41
Pushkin, Alexander 41
Rachmaninoff, Sergei 75, 102, 106
Ramey, Samuel 283
Ravel, Edoard 241
Ravel, Maurice 113, 142, 152, 196,
    241
Reagan, Nancy 178
Reagan, Ronald 178
Rebel, Jean-Fery 249
Reger, Max 266
Reichardt, Johann Friedrich 357
Renoir, Pierre Auguste 169, 236
Respighi, Ottorino 22, 366
Richter, Hans 230, 360
Ries, Ferdinand 268

Rimsky-Korsakov, Nikolai 54, 75, 100, 125, 149, 298, 332
Rodrigo, Joaquin 30
Rodrigo, Victoria 30
Roger, Thérèse 338
Roger-Ducasse, Jean Jules 164
Rogier, Charles 238
Roosevelt, Eleanor 184
Roosevelt, Theodore 15
Roseingrave, Thomas 339
Rosenzweig, Maxie 349
Ross, Harry 14
Rossini, Gioacchino 19, 60, 92, 124, 127, 332, 355
Rostova, Natasha 13
Rothwell, Walter 31
Rouget de Lisle, Claude-Joseph 195
Rourke, Michael E. 76
Rousseau, Jean-Jacques 33
Roussel, Albert 361
Rubinstein, Anton 58, 153, 254, 323
Rubinstein, Arthur 294
Rubinstein, Ida 241
Rubinstein, Nikolai 153
Russell, Karl 301
Russell, Lilian 208
Saint-Georges, Joseph Boulogne 63
Saint-Saëns, Camille 15, 54, 119, 139, 159, 252, 309, 355
Salerno-Sonnenberg, Nadja 356
Salieri, Antonio 7, 136, 144, 332
Salome 23
Salomon, Johann Peter 1, 74
Sanderson, Sibyl 204
Sarasate, Pablo de 248
Sargent, Malcolm 301
Satie, Eric 169, 297
Scarlatti, Alessandro 62, 339
Scarlatti, Domenico 112, 339
Schalk, Josef 274
Scharwenka, Xavier 347

Schede, Paul 243
Schloezer, Tatyana 69
Schobert, Johann 97
Schoenberg, Arnold 215, 266
Schubert, Franz 91, 143, 221, 246, 265, 301, 332, 342
Schultz, George 178
Schumann, Clara Wieck 45, 80, 153, 212, 218, 262
Schumann, Robert 45, 80, 195, 262, 309, 341
Schütz, Heinrich 227
Scott, Cyril 300
Scott, Walter 177, 233
Scott, William 325
Scriabin, Alexander 69
Scribe, Augustin-Eugène 238, 277
Segovia, Andrès 181
Sgambati, Giovanni 117
Shaffer, Peter 332
Shakespeare, William 25, 93, 168, 206, 348
Shostakovich, Dmitri 100, 229, 304
Sibelius, Jean 66, 203
Simon, Abbey 8
Smetana, Bedřich 172, 256, 327, 362
Smith, John Stafford 186
Smithson, Harriet 37
Sor, Fernando 16
Sousa, John Philip 76, 111
Spohr, Dorette 85, 202
Spohr, Louis 77, 85, 148, 202, 268
Spontini, Luigi 63
Stadler, John 53
Stalin, Joseph 214, 304
Stanford, Charles Villiers 142
Stehmann, Gerhardt 347
Steinbeck, John 313
Steininger, Emil 365
Steinway, William 254
Stendahl, Marie 19

Stern, Isaac 178
Still, William Grant 132
Stirling, Jane 275
Stockley, W.C. 253
Stokowski, Leopold 109, 352
Stradella, Alessandro 197
Straus, Oskar 365
Strauss, Johann I 59
Strauss, Johann II 59, 65, 266
Strauss, Richard 23, 129, 365
Stravinsky, Igor 149, 150, 184, 294
Sullivan, Arthur 246
Svendsen, Johan 348
Takemitsu, Toru 282
Taneyev, Sergei 75
Tartini, Giuseppe 21
Tchaikovsky, Anatol 312
Tchaikovsky, Modest 2, 43, 117, 200,
      207
Tchaikovsky, Peter 2, 41, 43, 102,
      114, 117, 195, 200, 207, 228,
      252, 312, 329
Telemann, George Philip 140
Telemann, Maria Catharina 140
Thalberg, Sigismond 38
Thibaud, Jacques 269
Thomas, Ambroise 139, 354
Thomas, Theodore 208
Thomson, Virgil 141, 350
Thun, Count Joseph Johann von 20
Thurber, Jeanette 258
Tolstoy, Leo 2, 13, 177, 343
Tomkins, Thomas 276
Tomlinson, Ralph 186
Toscanini, Arturo 135, 182, 241,
      299, 308
Treigle, Norman 283
Trossi, Agostino 60
Truman, Harry S. 214
Truman, Margaret 214
Tuckwell, Barry 110

Turgenev, Ivan 159
Turina, Joaquin 29
Tyler, John 279
Urusov, Prince 337
Valadon, Suzanne 169
Van Cliburn 102
Vanhall, Johann Baptist 53
Varèse, Edgar 6, 132, 313
Vaughan Williams, Ralph 142, 316
Veracini, Francesco Maria 226
Verdi, Giuseppe 39, 98,128, 157,
      284-285
Verne, Jules 73
Viardot, Pauline 159
Viardot, Louis 159
Victoria, Princess Royal 25
Victoria, Queen 25
Vieuxtemps, Helena Gorska 104
Vieuxtemps, Henri 104
Vieuxtemps, Josephine Eder 104
Villa-Lobos, Heitor 181
Visee, Robert de 249
Vivaldi, Antonio 250, 314
Vogl, Michael 265
Vorontsov, Prince 337
Vuillaume, J.B. 32
Wagner, Cosima 145, 360
Wagner, Minna 281
Wagner, Richard 35, 54, 57, 98, 143,
      145, 147, 149, 214, 230, 239,
      252, 257, 281, 331, 338, 342,
      343, 347, 360
Waldstein, Count Ferdinand 84
Walpole, Horace 189
Walpole, Robert 12, 55
Walton, William 273
Ward, Thomas F. 28
Warlock, Peter 263
Washington, Booker T. 68
Washington, George 53
Washington, Martha 53

Weber, Aloysia 50
Weber, Carl Maria von 10, 11, 51,
        63, 70, 120, 332
Weber, Konstanze 50
Webern, Anton 266
Weelkes, Thomas 88, 276
Welles, Orson 137
Westinghouse, George 359
Whistler, James 138
Wieck, Friedrich 262
Wieniawski, Henri 254
Wilbye, John 276
Wilde, Oscar 23, 125
Wilson, Edith 86
Wilson, Woodrow 86
Wolf, Hugo 101, 168
Wood, Henry 161
Ysaÿe, Eugene 95, 272, 331
Ysaÿe, Gabriel 95
Zangarini, Carlo 345
Ziegfeld, Florenz 208
Ziloty, Alexander Ilyich 43

About the Author

Norman Gilliland has hosted weekday classical music broadcasts since 1977, beginning in Florida and continuing in Wisconsin. He's the creator of *Grace Notes*, which has become a daily feature on a number of public radio stations nationwide. In 1999 his historical novel, *Sand Mansions*, was a selection of Wisconsin Public Radio's prestigious *Chapter A Day*. In 2002 he began performing in the stage production of *Feuding Founders*, a dramatization of the correspondence between John Adams and Thomas Jefferson. He lives in Madison, Wisconsin.